THE ART OF
Distressed
M&A

THE ART OF
Distressed
M&A

Buying, Selling, and Financing
Troubled and Insolvent Companies

H. Peter Nesvold

Jeffrey M. Anapolsky

Alexandra Reed Lajoux

New York   Chicago   San Francisco   Lisbon   London
Madrid   Mexico City   Milan   New Delhi
San Juan   Seoul   Singapore
Sydney   Toronto

ISBN   978-0-07-175019-6
MHID   0-07-175019-3

This publication is designed to provide accurate and authoritative information in regard to the subject matter covered. It is sold with the understanding that neither the author nor the publisher is engaged in rendering legal, accounting, securities trading, or other professional service. If legal advice or other expert assistance is required, the services of a competent professional person should be sought.

—From a Declaration of Principles Jointly Adopted by a Committee of the American Bar Association and a Committee of Publishers and Associations

Library of Congress Cataloging-in-Publication Data

Nesvold, H. Peter.
    Art of distressed M&A / by H. Peter Nesvold, Jeffrey M. Anapolsky, Alexandra Reed Lajoux.
        p.   cm.
    Includes index.
    ISBN 978-0-07-175019-6 (alk. paper)   1. Consolidation and merger of corporations.
2. Consolidation and merger of corporations—Finance.   I. Anapolsky, Jeffrey M.
II. Lajoux, Alexandra Reed.   III. Title.   IV. Title: Art of distressed M & A.
V. Title: Art of distressed M and A.
    HG4028.M4N49 2011
    338.8'3—dc22   2010029965

McGraw-Hill books are available at special quantity discounts to use as premiums and sales promotions or for use in corporate training programs. To contact a representative, please e-mail us at bulksales@ mcgraw-hill.com.

This book is printed on acid-free paper.

CONTENTS

PREFACE   vii

SECTION ONE   THE BIG PICTURE   1
Chapter 1   Business Failures   3

Chapter 2   Alternatives for Distressed Companies   31

Chapter 3   Trends in Distressed M&A and Investing   67

SECTION TWO   THE BANKRUPTCY PLAYERS   97
Chapter 4   A Debtor and Creditor Overview   99

Chapter 5   Secured Creditors   127

Chapter 6   Unsecured Creditors   151

Chapter 7   Advisors and Other Parties   173

SECTION THREE   AVOIDING COMMON PITFALLS   211
Chapter 8   Accounting for Workouts: TDRs, Extinguishments,
and Modifications   213

Chapter 9   Accounting for Bankruptcy: NOLs and Fresh Start Reporting   235

Chapter 10 Mitigating Legal Risks in Distressed M&A: Fiduciary Duties, Antitrust, and Fraudulent Transfers 269

SECTION FOUR   DEAL STRUCTURES THAT WORK   303

Chapter 11 Principles of Distressed Company Valuation 305

Chapter 12 Distressed M&A Strategy: The Plan of Reorganization 333

Chapter 13 Distressed M&A Strategy: 363 Sales and Loan-to-Own Transactions 373

Chapter 14 Distressed M&A Strategy: Financing and Refinancing Considerations 403

Conclusion 457

INDEX   461

PREFACE

Every community has its hospitals, its graveyards, and its institutions offering salvation. Business is no different. Blocks from the New York Stock Exchange, where public companies go to be born, stands the Bankruptcy Court for the Southern District of New York, where companies go to die—or to be reborn.

A business does not become "distressed" overnight, nor can it recover in a day. There is a long period before, during, and, for the happy few, after bankruptcy. This book focuses on what happens *during* distress—and even more narrowly, during the purchase or sale of a distressed entity. All too often, the owner or potential acquirer of a business will perceive it as being healthy until reality proves otherwise. Few experiences are as disappointing as the recognition that a once-thriving business is going down the tubes. Such recognition can bring out both the best and the worst in business managers. One CEO may work for a dollar a year; another may cook the books. For most, the reality is something in between: an effort to save costs while putting the best possible face on things within the limits of the law.

This book is for those who, by destiny or by choice, have found themselves dealing with an unmistakably distressed property. Transacting business in such a climate requires a balance between passionate commitment and cold detachment. All parties involved must be committed to preserving as much value as possible, yet they must refrain from throwing good money after bad. There comes a time when the bankruptcy pros must take over and practice their art during the process of reorganization under bankruptcy laws. We call this the *art of distressed M&A*.

THE ART OF DISTRESSED M&A

While there are many books about the process of going public, there are few guides to the other side of town—the difficult process of unwinding a business after years and sometimes decades or even centuries of operation.

While many investors, executives, advisors, and academics are familiar with traditional mergers and acquisitions, the world of distressed M&A remains a niche business that has been left to specialists. However, as one M&A commentator recently noted:

> For many years, the business of advising and financing bankrupt companies was small, specialized, and isolated. No more. If the insolvency wave of 2009 demonstrated anything, it's how tightly linked it is to the larger fluid deal economy. That makes the historic surge of bankruptcies [in that] year a watershed moment.[1]

Another industry expert noted that recovering from this watershed will take time: "Even if there's an economic recovery, an up-tick, it's going to take time for us to work through all of the companies that are highly levered. . . . Recovery is one thing, but recovery from the distressed cycle I think is going to be prolonged."[2]

As we go to press in early 2011, distressed mergers and acquisitions continue to be a part of the M&A landscape after a year of notable increase. According to Thomson-Reuters Legal Advisory League Tables, M&A transactions involving bankrupt U.S. companies in 2009 rose to 17 percent of all deal volume during that year (versus 2 percent in 2008).[3] Pessimists will see *distressed* M&A; optimists will see distressed *M&A*, noticing that financial markets are willing to fund recovery. Dubbed "bankruptcy beauties,"[4] companies like Visteon, General Growth Properties, and Six Flags are making news as comebacks.

Even well into an eventual economic recovery, a thorough knowledge of the unique complexities of distressed M&A is a "must have" tool for nearly every M&A professional. Consider, for instance, the current maturity schedule for corporate debt—an alarming $448 billion of corporate loans and a staggering $467 billion of high-yield bonds will mature between 2011 and 2017 (see Exhibit P-1). Not all of these issuers will be able to improve their operating performance or refinance their balance sheets to address these looming maturities. As of the end of 2010, the maturity situation with corporate loans is projected to peak in 2014 whereas

Exhibit P-1 Projected Corporate Debt Maturity Schedules

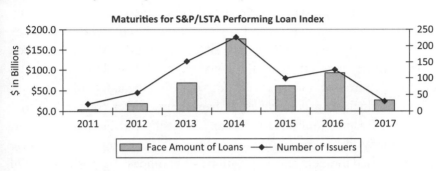

Maturities for S&P/LSTA Performing Loan Index

Face Amount of Loans — Number of Issuers

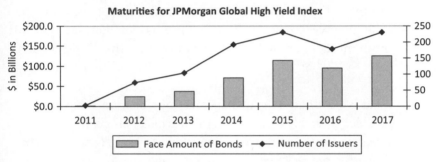

Maturities for JPMorgan Global High Yield Index

Face Amount of Bonds — Number of Issuers

Note: As of November 30, 2010. JPMorgan Global High Yield Index includes defaulted securities.

Sources: JPMorgan, BofA Merrill Lynch.

high-yield bond issuers appear to have postponed most of their problems to 2015 and beyond.

Much of this debt was issued in an environment in 2005–2008 with historically tight credit spreads and covenant flexibility—an environment that few credit professionals expect to see again in their lifetimes. A wave of refinancing and amendments in 2009–2010 allowed many issuers to extend maturities and lower their interest rates, providing additional breathing room to restructure operations and pursue growth opportunities. Even though credit spreads widened, the Federal Reserve kept interest rates at historical lows, which helped to improve cash flow for many leveraged businesses. While these transactions alleviated approximately 40 percent of loan maturities and 20 percent of the high-yield bond maturities through 2014, there is no guarantee they will continue. Once the capital markets lose patience for refinancing and amendments and when interest rates inevitably rise, opportunities for distressed M&A will be revealed. In a nutshell, the credit excesses of the last decade have set the stage for a protracted distressed M&A cycle.

As a result, an ever-increasing number of financial and strategic investors are being presented with deals for distressed companies. In fact, one could argue that *every* company that is in Chapter 11 bankruptcy is "for sale"—that is, it will be sold either to a third party or, in effect, to the company's creditors by the conversion of their debt into equity. Many asset purchasers have known for years that the assets of distressed businesses, including companies in bankruptcy, offer tremendous opportunities for potential buyers in many respects. But buying the assets of a company in bankruptcy is not as simple as haggling at a rummage sale. Distressed mergers and acquisitions—encompassing a wide array of transactions related to bankruptcies, restructurings, recapitalizations, and liquidations—involve seemingly innumerable issues that are typically not present in more traditional M&A of going concerns. Consider some examples:

- What issues should the management of a distressed business consider when choosing among its various options for selling assets: out-of-court restructurings, loan-to-own scenarios, debt buybacks, prepackaged bankruptcies, and so on?
- How do fiduciary duties of care and loyalty apply when directors are contemplating the purchase or sale of a distressed company? How can directors balance the interests of shareholders with other stakeholders in their deliberations?
- How does the valuation of a business that is in financial distress differ from that of a going concern? What is the legal framework for valuation that a bankruptcy court will apply during a Chapter 11 proceeding, and why is it critical to understand this?
- How should a distressed business approach cash management and debtor-in-possession (DIP) financing issues before filing and during bankruptcy?
- How can a purchaser protect against potential successor liability claims—i.e., future tort claims that, although they arose pre-petition, do not become known until after the bankruptcy filing?
- Under what circumstances might the target's tax attributes, including a history of net operating losses, survive a potential sale?
- What steps can a buyer of a distressed business take to mitigate the risk that creditors may attempt to set aside the deal, post-closing, on "fraudulent transfer" grounds?

- Under what circumstances might a bankruptcy court void a pre-petition sale? What steps can a proposed buyer take to mitigate this risk?
- What are some best practices for navigating a Chapter 11 sale process without acquiring the taint of being considered "damaged goods" by suppliers, customers, and other constituents? By the same token, how can a buyer manage the risk of the loss of key employees?
- What strategies for mitigating legal risks should a buyer consider, given the complexity of a Chapter 11 process and the smaller number of representations, warranties, and post-closing indemnifications that are common in such processes?
- What are some other "ticking time bombs" that need to be detonated before getting involved in a distressed company sale?

A PERENNIAL CONCERN

Contrary to popular belief that distressed M&A is countercyclical to the overall economy, companies become distressed in all economic periods. While all industries are likely to experience more pronounced distress when the economy enters a recession, and distressed acquisitions should be more plentiful during these periods, distressed M&A occurs during robust economic periods as well.

As B.C. Forbes, the founder of *Forbes* magazine, quipped, "If you don't drive your business, you will be driven out of business." Indeed, while there has always been change in business, the rate of change has accelerated in each decade as a result of technological innovation, globalization, deregulation, financial engineering, and other factors that are designed to promote capitalism. In prior periods, executives and directors could take a cautious wait-and-see approach to managing the changes in their industry by letting others lead and learning from their mistakes. No more. Today, industry laggards who fail to adjust quickly to their markets no longer enjoy the luxury of a second chance. Complacency is penalized, and risk taking is mandatory. Increased pressures from lenders, heightened shareholder demands for returns, intensified competition with lower barriers to entry, more efficient supply chains, and higher expectations for worker productivity make effective decision making more and more complex for executives and boards of directors. As a result, fewer and fewer are getting it right the first time.

Taking calculated risks and making educated guesses may work most of the time, but not all the time. As businesses increasingly are operating in a zone of "one strike and you're out," the rise of distressed M&A is inevitable.

In this book, we seek to reveal the terminology, concepts, trends, and techniques involved in distressed M&A. While becoming conversant in these areas is an important start, distressed M&A will inevitably require the skill and expertise of advisors such as bankruptcy attorneys, restructuring advisors, and turnaround consultants, because these areas are constantly evolving. This evolution in the art of distressed M&A is being driven by new rulings by bankruptcy courts, changes in the capital markets, increasing sophistication among distressed investors, the growing internationalization of corporate entities, and regulatory updates by Congress. As a result, it is impossible to completely master every aspect of distressed M&A, which is why we characterize this area as an art, not a science.

In the first section, we seek to explain the general concepts and provide a background for distressed M&A, including the nature of business failure, alternatives for the distressed business, and recent trends and useful statistics. Our goal is to provide the big picture before getting into details. We also highlight the key differences between traditional M&A and distressed M&A.

In the second section, we delve into the bankruptcy players. While some of these players may be similar to those in traditional M&A, there are several unusual twists that arise in distressed M&A. We do not assume that the reader has a law degree, but having formal training in legal concepts concerning debtors, creditors, contracts, and bankruptcy is always helpful. In this section, we first review general concepts regarding debtors and creditors. Next, we discuss secured creditors in greater detail. We then focus on several issues involving unsecured creditors. Finally, we explain the role of advisors and other players in the distressed M&A process.

In the third section, we focus on the common pitfalls of a distressed M&A transaction, including accounting, tax, and legal issues. As the reader may be aware, we have also written other books in The Art of M&A series that provide significantly greater detail on each of these topics. Therefore, we designed this section of this book to highlight the special aspects of these topics that are involved in distressed M&A and assume that the reader either is generally familiar with each topic already or is planning on reading one of our other books as well.

In the fourth section, we integrate all of the material on the bankruptcy players and the mechanics of a distressed M&A transaction into deal strategies, including principles of distressed company valuation, sponsoring a plan of reorganization, bidding in a 363 sale, and loan-to-own investing. Often a potential acquirer needs to consider all three of these techniques and others as well as part of an overall strategy in order to choose the best path and to adjust course as a situation develops. In this section, there are many additional terms, concepts, and issues that assume that the reader has reviewed the prior chapters. In our last chapter, we discuss financing and refinancing. Cash is the lifeblood of companies. Just as its absence can cause a death spiral, so an infusion can spark recovery. Finally, our conclusion offers some principles for business before, during, and after times of distress.

This book provides instruction from both the buyer's and the seller's points of view. As in all M&A transactions, it is essential for each side to understand the other's perspectives, motivations, and relationships in order to negotiate a deal. Unlike traditional M&A, however, distressed M&A typically involves many more twists and turns in navigating between the beginning of the process and the closing of the deal.

Unlike other texts, this book has an unusual amount of cross-references because many terms, concepts, and issues are touched upon in multiple chapters. While we naturally recommend reading this book from start to finish at least once, we expect that in practice, a reader will often move nonsequentially from chapter to chapter. Therefore, we attempted to provide a logical outline of various complex topics, but also noted when we anticipated that the reader would want to also refer to another part of the book in order to understand the overall issue.

We sought to differentiate this book from other publications on similar topics by creating a cross-disciplinary narrative that spans finance, accounting, law, tax, negotiations, and management. We distill these disciplines down to the topics that are most relevant to M&A, leaving the other issues that debtors and creditors may face in distressed situations for other authors to address. While there are other texts that may address these disciplines in greater depth than this book, we believe that this book is unique in integrating them in one package. Regarding bankruptcy, unlike the leading bankruptcy treatises, outlines, and textbooks, we focus exclusively on business bankruptcy topics and deliberately avoid consumer bankruptcy issues. With respect to the geographic scope of this book, we limit our discussion to U.S. law and domestic M&A, and do not address international and multinational issues.

ADDITIONAL INFORMATION

Our research has benefited from a variety of resources and forums. While there are many excellent sources of information on bankruptcy law and distressed M&A, we suggest three organizations in particular:

- The *Turnaround Management Association (TMA)*, which bills itself as the only international nonprofit association dedicated to corporate renewal and turnaround management. Established in 1988, TMA has more than 9,000 members in 46 chapters, including 32 in North America and 14 abroad. For additional information, see www.turnaround.org.
- The *American Bankruptcy Institute (ABI)*, one of the largest multidisciplinary, nonpartisan organizations dedicated to research and education on matters related to insolvency. Founded in 1982, ABI membership today includes more than 12,000 attorneys, auctioneers, bankers, judges, lenders, professors, turnaround specialists, accountants, and other bankruptcy professionals. The organization publishes the *ABI Journal* (10 times per year) and the *ABI Law Journal* (semiannually), among other electronic and print publications. For more information, see www.abiworld.org.
- The *Association for Corporate Growth (ACG)*, which deems itself a community for middle market M&A deal makers and business leaders focused on driving growth. The organization, founded in 1954, has subsequently grown to more than 12,000 members organized in 54 chapters throughout North America, Europe, and Asia. For more information, please visit www.acg.org.

In terms of bankruptcy data and related editorial information, we also recommend a handful of sources:

- Subscription sources such as *The Deal* (also available online at www.thedeal.com), *Bankruptcy Week* (and its related Web site, www.bankruptcydata.com), and Debtwire (www.debtwire.com).
- Government information provided to the public, such as the U.S. federal bankruptcy courts' Web site, which provides basic information on different aspects of the federal bankruptcy laws,

along with composite data on bankruptcy filings. For more information, visit www.uscourts.gov/bankruptcycourts.html.

- Finally, we suggest that readers watch for the launches of www .ArtofMA.com and www.macouncil.org, online resources that will provide additional resources and updates on broader M&A subject matter.

We hope that this book will be a useful reference for readers in many situations, including

- Executives who are concerned that their companies' futures are uncertain
- Owners who want to sell underperforming portfolio companies
- Corporate attorneys seeking to specialize in bankruptcy law
- Investment bankers interested in becoming restructuring advisors
- Seasoned operators making the transition to becoming turnaround consultants
- Hedge fund managers who want to understand bankruptcy sales for event-driven investing
- Buyout professionals who want to expand into turnaround investing
- Traditional lenders who are seeking to make DIP loans or provide exit financing
- Business and law school students who want to enter distressed M&A markets

The Art of Distressed M&A: Buying, Selling, and Financing Troubled and Insolvent Companies attempts to provide accurate, practical, and up-to-date answers to hundreds of questions that deal makers may have in this new environment. Like the preceding texts in The Art of M&A series, this one is organized in a question-and-answer format, moving from general to specific questions in each topic area.

What is your burning question of the moment? It may be as basic as "What is Chapter 11 bankruptcy?" or "Why do companies fail?" or as arcane as "What is a bankruptcy remote entity?" Whatever you want to know about distressed mergers and acquisitions, you are likely to find the answers here—or at least a useful reference.

ACKNOWLEDGMENTS

Throughout this book, we have cited expert sources, and these are acknowledged in our notes. However, several individuals deserve special mention as reviewers of significant portions of this book. Myron "Mickey" Sheinfeld, a noted bankruptcy practitioner and scholar, kindly read Sections One, Two, and Four and provided wise counsel. Other expert reviewers and sources of good counsel included Janet Pegg, managing director, UBS Investment Bank; Deborah Hicks Midanek, principal, Solon Group; and Kevin Sullivan, managing director, Aon Corporation.

The authors wish to acknowledge the full McGraw-Hill team, including Mary Glenn, Jennifer Ashkenazy, Morgan Ertel, Pattie Amoroso, and Maureen Harper. We also thank copyeditor Alice Manning, proofreader Maggie Warren, and indexer Kay Schlembach.

Endnotes

1. Anthony Baldo, editor, *The Deal* (2010).
2. John Rapisardi, co-chair, Financial Restructuring Department, Cadwalader, Wickersham & Taft, LLP.
3. For 2009 trends, see "Mergers and Acquisitions Review: Legal Advisors," Thomson-Reuters League 3. Tables for M&A, First Quarter 2010; available at http://online.thomsonreuters.com/DealsIntelligence/Content/Files/1Q10_MA_Legal_Advisory_Review_Final.pdf, last accessed November 2, 2010. For the new 2010 League Tables see *Distressed Debt and Bankruptcy Restructuring Review*, which includes all bankruptcy sales. See http://online.thomsonreuters.com/DealsIntelligence/Content/Files/3Q10_Distressed_Debt_Bankruptcy_Restructuring_Review.pdf. In announcing the new League Table, Thomson_Reuters stated "In the face of an *uptick in distressed company transactions in recent years*, we have worked with leading restructuring advisory firms to create a standardized set of restructuring league tables, which cover all global regions and generate rankings of financial and legal advisors to distressed companies in connection with debt exchange offers, debt tender offers, bankruptcy sales, loan modifications, and debt retirement funded by equity offerings." See http://online.thomsonreuters.com/DealsIntelligence/Content/Files/3Q10_MA_Legal_Advisory_Review.pdf
4. Mike Specter, "Bankruptcy Beauties: Once-Shunned Companies Look More Attractive—Once-Forsaken Firms under Bankruptcy Protection Are Looking More Attractive, and Generating Recoveries for Stakeholders Unheard of a Year Ago," *Wall Street Journal*, May 13, 2010.

THE ART OF
Distressed
M&A

The Big Picture

Before buying or selling a business with financial woes, it is helpful to start with some perspective regarding corporate bankruptcy.

Why do businesses fail? Chapter 1 of this book provides some basic statistics on how many have gone sadly south, and explains some of the fundamental differences between buying a healthy company and buying one that is distressed.

Chapter 2 of *The Art of Distressed M&A* explores restructuring alternatives for distressed businesses, including (1) workouts outside of bankruptcy court, (2) Chapter 7 liquidation for the orderly sale of a debtor's assets by a trustee, and (3) the better-known Chapter 11, which allows the debtor to continue operating while the company's capital structure is revamped in court.

In Chapter 3 of this book, we discuss some of the largest corporate bankruptcy filings to date, highlighting lessons that can be learned from those filings. We conclude with an overview of ways of investing in distressed debt and equity.

CHAPTER 1

Business Failures

Failure is simply the opportunity to begin again, this time more intelligently.

—*Henry Ford, Founder, Ford Motor Company*

OVERVIEW OF BUSINESS FAILURES

Why do businesses fail?

Businesses fail for the same reasons that they can succeed; failure and success are the two sides of the coin called risk. Just as the risks that businesses take are many and varied, so too are the reasons for business failure. However, the issues driving such failures fall into three general categories: industry, company, and management issues.

- *Industry.* Many businesses fail because of issues affecting their entire industry, such as macroeconomic factors, overcapacity, technological innovation, commodity cost spikes, foreign competition, turmoil in the capital markets, and regulatory change.
- *Company.* In other cases, the industry may be performing well, but a particular company experiences one or more problems, such as an overleveraged balance sheet, a product recall, an environmental disaster, a botched IT upgrade, the loss of a key employee, a union strike, uncollectable receivables, or unfavorable litigation.
- *Management.* Finally, even though the industry and the company are experiencing strong performance, financial distress may nevertheless be caused by issues related to mismanagement. These issues might involve fraud, generational transition, petty politics, and various instances of poor judgment, lackluster decision making, or misguided strategies.

Often the root causes involve more than one of the three categories, such as the failure to integrate a prior acquisition, which includes both the company's worsening performance and management's inability to execute its plan. This three-part framework is typically a good place to start when evaluating a distressed business for acquisition:

1. If problems within the industry are the main cause of the company's distress, the potential buyer will need to develop a view of how the trends affecting the industry will progress in the future. If the industry is cyclical, investing at the bottom of the cycle can yield solid returns. On the other hand, if the industry is plagued by chronic problems, then it may be difficult for an investor in a particular company to change the company, let alone the industry.
2. If issues within the company are the main cause of its distress, the potential buyer will need to assess whether an ownership change can fix these issues sufficiently to generate an attractive return on the overall investment (the current valuation plus any additional capital investment needed).
3. Financial distress that is primarily caused by management's ineptitude can often be the most attractive investment opportunity. If the new owner inherits a strong industry and company, then its key strategy may be to simply discontinue discredited decisions and encourage sound business judgment going forward.

Isn't bad management really the underlying cause of all these explanations?

There are certainly many investors who believe that good management can solve every business problem, but no human being can realistically be expected to work miracles. It seems unreasonable to expect management to be able to pinpoint the rise and fall of an industry cycle with complete accuracy. Similarly, it seems unfair to expect management to predict the precise outcome of every lawsuit, the customer reaction to every product launch, the impact of every competitive threat, and the severity of every product recall. While management may strive relentlessly to navigate perfectly through both calm and troubled waters, even the *Titanic* hit an iceberg. On the other hand, management teams will too often blame "a perfect storm" for their misfortune and go too far in excusing their reckless behavior, inattention to detail, and flawed strategies.

Rather than simply blaming management for a company's downfall, it seems more reasonable to acknowledge that businesses need different types of talent to manage different challenges in different periods of their development. More entrepreneurial executives have strong talents for growing businesses, developing products and services, building new facilities, strengthening relationships, recruiting new employees, mentoring existing employees, and expanding profitability through top-line growth. Other business leaders excel at fixing broken processes, improving operational efficiencies, rationalizing products and services, managing change, shutting down facilities, downsizing headcount, overhauling business strategy and positioning, and expanding profitability through cost reduction. Rarely is the same individual able to exhibit strength in both sets of skills. In fact, the person who created some aspect of a business—designed a new product, built a new facility, hired a new employee, or negotiated a new contract—is often the worst person to fix that area when things go wrong. Since no one likes to admit that he made a mistake, achieving real change often requires a fresh perspective.

Many of the practices taught in business schools and management training programs implicitly assume that a company has ample liquidity to pursue the various initiatives that are being described. Day-to-day operations also proceed on the assumption that the company has ample liquidity. Therefore, the vast majority of talented managers may never have experienced or even thought about a financial crisis, where everyday decisions need to be made in the context of extremely tight liquidity. Indeed, they may simply lack the training to analyze the underlying causes of the company's financial distress, derive alternatives for fixing the company's problems, and lead the investigation into and implementation of the best solutions. With the right turnaround advice, however, the managers who are most familiar with their business may be the best choice for leading the company through a financial crisis. If the existing management team stubbornly resists change and remains fixated on the same vision, however, then that team may be unable to fix the business no matter what advice it receives.

As Steve Jobs, cofounder of Apple Computer, explained, "Sometimes when you innovate, you make mistakes. It is best to admit them quickly, and get on with improving your other innovations." Despite such advice, many leaders of companies that are facing financial distress remain in denial about the severity of the situation. They may whine that all they need to fix the company's woes is another day and another dollar, they may resist any suggestion that their strategy is flawed or that they need to change direction, or they may dismiss any downside scenarios as being overly pessimistic and based upon unrealistic assumptions. Any mention of bankruptcy may get someone fired on the spot. After all, throughout the executive's career and the company's history, there have been ups and downs, but the company's fundamental survival has never been a concern. Under most dire circumstances, some fortunate turn of events—a last-minute big order by a customer, for example—has saved the day. This state of denial among executives and boards of directors may cause a company to defer action, hoping that the situation will improve. However, as the saying goes, hope is not a strategy. The reality is that, in most cases, the options available to businesses to deal with their predicaments become more limited over time rather than more plentiful. For these reasons, many observers use the analogy of a melting ice cube to illustrate a company's financial distress. For both, time is of the essence.

Therefore, some of the most compelling opportunities for distressed M&A arise when business leaders fail to act in time. In these circumstances, a potential buyer's turnaround strategy may be simply to replace the existing growth-oriented management team with a fix-oriented turnaround team.

Aren't business failures caused by companies' taking on too much debt?

While many business failures are directly related to companies becoming overleveraged, with the result that too much debt is burdening their operations, debt is neither a requirement for nor a cause of business failure. Solvency and liquidity are better ways to measure the health of a business. Simply speaking, businesses fail because they run out of cash, meaning that they can no longer conduct their daily operations because they can no longer pay their employees and vendors. These companies are illiquid. Illiquidity can arise whether a company is financed with a combination of debt and equity, such as a leveraged buyout, or with equity only, like a venture capital start-up. The issue is whether a company can tap additional capital resources—whether debt, equity, trade credit, or government grants—to increase its liquidity when necessary. In fact, financial distress can sometimes arise if a company takes on too little debt during good times and is unable to pass lenders' underwriting examinations in bad times. Indeed, the primary reason why many small businesses fail is a lack of financing, not too much.

Saying that an overleveraged balance sheet causes a company's financial distress is really mistaking cause and effect. By "overleveraged," finance professionals are usually referring to the level of a company's debt relative to its earnings strength, such as its debt/EBITDA (earnings before interest, taxes, depreciation, and amortization) ratio or its interest coverage ratio (EBIT/interest expense). While a company's leverage ratio (debt/equity) can also be helpful for monitoring its balance sheet over time or comparing it to competitors' balance sheets, it is not as useful for detecting financial distress because earnings are excluded from this measure. When a company completes its debt financing, both lender and borrower usually expect the company's leverage ratios to remain within healthy limits until the maturity of the debt. When unexpected issues arise with the company's operations, declining profitability and cash flow result in the balance sheet appearing overleveraged. The denominator in the applicable ratios decreases, while the numerator may increase as a result of missed amortization payments, accrued interest expenses, and additional advances to cover losses. When these ratios become too stretched, the company may be nearing insolvency.

In 1968, Edward Altman, now a professor at New York University Stern School of Business, published his Altman Z-Score formula for predicting the probability that a firm will go into bankruptcy within two years. The Altman Z-Score uses multiple corporate income and balance sheet values to measure the financial health of companies in most industries except financial institutions. To calculate a particular company's Altman Z-Score, enter the required variables at http://www.creditguru.com/CalcAltZ.shtml.[1] The Z-Score is another indication of solvency and liquidity.

Finally, even companies with no debt still have creditors. Whenever a company does business with a vendor on payment terms, that vendor becomes a creditor between the time when the goods are shipped or the services are provided and the time when payment is received. If a company pays its workers periodically, the employees become creditors between the time when they work the hours and the time when they receive a paycheck. If a company loses a lawsuit, the plaintiff becomes a creditor. If the amounts due to these creditors overwhelm a company's resources, it can become insolvent, illiquid, or both.

Overall, rather than focusing on whether a company is overleveraged, it is more constructive to determine if it is insolvent or illiquid.

What is insolvency?

Insolvency, which is discussed at length in Chapter 10 of this book, is another way of saying that a company is overleveraged. Different authorities define insolvency in different ways. The *Bankruptcy Code*, found under Title 11 of the United States Code (11 U.S.C.), defines the term *insolvent*, as it applies to a corporation, as a "financial condition such that the sum of [the] entity's debts is greater than all of such entity's property, at a fair valuation."[2] In this definition, debts include contingent liabilities. A *fair valuation* of an entity's property refers to the amount of cash that could be realized from a sale of the property "during a reasonable period of time."[3] A *reasonable period of time* is an amount of time that "a typical creditor would find optimal: not so short a period that the value of goods is substantially impaired via a forced sale, but not so long a time that a typical creditor would receive less satisfaction of its claim, as a result of the time value of money and typical business needs, by waiting for the possibility of a higher price."[4]

The Uniform Fraudulent Transfer Act (UFTA) also defines *insolvency* as having more liabilities than salable assets, but also deems insolvent any debtor "who is generally not paying his debts when they become due."[5] This is sometimes referred to as the *equity definition* of insolvency.[6] Most state laws have a definition that resembles that of the Bankruptcy Code, but some states (e.g., New York) follow the equity definition for certain situations other than fraudulent transfers.[7] Fraudulent transfers are discussed in depth in Chapter 10.

Under generally accepted accounting principles (GAAP), a company can be considered solvent if it has sufficient assets to pay its debts as they come due or if it has book assets that are greater than book liabilities. This GAAP definition is more lenient than other definitions because it does not count contingent liabilities. It may be significantly misleading if the market value of the assets declines in a manner that was not predicted by the applicable accounting principles. Therefore, merely examining whether book equity (i.e., the difference between book assets and book liabilities) is positive is usually insufficient to determine whether a company is solvent.

When does a pattern of late payments cross the line into insolvency?

Generally, insolvency begins when creditors stop trusting the entity to pay within an acceptable time frame. One or even two or three missed or late payments may not trigger an extreme response from creditors if the company has no history of financial difficulty or misdeeds. Companies stretch their accounts payable all the time, and a late fee or other minor penalty will frequently be sufficient to maintain the relationship. However, a recurring pattern of missed or late payments will usually trigger some kind of action. The action will vary, depending on the type of debt involved.

- If the debt is a bank loan, a loan officer will call, point out that the borrower is in violation of a loan agreement, and ask for an immediate meeting, which usually includes someone from the bank's workout department.
- If the debt is a commercial bill for merchandise or services, usually someone from the vendor's accounts receivable department will telephone and follow up by letter to inquire about the missed or late payments.

What are some warning signs that a company is in financial distress?

When a company is in financial distress, there are no obvious solutions to its problems. If the answers were obvious, then the crisis could have been averted. Perhaps the board of directors would have solved the company's problems by refinancing to lengthen debt maturities, changing management, discontinuing certain operations, pursuing strategic acquisitions, approving capital expenditures, revamping marketing strategies, or hiring a turnaround manager or management consultant. When the traditional defenses and normal course corrections prove to be inadequate, a company can enter the dreaded "death spiral," where one issue spawns another and another until there is a full-blown crisis. The common theme as a company sinks through the depths of the death spiral is shrinking liquidity leading to tougher choices and fewer alternatives.

Warren Buffett has a point when he notes, "It's only when the tide goes out that you learn who's been swimming naked." During periods of strong revenue growth, executives, directors, investors, and lenders may miss the warning signs that a company is approaching financial distress, especially if its lenders agreed to weak financial covenants or, worse, if the debt is *covenant-lite* (issued with no or few covenants). Strong revenue growth can mask a lot of issues inside a company. When the drivers of strong pricing and rising volume begin to change direction, however, mismanagement often becomes evident. As revenue growth flattens and then declines—often sharply in an industry downturn or economic recession—companies are frequently unable to contain their costs sufficiently to maintain profitability. Executives may have approved rapid expansion of new facilities, new equipment, long-term supply contracts, and bold marketing programs that sounded ideal when revenue growth was strong, but that burden the company with high fixed costs when revenue is declining. Management may have tolerated lax accounting practices, making it difficult to identify the profitability of each product or service, and therefore impossible to decide quickly which operations to discontinue. In other cases, management may have been in a rush to recruit new hires as soon as talented candidates became available, and determining which employees should be retained and which laid off may not be straightforward. Naturally, hindsight is 20/20, but companies that are going through these transitions lack a crystal ball to predict the future—even the near future—and may misread the warning signs.

Even when revenue growth appears to be healthy, there are many potential warning signs that a company may be in real trouble. These warning signs may include

- *Deterioration of cash flow.* Always, always, always keep an eye on cash flow. Things to watch for are free cash flow beginning to diverge from net income as measured under GAAP, accounts payable being increasingly stretched to abnormally high levels

compared to the industry norm, and/or capital expenditures
trending toward, or going below, replacement levels. An unexpected dividend cut can also be a harbinger of growing cash
flow problems. It's prudent to track common financial ratios
such as the company's fixed charge coverage (EBITDA as a
multiple of fixed charges, such as debt repayments, interest
expense, lease payments, and so on) and its current ratio (current assets divided by current liabilities).

- *Change of auditors.* It's generally uncommon for a company to
  switch auditors, except perhaps in cases in which there are consulting conflicts or when the company has outgrown its auditor
  and is upsizing to a larger outfit. As a general rule, scrutinize
  the reasoning behind an auditor change; you may discover that
  the auditor has raised a going-concern issue, internal control
  problems, or aggressive accounting interpretations.[8]

- *Unexplained departures of executives.* Like rats fleeing a sinking
  ship, it's not uncommon to see senior managers leaving in droves
  when a business starts to falter. This dynamic plays out quickly
  in publicly traded companies, particularly in this post-Sarbanes-
  Oxley era, when management must personally sign off on the
  financial statements. Often, if a CEO or CFO suddenly resigns
  with little or no credible explanation from the remaining management, many public shareholders assume the worst (e.g., mal-
  feasance) by selling first and asking questions later.

- *Sale of crown jewels.* Be wary of a company that begins to pare
  off high-return product lines, facilities, or business units. This
  is particularly concerning if the assets divested were part of the
  core focus of the enterprise.

- *Constant restructuring charges.* It's reasonable to be concerned about companies that constantly post restructuring
  charges related to severance, material changes in plan benefits, plant closures, and so forth. This suggests that there is a
  risk of substantially underutilized capacity, and, consequently, begs the question, *Why?* Is management in the process of legitimately trying to turn the business around, or is
  it merely "kicking the can down the road" with only incremental changes?

- *Unusual credit-related developments.* There are a handful of items to watch for along these lines. For instance, if a company draws down a substantial amount of its revolving credit facility (not in the ordinary course of business), this may indicate that management is preparing to file for bankruptcy and is seeking to maximize its cash just prior to entering the process. Other warning signs might be if the company violates a financial covenant or seems precariously close to doing so in the near future. Finally, it's worth considering the company's future debt maturity schedule. Are there any sizable repayments coming due in the next few years that cannot be made out of internal free cash flow? If so, it's advisable to consider the potential terms of this debt rollover; after all, many companies that levered up in recent years were able to do so at unusually tight spreads and with limited covenants. It's highly unlikely that many such capital structures could be replicated today. For these reasons, looming repayment obligations could portend future financial distress.
- *Competitors experiencing financial distress.* If a company's competitors are experiencing any of these issues, then the company itself may be next. Understanding the root causes of the competitors' distress will help determine whether the overall industry is experiencing negative developments or whether the issues are isolated.
- *Ratings downgrade.* If a company's securities receive a negative report or negative ratings from a credit rating agency like Standard & Poor's, Moody's, or Fitch,[9] this is a clear warning sign that the company is heading into trouble. For example, if the company's debt securities have a low rating, beware, especially if they are *high-yield bonds.* In an extreme case, the credit rating agencies may lower a company's rating by multiple notches at once, demonstrating serious concern about impending distress. For example, in June 2010 Fitch downgraded BP from AA- to BBB once the extent of the company's liability became clearer weeks after the explosion of an oil rig in the Gulf of Mexico, which commentators have labeled the largest manmade disaster in history.

A PRIMER ON HIGH-YIELD BONDS

What are high-yield bonds?

Before they became distressed, many troubled companies were financed with high-yield bonds, which are medium- to long-term obligations that (1) are subordinated to senior debt, (2) are normally unsecured, and (3) bear high interest rates. Historically, such bonds were also referred to as *junk bonds*, a term that was reportedly coined by famed financier Michael Milken. High-yield bonds are normally not prepayable for an initial period (usually three to five years, but some are not callable until maturity), and thereafter are prepayable only at a premium, which is called *call protection* (see Chapter 14 of this book for further discussion on call protection and *make-whole provisions*).

The main purpose of high-yield bonds is to provide mezzanine financing, filling in the gap between senior secured debt, which pays a lower interest rate, and the seller's takeback financing or the buyer's equity financing, which is the last to be paid back. There is sometimes more than one layer of high-yield debt, with one being senior subordinated and the other junior subordinated debt.

In the high-risk, high-reward gambles enabled by issuing high-yield bonds—such as leveraged buyouts (LBOs)—there will inevitably be some winners and many losers. The losing bets will produce distressed companies rather than investment gains.

To whom and how are high-yield bonds sold?

High-yield bonds are commonly sold to large financial institutions—insurance companies, pension funds, and mutual funds, including overseas investors—usually in blocks of $500,000 or more; they are primarily for sophisticated investors. Funds that invest in high-yield bonds often attract super-sophisticated portfolio managers who are known to go into and out of the high-yield bond market rapidly, causing volatility in prices. Often, but not necessarily, the offerings are registered under the federal securities laws to increase their marketability and are sold in a package with warrants to acquire common stock in the target. If they are privately placed, they often carry registration rights that will enable the holders to require the borrower to register the debt for sale in a public offering.

When issuers of high-yield bonds experience signs of distress, the bonds will typically trade downward, perhaps sharply, as risk-averse portfolio managers exit before the situation worsens. Indeed, certain mutual funds and other bond funds may be prohibited from holding the bonds of companies that have defaulted or entered bankruptcy, motivating the portfolio managers to sell the high-yield bonds indiscriminately at the first signs of trouble. For buyers of distressed companies, seeing bonds trade down can be one of the best indicators that a company may become an acquisition target.

What is a bond indenture?

The *indenture* is the basic agreement setting forth the terms of the high-yield bonds. It is entered into between the borrower and a bank, which acts as trustee for the bondholders. It serves the same function as the credit or loan agreement executed with the senior secured lender and the note purchase agreement executed with an institutional mezzanine lender. The indenture contains the covenants, events of default, and other material terms of the transaction, including the various responsibilities and rights of the issuer, the trustee, and the bondholders. If the bonds are issued or subsequently sold pursuant to a public offering, the indenture must qualify under the Trust Indenture Act of 1939. Much of the boilerplate in the indenture is derived from requirements under that law.

The principal objectives of the covenants are to prevent the borrower from disposing of its assets (unless the borrower reinvests the sale proceeds in assets that are used in the same business or uses them to pay down its debt); to ensure that if any merger, consolidation, or change affecting the borrower occurs, the successor entity is obligated to repay the bonds on the same terms and is in as strong a financial position after the transaction as before; to limit the creation of additional debt and liens (particularly secured debt that is senior to the bonds); to limit payments of dividends and distributions to stockholders; and to restrict transactions with affiliates.

What covenants do high-yield bonds normally contain?

Compared with senior debt agreements, unsecured high-yield bond indentures are simpler, fitting the classic bond indenture mold. Unlike senior debt instruments, which provide for total information flow to lenders, hair-trigger default provisions, and, in theory, extensive second-guessing and approval of management decisions, high-yield bond indentures tend to rely more on the borrower's good judgment and the value of the company as a going concern. As such, these indentures limit themselves to protecting the bondholders against major restructurings, asset transfers, or increases in the amounts of senior or secured debt. Typical financial covenants for this purpose include fixed charge coverage ratio, minimum EBITDA, maximum capital expenditures, debt/EBITDA ratio, interest coverage ratio, leverage ratio, and other measurements of financial performance. This relatively simple approach reflects the longer-term nature of such debt and the impracticality of obtaining consents from a large, diverse group of public bondholders.

In the rare case that the high-yield bonds are *secured,* however, a more elaborate set of covenants relating to the protection of collateral will be included.

Generally, borrowers should try to limit the financial covenants in high-yield bond issues to "incurrence" tests rather than "maintenance" tests. In other words, the covenants should not require that any specified level of financial health be maintained and should be breached only by a voluntary act by the company, such as paying a prohibited dividend, incurring prohibited debt, merging or combining with another company or selling assets unless certain tests are met, or dealing with affiliates other than at arm's length. These covenants will often closely restrict operating subsidiaries of the borrower to ensure that all debt is incurred on the same corporate level.

Depending on the conditions of the credit markets at the time the high-yield bonds are issued, the covenants may go much further. These tighter covenants may include detailed financial maintenance covenants relating to net worth, current ratios, interest coverage, and the like; limitations on investments; and application of proceeds from asset sales outside the ordinary course of business.

But won't it be possible to just waive these covenants if they prove to be too restrictive?

No. Prepaying the high-yield bonds is very likely to be either impossible or very expensive because of prepayment restrictions and penalties. In addition, unlike the case with senior lenders, it is often impossible, or at the least very difficult, to obtain waivers of covenants from a multitude of public bondholders. Therefore, the restrictions contained in the high-yield bond indenture should be something that the borrower can live with for a long time. Special care must be taken to ensure that the covenants fit the company's long-term plans with respect to acquisitions, dispositions of assets, expansions, and so on. Once the covenants are in place, the borrower will have to live with them pretty much unmodified. If the borrower violates the covenants, it may default.

DEFAULTS

What does it mean to default?

Legal documents related to debt issuance, such as credit agreements and bond indentures, typically define *events of default* that, if not cured, result in a default on the borrower's obligations. Defaults may relate to any kind of fixed income security, including high-yield bonds, leveraged loans, and other types of debt. A default usually provides the company's creditors with enhanced access to information, higher interest rates called *default interest*, and opportunities to renegotiate the terms of the debt going forward. In dire situations, a default may trigger an acceleration of the maturity of the debt such that the principal amount is immediately due and payable. Default interest, which may begin upon the event of default or at the time of acceleration of the debt, may involve a premium of 2 or 3 percentage points above the rate normally in effect. See Chapter 14 for a discussion on "amend and extend" agreements regarding defaults. There are three types of default that are relevant to distressed M&A: *payment default, technical default,* and *cross default.*

A *payment default* arises when a company fails to make a scheduled payment to one or more of its creditors. Usually, creditors give companies a *grace period* within which to make a late payment after the scheduled due date. If a company still has not made the payment by the end of the grace period, then a payment default occurs.

Technical defaults occur when a company's declining performance triggers one or more defaults with respect to its covenants (often called "tripping covenants"). When a company takes out a revolving line of credit or a term loan with its senior lenders or issues debt, such as bonds, with its unsecured creditors, the legal agreements between the company and its creditors specify certain covenants relating to financial, legal, administrative, and other issues. By defining minimum expectations, these covenants are a primary means for a creditor to remain a passive investor and allow the borrower to exercise its *business judgment* for managing day-to-day operations. When a borrower's performance falls below these minimum expectations, however, creditors understandably become concerned about the company's future performance. Therefore, when a company breaches one or more of these covenants, there is a technical default. A technical default can arise even if the company makes all of its payments on time.

A *cross default* occurs when a default with one group of creditors triggers defaults with other creditors. Companies with more complicated capital structures have multiple *tranches* of debt, with different legal agreements for each tranche. In such situations, it is typical for each tranche of debt to have as a covenant that the company is not in default with any other tranche of debt. If one group of creditors gains rights as a result of a default, the other creditors want to level the playing field by gaining those rights as well. Also, if one group of creditors is on notice that a company's performance is declining below minimum expectations, then other groups of creditors want that same notice. When a cross default occurs, a company's distress may accelerate if it finds itself simultaneously negotiating with multiple groups of creditors, causing a major distraction for management as it tries to run the day-to-day operations of the business.

How common are defaults?

As discussed previously, companies fail for a variety of reasons, meaning that defaults occur in every economic period. To illustrate this point, Exhibit 1-1 shows the volume and number of high-yield bonds that defaulted over three decades. Not surprisingly, though, default rates tend to spike in recessionary periods, as illustrated by Exhibit 1-2.

Default rates differ across industries, reflecting the wide variety of risk factors involved. Exhibit 1-3 summarizes default rates by industry from 2000-2009. During this decade, the financial, diversified media, and transportation sectors experienced the highest rates of default, while the energy, broadcasting, and healthcare sectors experienced the lowest rates of default. Overall, high-yield bonds experienced an average default rate of 4.17 percent across all industries during this period. Any particular year or decade, however, may generate vastly different results.

Exhibit 1-1 High-Yield Bond Defaults 1980–2009

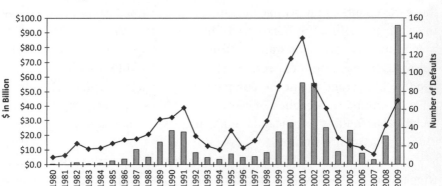

Note: Includes grace-period defaults.

Source: J.P. Morgan.

Another way to analyze default rates of high-yield bonds is to consider the year of issuance. Trends in interest rates, debt levels, leveraged buyouts, and covenants often impact the credit quality of bonds issued in the same period. Depending on the appetite for risk, investors may follow more rigid standards in some periods while permitting looser terms in others. Exhibit 1-4 highlights the average number of years to default for

Exhibit 1-2 High-Yield Bond Default Rates

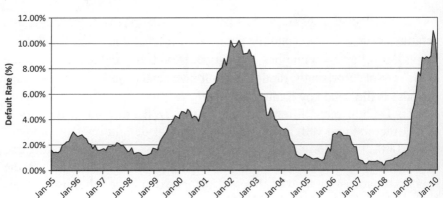

Note: Includes grace-period defaults.

Source: J.P. Morgan.

Exhibit 1-3 Average High-Yield Bond Default Rates by Industry, 2000–2009

Industry	2000–2009 Average	Industry	2000–2009 Average	Industry	2000–2009 Average
Diversified Media	9.15%	Aerospace	4.01%	Chemicals	2.83%
Financial	8.76%	Food and Drug	3.81%	Information Technology	2.75%
Transportation	7.05%	Wireless Telecom	3.37%	Service	2.31%
Cable/Wireless Video	5.90%	Manufacturing	3.29%	Utility	1.96%
Wireline Telecom	5.65%	Retail	3.11%	Healthcare	1.87%
Metals/Minerals	5.20%	Forest Products	3.05%	Broadcasting	1.51%
Consumer Products	4.64%	Gaming/Leisure	3.04%	Energy	0.71%
Food/Tobacco	4.33%	Housing	2.91%	All Industries	4.17%

Source: J.P. Morgan.

high-yield bonds to show the number of years since the defaulted issuer last issued new debt in the capital markets. During this 15-year period, the average time to default was 3.8 years.

How are defaults related to bond ratings?

Most bonds are rated by credit rating agencies, such as Standard & Poor's (S&P), Moody's, and Fitch. In general, investors expect these ratings to indicate a bond's credit quality, likelihood of default, and expected recovery in a distressed situation. Also, credit ratings enable investors to compare bonds across different industries and in different parts of the capital structure.

Exhibit 1-4 Average Number of Years to Default for High-Yield Bonds

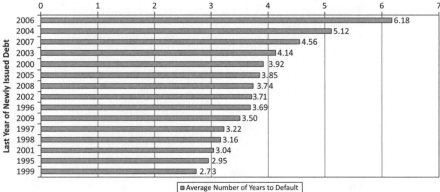

Source: J.P. Morgan.

This discussion will focus on S&P's ratings symbols, which label investment grade bonds AAA, AA, A, and BBB and speculative grade (i.e., high yield) bonds BB, B, CCC, CC, C, and D.[10] Just because debt may be rated investment grade does not mean that it cannot default. When a security's rating has a "+" or "−" after the symbol, this shows the relative standing of the security within the major rating category. The other credit rating agencies use symbols that are comparable to S&P's. Rating agencies are constantly monitoring the debt that they rate and periodically change their ratings. When credit rating agencies arrive at different conclusions for the same bond, the bond becomes known as *split rated*.

Exhibit 1-5 examines the default rates by credit rating from 1981–2009 by showing the likelihood of default during the time horizon since the bonds were issued. In general, the lower the credit rating and the longer a bond remains outstanding, the more likely a default will occur.

Exhibit 1-6 shows the default rates for speculative grade bonds by year of issuance regardless of when such debt ultimately defaulted. These calculations use par amounts.

How can a bond default if it is covenant-lite?

Investors use the term *covenant-lite* to describe bonds with minimal covenants in the bond indenture. In a situation in which debt is covenant-lite, a company can spiral out of control without triggering a technical default on its bonds or a cross default. However, it must still generate sufficient cash flow to make the scheduled interest and principal payments.

Exhibit 1-5 Cumulative Average Default Rates by Credit Rating, 1981–2009

Rating	Time Horizon (Years)						
	1	2	3	4	5	10	15
AAA	0.00%	0.03%	0.14%	0.26%	0.39%	0.82%	1.14%
AA	0.02%	0.07%	0.14%	0.24%	0.33%	0.74%	1.02%
A	0.08%	0.21%	0.35%	0.53%	0.72%	1.97%	2.99%
BBB	0.26%	0.72%	1.23%	1.86%	2.53%	5.60%	8.36%
BB	0.97%	2.94%	5.27%	7.49%	9.51%	17.45%	21.57%
B	4.93%	10.76%	15.65%	19.46%	22.30%	30.82%	35.74%
CCC/C	27.98%	36.95%	42.40%	45.57%	48.05%	53.41%	57.28%

Source: Standard & Poor's Leveraged Commentary & Data.

Exhibit 1-6 Default Rates for High-Yield Bonds by Credit Rating

Rating	1995	1996	1997	1998	1999	2000	2001	2002	2003	2004	2005	2006	2007	2008
Split BBB	0.00%	12.20%	34.70%	2.20%	32.20%	22.20%	16.80%	0.00%	0.00%	4.60%	4.50%	0.00%	0.00%	0.00%
B B	7.40%	14.30%	25.50%	13.60%	28.40%	11.10%	17.60%	4.80%	3.20%	3.30%	2.00%	4.90%	0.00%	0.00%
Split BB	26.00%	33.80%	11.00%	22.00%	45.50%	19.20%	20.40%	2.10%	2.90%	5.90%	0.50%	3.90%	0.00%	0.00%
B	26.60%	28.80%	39.10%	45.10%	35.00%	56.50%	17.70%	13.40%	12.20%	12.50%	5.40%	15.10%	7.50%	17.00%
Split B	26.00%	17.60%	37.00%	39.80%	31.50%	87.10%	0.00%	15.30%	19.90%	5.00%	7.60%	16.40%	4.90%	5.20%
CCC	27.80%	0.00%	40.70%	60.40%	46.30%	81.00%	35.80%	0.00%	4.30%	5.80%	6.00%	13.50%	7.60%	0.00%
Not Rated	78.50%	42.30%	61.30%	74.80%	44.10%	57.60%	0.00%	0.00%	5.00%	75.20%	21.50%	4.70%	0.00%	0.00%

Source: J.P. Morgan.

21

Therefore, while it may be unlikely—or even impossible—for a covenant-lite bond to experience a technical default, the borrower may still trigger a payment default when it eventually runs out of cash.

In most periods, investors require meaningful covenants in bond indentures, but capital markets sometimes become so competitive that borrowers convince investors to accept covenant-lite bonds. For example, in 2006 to 2007, borrowers issued nearly $125 billion of covenant-lite bonds.[11] As noted previously, these frothy capital markets led to record high defaults in 2009.

NEVER LET A CRISIS GO TO WASTE

Why would anyone want to voluntarily get involved with all of these messy issues by buying a distressed company?

In a nutshell, price. The most compelling advantage of buying a troubled business is that the company should be trading at a relatively cheap price. If the current owners are in a panic and feel that their options are limited, a buyer can have significant leverage when negotiating a transaction. In a properly functioning market, a fair price is determined by a willing seller and a willing buyer. In a distressed situation, however, the seller is under duress, and the M&A market is almost always not working well. Indeed, the distressed M&A markets can be some of the most inefficient markets for conducting transactions because of confusing information, intense time pressure, uncertain issues, and unfamiliar procedures. Most potential buyers simply avoid the hassle of figuring it all out and prefer cleaner M&A targets with more orderly sale processes. Other potential buyers simply cannot move quickly enough to deal with the fast sale process that distressed M&A markets may demand. These buyers may need to have multiple levels of executives and directors involved in the decisions or may need more time to raise financing. As a result, demand among potential buyers is sufficiently suppressed to make distressed M&A markets inefficient, causing the prices of these companies to appear cheap relative to traditional M&A valuations.

Those few brave investors who are willing to participate in distressed M&A transactions are betting that inefficient markets and relatively cheap prices at the beginning of their investment will lead to above-average returns when they exit their investment. What other investors perceive as extraordinarily high risks, investors in distressed companies see as particularly attractive opportunities. At the most basic level, these investors believe that turning a bad company back into a good company offers a superior risk/reward profile to transforming a good company into a great company. Investors in distressed companies believe that refocusing management on "basic blocking and tackling" is actually less risky than creating and implementing ingenious growth strategies. We provide additional perspective on investing in distressed companies in Chapter 3 of this book.

What are the key differences between traditional M&A and distressed M&A?

The most obvious difference between traditional and distressed M&A is that a distressed company is experiencing a liquidity and solvency crisis, so the interaction between debtors and creditors is different. Another clear difference between traditional and distressed M&A is the role of the judiciary, such as bankruptcy courts, in addressing these tensions between debtors and creditors. Distressed M&A probably requires more creative, out-of-the-box thinking regarding both the company and the transaction. Like traditional M&A, successfully completing a distressed M&A transaction involves complicated game theory and savvy negotiations.

The key differences between traditional M&A and distressed M&A are summarized in Exhibit 1-7.

Exhibit 1-7 Key Differences between Traditional and Distressed M&A

	Traditional M&A	Distressed M&A
Diligence	Available and organized data	Opaque and confusing data
Timing	Quick	Urgent
Valuation	At or above market	Below market
Competition	Relatively high number of bidders	Relatively low number of bidders
Liabilities	Probably need to assume	Probably able to avoid
Legal	Out of court	In court or out of court
Management	Probably retain	Probably replace
Strategy	Grow	Fix

Doesn't distressed M&A simply involve buying good companies with bad balance sheets?

While this makes sense intuitively, these opportunities are fairly rare in practice. Years ago, distressed M&A may have involved buying good companies with bad balance sheets, but M&A and credit markets today are too sophisticated. There are many investors and acquirers who are seeking such opportunities, so good companies with bad balance sheets can be adequately addressed with traditional M&A transactions. In addition, lenders in today's markets will typically work with a fundamentally good company to refinance its balance sheet rather than force a distressed sale. Both the borrower and the lender should prefer avoiding the uncertainties and costs of bankruptcy or some other type of distressed sale. The credit-friendly environment of the past decade has given failing businesses staying power, enabling even weak businesses to work out their balance sheets. Every once in a while, circumstances may indeed produce a good company with a bad balance sheet, so investors should pay careful attention and watch for these situations, but they should probably not form their entire investment thesis around them.

Therefore, in the current environment, distressed M&A very often involves a company with both troubled operations and an overleveraged balance sheet. As a result, an important aspect of distressed M&A is determining whether a company's troubled operations can be saved and, if so, the amount of time, effort, and capital that will be required. If a business is worth saving, the distressed M&A process offers a key advantage over and above deleveraging the balance sheet. If the burdens of certain legacy costs are handicapping the company's competitiveness and hindering its ability to change, the company may be salvageable if it can use the distressed M&A process to fix its cost structure. Costs that are adjusted might include unfavorable customer agreements, vendor commitments, leases, product liability, union contracts, pension plans, or other claims. Shedding these sorts of liabilities—as well as debt—can transform an unattractive business into a highly desirable acquisition for prudent investors who recognize a fundamentally good franchise underneath.

How does a potential buyer know if a target company is worth saving?

Whether a business is worth saving is highly subjective. Financial buyers (such as private equity firms) and strategic buyers (such as competitors) may view a company's operations very differently. To begin, interested buyers should identify the company's core franchise and evaluate its strength relative to its competition. Key questions to ask are

- Who will care if this company ceases to exist?
- Where would customers go if this company were no longer around?
- Why have customers chosen this company in the past?
- Where does this company's market share rank today as compared to five years ago?
- Is the company's industry highly fragmented?
- What are the barriers to entry to compete with the company?
- Does the company have any unique intellectual property, such as patents?
- Does the company have any long-term contracts with its customers?
- What does the company's brand mean to customers?

Many companies become financially distressed because they have allowed themselves to become undifferentiated in the middle of their markets. Over time, the company's value proposition to its customers, which may have been very strong for a long time, has been eroded by more formidable competition and a changing marketplace. Rather than proactively refreshing its value propositions, the company has allowed its competitors to outflank it in both (1) the low-price, high-volume, commoditized portions of the market and (2) the premium-price, low-volume, value-added portion of the market (see Exhibit 1-8). Midpriced, mediocre volume is often a road to financial distress as customers decide that they would rather either pay less for more basic products and services or trade up to gain the compelling benefits of the higher end of the market. In these situations, a company that is stuck in the middle may be worth saving if it can be reorganized by fixing its cost structure so that it can compete in the low-price market segments or improving its products and services so that it can compete in the premium market segments. If the company cannot pursue either path, then liquidation may be preferable to reorganization.

Exhibit 1-8 Competitive Positioning of Companies Vulnerable to Financial Distress

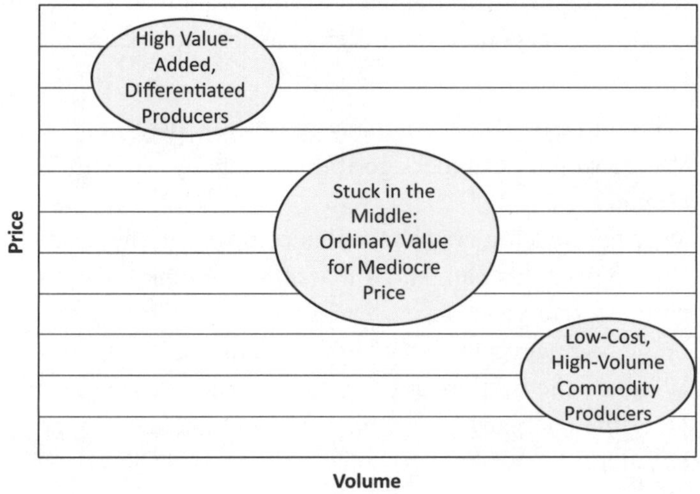

Volume

There are many examples of companies that have been stuck in the middle. In retail, concepts like Montgomery Ward, Ames, Caldor, Bradlees, Hechinger, Circuit City, Tower Records, and Lechmere enjoyed customer loyalty for decades, but then mass merchants attacked on one side and niche retailers struck on the other. All of these companies ultimately were liquidated, but others, like Kmart and Filene's Basement, reorganized. Among restaurants, Bennigan's and Steak & Ale succumbed to competition, but Schlotzsky's, Planet Hollywood, Mrs. Fields, and Sizzler lived to fight another day.

Even if a company avoids being stuck in the middle, it may still experience financial distress if its business model is fundamentally flawed or if it loses its competitive edge. Some recent examples of niche businesses that were unable to reorganize and were liquidated include, among retailers, Linens 'n Things, The Custom Shop, The Museum Store, Ritz Camera, The Sharper Image, and Today's Man.

So as you look for bargains, ask yourself:

- Are there structural fault lines within the industry?
- Has the company's primary offering reached the end of its life cycle?

- Is volume below critical mass to support the company's fixed costs, and, if so, what are likely scenarios as to how it will rebound?
- Has regulatory change forever dimmed the company's prospects?
- Are there successful competitors with business models that the company can emulate?
- Are the company's assets being put to their highest and best use?
- Is there an upcoming wave or a new trend that can benefit the company?
- Has the brand, trademark, and other intangible franchise value been irreparably damaged?
- Have the best employees already left the company, with the result that key customer relationships, operational wisdom, and competitive intelligence have been drained from the business (and have prior employees already taken this "tribal knowledge" to the company's competitors)?
- Overall, is the company past the point of no return, or is there still a realistic chance for recovery?

What are the differences between the terms used to describe troubled companies?

There are many terms of art that professionals use to describe troubled companies, including

- *Special situations.* This is usually the broadest term; it encompasses any and all of the ones below, and it is often chosen by professionals to remain opportunistic in selecting target investments and nonthreatening when soliciting clients.
- *Workouts.* This typically refers to out-of-court processes where a bank's workout group gets involved following a default by the company (see Chapter 2 of this book).
- *Underperformers.* While this term may refer to the company's current state as compared to its prior financial results or the company's performance vis-à-vis its competitors, it usually means that the company is on a negative trajectory, but is not yet in distress or bankruptcy and has not yet defaulted on its credit agreements.

- *Restructurings.* This term typically refers to a balance sheet restructuring, such as a debt-for-equity exchange, whether out of court or in bankruptcy, but it may also be used more generically, like special situations.
- *Turnarounds.* This optimistic term usually refers more to the operational aspects of a distressed company than to the balance sheet, but it may also be used more generically, like special situations.
- *Stressed companies.* Like underperformers, companies with this description have certain warning signs that indicate that there are potentially serious problems on the horizon that management and owners should proactively address, but that the company is not yet in crisis mode or in default with its creditors.
- *Distressed companies.* This is usually a broad, pessimistic term that is meant to include deeply troubled companies in a variety of situations where the company has defaulted on its commitments to its creditors, including out-of-court workouts, bankruptcies, and liquidations.

What are some of the key pitfalls of acquiring a troubled business?

Far and away, the key pitfall to overcome is uncertainty. Why is the business troubled in the first place? If you don't know, you could be taking on more than you can handle. The worst-case scenario is often referred to as "catching a falling knife," where the company continues through the death spiral even after the closing of a distressed M&A transaction. Buyers may be unpleasantly surprised to find that the seller's temporary fixes to the cost structure masked chronic problems that will be costly and time-consuming for the buyer to repair permanently. In other cases, buyers may unfortunately realize that an industry's cycle still has further to fall when they thought it had already hit bottom. Sometimes a buyer may have misjudged the valuable roles played by key employees and mistakenly cut muscle and not just fat during headcount reductions. Buyer's remorse can be just as painful when overpaying for a distressed company as when overbidding for a healthy one.

Such fundamental analysis aside, the distressed M&A process itself has its own set of potential pitfalls. While all potential acquirers will have to expend significant amounts of time, effort, and cost, only one bidder can ultimately be successful. Many bidders may chase a potential troubled company and wind up with nothing to show for their perseverance. Other bidders may decide to drop out of the distressed M&A process when they learn that the target company is worse than they expected, leaving them with similar sorts of "dead deal" costs.

In other cases, a company may begin down the distressed M&A path and then reconsider restructuring on its own if its operations or the capital markets improve and a distressed valuation is no longer the best option. Sometimes potential buyers may inadvertently reveal their turnaround strategies for a particular business to the existing owner, causing the seller to change its mind and try to fix the business itself.

Finally, another pitfall is that a buyer may attempt to drive down the valuation too far, leading the seller to investigate liquidation alternatives further. If a seller's initial estimates of the attainable value, professional costs, and time commitment involved in liquidation prove to be overly pessimistic, the seller may decide that it prefers liquidation to selling the troubled company as a going concern.

Sellers need not rush this decision. Instead, they should weigh their alternatives. The next chapter shows how.

Endnotes

1. See Edward I. Altman, "Financial Ratios, Discriminant Analysis and the Prediction of Corporate Bankruptcy," *Journal of Finance*, September 1968, pp. 189–209; and Edward I. Altman, "Predicting Financial Distress of Companies," July 2000; http://pages.stern.nyu.edu/~ealtman/Zscores.pdf, last accessed May 16, 2010.
2. 11 U.S.C. §101(32)(A).
3. *Travellers International AG v. Trans World Airlines, Inc.* (*In re Trans World Airlines*), 134 F.3d 188, 194 (3d Cir. 1998), *cert. denied*, 523 U.S. 1138 (1998).
4. Ibid. at 195.
5. Uniform Fraudulent Transfer Act §§2(a) and (b).
6. *Brandt v. Hicks, Muse & Co.* (*In re Healthco Int'l, Inc.*), 208 B.R. 288, 300 (Bankr. D. Mass. 1997), noted that "insolvency in the bankruptcy sense [is] an excess of liabilities over the value of assets," but in the context of fiduciary obligations of directors to creditors, "another form of insolvency is equally relevant—insolvency in the equity sense," that is, "an inability to pay debts as they mature. Even though not insolvent in a bankruptcy sense, a business is insolvent in the equity sense if its assets lack liquidity."

7. New York Business Corporation Law (§102(a)(8)) defines *insolvent*, in part, as "being unable to pay debts as they become due in the usual course of the debtor's business."

8. Public companies are required to disclose a change in auditors on Form 8-K as soon as it occurs, along with the reasons for the change. See Sections 13 and 15D of the Securities Exchange Act of 1934. For Form 8-K, see http://www.sec.gov/about/forms/form8-k.pdf, last accessed March 13, 2010. For disclosure details, see U.S. Code, Title 17, §229.304 (Item 304), "Changes In and Disagreements with Accountants on Accounting and Financial Disclosure"; available at http://law.justia.com/us/cfr/title17/17-2.0.1.1.11.4.30.4.html, last accessed March 13, 2010.

9. The major bond rating services—Standard & Poor's (S&P), Moody's Investor Services, and Fitch—use different symbols and sometimes arrive at different conclusions, known as a split rating. The best-known rating system is S&P's, which is, from the top, as follows: AAA, AA, A, and BBB for investment grade; BB, B, CCC, and lower for non–investment grade. S&P uses an "r" rating for bonds of any grade that carry a relatively high risk factor.

10. See http://www.standardandpoors.com/ratings/definitions-and-faqs/en/us (last accessed October 6, 2010) for more details.

11. As reported by J.P. Morgan and Standard & Poor's Leveraged Commentary & Data.

CHAPTER 2

Alternatives for Distressed Companies

You either need to raise the bridge or lower the water.

—Henry S. Miller, Managing Director,
Chairman, Miller Buckfire & Co., LLC

OVERVIEW OF RESTRUCTURING ALTERNATIVES

What are the main legal alternatives for troubled companies?

Fundamentally, all of the parties involved must decide whether a troubled business should continue as a going concern or whether it should be liquidated. Often, this fundamental question is not easily answered because of significant uncertainty, confusing information, and volatile values. Some creditors might want to liquidate and receive a prompt and clear monetary recovery. Other creditors might reason that if the company is liquidated, they may not receive any recovery whatsoever because the costs of administration, including fees for legal and accounting services, may consume what little value might remain.[1] Certain parties might want the business to continue so that it can be a source of future business and profits. If the parties choose continuing as a going concern (which often simply means that the parties could not agree to liquidate), then the company will need breathing room to prepare and implement an operational turnaround, sale of the company, or both. In order to create this breathing room, the company will need to restructure its arrangements with its creditors because it is in or near default. The main restructuring alternatives that are available to a defaulting entity are (1) an out-of-court workout, (2) federal bankruptcy protection, and (3) state insolvency proceedings.

A payment default, technical default, or cross default may trigger an *acceleration* of the entire balance of the defaulted debt, so that it becomes due and payable immediately. If a company that is experiencing distress is able to refinance the defaulted debt with new creditors on improved terms, the company may have negotiating leverage to pursue an out-of-court workout with its existing creditors. If alternative sources of financing are unavailable, however, the existing creditors will probably have the negotiating advantage and may demand unreasonable terms for an out-of-court workout. In this case, the company can resist these demands by opting for either federal bankruptcy protection or state insolvency proceedings. Whether the company ultimately resolves its issues with its creditors in an out-of-court workout or an in-court proceeding depends on many factors, including

- Will all creditors agree to cooperate without court supervision?
- Is it possible to identify all of the company's creditors, or are some liabilities contingent and unknown?
- Are creditors organized so that they can negotiate collectively with the company?
- Do some creditors need to be forced to consent?
- Are there benefits to keeping a restructuring out of the courts?
- Are there useful legal powers, rights, and remedies that would be provided by federal bankruptcy law or state insolvency law?
- Will a court proceeding harm the operations of the business, making all creditors worse off?
- How fatigued are the lenders with the company and its management?
- Does the company's management have any credibility left with the creditors?
- What is the risk tolerance of each of the parties involved?
- What regulatory concerns do the lenders have?

This chapter discusses these questions in detail. Overall, each of these three alternatives alters the capital structure of the company in order to give the business time to design, implement, and complete a turnaround strategy. Faced with fixed charges, such as interest and amortization payments, that overwhelm its cash flow, the company needs to redirect that precious cash flow to fixing itself rather than paying creditors. Instead of drowning in debt, the company must seek to either raise the bridge or lower the water in order to survive.

DEFINING WORKOUTS

What is a workout?

A *workout*, also called a *debt restructuring*, is an out-of-court process through which a defaulting entity negotiates a payment schedule or plan with its creditors. It is a strictly consensual process that is controlled by the parties involved. The outcome of a workout depends on the relative negotiating leverage of the company and its creditors, the availability of alternative capital sources for refinancing, and the parties' understanding of their rights and remedies under federal bankruptcy law or state insolvency law. Therefore, out-of-court workouts always occur in the context of the capital markets and the law, as each of the parties is seeking a superior outcome by completing the workout instead.

In summary, a workout involves putting the company on a shorter leash with tighter restrictions because the creditors are concerned about the future implications of the borrower's recent poor performance. In addition, a workout may increase the company's reporting requirements to its creditors so that they can monitor the situation more closely.

A workout generally involves multiple creditors—and, often, a committee to represent them. In a workout, these creditors refrain from forcing immediate payment in full from a defaulting entity. Instead, creditors may consent to any or all of the following:

- Increasing the interest rate
- Dividing the interest expense into cash interest and payment-in-kind interest
- Revising the amortization schedule
- Extending the maturity
- Permitting a partial paydown or refinancing
- Acquiring a security interest in additional collateral
- Granting warrants for equity appreciation
- Changing management

What are the key advantages of a workout?

Because the parties' decisions are not subject to court supervision, the major advantages of a workout include

- Greater control over the process by the participants
- Faster and more flexible solutions
- Substantially lower administrative costs
- Confidentiality, because there are no public hearings or public records

This last point, confidentiality, can be a significant issue for the parties. The company probably wants the privacy of an out-of-court workout to avoid tarnishing its reputation with its customers, suppliers, employees, partners, and investors. The management of an already distressed company almost certainly does not need the additional distractions that are the inevitable result of the publicity surrounding a bankruptcy filing, such as being inundated with inquisitive calls. Competitors will undoubtedly relish the opportunity to exploit a company's public woes. Meanwhile, the senior lenders want to avoid the embarrassment of having made a troubled loan, which can create negative ramifications with the lender's regulators and investors.

Choosing an out-of-court workout also offers the advantage of keeping other options open. If the parties fail to reach agreement in a workout, they can always opt for federal bankruptcy protection or a state insolvency proceeding instead. On the other hand, once the parties are in federal or state court, it is difficult to revive the out-of-court workout option.

How does a workout operate?

Typically, a business that is faced with defaults or impending defaults asks to meet with representatives of the affected creditors in private. The company will probably have separate meetings with secured creditors and unsecured creditors. When a company has a complicated capital structure, it may meet with representatives for each tranche of debt. Management should repeat these meetings as often as needed in order to build the trust necessary for cooperation. It is far better to admit mistakes, acknowledge problems, and disclose issues than to try to conceal, deny, and distract. No downside surprises!

At the meeting, the company and its advisors present the current status of its operations and details of its financial condition. In addition, the company distributes a plan detailing how it intends to meet its current and future financial obligations. Usually, the creditors will want to understand the key elements of management's operational turnaround plan, a revised annual budget, and a detailed weekly cash flow projection. The plan is likely to include a debt restructuring designed to create breathing room to enable the company to implement its plan. The debt restructuring may range from requesting minor concessions from creditors to a drastic transformation of the capital structure.

An important part of the workout plan is a realistic estimate of the length of time needed for an operational turnaround, a sober assessment of the risks involved for each aspect of the turnaround, and a satisfactory approximation of the recovery for both the secured and unsecured creditors if the creditors agree to the debt restructuring. Each part of this analysis should consider the creditors' options in a federal bankruptcy case or state insolvency proceeding.

Separately, the workout plan should include a realistic estimate of the recovery that the creditors—both secured and unsecured—could expect if they forced the company into liquidation. The number should not be unrealistically low, but at the same time, it should account for the cash drain caused by the administration of the liquidation itself. Usually, the news is not pretty. The conventional view is that the average secured loan recovery is in the 75 to 80 percent range, while the average unsecured loan recovery is only about 2 percent.[2] However, generalities and averages have little bearing on any specific situation.

A company that is going through a workout must, above all, be honest with its creditors. Ultimately, the creditors' level of confidence in management's presentation of its strategy and its financial analysis will heavily influence the ability to complete a workout. Therefore, management, which has already shaken creditors' confidence by performing below expectations, needs to present a balanced view of the company's situation and outlook. On the one hand, if the estimate of time and recovery required for a turnaround is too slow or too low, creditors might prefer to liquidate rather than work matters out. On the other hand, if the estimates show wildly optimistic forecasts, demonstrate a state of denial regarding the issues plaguing the company, fail to present effective solutions for the company's predicament, or otherwise seem unrealistic, then the creditors will probably not agree to the debt restructuring. If the creditors' faith in current management is irreparably damaged, then the creditors may press for a change in management, engagement of a *turnaround consultant*, or employment of a *chief restructuring officer*.

For these reasons and others, a company would be wise to retain a seasoned restructuring advisor and experienced bankruptcy attorney to assist it in striking the right balance and navigating thorny negotiations. Moreover, the stamp of approval provided by such outside advisors helps enhance management's credibility. Furthermore, the advisors may have relationships with the company's creditors that can help smooth the process of reaching agreement.

What are some noteworthy out-of-court workouts?

Probably the most noteworthy out-of-court workouts occurred amid the 2008–2009 financial crisis: the federal government bailout of American International Group (AIG) and the rescue of Bear Stearns & Co.

DEFINING BANKRUPTCY

What is federal bankruptcy protection?

In the United States, bankruptcy is permitted by Article 1, Section 8, Clause 4 of the U.S. Constitution, which authorizes Congress to enact "uniform Laws on the subject of Bankruptcies throughout the United States." Accordingly, protection for debtors is accomplished under federal laws governing bankruptcy, which are known as the *Bankruptcy Code*. Throughout this book, we note the relevant Bankruptcy Code sections using references like 11 U.S.C. §###, or 11 U.S.C. section ###. The same Bankruptcy Code applies to both companies and individuals, but in this book, we are focusing only on those aspects that affect businesses. When a company seeks federal bankruptcy protection, it files a bankruptcy petition with a bankruptcy court to commence a bankruptcy case. The date on which the filing occurs is known as the *petition date*. The petition date has significant legal consequences because several sections of the Bankruptcy Code refer to *pre-petition* and *post-petition* periods. As of the petition date, the company is known as the *debtor*, which is more fully discussed in Chapter 4 of this book.

Are all bankruptcies voluntary?

The filing of a bankruptcy petition can be either voluntary or involuntary.[3] A *voluntary bankruptcy* petition is one filed by the company itself in order to gain protection from its creditors and a discharge of certain of its debts. In contrast, an *involuntary bankruptcy* petition is one that is filed against the company by creditors who are seeking to prevent or limit their losses by imposing bankruptcy court supervision on the company and its management.

An involuntary bankruptcy petition is a serious undertaking with potential ramifications for the instigating creditors. Bankruptcy Code section 303(b) creates certain requirements for an involuntary bankruptcy petition to be valid and enforceable:

- First, if a company has at least 12 unsecured creditors (excluding employees, insiders, and certain other parties), a minimum of 3 must sign the involuntary bankruptcy petition. If there are fewer than 12 unsecured creditors (excluding employees, insiders, and certain other parties), only 1 is needed to file the involuntary bankruptcy petition.
- Second, the signing creditors must, in aggregate, have total unsecured claims of more than $14,425.[4] See Chapter 4 of this book for a discussion of creditors' claims in general and the differences between secured and unsecured creditors. See Chapter 6 for an in-depth discussion regarding unsecured creditors.
- Third, each of these creditors must have unsecured claims that are not contingent as to liability or subject to a bona fide dispute as to amount. See Chapter 4 of this book for a discussion of contingent and disputed claims.

If creditors improperly file an involuntary bankruptcy petition by violating any of these requirements or others, the bankruptcy court may impose penalties against the petitioning creditors, such as reimbursing other parties for their costs and reasonable attorneys' fees. Furthermore, if the bankruptcy court finds that the petitioning creditors have acted in bad faith, then the creditors may be liable to the company for a wide variety of damages, including punitive damages. For these reasons, involuntary bankruptcies are a rare last resort for creditors who are frustrated with an out-of-court workout.

Why are corporate bankruptcies often called Chapter 11?

The Bankruptcy Code contains two primary means for a company to address its distress:

- *Chapter 11 reorganization*, in which the company continues to conduct business and attempts to return to solvency by restructuring its financial position. The debtor submits a plan to creditors and the court and, if this plan is affirmed, can operate under the plan. Chapter 12 of this book provides a detailed discussion of the plan of reorganization process under Chapter 11 of the Bankruptcy Code.
- *Chapter 7 liquidation*, in which the company's assets are liquidated to satisfy the claims of creditors. A Chapter 7 process involves the appointment of a trustee by the bankruptcy court to manage the day-to-day operations and liquidation of the company's assets.

There is also a hybrid scenario, known as a *liquidating Chapter 11*. Sometimes a company's bankruptcy case begins as a Chapter 11 reorganization, but at some point it becomes apparent that the business is not viable. The debtor and its creditors may agree to permit the debtor's management, which is very knowledgeable about the company's assets, to preside over the liquidation, rather than convert the bankruptcy case to a Chapter 7 liquidation. In these situations, the parties will agree that the appointment of a trustee, which is required in a Chapter 7 liquidation, is not warranted or desired.

As shorthand, businesspeople sometimes refer to bankruptcies as Chapter 11 or Chapter 7. Both Chapter 7 and Chapter 11 cases can involve either a voluntary or an involuntary bankruptcy petition.

Overall, the Bankruptcy Code contains nine operating chapters:

1. Chapter 1 contains general provisions and definitions.
2. Chapter 3 describes case administration.
3. Chapter 5 explains rules for handling creditors, debtors, and estates.
4. Chapter 7 covers liquidation, or the orderly sale of the assets of a debtor by a trustee.
5. Chapter 9 applies to the debts of municipalities.

6. Chapter 11 addresses reorganization of a debtor.
7. Chapter 12 provides relief for family farmers.
8. Chapter 13 provides a process by which an individual with regular income may repay all or a portion of her indebtedness under a new structure.
9. Chapter 15, which became the newest chapter in 2005, covers ancillary and other cross-border cases, enabling a corporate insolvency proceeding outside the United States to gain access to the U.S. court system.[5] Chapter 15 updated and replaced the prior section 304 of the Bankruptcy Code. Recent cases filed under Chapter 15 include those of the international advertising firm Quebecor World (2008, Southern District of New York), the Canadian forest products company Pope & Talbot (2008, District of Delaware), an Israeli jewelry manufacturer named Gold & Honey (2009, Eastern District of New York), and two Kazakhstani banks, BTA Bank (2010, Southern District of New York) and Alliance Bank (2010, Southern District of New York).[6]

There are no even-numbered chapters of the Bankruptcy Code except for Chapter 12. The chapters used for business bankruptcies are Chapters 7, 11, and 15. Debtors can change their status from one chapter to the other during the course of their insolvency, which is known as conversion of the case.[7] This book concentrates on Chapter 7 and 11 bankruptcies because they are the most common types of business bankruptcies.

What are the main purposes of Chapter 11 reorganization?

In the United States, businesses are given a second chance to reorganize under Chapter 11 of the Bankruptcy Code because Congress believes that reorganization preserves businesses that create jobs, pay taxes, and benefit communities. Other countries, such as those in Europe, favor creditors' rights through laws focusing on liquidation rather than reorganization.

Overall, the main purposes of a Chapter 11 reorganization are to give the debtor a fresh start and to provide creditors with fair and equitable recoveries. Other important purposes are to consolidate all disputes involving the debtor into one forum, to enable the debtor to have breathing room to create and carry out its plan, to empower the debtor to unravel uneconomical business arrangements, to grant the debtor a discharge from its pre-petition debts, and to achieve greater recoveries for creditors than they would have received in a liquidation.

Finally, and perhaps most relevant to distressed M&A, a key purpose of Chapter 11 reorganization is to determine whether the business should be partially or entirely sold.

Isn't there also a Chapter 22?

No. The term *Chapter 22* is a tongue-in-cheek reference to companies that file petitions for Chapter 11 reorganization more than once. It is not an actual chapter in the Bankruptcy Code. While it is still unusual for companies that have reorganized once to try to do so again, there are more and more examples as the current Bankruptcy Code enters its fourth decade.

The number of Chapter 22 cases is now over 200. Some key examples of such cases are

- Aloha Airlines (2004, 2008)
- American Pad & Paper (2000, 2002)
- Avado Brands (2004, 2007)
- Birch Telecom (2002, 2005)
- Continental Airlines (1983, 1999)
- Dan River (2004, 2008)
- Datapoint (1994, 2000)
- Eagle Geophysical (1999, 2009)
- FastComm Communications (1998, 2002)
- Foamex (2005, 2009)
- Hayes Lemmerz (2001, 2009)
- High Voltage Engineering (2004, 2005)
- London Fog (1999, 2006)
- LTV (1986, 2000)
- Key Plastics (2000, 2008)
- McLeodUSA (2002, 2005)
- Midway Airlines (1991, 2001)
- Moll Industries (2002, 2010)
- Orius (2002, 2005)

- Pan Am (1991, 1998)
- Planet Hollywood (1999, 2001)
- Pliant (2006, 2009)
- Polaroid (2001, 2008)
- Resorts International (1989, 1994)
- Roadhouse Grill (2002, 2008)
- Schwinn Bicycle (1992, 2001)
- Silicon Graphics (2006, 2009)
- Sunshine Mining (1992, 2000)
- US Airways (2002, 2004)

There have even been several "Chapter 33" cases, such as Anchor Glass Container (1996, 2002, 2005), Memorex Telex (1992, 1994, 1996), Salant (1985, 1990, 1998), and Trans World Airlines (1992, 1995, 2001). So far, there have been only two "Chapter 44" cases: Harvard Industries and TransTexas Gas. Clearly, in bankruptcy, three strikes do not necessarily mean that you're out!

Exhibit 2-1 shows the number of Chapter 22 and Chapter 33 cases filed in each year from 1984 to 2009.

Why are there so many Chapter 22 cases?

Critics of the Bankruptcy Code will often cite Chapter 22 cases as proof that bankruptcy reorganization is an ineffective and misguided approach to business failures. The significant number of companies that have to reorganize after a previous trip through the bankruptcy process provides abundant examples of this. However, the frequency of so-called Chapter 22 filings begs the question, why does this happen? In some cases, bankruptcies are pushed through the process too quickly. Probably the most commonly cited reasons for a rushed process are to save jobs and to provide creditors with cash or other distributions. Ultimately, if the measure of success of a Chapter 11 bankruptcy filing is to restructure the business so that it becomes healthier and more stable, it may make more sense to take the time required to address its operations thoroughly as well as just recapitalizing the balance sheet. This underscores a critical point: companies that file Chapter 11 bankruptcy need to use the opportunity to thoughtfully and materially reorganize their capital structure, rather than rush through the process to appease various constituents.

Exhibit 2-1 Chapter 22 and Chapter 33 Bankruptcy Filings 1984–2009

Year	Number of Chapter 22s	Number of Chapter 33s
1984	3	--
1985	3	--
1986	4	--
1987	1	--
1988	3	--
1989	4	--
1990	10	--
1991	9	--
1992	6	--
1993	8	--
1994	5	--
1995	9	--
1996	12	2
1997	5	--
1998	2	1
1999	10	--
2000	12	1
2001	17	2
2002	11	--
2003	17	1
2004	6	--
2005	9	1
2006	4	--
2007	8	1
2008	19	--
2009	12	--
TOTAL	**209**	**9**

Sources: The Bankruptcy Almanac, annually; Boskin, *New Governance Research;* and Altman and Hotchkiss, *Corporate Financial Distress and Bankruptcy* (Hoboken, N.J.: Wiley, 2005).

According to a study coauthored by noted bankruptcy expert Edward Altman, firms that filed Chapter 22 had, on average, almost three times as much leverage as firms that permanently exited Chapter 11.[8] That is, Altman's Chapter 22 sample had $3.70 of debt for every dollar of equity, while the Chapter 11 firms had about $1.35 of debt for every dollar of equity.

When a potential purchaser encounters a Chapter 22 case, there is good news and bad news. The good news is that the purchaser can review all of the materials from the original Chapter 11 case, including the valuation at the end of that case, to become familiar with the company and its issues quickly.

More good news involves the fact that there will probably be fewer buyers interested in considering an acquisition the second time around, and the sellers will probably be more reasonable regarding price. The bad news can be summarized with the phrase *caveat emptor*—let the buyer beware!

Aren't there also Bankruptcy Rules in addition to the Bankruptcy Code?

The Federal Rules of Bankruptcy Procedure (*Bankruptcy Rules*) are meant to ensure a "just, speedy, and inexpensive determination of every case and proceeding" under the Bankruptcy Code. In addition, the Federal Rules of Civil Procedure and the Federal Rules of Evidence, both of which apply to all federal courts, including bankruptcy courts, are relevant to all bankruptcy cases.

The Bankruptcy Rules comprise nine clusters, with rules numbered according to the clusters (the 1,000s are in Part I, the 2,000s are in Part II, and so forth):

1. Part I, commencement of the case
2. Part II, officers and administration, notices, meetings, examinations, elections, and attorneys and accountants
3. Part III, claims and distribution to creditors and equity interest holders; plans
4. Part IV, the debtor; duties and benefits
5. Part V, bankruptcy courts and clerks
6. Part VI, collection and liquidation of the estate
7. Part VII, adversary proceedings
8. Part VIII, appeals
9. Part IX, general provisions

Who may file a voluntary bankruptcy petition?

While anyone can file a voluntary bankruptcy petition, the bankruptcy court will not accept it unless the filing entity is a proper *debtor* pursuant to the Bankruptcy Code. Regarding corporate entities, any company may become a debtor if it is incorporated or has property in the United States.[9]

As a matter of corporate law, companies need to follow the formal procedures in their bylaws for taking an extraordinary step like filing a voluntary bankruptcy petition. These procedures usually involve a majority vote of the disinterested directors on the company's board, and sometimes a supermajority vote. Normally, the CEO cannot unilaterally decide that pursuing bankruptcy is in the best interests of the company, but must receive formal direction from the board of directors to file the voluntary bankruptcy petition.

What is a bankruptcy remote entity?

A *bankruptcy remote entity* (also known as a *special-purpose entity, singlepurpose entity, SPE,* or *bankruptcy remote vehicle*) is a company structured in such a way that it is unlikely to become insolvent as a result of its own activities, insulating it from the consequences of the insolvency of its affiliates. Structuring a company as a bankruptcy remote entity gives its creditors greater control in a potential insolvency by restricting the entity's ability to enter bankruptcy. The entity usually has an independent director on its board whose vote is required if the entity is to file a voluntary bankruptcy petition, effectively nullifying the company's constitutional right to seek bankruptcy protection. Other SPEs require the vote of the holder of a "golden share" to approve a bankruptcy filing. In these situations, the creditors find direct or indirect ways to influence the decision makers. These structures are designed to benefit creditors by circumventing bankruptcy laws, protecting the entity's assets from being affected by the bankruptcy of a related entity, and encouraging an out-of-court workout in distressed situations.

A primary purpose of creating bankruptcy remote entities is to attract debt investors through improved credit ratings and more favorable remedies upon default. For example, the creditors may prefer their remedies in state court rather than federal court. In other situations, the creditors may want to protect the assets of the SPE from being substantively consolidated with the assets of related entities in a plan of reorganization.

This area of bankruptcy law is changing. The decision in the General Growth Properties case in the Southern District of New York set forth various general principles that could permit a bankruptcy remote entity or SPE to file for bankruptcy protection. This is good news for SPE debtors—but bad news for SPE creditors who had counted on the so-called bankruptcy remoteness of SPEs to structure what they believed was a safe haven for financing. Therefore, a buyer who is contemplating a situation involving a bankruptcy remote entity or other SPE should consult with a seasoned bankruptcy attorney who understands the status of the law in the appropriate jurisdiction.

Where may a company file a voluntary bankruptcy petition?

The proper location for filing a bankruptcy petition is called the *jurisdiction*. Generally, a company can file its voluntary bankruptcy petition in the jurisdiction of its headquarters, its principal place of business, or its incorporation. Thus, there are often many places that a company can select to file its voluntary bankruptcy petition. According to one analysis, there has been an increase in *forum shopping*, or selecting the jurisdiction that most benefits the debtor, over the past several years. This is illustrated in Exhibit 2-2.

The U.S. court system operates 92 federal bankruptcy courts, authorized under section 151 of Title 28 of the United States Code (28 U.S.C. §151), that are organized into 11 federal circuits nationwide, as shown in Exhibit 2-3.

As illustrated on the map in Exhibit 2-3, each federal circuit includes several states. Many states are divided into districts, such as the Central

Exhibit 2-2 Rate of Forum Shopping, 1980–2009

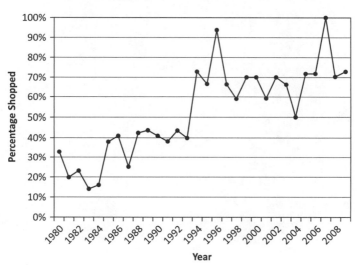

Source: LoPucki's Bankruptcy Research Database.

Exhibit 2-3 U.S. Circuit Courts

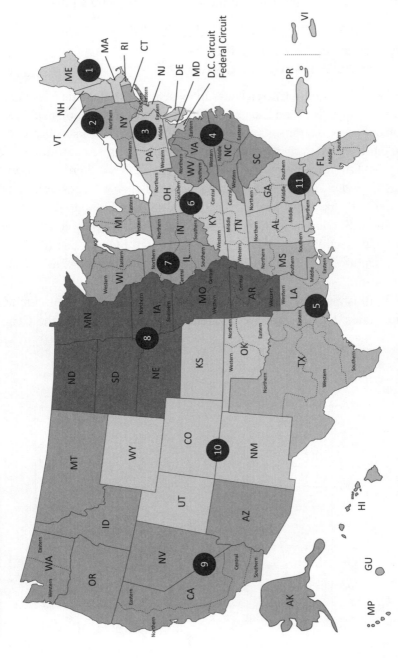

District of California, whereas other states have just one district, such as the District of Massachusetts. Each district has a bankruptcy court located within it. A bankruptcy petition is filed with a particular bankruptcy court, which will assign the case to an individual bankruptcy judge. This assignment is usually based on a lottery, taking into account availability and conflicts.

Currently, the most common jurisdictions for filing business bankruptcy cases are the Southern District of New York and the District of Delaware. Delaware is a popular jurisdiction because it is the state in which many companies are incorporated. Once a jurisdiction becomes popular, it develops a robust body of case law, making legal precedent more certain and less risky and, in turn, fueling the continued popularity of the jurisdiction.

What are the legal precedents that each bankruptcy court must follow?

Each jurisdiction maintains its own case law, so the legal precedents in one jurisdiction may differ from those in other jurisdictions. The bankruptcy courts in each district must follow the legal precedents of that district and its circuit, but the legal precedents of other districts in its circuit are not binding. For example, the Bankruptcy Court of the Southern District of Texas must follow the precedents of the Bankruptcy Court of the Southern District of Texas, the District Court of the Southern District of Texas, and the Fifth Circuit Court of Appeals, but it can disagree with the precedents established in the Northern District of Texas or the Western District of Texas. However, while a bankruptcy court in a certain circuit is not bound by the decisions of circuit courts in other jurisdictions, it may nevertheless find these opinions persuasive, particularly if the facts and issues are similar. All bankruptcy courts must follow the legal precedents set by the U.S. Supreme Court.

Where can I find more information about a particular bankruptcy court?

Each bankruptcy court maintains its own Web site, which includes the local rules and the docket for each bankruptcy case. The Web addresses for these sites are given in Exhibit 2-4.

Exhibit 2-4 Bankruptcy Court Web Sites

Bankruptcy Court	Circuit	Bankruptcy Court Web Site	# of Business Bankruptcies 1999–2008
Alabama—Middle	11th	www.almb.uscourts.gov	1,104
Alabama—Northern	11th	www.alnb.uscourts.gov	2,083
Alabama—Southern	11th	www.alsb.uscourts.gov	505
Alaska	9th	www.akb.uscourts.gov	921
Arkansas—Eastern	8th	www.arb.uscourts.gov	1,997
Arkansas—Western	8th	www.arb.uscourts.gov	1,532
Arizona	9th	www.azb.uscourts.gov	6,570
California—Central	9th	www.cacb.uscourts.gov	21,490
California—Eastern	9th	www.caeb.uscourts.gov	10,179
California—Northern	9th	www.canb.uscourts.gov	10,237
California—Southern	9th	www.casb.uscourts.gov	2,574
Colorado	10th	www.cob.uscourts.gov	6,280
Connecticut	2nd	www.ctb.uscourts.gov	1,968
Delaware	3rd	www.deb.uscourts.gov	28,205
DC	3rd	www.dcb.uscourts.gov	492
Florida—Middle	11th	www.flmb.uscourts.gov	9,672
Florida—Northern	11th	www.flnb.uscourts.gov	1,003
Florida—Southern	11th	www.flsb.uscourts.gov	7,476
Georgia—Middle	11th	www.gamb.uscourts.gov	1,667
Georgia—Northern	11th	www.ganb.uscourts.gov	12,133
Georgia—Southern	11th	www.gasb.uscourts.gov	2,416
Guam	9th	ecf.gub.uscourts.gov	145
Hawaii	9th	www.hib.uscourts.gov	638
Idaho	9th	www.id.uscourts.gov	2,085
Illinois—Central	7th	www.ilcb.uscourts.gov	1,746
Illinois—Northern	7th	www.ilnb.uscourts.gov	7,238
Illinois—Southern	7th	www.ilsb.uscourts.gov	3,969
Indiana—Northern	7th	www.innb.uscourts.gov	2,298
Indiana—Southern	7th	www.insb.uscourts.gov	4,029
Iowa—Northern	8th	www.ianb.uscourts.gov	1,788
Iowa—Southern	8th	www.iasb.uscourts.gov	1,196
Kansas	10th	www.ksb.uscourts.gov	2,413
Kentucky—Eastern	6th	www.kyeb.uscourts.gov	2,027
Kentucky—Western	6th	www.kywb.uscourts.gov	1,615
Louisiana—Eastern	5th	www.laeb.uscourts.gov	1,408
Louisiana—Middle	5th	www.lamb.uscourts.gov	417
Louisiana—Western	5th	www.lawb.uscourts.gov	4,203
Maine	1st	www.meb.uscourts.gov	1,415
Maryland	3rd	www.mdb.uscourts.gov	6,144
Massachusetts	1st	www.mab.uscourts.gov	3,939
Michigan—Eastern	6th	www.mieb.uscourts.gov	5,524
Michigan—Western	6th	www.miwb.uscourts.gov	3,244
Minnesota	8th	www.mnb.uscourts.gov	12,006
Mississippi—Northern	5th	www.msnb.uscourts.gov	1,144
Mississippi—Southern	5th	www.mssb.uscourts.gov	1,31?

Bankruptcy Court	Circuit	Bankruptcy Court Web Site	# of Business Bankruptcies 1999–2008
Missouri—Western	8th	www.mow.uscourts.gov	2,112
Montana	9th	www.mtb.uscourts.gov	1,949
Nebraska	8th	www.neb.uscourts.gov	1,959
Nevada	9th	www.nvb.uscourts.gov	3,255
New Hampshire	1st	www.nhb.uscourts.gov	3,056
New Jersey	3rd	www.njb.uscourts.gov	7,563
New Mexico	10th	www.nmcourt.fed.us/usbc	5,148
New York—Eastern	2nd	www.nyeb.uscourts.gov	3,406
New York—Northern	2nd	www.nynb.uscourts.gov	3,285
New York—Southern	2nd	www.nysb.uscourts.gov	11,370
New York—Western	2nd	www.nywb.uscourts.gov	3,382
N. Carolina—Eastern	4th	www.nceb.uscourts.gov	2,293
N. Carolina—Middle	4th	www.ncmb.uscourts.gov	2,107
N. Carolina—Western	4th	www.ncwb.uscourts.gov	1,233
N. Dakota	8th	www.ndb.uscourts.gov	865
Ohio—Northern	6th	www.ohnb.uscourts.gov	9,069
Ohio—Southern	6th	www.ohsb.uscourts.gov	5,782
Oklahoma—Eastern	10th	www.okeb.uscourts.gov	801
Oklahoma—Northern	10th	www.oknb.uscourts.gov	2,353
Oklahoma—Western	10th	www.okwb.uscourts.gov	2,818
Oregon	9th	www.orb.uscourts.gov	11,985
Pennsylvania—Eastern	3rd	www.paeb.uscourts.gov	3,365
Pennsylvania—Middle	3rd	www.uslawcenter.com/usmiddle	4,349
Pennsylvania—Western	3rd	www.pawb.uscourts.gov	4,581
Puerto Rico	1st	www.prb.uscourts.gov	2,942
Rhode Island	1st	www.rib.uscourts.gov	874
S. Carolina	4th	www.scb.uscourts.gov	1,641
S. Dakota	8th	www.sdb.uscourts.gov	1,215
Tennessee—Eastern	6th	www.tneb.uscourts.gov	2,437
Tennessee—Middle	6th	www.tnmb.uscourts.gov	2,298
Tennessee—Western	6th	www.tnwb.uscourts.gov	1,870
Texas—Northern	5th	www.txnb.uscourts.gov	10,918
Texas—Eastern	5th	www.txeb.uscourts.gov	3,765
Texas—Western	5th	www.txwb.uscourts.gov	6,096
Texas—Southern	5th	www.txs.uscourts.gov	7,783
Utah	10th	www.utb.uscourts.gov	4,009
Vermont	2nd	www.vtb.uscourts.gov	733
Virginia—Eastern	4th	www.vaeb.uscourts.gov	3,828
Virginia—Western	4th	www.vawb.uscourts.gov	3,753
Washington—Western	9th	www.wawb.uscourts.gov	3,971
Washington—Eastern	9th	www.waeb.uscourts.gov	2,498
W. Virginia—Northern	4th	www.wvnb.uscourts.gov	1,204
W. Virginia—Southern	4th	www.wvsb.uscourts.gov	1,266
Wisconsin—Eastern	7th	www.wieb.uscourts.gov	2,296

What court hears the appeals
of decisions by a bankruptcy court?

Appeals of a bankruptcy court's decisions may be made to the district court, which is a federal court located in the same district, unless applicable special exceptions apply.[10] Further appeals from the district court may be made to the circuit court of appeals, which is a federal court that presides over the entire circuit in which the district is located, unless special exceptions apply.[11] Final appeals from the circuit court of appeals may be made to the U.S. Supreme Court, which has jurisdiction over all circuits.

In certain jurisdictions, the courts have decided to establish a Bankruptcy Appellate Panel, known as a BAP, to hear appeals from the bankruptcy court.[12] The BAP conserves the scarce judicial resources of the district court and consists of judges with greater bankruptcy expertise. Appeals from decisions by a BAP are made to the relevant circuit court of appeals.[13]

Must a company be insolvent
to file a bankruptcy petition?

No. Insolvency is not a formal requirement for filing either a voluntary or an involuntary bankruptcy petition. As a practical matter, however, all or nearly all companies that file for bankruptcy are insolvent.

Why would a solvent company want to file a voluntary bankruptcy petition when less costly, more efficient, and less embarrassing alternatives for resolving disputes with creditors exist, such as an out-of-court workout? Perhaps the solvency or insolvency of the company is not entirely clear because of the uncertainty of contingent and disputed liabilities. In other situations, a company may be solvent, but illiquid. If a solvent company files a voluntary bankruptcy petition, it may breach its fiduciary duties to equity holders (see Chapter 10 of this book). In general, a bankruptcy court will be averse to wasting precious judicial resources on a solvent company that is seeking bankruptcy protection and is likely to demand a compelling reason for approving the voluntary bankruptcy petition.

Why would the creditors of a solvent company want to risk harming their investment by filing an involuntary bankruptcy petition against a debtor and incurring high administrative expenses, distracting management, and giving the company new rights and remedies? Perhaps the creditors believe that the management is committing bad acts, such as embezzlement or fraud. If creditors file an involuntary bankruptcy petition against a solvent company, then its solvency may be evidence of bad faith.

What are the key components of a Chapter 11 reorganization?

While there are a wide variety of motions, objections, petitions, affidavits, orders, and other filings in a bankruptcy case, the broad outline of a Chapter 11 reorganization is as follows:

- Filing the bankruptcy petition
- Opening of the bankruptcy case by the bankruptcy court
  - Assignment of a case number
  - Assignment of a bankruptcy judge
- Filing of first-day motions by the debtor
  - First-day affidavit
  - Motion for joint administration
  - Motion for use of cash collateral
  - Motion for post-petition financing (debtor-in-possession loan)
  - Motion to provide adequate assurance to utilities
  - Motion to use and maintain existing cash management systems and bank accounts
  - Motion to pay pre-petition employee wage claims
  - Motion to pay pre-petition critical vendor claims
  - Motion to retain attorneys and advisors for debtor
- Holding first-day hearing before bankruptcy court
- Holding 341 meeting by the U.S. trustee for the unsecured creditors
- Appointment of the official committee of unsecured creditors by the U.S. trustee
- Retaining attorneys and advisors for the official committee of unsecured creditors
- Accepting or rejecting executory contracts and unexpired leases by debtor

- Submitting proofs of claim by creditors prior to claims bar date
- Filing the disclosure statement
- Filing the plan of reorganization
- Voting on the plan of reorganization by creditors
- Confirmation of the plan of reorganization by the bankruptcy court
- Exiting from bankruptcy by the debtor
- Filing voidable preference claims by the debtor
- Distributing proceeds to creditors
- Closing of the bankruptcy case by the bankruptcy court

How is a sale of the company as a going concern accomplished in bankruptcy?

Section 363 is the part of the Bankruptcy Code that provides a way for a debtor to sell some or all of the assets of the business free and clear of liens and most claims in a quick cash sale. Often, such sales can be completed without any of the complications of a plan of reorganization, such as voting by the creditors and confirmation by the bankruptcy court. Bankruptcy cases involving sales of the company—known as *363 sales*—are discussed in detail in Chapter 13 of this book.

Legal experts are predicting a continuing rise in distressed M&A via 363 sales as a result of changes in bankruptcy law.[14] The recent Lehman Brothers bankruptcy in 2008 and the General Motors bankruptcy in 2009 are notable examples. Although these cases were among the largest bankruptcies ever filed, they utilized the bankruptcy sale procedures under Section 363. For more details about these noteworthy bankruptcy cases and others, see Chapter 3 of this book.

How much does a bankruptcy case cost?

High overall cost is the primary deterrent to filing a bankruptcy petition, which makes it a last resort for most companies. Bankruptcy filings reflect the complexity of the situations that precipitate them. In some Chapter 11 cases, literally thousands of separate creditors have claims against the debtor. Not surprisingly, the need for professional assistance rises with each level of complexity. Some of the professionals that might be needed include, among others,

- Accountants
- Appraisers
- Attorneys
- Investment bankers
- Turnaround consultants

Each of these types of advisor is discussed in greater detail in Chapter 7 of this book. Both the debtor and the creditors may need to hire each of these professionals. Other direct administrative costs of the bankruptcy proceeding include the filing fee for the bankruptcy petition, fees to the U.S. trustee, and fees and expenses of a claims agent.

In addition, there are *indirect costs* of bankruptcy. These include such factors as tarnished reputation, lost sales from concerned customers, deteriorating margins because of heightened supplier demands, loss of key personnel, and management distraction. While these costs are particularly difficult to measure, some studies estimate that indirect costs range from 5 percent to 25 percent of the firm's value.[15] In addition, indirect costs include the unreimbursed fees and expenses of attorneys and other advisors that individual creditors and potential purchasers hire to provide separate advice.

The precise cost of a bankruptcy case will likely be correlated to its size and complexity. A smaller business might cost at least $100,000 for basic filing fees, attorney's fees, and assistance with a plan of reorganization. For larger organizations, the amounts can run in the millions—one study pegged the cost as roughly 8 percent of a firm's value.[16] As legal specialists, senior partners at top bankruptcy law firms now bill at $1,000 per hour.

The Lehman Brothers bankruptcy case presents an extreme example. From the beginning of the case in September 2008 through April 2010, more than $730 million in fees and expenses were submitted, driving the final estimates to more than $1 billion. The *New York Times* reported several circumstances of possible abuse by professionals, including more than $263,000 for photocopies in four months, over $2,100 in limousine rides by one law firm partner in one month, $48 just to leave a voicemail message, $364.14 in dry cleaning, and more than a week at a luxury Manhattan hotel at a cost of $685 per night.[17] As a result, President Obama's "pay czar,"

Kenneth Feinberg, whom the bankruptcy court appointed as fee monitor for the Lehman case, imposed new rules: air travel must be in coach class only, ground transportation is limited to $100 a day and only after 8 p.m., hotel rooms are capped at $500 a night, photocopy charges are limited to 10 cents a page, and late meals cannot exceed $20 each.

In liquidation, the trustee appointed under Chapter 7 of the Bankruptcy Code is paid an incentive fee calculated in accordance with Bankruptcy Code section 326(a) using the amount of proceeds achieved from the sale of assets, as follows:

- Not to exceed 25 percent on the first $5,000 or less
- 10 percent on any amount in excess of $5,000 but not in excess of $50,000
- 5 percent on any amount in excess of $50,000 but not in excess of $1,000,000
- Reasonable compensation not to exceed 3 percent of such moneys in excess of $1,000,000, upon all moneys disbursed or turned over in the case by the trustee to parties in interest, excluding the debtor, but including holders of secured claims[18]

How long does a bankruptcy process typically take?

It is very difficult to draw broad conclusions, as the answer will depend on the level of complexity of the case, as well as many other factors. Exhibit 2-5 illustrates the results of one analysis that looked at the average duration of nonprepackaged, nonnegotiated large public company filings from 2000 through 2009. This analysis suggests that the typical duration might be roughly 500 to 1,000 days, although changes to the Bankruptcy Code implemented via the Bankruptcy Abuse Prevention and Consumer Protection Act of 2005 (2005 BAPCPA) have sought to lower that range.

Does the bankruptcy process improve the quality of information available on a troubled company?

When a company is approaching insolvency but is not yet in a formal bankruptcy proceeding, the quality and quantity of information that is available to creditors can deteriorate rapidly and perhaps even become fraudulent.

Exhibit 2-5 Average Duration of Nonprepackaged, Nonprenegotiated Large Public Company Bankruptcies Concluded 2000–2009

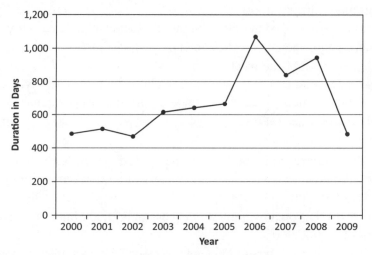

Source: UCLA–LoPucki's Bankruptcy Research Database.

A private company may try to avoid revealing the severity of its problems to creditors. If the company is public, it may delay filing required quarterly and annual reports.

Once a company files for bankruptcy and comes under the supervision of the bankruptcy court, the quality of the information that it provides to creditors usually improves. All formal financial reporting in a bankruptcy is done under oath, and there are criminal penalties for falsification of records and statements. Furthermore, by law, the debtor must file detailed reports on its finances, which are a matter of public record. Also, debtors may be compelled to testify in more detailed examinations dictated by Bankruptcy Rule 2004.

Bankruptcy Rule 2004 states, "On motion of any party in interest, the court may order the examination of any entity."[19] Further, it says that this examination may relate to "the acts, conduct or property or the liabilities and financial condition of the debtor, or to any matter which may affect the administration of the debtor's estate, or to the debtor's right to a discharge." In some cases, such as Chapter 11 cases, "the examination may also relate to the operation of any business and the desirability of its continuance, the source of any money or property acquired or to be acquired by the debtor for purposes of consummating a plan and the consideration given or offered [for this money or property], and any other matter relevant to the case or to the foundation of a plan."

Information on bankrupt entities is so good, in fact, that in some circumstances, securities issued to creditors in a federal bankruptcy case are tradable without registration. This exception enables some firms to go public without the expense of a registration.

Of course, in a transaction with a distressed entity, all the normal deal imperatives apply, including thorough financial, legal, operational, and transactional due diligence. This subject is beyond the scope of this book, but we urge buyers to hire experts in this area and to master it themselves to the extent possible.[20]

What is the exact status of bankruptcy law right now? Isn't it undergoing some changes?

Bankruptcy law is a fairly stable area of law, especially where businesses are concerned. Most of the legislation passed in recent years has focused on the reform of laws affecting consumer bankruptcy. The laws controlling business bankruptcy were also made less hospitable, but they still encourage reorganization over liquidation.

The current Bankruptcy Code was enacted in 1978 to replace the prior Bankruptcy Act of 1938, which was the first major revision of the original Bankruptcy Act of 1898. The following laws have amended (but not replaced) the 1978 law:

- The Bankruptcy Judges, United States Trustees, and Family Farmer Bankruptcy Act of 1986. This law added an item for Chapter 12 of Title 11.
- The Bankruptcy Reform Act of 1994.[21] This law, considered to be the first comprehensive revision of the Bankruptcy Code, contained provisions to expedite bankruptcy cases and to help creditors recover claims against bankrupt estates. It also created an independent National Bankruptcy Review Commission to investigate further changes in bankruptcy law until November 1997 when the commission automatically ceased to exist.

- The Bankruptcy Abuse Prevention and Consumer Protection
  Act of 2005.[22] This get-tough bill, discussed further in the next
  section, was an outgrowth of an October 1997 report of the
  National Bankruptcy Review Commission.
- The Credit Card Accountability, Responsibility, and Disclosure
  Act of 2009. This act focused on consumer bankruptcy, and
  could affect the number of small business bankruptcies
  because many small businesses use credit cards for funding.
- The Wall Street Reform and Consumer Protection Act of
  2010. Known as the Dodd-Frank Act, it addresses bankruptcy
  of financial institutions—namely publicly held bank holding
  companies and "nonbank financial companies," a broad term
  that could conceivably cover any financial firm. Title II of the
  Dodd-Frank Act, entitled Orderly Liquidation Authority,
  names the Federal Deposit Insurance Corporation (FDIC) as
  the receiver for certain bankrupt financial firms, and gives it
  superpowers in this regard. The FDIC may "disaffirm or repu-
  diate any contract or lease to which the covered financial
  institution is a party" if the FDIC finds it "burdensome."
  Furthermore, the FDIC may recover from any current or former senior executive or director "substantially responsible for
  the failed condition of the covered company" any compensation received in the two years prior to receivership. The law
  defines compensation broadly to include salary paid under a
  contract—typically exempted from such clawback regulations.
  The law also calls for studies regarding secured creditor hair-
  cuts, the bankruptcy process for financial institutions, and
  the international bankruptcy process for nonbank financial
  institutions—all areas that could become the focal points for
  future regulations under the authority of this law.[23]

On the horizon is the Protecting Employees and Retirees in Business
Bankruptcies Act (pending as we go to press), which would amend the
Bankruptcy Code to improve protections for employees and retirees in
business bankruptcy cases. Of 14 pending bills and resolutions pertaining
to bankruptcy in the current Congress, this one has the greatest relevance
to business bankruptcy cases.

What were the implications of the 2005 BAPCPA?

Although the 2005 BAPCPA focused mainly on consumer bankruptcy cases, experts called it the equivalent of a new commercial bankruptcy code. Among other features of this new law were the following:

- It imposed substantial additional costs or burdens on debtors, such as the requirement for early cash settlements and higher utility security deposits, making it more difficult to emerge from bankruptcy.
- It capped the length of extensions to a debtor's period of exclusivity to propose and solicit votes for a plan of reorganization that a bankruptcy court can grant.
- It required the unsecured creditors' committee to receive input from all creditors.
- It transferred elements of control to certain nondebtor stakeholders—for example, it lengthened the reclamation period for vendors, shifting the balance of power from financial creditors to trade creditors.

The improved status of vendors could help companies, because their vendors may keep shipping rather than defecting to other customers. On the other hand, it may make it more difficult to obtain debtor-in-possession (DIP) financing by destabilizing the debtor's ownership of assets in its possession.

Another practical consequence of the 2005 BAPCPA was that, combined with the tightening credit markets of 2008 and beyond, it meaningfully compressed the bankruptcy timeline.

Are there any unusual concepts or unique terms that arise in bankruptcy?

Yes, there are many. Throughout this book, we explain those concepts and terms that are most relevant to distressed M&A. In Chapters 4 through 7 of this book, we review the concepts and terms for debtors, secured creditors, unsecured creditors, and advisors. In Chapters 8 and 9, we address concepts and terms involving tax and accounting. In Chapter 10, we refer to fiduciary duties, antitrust, and fraudulent transfers in the context of distressed transactions. In Chapter 11, we discuss principles of distressed-company valuation. Chapter 12 outlines plans of reorganization in depth. In Chapter 13, we discuss sales processes under Bankruptcy Code section 363. Finally, in Chapter 14, we consider financing considerations in the bankruptcy context.

There are a few bankruptcy concepts that are worth mentioning briefly even though they do not directly involve distressed M&A and will not affect the rest of this book. Each of these topics is complicated, with many exceptions and nuances that a bankruptcy attorney can explain in greater detail. These concepts include

- *Automatic stay.* Bankruptcy Code section 362 provides protection for the debtor from the attempts of creditors to seize collateral, demand payment, and litigate disputes outside of bankruptcy court. In other words, these attempts are "stayed" from further action to enable an orderly resolution of creditors' claims in accordance with the provisions of the Bankruptcy Code and the Bankruptcy Rules. By enacting section 362 of the Bankruptcy Code, Congress wanted to avoid a free-for-all grab for assets among creditors and to consolidate all legal proceedings in one forum, the bankruptcy court. This protection arises automatically as a matter of law upon the filing of a bankruptcy petition. Creditors can petition the bankruptcy court for relief from the automatic stay, such as requesting that the automatic stay be lifted, under special circumstances.
- *Executory contracts and unexpired leases.* Bankruptcy Code section 365 provides a debtor in possession with extraordinary power to assume or reject executory contracts and unexpired leases. Often, a company enters pre-petition agreements with counterparties that it initially expects will be beneficial but that eventually become uneconomical or otherwise burdensome as the business environment changes. Indeed, these undesirable agreements may be a primary cause of the company's financial distress. *Unexpired leases* refer to landlord-tenant agreements where the maturity occurs post-petition. *Executory contracts* encompass all agreements besides unexpired leases and may include supply agreements with vendors, service agreements

with customers, arrangements with consultants, licenses covering intellectual property, and understandings with business partners. The Bankruptcy Code does not define the term *executory*, so case law provides a flexible definition that is interpreted by bankruptcy courts. Not all contracts are executory, which means that both parties must still have performance required in some form other than financial payment. Therefore, credit agreements, letters of credit, and other financial contracts are not executory contracts. If the debtor in possession rejects an executory contract or unexpired lease, the damages owed to the counterparty become an unsecured claim in the bankruptcy proceeding. If the debtor in possession assumes an executory contract or unexpired lease, it must "cure" any defaults, including nonpayment, and provide adequate assurance of future performance at the time of the assumption. If the debtor assumes an executory contract or unexpired lease, it may then assign it to a third party in exchange for cash or other value. It is important to note that the debtor has the right to assume or reject regardless of whether the contract or lease contains common language that it is automatically terminated in the event of the debtor's insolvency, the commencement of a bankruptcy case, or the appointment of a trustee (known as *ipso facto* clauses).[24] The Bankruptcy Code contains special provisions for certain types of contracts used by financial participants [as defined in Bankruptcy Code section 101(22A)] in the financial markets, such as securities contracts [see Bankruptcy Code sections 555 and 741(7)], forward contracts [see Bankruptcy Code sections 101(25), 101(26), and 556], repurchase agreements [see Bankruptcy Code sections 101(46), 101(47), and 559], swap agreements [see Bankruptcy Code sections 101(53B), 101(53C), and 560], and master netting agreements [see Bankruptcy Code sections 101(38A), 101(38B), and 561].

- *Voidable preferences.* As a company spirals toward bankruptcy, vendors and other creditors may become aware of the situation and try to engage in self-help. It would be unfair for these creditors to receive recoveries superior to those received by similarly situated creditors just because they were luckier or quicker. Moreover, it would undermine the principle of the bankruptcy process, which is to provide fair and equitable recoveries to all creditors. Furthermore, if this unruly practice were allowed, it would encourage more and more creditors to engage in self-help and probably hasten the company's demise. Finally, it would invite the company to give preferential treatment to friendly creditors and insiders. Therefore, Bankruptcy Code section 547 codifies a bankruptcy concept called a *voidable preference*, whereby creditors who received more than their fair recoveries are required to return the excessive amounts to the debtor in possession.[25] Specifically, all transactions greater than $5,475 (adjusted periodically) between the company and its pre-petition creditors within the 90 days prior to the bankruptcy filing (one year for insiders) are considered to be potential preferential transfers. If they are proven to be such by the debtor, then the bankruptcy court can void the transfers, and the creditor must return the amounts involved to the debtor's estate. Because this process is not automatic, these transfers are called *voidable*, not void. The main defenses by creditors against preference claims include transactions in the ordinary course of business, transactions involving a contemporaneous exchange for new value, granting new security interests that secure new value, receiving an amount that was not more than the amount the creditor would have received anyway in the bankruptcy case, and other such technicalities.[26] Since secured creditors cannot have liens on a debtor's preference claims because they arise post-petition, these claims may provide recoveries for unsecured creditors. However, considering the probability of success, legal fees, and collection expenses, the net amount is usually relatively minor.

DEFINING STATE INSOLVENCY PROCEEDING

What is a state insolvency proceeding?

A state insolvency proceeding is an alternative to federal bankruptcy law that enables the debtor to reorganize or liquidate. The biggest differences between state insolvency and federal bankruptcy are that (1) the proceedings must be voluntarily initiated by the debtor (i.e., there are no involuntary state insolvency proceedings) and (2) the outcome is binding only in the state in which the action is filed.

The relatively narrow application of state insolvency proceedings is due to the fact that states cannot grant discharges of debt because such action would infringe upon the bankruptcy powers granted solely to the federal government by the U.S. Constitution. As a result, such proceedings merely involve a negotiated agreement among the creditors and the debtor. There is minimal direct court involvement, unless there are issues in dispute among the parties.

What are the main advantages and disadvantages of a state insolvency proceeding?

The main advantage of a state insolvency proceeding is that it is typically inexpensive and fast. Arguably, it also avoids the stigma of bankruptcy (although this stigma has receded in recent years, which is a reflection of both the state of the U.S. economy and the increased acceptance of bankruptcy as a tool for optimizing a company's capital structure).

The main disadvantage is that the discharge of debts is not binding on creditors located in other states. This can be a major drawback for a distressed entity with creditors outside its home state, as their claims will not be discharged. By contrast, in a Chapter 7 or Chapter 11 bankruptcy proceeding under federal law, all claims within the United States will be discharged.

In addition, state insolvency proceedings generally require the cooperation of both the debtor and the creditors, whereas the federal bankruptcy court has substantially greater authority to compel these parties to participate. A bankruptcy court can force all of the creditors to accept the terms agreed to by the majority of the creditors, whereas a state court cannot.

Despite these disadvantages, however, a debtor might initiate state insolvency proceedings in certain circumstances (e.g., the desire to keep a low profile; having a limited number of creditors, most of whom are in agreement, and who are concentrated in one state). If a state insolvency proceeding results in a stalemate, the debtor preserves the option of subsequently filing for bankruptcy under federal law.

What is an assignment for the benefit of creditors?

An *assignment for the benefit of creditors*, also known simply as an *ABC*, is a voluntary action in which the debtor assigns its property to creditors or to a neutral third party (an *assignee*) who serves as a fiduciary on behalf of such creditors. The assets are then liquidated, with the proceeds being distributed to the creditors who have filed claims with the assignee, leading to a total discharge of debts in that state. Most states have laws that assign priorities to the payments from the ABC. Essentially, an ABC amounts to the equity holders tossing the keys to the company to the creditors and walking away in defeat. Creditors may then decide whether to retain the current management to assist them in disposing of the assets.

If a creditor decides to participate in the action by filing a claim, it is bound by the terms of the ABC. If the creditor decides not to participate (known as a *nonassenting creditor*), it may pursue collection actions on its own. However, the nonassenting creditor generally cannot levy upon any property in the ABC. As a result, a creditor that does not participate is unlikely to be repaid because the debtor must transfer all of its nonexempt property to the ABC.

The only exception that allows a nonassenting creditor to challenge the validity of the ABC is if one of the following three scenarios occurs:

1. The debtor does not transfer all of its nonexempt property to the ABC.
2. The debtor tries to retain control or exercise rights over the transferred assets, such as revoking or stipulating the use of the property or taking too long in providing for its liquidation.
3. The debtor makes preferential payments in exchange for a release of its debts or excludes specific creditors.

What is foreclosure?

Foreclosure is a legal proceeding initiated by a secured creditor (such as a mortgage holder or other third-party lien holder) under state law to repossess its collateral for a loan that is in default and/or to sell the property and use the proceeds to pay off the loan. The process can be rapid or lengthy, depending on the type of foreclosure sought, the specific circumstances, and the law of the state in which the action was filed. The *automatic stay* provided by Bankruptcy Code section 362 prevents a secured lender from pursuing foreclosure and is often a key reason why a borrower seeks bankruptcy protection.

The concept of foreclosure dates back many centuries. Early on, the law generally allowed the creditor to automatically take ownership of the secured asset. Over time, the law evolved to allow the debtor time to repay the debt before being forced to hand over the asset.

What are the different types of foreclosure?

There are two types of foreclosure that are available in nearly all U.S. jurisdictions. *Foreclosure by judicial sale*, also known as *judicial foreclosure*, is available in every U.S. state and is the more important form. In fact, in most states, it is the required means of foreclosure in cases involving a personal residence, unless the mortgage documents expressly indicate otherwise. In such an action, the secured creditor files a motion with the relevant court and notifies all applicable parties. Notice requirements vary by jurisdiction. Typically, the state court hands down its decision after a brief hearing and supervises the sale of the asset. Sale proceeds initially go to satisfy the first mortgage, then to other lien holders. If the proceeds exceed the amount of all debts on the asset, the residual cash reverts to the debtor.

The second most common type of foreclosure is *foreclosure by power of sale*. In the states in which this foreclosure process is available, it allows the secured creditor to sell the asset without court supervision—provided that the mortgage on the asset includes a *power of sale clause* or the parties used a deed of trust instead of a mortgage. Also, while a court does not oversee the sale process, the foreclosure can be subject to judicial review after the fact. In terms of priority of payments, as with foreclosure by judicial sale, sale proceeds are initially paid to the holder of the first mortgage and then to other lien holders. However, because court supervision of the sale is not involved, foreclosure by power of sale is generally faster than foreclosure by judicial sale.

These twists and turns in bankruptcy law have made bankruptcy and distressed M&A more viable as alternatives for businesses in financial distress. The next chapter proves the point by showing some major "big picture" trends in this regard.

Endnotes

1. On the other hand, creditors should not allow the threat of a bankruptcy filing to force them into unreasonable concessions. See Dan Torrez, "Desperate Companies Cry Wolf with Faux Filings," *Austin Business Journal*, June 2003.
2. Although 75 to 80 percent is the average secured loan recovery, the dispersion around that average is substantial. In fact, the typical secured recovery is closer to 100 percent, with the occasional total loss or minimal recovery (20 to 30 percent) dragging down the average. In many cases where the recovery is 100 percent, the creditors are secured by highly liquid assets (like accounts receivable) that can be turned into cash very quickly. In other cases, where the creditors are not secured by easily liquidated assets, they still collect most or all of their loan because they are able to sell or reorganize the bankrupt company as a "going concern," realizing its full "enterprise value."
3. See 11 U.S.C. §303.
4. These dollar figures were effective April 1, 2010, and are updated every three years.
5. Chapter 15, the newest edition (from 2005), incorporates the Model Law on Cross Border Insolvency drafted by the United Nations Commission on International Trade Law. For the full text of all the Bankruptcy Code chapters, see http://www4.law.cornell.edu/uscode/11/, last accessed March 13, 2010.
6. More information on Chapter 15 can be found at www.uscourts.gov/bankruptcycourts/bankruptcybasics/chapter15.html and www.chapter15.com.
7. For a case involving the carryover of one bankruptcy to another, see *Young v. United States*, 535 U.S. 43 (2002).
8. Edward Altman and Thongchai Rattanaruengyot, "Post-Chapter 11 Bankruptcy Performance: Avoiding Chapter 22," *Journal of Applied Corporate Finance*, Summer 2009, p. 51.
9. 11 U.S.C. §109(a).
10. 28 U.S.C. §158(a).
11. 28 U.S.C. §158(d).
12. 28 U.S.C. §158(b).
13. 28 U.S.C. §158(d).
14. See Frank B. Reilly, Jr., and David N. Crapo, "Distressed M&A: Bankruptcy Code Section 363 Sales," *Corporate & Finance Alert*, December 23, 2008; available at http://www.gibbonslaw.com/news_publications/articles.php?action=display_publication&publication_id=2640, last accessed March 29, 2010.
15. Stephen E. Cays, "A Study on the Measurement and Prediction of the Indirect Costs of Bankruptcy," white paper, Glucksman Institute for Research in Securities Markets, Leonard N. Stern School of Business, April 2, 2001; available at http://w4.stern.nyu.edu/glucksman/docs/Cays.PDF, last accessed April 26, 2010.

16. Michael E. Bradbury and Suzanne Lloyd, "An Estimate of the Direct Costs of Bankruptcy in New Zealand," *Asia Pacific Journal of Management*, 11, no. 1, pp. 103–111.

17. Nelson D. Schwartz and Julie Creswell, "Who Knew Bankruptcy Paid So Well?" *New York Times*, April 30, 2010; http://www.nytimes.com/2010/05/02/business/02workout.html?pagewanted=all, last accessed September 11, 2010.

18. 11 U.S.C. §326(a).

19. See Fed. R. Bankr. P. 2004.

20. See, for example, Alexandra R. Lajoux and Charles M. Elson, *The Art of M&A Due Diligence: Navigating Critical Steps and Uncovering Crucial Data,* 2nd ed. (New York: McGraw-Hill, 2011).

21. Public Law 99-554, Title II, Section 257(a); October 27, 1986.

22. Public Law 109-8. For a good analysis of this law, see "Establishing Rules of Engagement," *The Deal*, October 17–23, 2005, pp. 26–27. Comments about the impact of this law are based in part on this article.

23. See The Wall Street Reform and Consumer Protection Act of 2010, known as the Dodd-Frank Act after sponsors Sen. Christopher Dodd and Rep. Barney Frank. For the full text of the law, which is over 2,300 pages, see http://docs.house.gov/rules/finserv/111_hr4173_finsrvcr.pdf. Heath P. Tarbert, Counsel, Weil, Gotshal & Manges LLP in Washington, DC, in a conversation with one of the authors, warned that almost any financial firm might be vulnerable to FDIC action under this broad provision—including even a hedge fund.

24. 11 U.S.C. §365(e).

25. 11 U.S.C. §547.

26. 11 U.S.C. §547(c).

CHAPTER 3

Trends in Distressed M&A and Investing

"How did you go bankrupt?"

"Two ways. Gradually, and then suddenly."

—Ernest Hemingway, The Sun Also Rises *(1926)*

OVERVIEW OF TRENDS IN DISTRESSED M&A AND INVESTING

How is the perception of bankruptcy changing on the heels of the Great Recession of 2007–2009?

Hemingway's words aptly sum up the shape of the bankruptcy wave during the recent economic downturn. Many companies that had been struggling for survival for years before the fall of Wall Street's titans fell victim almost overnight to one of the fastest and largest deteriorations of economic conditions in several generations. As a result, the art of buying, selling, and financing companies in distress is undergoing a dramatic transformation. A recent cover story in *The Deal* sets the stage:

> Traditionally, bankruptcy was walled off from normal dealmaking, run by a group of specialists, defined by the stigma attached to insolvent companies. But the very harshness and scale of the current bankruptcy wave has shown just how "normal" Chapter 11 has become, how it has grown into a transitional chapter for many companies not unlike, say, raising venture capital or going public.[1]

Recent U.S. data back this comparison. In 2009, 91 large publicly traded companies filed for some type of bankruptcy protection,[2] compared to only 49 initial public offerings that same year.[3] Furthermore, the total number of all business bankruptcies for 2009—including over 55,000 cases involving approximately 25 percent Chapter 11 filings, and 75 percent Chapter 7 filings[4]—far exceeds the tally for venture capital investments (2,795) and acquisitions (7,585) *combined.*[5] To be sure, 2009 was an unusually gloomy year for business; not every year has so many bankruptcies and so few IPOs, venture financings, and mergers. Still, considering longer-term trends, it is clear that bankruptcy has become part of business life.

In the previous chapters, we discussed why businesses fail and what restructuring alternatives such businesses may have. In this chapter, we describe recent trends in bankruptcies and distressed M&A. We discuss the causes of some of the largest corporate bankruptcy filings to date, along with what acquirers can learn from those filings. This chapter also briefly describes trends in distressed debt and equity investing. While an extensive discussion of distressed investing in general is outside the scope of this book, this area is increasingly converging with distressed M&A—particularly as more capital flows into the hands of financial buyers.

How common are bankruptcies over time and which ones are relevant to distressed M&A?

Generating proprietary deal flow among bankrupt businesses can be especially tricky. Each year, there are hundreds of thousands of bankruptcy cases in the United States. In order to understand which bankruptcy cases are most relevant to distressed M&A, potential buyers must sort through a lot of data. In a given year, the entire universe of U.S. bankruptcy cases includes both consumers and businesses. Among bankrupt businesses, there are Chapter 7 liquidations, which are usually not relevant to distressed M&A, and Chapter 11 reorganizations, which may result in sales under section 363 of the Bankruptcy Code (so-called 363 sales) or other distressed investing opportunities. Within Chapter 11 cases involving bankrupt businesses, there are entrepreneurial ventures, middle market companies and public corporations, and a wide variety of different industries. Depending on an investor's size and industry focus, only a subset of these will be relevant. As discussed in Chapter 2, each of these cases is located in a particular jurisdiction that operates a unique Web site to publish the case's information on a bankruptcy docket. There is no straightforward way to search all of these Web sites for relevant bankruptcy cases. Therefore, it can be difficult to identify bankruptcy cases that are most relevant to a buyer's particular investment strategy. Certain newswires and data-bases are helpful, but typically cover cases that are widely followed and, thus, involve more competition.

As illustrated in Exhibit 3-1, business bankruptcies comprise a small portion of the number of bankruptcy cases filed each year. After a declining trend from 1990 to 2005 from 9.0 percent to 1.9 percent, there has been a notable rise through 2009 to 4.3 percent for the number of business bank-ruptcies as a percent of the total number of bankruptcy cases annually. In general, the number of business bankruptcies does not appear to be cor-related with the total number of bankruptcy cases.

Bankrupt businesses represent less than 1 percent of the total number of U.S. companies in any given year,[6] and most of these cases involve Chapter 7 liquidations. For example, in 2009 there were over three times as many Chapter 7 liquidations than Chapter 11 reorganizations involving businesses.[7] Liquidations may generate sales at attractive prices for certain assets, such as equipment and raw materials. While such asset sales may provide bargains for other companies in the same industry, these situations are typically less relevant for distressed M&A. Businesses going through Chapter 11 reorganizations are the most likely candidates for distressed M&A because the debtors and creditors believe that these companies still have value as going concern entities, meaning that the value of the whole is greater than the sum of the parts. As illustrated in Exhibit 3-2, each year

Exhibit 3-1 U.S. Business Bankruptcy Cases as Percent of Total U.S. Bankruptcy Cases

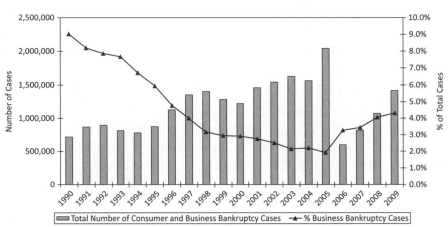

Source: U.S. Courts and American Bankruptcy Institute.

Exhibit 3-2 U.S. Business Chapter 11 Cases

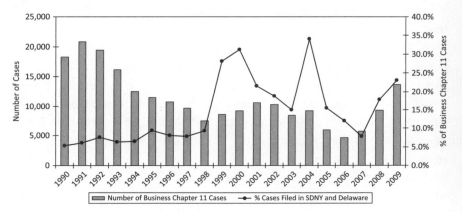

Source: U.S. Courts.

there are thousands of business bankruptcies that involve Chapter 11 reorganizations. Each Chapter 11 case involving a business is a potential target for distressed M&A because debtors and creditors will be seeking alternatives to their predicaments. Some of these cases will result in the companies exiting via a plan of reorganization (see Chapter 12 of this book for details), while others will sell some or all of their assets via 363 sales (see Chapter 13 of this book for details).

As previously noted in Exhibit 2-4, business bankruptcies are widely dispersed throughout the country in various jurisdictions. However, as shown in Exhibit 3-2, from 1999 onward, a high percentage of business Chapter 11 reorganizations were filed in the Southern District of New York (SDNY) and the District of Delaware, making these jurisdictions popular hunting grounds for distressed M&A. Indeed, over 20 percent of all businesses filing Chapter 11 cases chose these two jurisdictions from 2000 to 2009, compared to approximately 8.4 percent from 1990 to 1999.

For buyers who are interested in larger cases, Exhibit 3-3 illustrates the number of bankruptcies involving publicly traded companies with assets over $100 million.[8] The 2008 spike in mean assets for this category resulted from the unprecedented megacases of Lehman Brothers and Washington Mutual. These cases and others in the top ten largest bankruptcies in U.S. history are profiled later in this chapter.

Notably, while the economic downturn in 1990–1991 produced the peak years for the total number of business Chapter 11 cases in 1991 as shown

Exhibit 3-3 Bankruptcies of Large Publicly Traded Companies

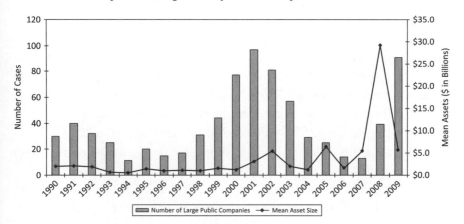

Source: UCLA-LoPucki's Bankruptcy Research Database.

in Exhibit 3-2, the economic downturns in 2000–2001 and 2008–2009 produced the peak years for the number of large public company Chapter 11 cases in 2001 and 2009 as shown in Exhibit 3-3. This outcome could be the result of more private businesses choosing Chapter 7 liquidation over Chapter 11 reorganization. Both exhibits illustrate that business bankruptcies are a lagging indicator of economic cycles as struggling businesses eventually succumb to financial pressures.

Some academic research suggests that the U.S. Court's methodology for categorizing bankruptcy filings as predominantly involving business versus nonbusiness assets undercounts the "true" number of business bankruptcies. One study suggests that as much as 15 percent of consumer bankruptcies come from business ventures—so the actual number of business bankruptcies (counting the self-employed, who may make consumer rather than business filings) can well exceed a quarter of a million per year.[9]

What are the chances of long-term recovery from a bankruptcy filing?

Only about one in five companies that file recovers, and of those, half fail again, according to the American Bankruptcy Institute. See Chapter 2 for a detailed discussion of companies with multiple bankruptcy cases, referred to as Chapter 22, Chapter 33, and even Chapter 44.

How common are distressed acquisitions?

The answer to this question, in a nutshell, is "increasingly." Exhibit 3-4 summarizes the number of bankrupt companies selling assets from 2001 to 2009, as well as the value of those transactions. From 2004 to 2007, the number of bankruptcy sales was relatively stable in the 325 to 350 range. This figure increased markedly to nearly 450 sales in 2008, then expanded to almost 600 in 2009. The value of such transactions has increased by an even greater amount—from a low of $24 billion in 2006 to $265 billion in 2009.

But even though distressed M&A volume nearly doubled from 2006 to 2009 (Exhibit 3-4), this still lagged the sixfold increase in business bankruptcy filings during this time. Aggregate deal value was much stronger, but it was skewed by a handful of disproportionately large transactions. This begs the question, why didn't the global economic recession of 2008–2009 (second in magnitude only to the Great Depression, by some measures) result in even more distressed M&A transactions?

The primary reason was that rather than pushing troubled companies into foreclosure or bankruptcy, banks widely engaged in a practice that was jokingly called "amend, extend, and pretend." In an unexpectedly large number of situations, when a borrower violated its financial covenants, banks agreed to amend the credit agreement and extend the maturity of the loan to give the borrower time to ride through the recession. In exchange, many such banks extracted an amendment fee plus an average spread

Exhibit 3-4 Assets Sold by Bankrupt Companies, 2001–2009

Year	No. of Deals	Volume ($ billions)
2001	75	28.8
2002	318	37.9
2003	296	47.4
2004	337	102.0
2005	346	54.6
2006	336	23.8
2007	326	53.3
2008	446	42.5
2009	597	265.5

Source: pipeline.thedeal.com.

Exhibit 3-5 Spread Increases in Selected "Amend and Extend" Transactions

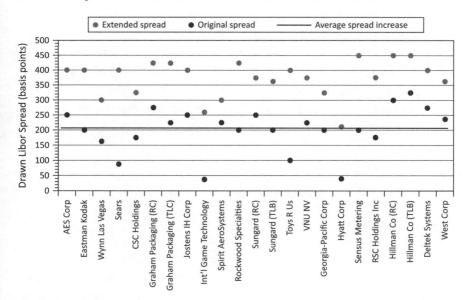

Source: Thomson Reuters PLC.

increase of roughly 200 basis points, according to one analysis. (See Exhibit 3-5.) However, although some borrowers may be able to make their interest payments during the extension period, it seems unlikely that they will ever be able to resume a normal amortization schedule and repay the loan balance in its entirety.

While it will be some time before research about the behavior of financial institutions in this period will be published, anecdotal evidence suggests that banks were so busy working out residential real estate in 2008–2009 that they sought to defer problems with their corporate loans to another period. In addition, banks may have been getting savvy about how to manipulate the timing of liquidating their collateral by enabling troubled borrowers to survive until valuations for the assets to be sold recovered. Furthermore, government regulators may have been encouraging banks to be patient and flexible with borrowers to avoid deepening the recession and increasing the number of bank failures. No matter what the reason, the "kicking the can down the road" strategy employed by the vast majority of lenders resulted in far fewer distressed M&A opportunities than potential buyers expected in this period.

It is currently unclear, however, whether the banks will repeat the "amend and extend" behavior if the reset financial covenants prove to be too stringent or the extended maturity finally arrives. It seems unlikely that these troubled companies have sufficient resources to actually fix their fundamental problems, so these problems will eventually need to be solved, perhaps through distressed M&A transactions. Rather than there being a peak in distressed M&A in 2008–2009, the transactions may be stretched over a longer period during 2010 and beyond.

What impact did the market rally of 2009 and into 2010 have on distressed investing?

Steve Martin, the actor, once quipped, "Comedy is all about ti-MING." The same could probably be said about valuations throughout the bankruptcy cycle. During the credit crisis that peaked shortly after Lehman Brothers' bankruptcy filing, the availability of credit tightened to such an extreme that many companies were forced into restructuring. Some companies, such as Delphi (which had filed back in October 2005), were "trapped" in Chapter 11 bankruptcy for a period, as the market for exit financing similarly tightened to extremes rarely seen in the past. This had the effect of sharply undercutting valuations for highly leveraged companies—both going concerns and those undergoing restructurings—as fears heightened that the crisis would outlast such companies' access to liquidity.

As the macroeconomy showed signs of bottoming around mid-2009, equity markets started to rally off decade lows, and credit availability started to ease. This set up an interesting dynamic: companies that had previously filed for bankruptcy, and all of whose equity value appeared to have been wiped out by the credit crunch, increasingly started to look more viable as conditions in the credit markets improved. In some cases, the fulcrum security moved all the way from the secured debt to the equity during the course of about a year.

Exhibit 3-6 reflects the key takeaway: expected net recoveries, using bond prices as a proxy, improved materially as the first wave of the recovery took hold, in some cases with bonds of bankrupt companies trading through par value in so-called "solvent debtor" cases. This illustrates the value proposition of both distressed M&A and distressed investing: those who get the timing right stand to make outsized returns!

Exhibit 3-6 Bond Prices for Selected Bankrupt Companies January 2009 to June 2010

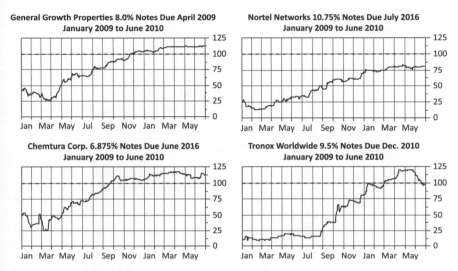

Source: FactSet.

While the stocks of bankrupt companies typically continue to trade on the over-the-counter exchange (the "Pink Sheets"), the equity markets are generally poor indicators of the outcome of a bankruptcy case. Overall, investing in the stocks of bankrupt companies is a very risky endeavor since these equity markets often behave more erratically than bond markets. As illustrated in Exhibit 3-7, the stocks for the same companies in Exhibit 3-6 did not always trade in line with the bond markets. There are many reasons why this disconnect may arise. Generally speaking, bond prices are a better indicator than stock prices to gauge anticipated results in a bankruptcy case.

NOTEWORTHY BANKRUPTCY CASES

What are some bankruptcies of historical note?

Before 1970, bankruptcies of very large companies were rare. When Penn Central failed in 1970 and W.T. Grant failed in 1975, these events sent shock waves throughout the business world. (Indeed, many people attribute the modern "corporate governance" movement to these pivotal events. This movement focuses on independent corporate boards and active shareholders as checks on management.) In 1980, Chrysler narrowly avoided bankruptcy

Exhibit 3-7 Stock Prices for Selected Bankrupt Companies January 2009 to June 2010

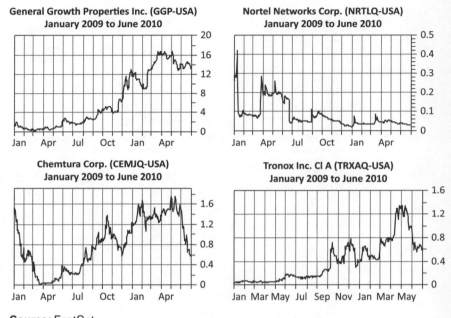

Source: FactSet.

through a government bailout. In the words of Mark Twain, history does not repeat itself, but it does rhyme. Chrysler, as well as General Motors, filed for government-supported bankruptcy in 2009.

The leveraged buyout cycle of the 1980s arguably drove a wave of mega-bankruptcies from 1990 to 1992, including $1 billion-plus debtors such as Southland Corp., LTV Corp., and R.H. Macy & Co. The next major wave—2001 to 2003—featured Enron and WorldCom, filers that were dragged down by corporate accounting scandals and by the Internet and telecom bubbles. The Enron bankruptcy, in particular, was notable not only for its size (at $63 billion), but also for its complexity. A total of 75 entities (the parent company and 74 subsidiaries) all filed for bankruptcy, affecting numerous creditors.

The current wave, to date, is most notable for megafilings from Lehman Brothers, General Motors, and Chrysler. In fact, as Exhibit 3-8 illustrates, six of the ten largest bankruptcy filings in U.S. history have occurred since September 2008. Moreover, the Lehman Brothers filing was more than six times the size of WorldCom's—which had had the (infamous) distinction of being the largest U.S. filing up through the last bankruptcy cycle.

Exhibit 3-8 The Ten Largest U.S. Bankruptcies

Company	Petition Date	Total Assets Prepetition	Industry
Lehman Brothers	Sept. 15, 2008	$639 billion	Financial Services
Washington Mutual	Sept. 25, 2008	$328 billion	Savings and Loan
WorldCom	July 21, 2002	$104 billion	Telecommunications
General Motors	June 1, 2009	$91 billion	Automotive
CIT Group	Nov. 1, 2009	$71 billion	Financial Services
Enron	Dec. 2, 2001	$66 billion	Energy
Conseco	Dec. 17, 2002	$61 billion	Insurance
Chrysler	April 30, 2009	$39 billion	Automotive
Thornburg Mortgage	May 1, 2009	$37 billion	Financial Services
Pacific Gas & Electric	April 6, 2001	$36 billion	Energy

Sources: CNN Money.com, bankruptcydata.com, and bankruptcy filings.

The main culprit and the primary victim of the current bankruptcy wave was the financial sector. Just four decades ago, the financial sector accounted for only 4 percent of the gross domestic product of the United States—a sensible level for a sector meant to enable other industries. Now this sector represents at least 8 percent, with two major consequences. First, the sheer size of the financial sector boosts the mathematical probability that, when corporate failures occur, they will be in this sector. Second, as a ripple effect, when failures do occur in this sector, they are more likely to have a broader economic impact. Notably, of the ten largest bankruptcies in American history, five were in the financial sector, and the remainder had some significant connection to it through their financing arms.

What can acquirers learn from these ten largest bankruptcies?

Every bankruptcy that occurs, large or small, is a complex web of events that defies easy description. Still, prime causes can be found for each event, and key lessons can be learned. Here are brief synopses of the ten largest bankruptcies, all of which involved publicly traded companies, including key events, causes, and lessons learned.

Lehman Brothers Holdings—$639 billion

Lehman, headquartered in New York City, and its subsidiaries filed for a voluntary bankruptcy petition under Chapter 11 of the Bankruptcy Code with the Bankruptcy Court for the Southern District of New York on September 15, 2008, declaring $639 billion in total assets, $613 billion in total debts, and more than 100,000 creditors. As one way to repay creditors, the firm sold assets under Bankruptcy Code section 363.[10]

Causes. Lehman had experienced losses in its $60 billion mortgage-related loan portfolio, but risk was a deeper issue. In 2006, its senior management had decided (with board approval) to put more capital at risk in the hopes of achieving higher growth. One of the errors that management had made was to increase the "risk appetite limit" that had been set by the firm's risk committee.[11] As part of that strategy, it acquired Archstone, causing the firm to become more leveraged.

Key Lesson. Culture matters. An early crack in the foundations of Lehman had been identified a quarter century earlier by Ken Auletta in *Greed and Glory: The Fall of the House of Lehman* (New York: Random House, 1986), which depicted cultural clashes between transactional traders and relationship bankers, with the traders' victory weakening the firm and leading to a merger into Shearson/American Express in 1984. A decade later, American Express spun Lehman off, and it became its own company again. But the trading mentality persisted, leading to Lehman's bankruptcy in 2008; this was chronicled in *A Colossal Failure of Common Sense: The Inside Story of the Collapse of Lehman Brothers* (New York: Crown Business, 2009) by Lehman bond trader Lawrence G. McDonald. The last word on Lehman comes from the bankruptcy court. In his March 2010 report, Anton R. Valukas, Examiner, found that "Lehman was more the consequence than the cause of a deteriorating economic climate. Lehman's financial plight . . . was exacerbated by Lehman executives, whose conduct ranged from serious but nonculpable errors of business judgment to actionable balance sheet manipulation; by [the firm's] business model, which rewarded excessive risk taking and leverage; and by government agencies, which might have better anticipated or mitigated the outcome."[12]

Washington Mutual—$328 billion

Washington Mutual (WaMu), headquartered in Seattle, Washington, holds two distinctions—one proud, the other humbling. It was the largest mutual savings bank in history, and it was the largest bank failure in history as well. Its bankruptcy case began officially on September 25, 2008, when, after an alarming run on the bank's deposits following weak financial performance, the Office of Thrift Supervision seized the bank and placed it in the receivership of the Federal Deposit Insurance Corporation (FDIC), which promptly sold its subsidiaries to JPMorgan Chase. The next day, the holding company filed a voluntary bankruptcy petition with the Bankruptcy Court for the District of Delaware as a liquidating Chapter 11 case. In March 2009, WaMu sued the FDIC for unjustified seizure and for an unreasonably low sales price to JPMorgan. In March 2010, as a result of legal actions, JPMorgan said that it would return some $4 billion to WaMu, after adjustments for taxes.[13]

Causes. More than any other major bankruptcy of the past decade, this case can be blamed on the mortgage market. In 2006, the bank was profitable, reporting a profit of $3.6 billion. But the bank ultimately reported a net loss of $67 billion for 2007 as a result of defaulting mortgages.

Key Lesson. External economic trends are as important as internal controls. By all accounts, WaMu had strong management and a vigilant board, with no evidence of fraud or negligence. The bank's main problem was that it underestimated the riskiness of a core market—the subprime mortgage market.

WorldCom—$104 billion

WorldCom, headquartered in Clinton, Mississippi, and its subsidiaries, including the former MCI, Inc., filed a voluntary bankruptcy petition in July 2002 with the Bankruptcy Court for the Southern District of New York, in the wake of Enron's then-record bankruptcy. The two events speeded passage of legislative reform—namely, the Sarbanes-Oxley Act of 2002. Many of WorldCom's problems were documented in "Restoring Trust: Corporate Governance for the Future of MCI, Inc.," a report delivered in August 2003 by former SEC chairman Richard C. Breeden to the district court that was overseeing MCI's bankruptcy. (WorldCom acquired MCI in September 1998 in a transaction valued at $37 billion at the time of its announcement.) As corporate monitor of MCI-WorldCom, Breeden recommended a "governance constitution," with 78 specific corporate governance recommendations, that MCI would have to implement as a condition for its emergence from bankruptcy. Many of the recommendations became part of the company's articles of incorporation. When MCI-WorldCom's plan of reorganization became effective in 2004, it had $6 billion in cash and nearly that much in debt ($5.7 billion). It used the cash to pay severance to the workers it had laid off.[14] The court released the company from an obligation to pay 19 of the employees the $1.4 million they had been promised as senior managers. Bondholders ended up being paid 35.7 cents on the dollar, in bonds and stock in the new MCI company.[15] In 2005, after the debtor had emerged from bankruptcy, Verizon acquired MCI, which it operates as a subsidiary for wireless telephone service.

Causes.   The most probable causes of WorldCom's collapse were a failure to integrate acquisitions and a massive accounting fraud intended to conceal its losses. As for the first cause, WorldCom acquired more than 70 companies in two decades, including MFS Communications and MCI, but, as experts writing just before WorldCom declared bankruptcy said, "failed to meld its acquisitions into a coherent, value-producing whole."[16] The crowning blow to the company was a June 2002 disclosure that it had incorrectly accounted for $3.8 billion in operating expenses.

Key Lesson.   Directors need to do more to oversee the integration of acquisitions and to scrutinize financial reporting, including prospectuses offering new stock. The latter was a key finding in the Breeden report.

General Motors—$91 billion

On June 1, 2009, GM, headquartered in Detroit, Michigan, and its subsidiaries filed a voluntary bankruptcy petition with the Bankruptcy Court of the Southern District of New York. GM owed the U.S. government, its largest creditor, $19.4 billion. The company pursued a prepackaged plan of reorganization, receiving $24.2 billion in U.S. government funds for its DIP loan. In July 2009, its operations and core brands, including Chevrolet, Buick, GMC, and Cadillac, were transferred to a newly formed company, which became known as "New GM." New GM cherry-picked the most profitable assets and quickly exited bankruptcy protection under U.S. Treasury ownership in a highly controversial 363 sale process that generated approximately 750 written objections. The active participation of the U.S. Treasury as DIP lender and 363 sale bidder was unprecedented and involved the government pursuing an aggressive agenda to save GM. The remaining assets, such as Pontiac and Saturn, became known as Motors Liquidation Company or "Old GM." The U.S. Treasury provided approximately $1.2 billion to fund the wind-down of Old GM in Chapter 11, including resolving post-sale issues such as discontinuing the remaining operations and making distributions to creditors after reviewing their claims. Creditors received partial recoveries in common stock of New GM so that they could participate in an eventual initial public offering. On July 21, 2009, the SEC and the Financial Industry Regulatory Authority (FINRA) issued an alert explaining the difference between the two companies and discouraging investment in Old GM, which was misleading to some investors.[17]

Causes.   The economic structure of the auto industry makes it particularly vulnerable to bankruptcy. The industry has high fixed costs, and end market demand is closely linked with national prosperity. When the U.S. economy weakened, so did GM. GM once sold so many cars that its CEO was quoted (albeit incorrectly) as saying, "What's good for General Motors is good for the country."[18] One additional cause of GM's bankruptcy was its failure to adjust its strategy to changing times. Through a series of strategic missteps (a financing arm that ventured heavily into mortgages and relied on the securitization market, undisciplined customer rebates industrywide, shifting consumer preferences away from trucks and toward smaller vehicles, and so on), the company lost significant market share and all profitability.[19]

Key Lesson.   Focus on a sound strategic plan and adjust it to reflect changes in the business environment and changing customer tastes. In Chapter 11, never underestimate the unexpected, such as the U.S. government taking unprecedented action that may have distorted the fundamental tenets of bankruptcy law.

CIT Group—$71 billion

CIT Group, headquartered in New York City, and its subsidiaries filed a voluntary bankruptcy petition with the Bankruptcy Court of the Southern District of New York on November 1, 2009, announcing a prepackaged debt restructuring plan to reduce its debt by $10 billion. CIT emerged from bankruptcy weeks later, in December 2009. The prepackaged plan of reorganization resulted in (1) a $10.4 billion net reduction in debt obligations, reflecting the cancellation of senior and subordinated unsecured debt obligations and the issuance of new secured notes; (2) the cancellation of all preferred stock obligations and prior common shareholder interests; (3) the issuance of 200 million new common shares to eligible debt holders; and (4) an improved liquidity and capital position achieved through debt reduction and the deferral of significant debt maturities for three years.[20]

Causes.   As an old-line dividend-paying blue chip in the middle-market space, CIT does not present the profile of a prodigal firm. The cause appears to have been a heavy concentration of loans to businesses affected by the subprime mortgage crisis.

Key Lesson.   Find ways to hedge material risks that are inherent in your core business, in case that sector suffers a reversal.

Enron—$66 billion

Enron, headquartered in Houston, Texas, and its subsidiaries filed a voluntary bankruptcy petition with the Bankruptcy Court for the Southern District of New York on December 2, 2001, an event that, along with the WorldCom bankruptcy, precipitated major corporate governance reforms. The Powers report tells the story. On February 1, 2002, William C. Powers, Jr., presented to the Enron board of directors the Report of the Investigation by the Special Investigative Committee of the Board of Directors on Enron Corp. (Powers chaired the special investigative committee.) Enron had had substantial undisclosed arrangements (off-balance sheet transactions involving insiders) that hid the conditions that led to Enron's bankruptcy, and also contributed to it. Today, Enron is literally a shell of its former self, operating as Enron Creditors Recovery Corp. (ECRC), which is distributing the remaining assets of the bankrupt Enron to creditors.[21] ECRC continues to attempt to obtain funds from advisors that allegedly enabled Enron's fraud.[22] The thousands of derivative trades that remained unresolved at the time of Enron's demise eventually led to significant revisions in the sections of the Bankruptcy Code addressing forward contracts, swaps, master netting agreements, and other financial contracts.

Causes.   Hubris is the corrosive thread throughout the many accounts of Enron's demise. The "smartest guys in the room" took an energy and financial company with great potential and turned it into a house of cards held together by a web of financial structures of questionable purpose.

Key Lesson.   Ask questions. The main message of the Powers report is that the board of directors should have exercised stronger oversight of the company's special financial arrangements. Pride goes before a fall, but humility can prevent one. To avoid a future Enron, directors and others can ask questions if they don't understand the purpose of particular strategies, transactions, or vehicles.

Conseco—$61 billion

Conseco, headquartered in Carmel, Indiana, and its subsidiaries filed a voluntary bankruptcy petition under Chapter 11 with the Bankruptcy Court for the Northern District of Illinois on December 17, 2002. In September 2003, the court confirmed the plan of reorganization. The company, which was renamed CNO Financial Group, sold its finance operations and emerged to focus on its core insurance operations.

Causes.   Many analysts attribute the bankruptcy of Conseco, a multiline insurance company, to one main cause: the $7.6 billion acquisition of Green Tree Financial Corp., one of the largest financers of mobile homes, in April 1998. There was concern that not only had Conseco overpaid for Green Tree, but also it had strayed from its core business into an industry with which it was unfamiliar and inexperienced. On the day of the announcement of this stock-for-stock deal, the company's stock fell 15 percent. While the initial drop might have been attributable to the usual merger arbitrage upon the deal announcement, Conseco's stock continued to decline for the next three years, despite a variety of attempts to recover. These included insider purchases signaling confidence, debt restructuring, and cost savings through outsourcing. Then, in 2002, with the stock trading at under $1, the company disclosed that the SEC was investigating the company's accounting practices. Ultimately, Conseco divested Green Tree, which essentially was an admission that the acquisition had failed.

Key Lesson.   The Conseco saga underscores the importance of a prudent M&A strategy. The Green Tree deal was strategically sound, and there were no reported problems with integration; the problem, many believe, was that Conseco had overpaid for the deal, as well as for dozens of other transactions leading up to that 1998 purchase.[23]

Chrysler—$39 billion

Chrysler, headquartered in Detroit, Michigan, and its subsidiaries filed a voluntary bankruptcy petition under Chapter 11 with the Bankruptcy Court for the Southern District of New York on April 30, 2009, two years after a private equity firm had acquired it from Daimler, thus untangling an unsuccessful merger from a decade earlier.[24] Although the federal government had loaned Chrysler money earlier in the year, the Presidential Task Force on the Auto Industry rejected Chrysler's restructuring plan and virtually forced the automaker to find an overseas merger partner. The group, showing little commitment to U.S. autos (not even as consumers),[25] gave Chrysler 30 days to complete an alliance with Fiat as a condition for receiving more government funding. In June 2009, the company merged with Fiat, despite legal challenges. Fiat assumed control of most of Chrysler's assets; the remaining assets were sold off under court supervision, with the proceeds to be distributed to creditors with claims against Chrysler LLC.[26]

Causes.   In addition to the structural issues cited earlier for GM, the cause of this bankruptcy may have been chronic underinvestment in product development. While Chrysler had had a handful of "hits" in recent years (Chrysler 300C, PT Cruiser, Town & Country minivan), these were few and far between.

Key Lesson. Determine whether the company has a salvageable franchise. Like Conseco, the Chrysler case highlights the result of failed M&A. In this case, both a strategic and a financial buyer underestimated the challenges of turning around a troubled company. As with GM, industry woes combined with an inability to develop a sound strategic plan were key ingredients for financial disaster. Without a viable independent business, sale to a buyer may be the only realistic solution.

Thornburg Mortgage—$37 billion

On May 1, 2009, Thornburg Mortgage, headquartered in Santa Fe, New Mexico, and its subsidiaries filed a voluntary bankruptcy petition to pursue a liquidating Chapter 11 case with the Bankruptcy Court for the District of Maryland. Its assets were subsequently sold pursuant to Bankruptcy Code section 363, and the company officially ceased operations. Previously, from 2000 to 2006, Thornburg's profit had risen tenfold and the stock had tripled, compared with the 54 percent gain for the S&P 500 Financials Index.

Causes. Thornburg's downfall can be attributed to a combination of creditor panic and lack of insider loyalty. This real estate investment trust (REIT) had relatively high-quality mortgages, but creditors concerned about the subprime mortgage crisis and mortgage-backed securities made margin calls that the firm was unable to meet. The trustee in charge of the bankrupt company has alleged that one cause of the bankruptcy was self-dealing by insiders. The trustee has stated that four top executives of Thornburg paid themselves handsome bonuses shortly before the mortgage lender filed for bankruptcy in 2009, and misappropriated funds from Thornburg in a hidden plan to launch a new firm.[27]

Key Lesson. Trust but verify—and vice versa. If creditors had been more patient, and if the board had been more alert to potential conflicts of interest on the part of key managers, Thornburg might still be an operating company.

Pacific Gas & Electric—$36 billion

On April 6, 2001, Pacific Gas & Electric Co (PG&E)., headquartered in San Francisco, California, and its subsidiaries filed a voluntary bankruptcy petition under Chapter 11 of the Bankruptcy Code with the Bankruptcy Court for the Northern District of California. After more than two years of negotiation over competing plans of reorganization, PG&E, the California Public Utilities Commission (CPUC), and the Official Committee of Unsecured Creditors agreed to a settlement that paved the way for the utility to exit bankruptcy. The June 2003 settlement included (1) PG&E's abandoning efforts to divide the utility into four parts, with three under federal control, and instead remaining intact under CPUC regulation, (2) agreement on a multiyear declining schedule for utility rates, (3) dedication of 140,000 acres of watershed lands and $70 million to a nonprofit corporation for maintaining PG&E's hydroelectric operations and for public purposes, (4) establishment of a $15 million venture capital fund to foster and promote new clean energy technologies, and (5) full recoveries for creditors.

Causes.   The company's insolvency followed an increase in the cost of wholesale power, combined with so-called deregulation that prevented the utility from raising its costs despite a heavy debt burden.

Key Lesson.   Scan the horizon. Sometimes running a business well for customers is not enough. Exogenous factors like the price of raw materials or new government policies can create a tipping point. After a crisis results in bankruptcy, building consensus with key constituents can eventually result in full recoveries for creditors.

Can you identify recent bankruptcy cases in various industries that involved distressed M&A?

Exhibit 3-9 highlights selected bankruptcy cases in different industries during the current global recession of 2008–2010. Overall, the clear conclusion is that no industry is immune from business failures when macroeconomic problems are severe.

Exhibit 3-9 Selected Bankruptcy Cases by Industry, 2008–2010

Apparel	Automotive	Aviation	Banking & Finance	Biotechnology	Building Products
Fashion House	EZ Lube	Alitalia S.p.A.	Advanta	Forticell Bioscience	MAAX
Hartmarx	Meridian	Aloha Airlines	Capmark Financial	Lipid Sciences	Masonite
Point Blank Solutions	Visteon	Mesa Air	IndyMac Bancorp	Microlslet	U.S. Concrete

Chemical	Consumer Products	Electronics	Energy	Entertainment & Recreation	Ethanol
Chemtura	Lenox Group	Sequiam	Applied Solar	Bally's Total Fitness	Northeast Biofuels
Ethanex Energy	Polaroid	Soyo Group	Technipower Systems	Midway Games	Otter Tail Ag Enterprises
Lyondell Chemical	Simmons Company	Syntax-Brillian	U.S. Energy	Six Flags	VeraSun Energy

Food & Beverage	Gaming	Grocery	Home Building	Hospitals	Hotels
Eurofresh	Herbst Gaming	Great Atlantic & Pacific	TOUSA	Forum Health	Extended Stay
Growers Direct Coffee	Legends Gaming	Bruno's Supermarkets	WCI Communities	Hospital Partners	Fountainbleu Las Vegas
Pilgrim's Pride	Trump Entertainment	Penn Traffic Company	WL Homes	Integra Hospital Plano	Tropicana Entertainment

Information Technology	Insurance	Law Firms	Medical Devices & Services	Mining	Oil & Gas
BearingPoint	BluePoint Re	Dreier	Artes Medical	Apex Silver Mines	Baseline Oil & Gas
Muzak	ING Re (UK)	Heller Ehrman	Scantek Medical	Buillion River Gold	Crusader Energy
Silicon Graphics	LandAmerica Financial	Thelen Reid & Priest	SurgiLight	Sterling Mining	Saratoga Resources

Packaging, Pulp & Paper	Plastics	Publishing	Real Estate	Recreational Vehicles	Restaurant
AbitibiBowater	ECO2 Plastics	Idearc	Crescent Resources	Fleetwood Industries	Buffets Holdings
Pope & Talbot	Moll Industries	Readers Digest	DBSI	Fountain Powerboat	Steakhouse Partners
Smurfit-Stone Container	Wellman	Tribune Company	General Growth Properties	Monaco Coach	Uno Restaurant

Retail	Semiconductors	Steel & Metals	Telecommunications	Transportation	Textiles
Circuit City	Aviza Technology	Almatis B.V.	Charter Communications	Jevic Transportation	Dan River
KB Toys	GSI Group	Stamford Industrial	Hawaiian Telecom	SIRVA	Foamex
Linens 'n' Things	Tvia	Neenah Enterprises	Nortel Networks	U.S. Shipping Partners	Propex

DISTRESSED INVESTORS

What types of investors deploy their capital in distressed businesses?

The United States has the most advanced market for investing in distressed securities. At least in part, this is because of a combination of well-settled bankruptcy laws and highly developed capital markets. As a result, the range of investor types in the distressed area is just as wide as that in more "traditional" markets.

Broadly speaking, one might divide the universe of potential distressed investors into three categories: (1) private equity funds that focus on control buyouts of distressed companies; (2) hedge funds that trade in the claims and credit of distressed entities; and (3) both hedge funds and long-only funds (e.g., mutual funds) that invest in the equity of reorganized businesses.

What is the appeal of investing in distressed companies?

"Cheap valuation" might be among the first reasons that come to mind. However, most investors measure their success on a risk-adjusted basis. As a result, low valuation in a vacuum is meaningless. That is, most companies with low valuations are cheap for a reason. (In fact, we devoted all of Chapter 1 to discussing the reasons why businesses fail.)

In our view, the appeal of distressed investing is largely a function of structural factors that can affect the market. These factors generally differ when an investor is evaluating the credit of a distressed company from their values for the equity of a postbankruptcy entity.

On the credit side, some lenders either become forced sellers at precisely the wrong time (i.e., the point of least market liquidity) or become less concerned with extracting full value on a defaulted loan. Consider, for instance, ratings-focused credit mutual funds. Such funds are often constrained by mandates setting minimum credit ratings for the assets they hold. When companies default or their ratings drop, these funds become forced sellers.

The typical commercial bank may also face structural incentives to sell a distressed loan prematurely. Once a loan "goes bad," it generally moves from performing to impaired (or defaulted) on the bank's balance sheet—thereby requiring a larger risk capital allocation. This higher allocation makes holding the loan more expensive for the bank. The bank also typically writes down the value of the loan internally (possibly to zero) before handing it off to the workout area. The workout team thus may have incentives to move the loan off the bank's books as quickly as possible, with relatively limited regard for the credit's face value.

Structural factors also frequently support investing in the equity of companies postbankruptcy. One commentator divides these factors into two areas: qualitative and fundamental. We summarize these factors in Exhibit 3-10.

Distressed investing also has the added benefit of potentially low correlation with investments in more liquid securities. This diversifies portfolio risk and creates hedging opportunities for investors with an appetite for alternative asset classes.

In addition, there is also a relatively large (and unregulated) market in *claims trading*, or the buying and selling of claims against a bankrupt corporate debtor. Relatively little has been written about claims trading, which is highly speculative and not subject to either securities or M&A

Exhibit 3-10 Structural Factors Supporting Distressed Equity Investing

---

GENERAL QUALITATIVE FACTORS

- *Information access.* While companies typically provide regular updates, the data are often confusing (there are multiple versions, and the sources are often courts themselves), and compilation of these data is not available. Also, a great deal of qualitative information is managed by creditors during a Chapter 11 bankruptcy process.
- *Investor skepticism.* Investors typically cringe and view reorgs as tainted companies.
- *Positive section bias.* Only one company in ten emerges from a Chapter 11 filing as a public company. Many good businesses are acquired in Chapter 11 bankruptcy, so many investors assume that the best offerings have been picked over.
- *Lack of research coverage.* Research coverage typically does not resume for one year.
- *Flowback.* Often, there is some initial selling pressure as some creditors rush to sell their holdings.

GENERAL FUNDAMENTAL FACTORS

- *Reduction in debt.* Debt is typically reduced by 20 to 80 percent, reducing the financial burden on "good" business models.
- *Asset structure changes.* During bankruptcy, companies will often close or sell underperforming assets and cancel leases.
- *New management teams.* Change in management can reinvigorate a company.
- *Monthly operating results.* This primarily mitigates risk. Monthly results are filed by the company with the bankruptcy court (for investors, generally available as 8-Ks).
- *Financial projections.* Financial forecasts are included in the disclosure statement.

Source: JP Morgan Chase & Co.

regulation. There is also little data or case law on the subject. As a result, nobody really knows the size of the market—although some have suggested that it is in the hundreds of billions.

Why would an investor be interested in buying a claim against a bankrupt company?

It's probably easy to understand why some creditors might be willing to sell claims, even at a discount, related to a bankrupt entity. Such creditors may have neither the appetite nor the ability to await a full payout; they may even be concerned about whether the claim will, in fact, ever be paid. (Certainly, bankruptcy is fraught with risk.) But what may be less clear is why another party might be willing to step in and buy that claim, given how speculative the investment inherently is likely to be.

Broadly speaking, there are three types of investors that might be interested in purchasing a creditor's claim:

1. Some investors will purchase claims solely for investment purposes. (A broker-dealer may also take this role if it is trying to match buyers and sellers of claims and pocket a commission or markup.) Such investors will compare the expected return on a claim (which incorporates anticipated recoveries and time to reorganize, among many other variables) with the cash outlay to purchase that claim. If the risk-adjusted return on the acquired claim exceeds the investors' hurdle rate, it may appear attractive.
2. Other investors may be seeking to influence the reorganization in some way. This might include purchasing the claims as the *fulcrum security*, buying a blocking position to extract a greater payout in the plan of reorganization. (Chapter 4 of this book discusses fulcrum securities in greater detail. In a nutshell, a fulcrum security is the debt instrument that is most likely to be converted to equity ownership in the restructuring.)
3. Finally, some claims purchasers might only be looking for information about the debtor. Examples might include a potential buyer of the debtor's assets in a contemplated *363 sale* (discussed at length in Chapter 13 of this book), or simply a competitor looking for market intelligence.

In general, the party buying a claim succeeds to all the rights and infirmities of the seller, including, of course, the right to the face value of the claim. *Infirmities* include all the defenses that the debtor and other parties at interest can assert to challenge the claim. Examples include voidable preference, fraudulent conveyance, failure to fulfill contractual terms, and so forth.

Once the parties reach agreement to sell a claim, the buyer must notify the bankruptcy court of the transaction. If the court is satisfied that all requirements have been met, it will validate the transfer and officially record the new owner of the claim. The details of the transaction, including price and terms, become part of the public record on the bankruptcy docket.

When during the bankruptcy process might distressed investors enter the picture?

As described in other parts of this book, investors can enter the process literally at any time. However, prior to plan confirmation or some other court order, such investors typically enter in one of three ways: (1) as a debtor-in-possession (DIP) lender, (2) as an investor in the bank debt, or (3) as an investor in the fulcrum security. Note that these are not necessarily mutually exclusive options; for instance, the bank debt may be the fulcrum security.

Has investing in postbankruptcy equities historically been a profitable strategy?

As a general rule, yes. For instance, JPMorgan compiled the 12-month gains of reorganizations by looking at 117 reorganizations over the 15-year period from 1988 to 2003.[28] The first 12-month gains of reorganizations during this period outperformed the S&P 500 by an average of 84 percentage points, with the greatest relative outperformance being concentrated in the first month of trading. Nonetheless, there was a dispersion of returns in this study: only half of the companies in the sample of 117 outperformed the market. Accordingly, the overall positive results were driven by a minority of the companies in the study. This suggests that investors looking to invest in postbankruptcy equities take a portfolio approach to buying such securities.

Are there any funds that buy insolvent entities?

Yes. Several kinds of funds have been formed that focus on the purchase of distressed entities; they are called variously *reorganization funds, turnaround funds, vulture funds,* or *workout funds.* But whatever the name they use, their focus is the same: to invest at bargain rates in an entity that is undergoing financial distress or is already bankrupt, and then to reap the benefits when the company emerges from this state. As recently explained by Marc Rowan, a founding partner of Apollo Management:

> [T]he strategy that we have relied on for the past 20 years is distressed. Most of the founders of our business come out of the debt business. Rather than looking for acquisitions in the traditional private equity fashion during these periods of time, we employ our fixed income skill set. We go in and we buy the debt, bank debt, subordinated debt, of fundamentally good businesses that are overlevered, and we work through a process with creditors—sometimes in bankruptcy, sometimes out of bankruptcy—and we end up, hopefully, backing into control of a fundamentally good capital structure at a good price.[29]

As might be expected, fund-raising activity in this area grew dramatically as economic conditions deteriorated during 2009. Exhibit 3-11 summarizes the amount of capital raised by such funds from 2001 to 2009.

Exhibit 3-11 Capital Raised by Private Equity Distressed Asset Funds

Year	No. of Funds	Aggregate Capital (US$ billions)
2001	11	7.9
2002	9	5.8
2003	17	5.9
2004	23	11.7
2005	21	10.9
2006	28	19.0
2007	38	47.5
2008	28	44.7
2009*	59	52.5

*Includes funds that were in the process of raising capital as of July 31, 2009.
Source: Preqin; *CFA Magazine*, November–December 2009, p. 42.

Leading private equity funds that focus on distressed buyouts are

- Apollo Management (www.apolloic.com)
- Bayside Capital (www.bayside.com)
- Industrial Opportunities Partners (www.iopfund.com)
- Insight Equity (www.insightequity.com)
- JLL Partners (www.jllpartners.com)
- KPS Special Situations (www.kpsfund.com)
- Matlin Patterson Global Advisors (secure.reportingsystem.com/ MatlinPatterson-home)
- Monomoy Capital Partners (www.mcpfunds.com)
- Questor (defunct)
- Prophet Equity (www.prophetequity.com)
- Sunrise Equity Investors (defunct)
- Sun Capital Partners (www.suncappart.com)
- Versa Capital Management (www.versa.com)
- Wayzata Investment Partners (www.wayzatainvestmentpartners .com)
- Wellspring Capital Management (www.wellspringcapital.com)
- WL Ross & Co. (www.institutional.invesco.com)
- Yucaipa Companies (www.yucaipaco.com)

In addition, there are numerous hedge funds that are attracted to distressed debt investing to produce higher-yielding strategies; some noteworthy funds are

- Angelo Gordon
- Appaloosa Management
- Black Diamond
- Cerberus
- Crystal Capital
- DDJ Capital Management
- D.E. Shaw
- Elliott Associates
- Garrison Investment Group
- Harbinger
- Highland Capital

- MHR Capital
- Oaktree Capital
- Paulson & Co.
- SilverPoint Capital
- Third Avenue Focused Credit Fund

These private equity distressed asset funds have emerged in an era in which private equity M&A and bankruptcies are both up.[30] Yet equity investors accounted for only about 6 percent of global M&A transactions in early 2010.[31] Most money for distressed deals comes from secured and unsecured creditors facilitated by advisors. The next section of our book introduces these important players.

Endnotes

1. Anthony Baldo, "The Bankruptcy Routine," *The Deal*, Jan. 25–Feb. 7, 2010, pg. 40.
2. This number includes both Chapter 7 and Chapter 11 cases. See UCLA-LoPucki's Bankruptcy Research Database.
3. Jay R. Ritter, "Some Factoids about the 2009 IPO Market," Cordell Professor of Finance, University of Florida (March 5, 2010); available at http://bear.warrington.ufl.edu/ritter/IPOs2009Factoids.pdf, last accessed March 7, 2010.
4. As reported by the U.S. Courts.
5. PricewaterhouseCoopers & National Venture Capital Association, MoneyTree Report 2009; available at https://www.pwcmoneytree.com/MTPublic/ns/moneytree/filesource/exhibits/National%20MoneyTree%20full-year%20Q4%202009.pdf, last accessed March 13, 2010.
6. Approximately 15 million business entities file U. S. tax returns as going concerns every year.
7. As reported by the U.S. Courts and American Bankruptcy Institute.
8. Includes companies who reported assets of more than $100 million (measured in 1980 dollars) on the last form 10-K that the debtor filed with the Securities Exchange Commission before filing the bankruptcy case.
9. Elizabeth Warren & Robert M. Lawless, "My Myth of Disappearing Business Bankruptcy," 93 *California Law Review* 745 (2005).
10. Frank B. Reilly, Jr., and David N. Crapo, "Distressed M&A: Bankruptcy Code Section 363 Sales," *Corporate & Finance Alert*, December 23, 2008; available at http://www.gibbonslaw.com/news_publications/articles.php?action=display_publication&publication_id=2640, last accessed March 7, 2010.
11. *In re Lehman Brothers Holding, Inc., et al.*, Report of Anton R. Valukas, Examiner, Chapter 11 Case No. 08-13555 (JMP), March 11, 2010 (hereinafter "Lehman Brothers Examiner's Report"), at 72; available at http://www.scribd.com/doc/28228424/Lehman-Brothers-Examiner-s-Report-Vol-1, last accessed April 26, 2010.

12. Ibid., at 2–3.

13. "Washington Mutual Resolves Lawsuit Battles with FDIC, JPMorgan Chase (JPM)"; available at http://www.tmcnet.com/usubmit/2010/03/13/4670263.htm, last accessed April 26, 2010. For an outline of the issues considered in the case, see *In re Washington Mutual Inc. et alia, Debtors. Washington Mutual Inc. and WMI Investment Corp., Plaintiffs v. JP Morgan Cash Bank, National Association, Defendant*; available at http://www.kccllc.net/documents/0812229/081222 9100302000000000008.pdf, last accessed April 26, 2010.

14. The workers formed a group called exWorldCom 5100, successfully mobilizing for repayment. Jim Crane, "Laid-Off WorldCom Workers to Get $36 Million," *Baltimore Sun*, October 1, 2002; available at http://www.baltimoresun.com/business/bal-worldcom1001,0,915132.story, last accessed April 26, 2010.

15. Steven Taub, "MCI Emerges from Bankruptcy," *cfo.com*, April 21, 2004; available at http://www.cfo.com/article.cfm/3013321/c_3042555, last accessed April 25, 2010.

16. Knowledge@Wharton, "Will WorldCom Rise Again," commentary from the Wharton School of Business at the University of Pennsylvania, May 26, 2002; available at http://news.cnet.com/Will-WorldCom-rise-again/2009-1033_3-922988.html, last accessed April 26, 2010.

17. "Trading in Motors Liquidation Company (Formerly Known as General Motors Corporation)," FINRA, July 2009; available at http://www.finra.org/web/groups/industry/@ip/@reg/@notice/documents/notices/p119826.pdf, last accessed April 26, 2010.

18. According to a *Time* magazine article from 1961, what GM's CEO actually said was, "For years I thought that what was good for our country was good for General Motors, and vice versa." *See* "Armed Forces: Engine Charlie," *Time*, October 6, 1961; available at http://www.time.com/time/magazine/article/0,9171,827790-1,00.html, last accessed May 13, 2010.

19. See, for example, Sharon Silke Carty, "Seven Reasons GM Is Headed to Bankruptcy," *USA Today*, June 2, 2009; available at http://www.usatoday.com/money/autos/2009-05-31-gm-mistakes-bankruptcy_N.htm, last accessed April 26, 2010.

20. "CIT Reports 2009 Financial Results," press release, March 16, 2010; available at http://phx.corporate-ir.net/External.File?item=UGFyZW50SUQ9Mjk1NzU4M3xDaGlsZElEPTM3MzA4MHxUeXBlPTI=&t=1, last accessed April 26, 2010.

21. See http://www.enron.com/.

22. In a lawsuit that is still pending as we go to press with this book, ECRC alleges that Citigroup helped certain Enron officers to manipulate and misstate Enron's financial condition in the five years leading up to Enron's bankruptcy in December 2001. Specifically, ECRC alleges that during this period, Citigroup entered into at least 13 structured finance transactions with Enron, knowing of the company's plans to account for them in a way that made Enron's financial state appear stronger than it really was. In his fourth and final report on the Enron bankruptcy, examiner Neal Batson concluded that all of the transactions between Enron and Citigroup share one or more of the following characteristics: no rational business

purpose; completion near the close of Enron's financial reporting period, and in an amount designed to assist Enron in meeting one or more targeted financial ratios; attempted disguise of cash flow from financing as cash flow from Enron's business operations, which ultimately allowed the overstatement of Enron's operating cash flow on Enron's financial statements; or attempted disguise of debt as price risk management liabilities (trading business liabilities), which ultimately allowed the understating of debt on Enron's balance sheet. If the courts agree with this report, Citigroup may be found liable for violation of securities laws.

23. For a detailed account of the Conseco story, see "Rebuilding Conseco," *Indianapolis Star*, August 13, 2004.

24. Germany's Daimler AG sold 80.1 percent of Chrysler to Cerberus for $7.4 billion, keeping 19.9 percent.

25. See Noel Sheppard, "Obama's Auto Task Force Owns Foreign Cars, Will Media Care?" *NewsBusters*, February 23, 2009; available at http://newsbusters.org/blogs/noel-sheppard/2009/02/23/obamas-auto-task-force-owns-foreign-cars-will-media-care, last accessed April 26, 2010. This article claims that most of the task force members owned foreign cars, and some did not own cars.

26. See "Chrysler Bankruptcy Ends; Supreme Court Clears Sale to Fiat," *U.S. News*, June 10, 2009; available at http://usnews.rankingsandreviews.com/cars-trucks/daily-news/090610-Chrysler-Bankruptcy-Ends-Supreme-Court-Clears-Sale-to-Fiat, last accessed March 7, 2010.

27. Emily Chasan, "Trustee Sues ex-Thornburg Mortgage Execs for Theft," Reuters, March 4, 2010, available at http://www.reuters.com/article/idUSN0412213220100304, last accessed April 26, 2010. For the full case, see *In re TMST, Inc.*, case No. 09-17787-DK, United States Bankruptcy Court, D. Maryland at Baltimore (February 16, 2010); available at http://www.leagle.com/unsecure/page.htm?shortname=inbco20100216515, last accessed April 26, 2010.

28. Thomas J. Lee, "The Chapter after Chapter 11," J. P. Morgan Equity Research, January 9, 2004.

29. Interview with Marc Rowan, founding partner of Apollo Management, "The Best Returns Follow Chaos"; available at http://knowledge.wharton.upenn.edu/arabic/article.cfm?articleid=1203, last accessed May 12, 2010.

30. See Thomson Reuters League Tables for Quarter 1 2010. Compared to Quarter 1 2009, the period showed an 89 percent increase in private equity M&A in the period, and a more than 800-fold increase in distressed M&A.

31. Ibid.

The Bankruptcy Players

When considering the purchase of a distressed business, a potential buyer should initially identify the various parties who are involved in the situation. Whether the target company has already begun a bankruptcy turnaround or is engaged in an out-of-court workout, the parties typically negotiate using bankruptcy concepts and terms.

In general, the bankruptcy process pits the debtor against its creditors, giving each certain rights and capabilities to enable them to negotiate a fair and equitable resolution of a number of complex issues. A potential buyer may decide to support the debtor, join with its creditors to oppose the debtor, or attempt to stay neutral. Therefore, a potential buyer should compare the interests, motivations, and negotiating leverage of all parties to determine where to align its interests to have the best chance of ultimately purchasing the company.

In this section, we examine the primary participants in the bankruptcy process: the debtor, the secured creditors, the unsecured creditors, the advisors, and other players. Because distressed M&A involves a constantly changing landscape with continuously evolving developments, we strongly encourage interested buyers to engage talented bankruptcy attorneys, restructuring advisors, and turnaround consultants with relevant experience dealing with the issues involved in a particular case.

Our intention here is to give potential purchasers a detailed appreciation of these issues so that they can differentiate among service providers, become knowledgeable participants in the bankruptcy process, pursue effective strategies, and make insightful decisions. We expect that this section will also prove useful for executives and owners of distressed companies who are contemplating the bankruptcy process. Nearly all of the issues that we explain from a potential buyer's perspective are also relevant from the seller's standpoint. Finally, we also hope that this section will be a useful quick reference that bankruptcy professionals can use to educate their clients and recruits, enabling more robust analysis and promoting more effective communication.

CHAPTER 4

A Debtor and Creditor Overview

Neither a borrower nor a lender be;
For loan oft loses both itself and friend.

—William Shakespeare, Hamlet *(1602)*

OVERVIEW OF THE DEBTOR

What is a debtor?

Both within and outside of the bankruptcy process, a *debtor* is a borrower or any other party that incurs liabilities or obligations to others and owes them a debt. The Bankruptcy Code's official definition is a "person or municipality concerning which a case under this title has been commenced."[1] The term *person* in bankruptcy law, as in corporate law, includes a corporation.

What is the debtor's estate?

When a company enters the bankruptcy process, all of its assets become known as the *debtor's estate*, which becomes subject to the authority of the bankruptcy court. The Bankruptcy Code broadly construes the concept of the bankruptcy estate as meaning all of the debtor's legal and equitable interests in any and all property as of the commencement of the bankruptcy case.[2] In general, a debtor's estate includes the assets that appear on the company's balance sheet. In addition, the Bankruptcy Code includes in the debtor's estate any interest in any property that the debtor acquires after the commencement of the bankruptcy case.[3]

Whether a debtor has actual possession of an asset is irrelevant to whether that asset becomes part of the debtor's estate. For example, even if a creditor refuses to turn goods over to the debtor because of overdue bills, those goods are nevertheless part of the debtor's estate.

Theoretically, the exact location of an asset is also irrelevant to whether it becomes part of the debtor's estate. However, as a practical matter, if a debtor has assets outside of the United States, its creditors and the bankruptcy court may be unable to recover them unless a foreign government and its courts cooperate in enforcing the debtor's property rights.

Who are related debtors?

Most companies of any appreciable size will have a complex financial structure—typically a pyramid of corporate entities involving various subsidiaries and affiliates, often intertwined in separate borrowing arrangements with creditors. Therefore, a distressed company will often have multiple debtors involved in a bankruptcy proceeding, with each corporate debtor in the pyramid having its own set of creditors. When there are multiple corporate entities involved in a company's bankruptcy proceeding, these entities are referred to as *related debtors*. Although the bankruptcy court will assign each related debtor its own case number, the court will typically identify one related debtor as the lead case and use its docket as the reference for all of the cases. Sometimes, a company will seek to pick an obscurely named entity as the lead debtor to protect its public brand image because the lead debtor's name is often the one referred to in the news. When researching a company's bankruptcy case, a potential buyer should be careful to make sure that it is reviewing the proper docket, or else it may miss important information and developments.

Who are nondebtors?

For strategic reasons, a company may seek to keep certain subsidiaries and affiliates out of the bankruptcy process. Also, if a subsidiary was established as a bankruptcy remote entity or special-purpose entity (SPE), which are discussed in Chapter 2 of this book, the parent may be unable to include it. In such circumstances, these entities are referred to as *nondebtors* or *nondebtor entities* and are not subject to the bankruptcy process. While there is no legal requirement that all of a company's subsidiaries and affiliates must necessarily become debtors, as a practical matter, it may be necessary for all of them to seek bankruptcy protection if they have overlapping liabilities. Also, if a plan of reorganization involves substantive consolidation (see Chapter 12 of this book), then it may be necessary for all entities to become debtors.

A potential buyer should examine a target company's entire corporate organization chart and determine which entities are debtors and which are nondebtors by cross-referencing the bankruptcy docket. If the potential buyer is seeking to acquire the entire company, it may need to purchase certain assets through the bankruptcy process and other assets outside of that process. Alternatively, the buyer's proposed transaction structure could require the target company to convert its nondebtor entities to debtors so that all of the assets can be acquired through the bankruptcy process.

What happens in a company with multiple subsidiaries in various states of financial health? Must they all file for bankruptcy?

Several options are possible. A parent company sometimes starts a Chapter 11 reorganization case while subsidiaries remain outside Chapter 11 to carry on day-to-day business; such subsidiaries may file subsequently if it becomes clear that they need to join the proceedings. In some cases, many affiliates of the Chapter 11 debtor in possession remain outside of Chapter 11 for long periods; in some instances, they may reorganize outside of Chapter 11 in tandem with the reorganization plans of the Chapter 11 debtors in possession. This is largely because creditors recognized that they could obtain greater value by proceeding in this manner. Doing so, however, requires the development of governance and financial protocols for dealing with conflicts of interest.

For example, many real estate investment trusts (REITs) reorganized their parent companies in Chapter 11 while their operating subsidiaries remained outside bankruptcy. Similarly, in the 1990s, Western Union operated outside bankruptcy while its parent corporation, New Valley Corporation, reorganized very successfully in Chapter 11.

RIGHTS AND RESPONSIBILITIES OF THE DEBTOR IN POSSESSION

What is a debtor in possession?

For most aspects of the distressed acquisition process, the terms *debtor* and *debtor in possession* may be used interchangeably. The concept of debtor in possession refers to the debtor's being in possession and control of the debtor's estate,[4] rather than being a trustee who is merely acting as its guardian. Most potential buyers of distressed companies will hear the term debtor in possession used when referring to post-petition loans, which are known as debtor-in-possession, or DIP, loans.

What authority does a debtor in possession have?

The debtor in possession is authorized to operate the business during the bankruptcy case.[5] Therefore, all of the decisions that are made in the ordinary course of business—processing new orders, managing employees, setting pricing, selecting vendors, marketing products and services, and so on—remain in the control of the debtor in possession. To facilitate the debtor in possession's atypical responsibilities in the bankruptcy case, the Bankruptcy Code also empowers the debtor in possession to retain one or more advisors, such as attorneys, accountants, investment bankers, consultants, and claims agents, subject to approval by the bankruptcy court.[6] In particular, these advisors assist the debtor in possession in exercising its authority to prepare a disclosure statement and a plan of reorganization, which may or may not involve a 363 sale of some or all of its assets.

The Bankruptcy Code also bestows upon the debtor in possession certain post-petition powers that are available only during a bankruptcy proceeding and are all subject to the approval of the bankruptcy court. These powers enable the debtor in possession to play a bit of offense rather than always being on the defensive. The debtor in possession may raise post-petition financing (a DIP loan) to fund its turnaround during the bankruptcy proceeding.[7] Moreover, the debtor in possession may assume (and assign) or reject executory contracts and unexpired leases in order to unwind uneconomical arrangements.[8] Also, the debtor in possession may seek to recover property of the estate by forcing third parties to turn over valuable property owned by the debtor (or the proceeds if the third party has already sold such property),[9] initiating voidable preference claims,[10] and pursuing fraudulent transfer claims.[11] Furthermore, the debtor in possession may abandon property of the estate if it determines that doing so would be beneficial.[12]

Finally, the debtor in possession is authorized to oppose the claims of individual creditors. The debtor in possession is also authorized to dispute the proofs of claims filed by creditors,[13] challenge the liens of secured creditors,[14] object to setoff attempts by creditors,[15] and commence litigation—known as adversary proceedings[16]—against creditors or other parties. These are powerful tools that the debtor in possession can use when negotiating a plan of reorganization with creditors.

Are there any decisions that only a debtor in possession may make?

Yes. The decisions that only a debtor in possession may make (at least, so long as the debtor in possession has not been replaced by a bankruptcy trustee), subject to approval by the bankruptcy court, include

- Deciding upon the firms to retain as the debtor's advisors (see Chapter 7 of this book regarding the various advisors)
- Determining the jurisdiction in which to file a voluntary bankruptcy petition (see Chapter 2 of this book for a discussion on jurisdictions)
- Picking the lender to finance the DIP loan (see Chapters 5 and 14 of this book for further discussion)
- Selecting which executory contracts and unexpired leases to assume (and assign) and which to reject
- Electing to sell some or all of the company in a 363 sale and, if so, proposing bidding procedures
- Choosing a *stalking horse* for a 363 sale (see Chapter 13 of this book for details)
- Proposing and soliciting a plan of reorganization during its exclusivity period (see Chapter 12 of this book for details)

Individual creditors, the creditors' committee, the U.S. trustee, and other parties may influence the decisions of the debtor in possession in any of these matters, but, ultimately, the debtor in possession determines what approval to seek from the bankruptcy court. However, if the debtor in possession is continually challenged by other parties, its credibility before the bankruptcy court will be diminished, which may hinder its ability to achieve its goals later in the bankruptcy proceeding. In addition, if the debtor in possession angers the creditors and other parties in the earlier stages of the bankruptcy case, it may be very difficult or impossible to attract their votes in favor of a plan of reorganization proposed by the debtor in possession later in the process.

What are the duties of a debtor in possession in a bankruptcy proceeding?

In addition to exercising the authority and discretion granted by the Bankruptcy Code, the debtor in possession is explicitly required by Bankruptcy Code section 521 to perform certain duties, including[17]

- Creating a comprehensive list of all creditors of the debtor
- Preparing a schedule of financial affairs (SOFA) for the company as of the petition date
- Submitting a schedule of assets and liabilities (SOAL) for the company as of the petition date
- Filing monthly statements of current income and expenditures
- Administering employee benefit plans under the Employee Retirement Income Security Act of 1974 (ERISA)

The filings that the debtor in possession makes regarding each of these duties provide potential bidders with key insights into the current status of the business, including comprehensive schedules on property, contracts, leases, lawsuits, names of financial advisors and auditors, and scheduled payments to creditors. Each of these disclosures is publicly available on the bankruptcy docket via the Public Access to Court Electronic Records (PACER) link on the bankruptcy court's Web site (see Chapter 2 for a list of bankruptcy court Web sites). Although these disclosures are supposed to be made within 15 days of the petition date,[18] bankruptcy courts routinely grant extensions for complex cases.

While performing these duties and attending to its responsibilities, the debtor in possession needs to pay careful attention to satisfying its fiduciary duties during a bankruptcy proceeding. Chapter 10 of this book discusses such duties in greater detail.

MANAGING THE DEBTOR

Who manages the debtor?

The same executive team that managed a company's operations in the prepetition period typically manages the company's operations in the postpetition period as well. Bankruptcy law generally respects the corporate law framework for governance. As under state corporate law, a company's board of directors selects the executives of the company to manage day-to-day operations. Together, the directors and officers of the company have wide discretion to make decisions based on their own judgment, provided that they do so with due care and loyalty—a concept referred to as the *business judgment rule*. (Chapter 10 of this book discusses the business judgment rule in greater detail.)

But here the similarity to corporate law ends. In a bankruptcy, while actions in the ordinary course of business are generally left to a company's management team, many significant actions, such as the sale of business units, are governed by the provisions of the Bankruptcy Code and may require the approval of the bankruptcy court. As a result, the directors and officers have little say in many important matters. Furthermore, nothing gives managers the right to keep running the company and determining its plans once the company has filed for bankruptcy; both presumptions can be challenged.

If a challenge to management's incumbency is successful, the bankruptcy court has the authority to remove certain executives and appoint a *bankruptcy trustee* to manage the debtor's operations. But note that the standard for challenging management incumbency is high—in some cases requiring proof of fraud, embezzlement, or criminal acts on the part of management. Also, creditors should exercise caution in seeking a change from current management to a bankruptcy trustee. As the saying goes, "The devil you know is better than the devil you don't."

An easier tactic is to challenge the debtor's exclusivity by convincing the bankruptcy court to give creditors (rather than the incumbent management) the right to propose a plan of reorganization. Yet another alternative is for creditors to try to control the debtor's use of cash collateral[19] or the terms of a DIP loan.

A potential buyer should evaluate the interaction between a debtor's management team and the creditors, paying special attention to attitudes toward management's continued (or discontinued) control of the debtor's operations. For example, creditors may support a quick sale to a third party to avoid continuing to deal with the existing management. Conversely, certain members of management may be motivated to sell the company in order to keep their jobs rather than wage a contentious battle with creditors.

Why does the Bankruptcy Code allow the management team that drove the company into bankruptcy to continue to operate it?

As a historical note, the presumption that the debtor should remain debtor in possession was not the case prior to 1978, when the current version of the Bankruptcy Code went into effect. Previously, at the start of a Chapter 11 reorganization, a bankruptcy trustee was automatically appointed by the bankruptcy court to take over the management of a debtor's day-to-day operations. While this is still the practice in Chapter 7 cases, the current Bankruptcy Code favors keeping the existing management team in Chapter 11 cases rather than automatically appointing a bankruptcy trustee. Both approaches are imperfect and involve many subjective factors.

On the one hand, allowing the existing management to remain in control of the debtor provides the advantage of that management's detailed familiarity with the most important aspects of the company, including not only financial aspects such as contracts and pricing and the company's relationships with customers, partners, vendors, creditors, and competitors, but also business fundamentals such as employees, plant and equipment, information systems, business segments, and the overall organization. This familiarity may counteract some or all of the business disruption that a bankruptcy process inevitably causes and thereby stabilize the valuation of the business (or at least prevent it from deteriorating further). Because many companies become financially distressed as a result of a macroeconomic crisis or an industry downturn, management should not automatically be blamed for causing a company's woes. A bankruptcy trustee, who is new to the business, requires a period of time to become acclimated to the business, digest its predicament, and determine a path forward. The inertia during this period can promote inefficiency and delay, giving competitors a prime opportunity to take advantage of the company's misfortune. Finally, the selection of a bankruptcy trustee can introduce politics, favoritism, and other complications into an already complex bankruptcy process. (Once again, the devil you know . . .)

On the other hand, automatically appointing a bankruptcy trustee to assume responsibility for day-to-day management of the debtor's operations can provide a fresh perspective on dire circumstances. Bankruptcy courts, which are designed to be independent and neutral from politics, can screen qualified candidates to ensure that bankruptcy trustees have the skills and experience required to manage competently. Appointing a new leader acknowledges that some managers are visionary dreamers who are skilled at growing, building, and cultivating businesses, whereas others are pragmatic fixers who are skilled at reducing costs, improving performance, and driving bottom-line results. A bankruptcy trustee will not be mired in justifying the poor decisions of prior management, continuing the pursuit of broken strategies, or harboring emotional grudges from past conflicts. A bankruptcy trustee can be a neutral decision maker and fact finder, enabling the bankruptcy process to operate more efficiently and transparently. As a new participant without any legacy issues, a bankruptcy trustee can be a friendlier and less controversial leader to orchestrate a consensual resolution with creditors, who may feel distrust, anger, and fatigue with existing management. A bankruptcy trustee also may have staying power: senior management turnover (whether caused by resignation or by termination) tends to increase following declines in financial performance.[20]

While there are pros and cons to both approaches, lawmakers show no serious signs of changing the status quo, which favors a continuation of the incumbent management. In most bankruptcies, participants presume that the value of a debtor's estate is best supported by permitting the current management to continue operating the company. To be sure, this presumption is *rebuttable*; still, it is often taken for granted.[21] Currently, bankruptcy trustees are rare, although the concept is often present as a threat (whether explicit or implicit) to keep existing management in line. But whether management goes or stays, most post-filing companies appoint a chief restructuring officer.

How are bankruptcy trustees appointed, and how are they responsible for managing debtors?

A bankruptcy trustee is an individual appointed by the bankruptcy court to take charge of the affairs of the debtor and manage the assets in the debtor's estate, as occurred with the Death Row Records, Dreier LLP, ER Urgent Care, Kobra Properties, Marvel Entertainment, SCO Group, and Sentinel Management Group cases. Under such circumstances, the bankruptcy trustee replaces the company's executives and board of directors.

If the case is a Chapter 11 reorganization, the bankruptcy trustee is known as a *Chapter 11 trustee*. The bankruptcy court may appoint a

Chapter 11 trustee at the request of any party in interest pursuant to Bankruptcy Code section 1104.[22] When the debtor becomes the debtor in possession, the debtor assumes the role and powers of the Chapter 11 trustee instead of an outside individual being appointed. To appoint a Chapter 11 trustee, the requesting party must demonstrate that such appointment is[23]

- For cause, including fraud, dishonesty, incompetence, or gross mismanagement of the debtor by current management
- In the interest of the creditors, the equity holders, or the debtor's estate in general
- Preferable to conversion of the Chapter 11 case to Chapter 7 liquidation

If creditors successfully convince the bankruptcy court to appoint a Chapter 11 trustee, the debtor's exclusivity period for filing a plan of reorganization ends immediately.[24] Therefore, creditors may benefit by promptly gaining the ability to propose their own plan—or competing plans—of reorganization.

The main duties of a Chapter 11 trustee include[25]

- Filing schedules of assets and liabilities for the debtor
- Investigating the financial affairs of the debtor
- Determining the financial condition of the debtor
- Assessing the desirability of continuing the business
- Filing a statement of any investigation conducted into fraud, dishonesty, incompetence, misconduct, mismanagement, or irregularity in the management of the debtor's affairs
- Examining creditors' proofs of claim and, when appropriate, filing objections
- Filing a plan of reorganization or recommending a conversion of the case to Chapter 7 liquidation
- Filing necessary reports after confirmation of the plan of reorganization

If the case is a Chapter 7 liquidation, the bankruptcy trustee is known as a *Chapter 7 trustee*. First, an interim Chapter 7 trustee is promptly appointed by the bankruptcy court at the beginning of the Chapter 7 proceeding.[26]

Next, creditors may vote to elect a candidate for Chapter 7 trustee under Bankruptcy Code section 702. Unlike in a Chapter 11 case, the debtor loses its right to become the debtor in possession in a Chapter 7 proceeding. The main duties of a Chapter 7 trustee include[27]

- Collecting the property in the debtor's estate
- Converting that property to cash
- Investigating the financial affairs of the debtor
- Examining creditors' proofs of claim and, when appropriate, filing objections

In all cases, the bankruptcy trustee must satisfy the eligibility requirements of Bankruptcy Code section 321.[28] The bankruptcy trustee must be accountable for all property received.[29] In addition, the bankruptcy trustee manages tax issues for the debtor and administers the debtor's employee benefit plans under ERISA.[30] Moreover, at the end of the bankruptcy case, the bankruptcy trustee must file a final report and a final accounting with the bankruptcy court and the U.S. trustee.[31] Furthermore, the bankruptcy trustee becomes the official representative of the debtor's estate and has the capacity to sue and be sued.[32] A person who has served as the *examiner* (explained in Chapter 7) in a particular case cannot serve as the bankruptcy trustee in either a Chapter 7 or a Chapter 11 proceeding.[33]

A bankruptcy trustee should not be confused with a U.S. trustee, which is explained later in this chapter. The U.S. trustee must qualify each bankruptcy trustee to serve in both Chapter 7 and Chapter 11 cases.[34] A person who is serving as a U.S. trustee in the jurisdiction of the bankruptcy case is eligible to serve as the bankruptcy trustee for the case, if necessary.[35]

For more information on bankruptcy trustees, see the National Association of Bankruptcy Trustees at www.nabt.com or call toll-free (800) 445-8629.

How does a chief restructuring officer assist in managing the debtor?

Rather than pursue the extreme tactic of removing the incumbent management and appointing a bankruptcy trustee, the parties may compromise by agreeing to hire a chief restructuring officer (CRO) to help manage the business. A CRO is an employee of the company who serves as the primary officer in charge of managing the reorganization, including producing information as required and requested, conducting internal analyses to produce reorganization strategies, retaining and managing outside professionals, and testifying before the bankruptcy court. An alternative to the appointment of a CRO is the engagement of a *turnaround consultant*, who is not an employee of the company. Both CROs and turnaround consultants may be engaged to assist in managing the debtor in either an out-of-court workout or a Chapter 11 reorganization. See Chapter 7 of this book for more information on CROs and turnaround consultants.

The increasing use and prominence of CROs in the bankruptcy process could be seen as the market forming its own balance between the rebuttable presumption of keeping existing management in place (i.e., the view of the Bankruptcy Code since 1978) and automatically appointing a bankruptcy trustee (i.e., the view of bankruptcy law prior to 1978).

Although the Bankruptcy Code does not refer to or define the role of a CRO, the practice of appointing a CRO has become increasingly commonplace, particularly in large, complex bankruptcies. For example, General Motors, Lehman Brothers, Kmart, and Dubai World each hired an outside expert to serve as CRO during their respective bankruptcy proceedings. Nortel Networks, on the other hand, appointed an insider, its finance director, to the role. Both a CRO and a turnaround consultant can enter the picture either pre-petition or post-petition. In general, a CRO has greater authority to direct the reorganization process than a turnaround consultant and has greater independence from the existing management.[36]

Generally, the CRO has experience with the bankruptcy process, creditor negotiation, and corporate reorganization to augment the experience of a company's existing management team. The exact role of a CRO and the exact reporting structure vary depending upon the company's situation. For example, the CRO may report to the CEO, to the COO, or directly to the board of directors. In the case of General Motors, the CRO oversaw the liquidation of assets that were deemed to be dead weight (i.e., Hummer, Saturn, Saab, and Pontiac), while the CEO managed the ongoing operations of the company (i.e., Chevrolet, Cadillac, Buick, and GMC).

The appointment of a CRO is often a response by the company to appease frustrated and concerned creditors, who may have lost confidence in the existing management. A senior lender, for example, may require the company to appoint a CRO as part of the negotiation about an amendment to a credit agreement following a default. Bondholders might require the company to appoint a CRO as a condition for deferring a debt amortization payment when cash flow is tight. While concerns about lender liability typically cause the creditors to avoid dictating the choice of CRO, it is common for the senior lender to provide a list of three names that the senior lender recommends for the role and for the company to choose one of these individuals. Therefore, although the CRO becomes an employee of and owes fiduciary duties to the company, he is often considered to be an agent of the creditors because the senior lenders drive repeat business throughout the CRO's career. Because of this potential conflict of interest, the CRO must balance his fiduciary duties and personal interests carefully.

Is it appropriate to ask a CRO, a turnaround consultant, or a bankruptcy trustee about sell-off plans for a particular company?

By all means, yes. Indeed, a potential purchaser of a distressed company should promptly determine whether a distressed company has appointed a CRO, turnaround consultant, or bankruptcy trustee because that individual is probably going to be an important decision maker regarding whether all or parts of the company will be sold.

Moreover, purchasers who want to focus on buying distressed assets would benefit from forging strong relationships with turnaround consulting firms so that they can receive notification when distressed assets are being considered for sale. Furthermore, establishing credibility with turnaround consultants in advance will enhance a potential purchaser's chances of being approached earlier in the sale process. Because time is of the essence in most distressed sale processes, an early word can provide a significant advantage.

What role does a debtor's board of directors have in managing the debtor during a bankruptcy case?

Prior to a bankruptcy filing, the board is a critical decision maker, working with management in striving to keep the firm solvent and considering how to respond to the evolving financial situation. To be sure, the board may not have a complete window on financial trends at the company;

management may be overly optimistic and may unconsciously or consciously suppress negative information. Nonetheless, a financially literate board, supported by an effective audit committee, can often detect and resolve financial problems well in advance of a crisis.[37] If bankruptcy is seen as the best option, a company's bylaws typically require the board of directors to authorize the company's executives to file a voluntary bankruptcy petition.

There are no particular requirements for changes to a board of directors in a bankruptcy case. Sometimes the board remains the same. At other times, there is a change in the identity of the chairperson, the CEO, and/or the directors, or a change in the structure of the board. For example, the board may decide to combine or split the chairman and CEO roles, may decide to appoint a lead director, or may decide to replace the entire board. These matters are decided on a case-by-case basis.

The individual directors serving on a company's board may decide to resign voluntarily as the business spirals toward bankruptcy. Chapter 10 of this book explores the directors' fiduciary duties as a company approaches insolvency and enters bankruptcy. After the bankruptcy case begins, if the company enters into a DIP loan, which is discussed in detail in Chapter 14 of this book, any change in control, defined to include a new majority of the board, is likely to be an event of default.

If the bankruptcy court appoints a bankruptcy trustee, however, the bankruptcy trustee replaces the board of directors and assumes control of the debtor's business.

Can the board of directors declare and pay dividends to equity holders during a bankruptcy case?

Normally, no. A bankrupt company typically has insufficient cash flow to pay dividends to shareholders, and it would be inappropriate to provide payment to equity holders when debt holders are impaired.

However, in unusual circumstances, companies have been permitted by a bankruptcy court to pay dividends during a bankruptcy proceeding. In the extraordinary case of General Growth Properties (GGP), the debtor was a real estate investment trust (REIT) that was required by applicable nonbankruptcy law to distribute 90 percent of its taxable income to shareholders to avoid regulation under the Investment Company Act of 1940 (the 1940 Act) and maintain its tax-advantaged structure.[38] GGP, along with 158 of its properties, filed a voluntary bankruptcy petition in April 2009, creating the largest real estate bankruptcy in U.S. history, with nearly $30 billion in assets and approximately $27 billion in debt. As a result of the bankruptcy filing, GGP suspended its dividend. However, when the economy improved and GGP's financial performance stabilized as the case progressed, the company once again needed to satisfy dividend payout requirements in order to maintain its exempt status under the 1940 Act, even though it was in bankruptcy. Therefore, in December 2009, the bankruptcy court approved GGP's motion for a 19-cent dividend in a combination of cash and common stock, which GGP paid to shareholders in January 2010. The bankruptcy court's approval was necessary to avoid GGP's being disqualified for the 1940 Act exception and risking becoming a registered investment advisor making taxable investments, which would have been detrimental to all stakeholders in the bankruptcy case. Importantly, it was already clear that GGP's shareholders were "in the money" and would ultimately receive distributions in an eventual plan of reorganization.

OVERVIEW OF THE CREDITORS

What is a creditor?

A creditor is a party to whom the debtor has a liability. The most obvious kind of creditor is a lender who loaned money to the debtor and has not yet been paid back. Many other parties can become creditors, however, even if they never lent money to the debtor. Vendors who have shipped goods to the debtor and are awaiting payment become creditors. Employees who are due unpaid wages become creditors. Landlords who entered leases with the debtor with future rental periods still remaining become creditors. Plaintiffs who have been awarded damages from the debtor become creditors. Utilities that have provided unbilled services to the debtor become creditors. Governments that are due unpaid taxes from the debtor become creditors. Even counterparties to derivative instruments, such as open swaps or futures, with the debtor become creditors, assuming that they are *in-the-money* as of the petition date. (Being in-the-money means that an instrument's current market price is high enough to yield a gain; the opposite is being out-of-the-money.) Clearly, there can be many and diverse kinds of creditors in a given bankruptcy.

Which creditors become the active decision makers during the bankruptcy process?

Determining which creditors become the active decision makers really comes down to which creditors hold the *fulcrum security*—where they are partially in-the-money and partially out-of-the-money, and thus may be repaid at least partly with equity in the reorganized debtor. This is one of the most important considerations early on. In general, creditors who are clearly in-the-money remain passive because their interests are already protected, while creditors who are clearly out-of-the-money lack the motivation to become active.

The framework of the Bankruptcy Code—and, indeed, nearly all of debtor-creditor law—is premised on the notion that the fulcrum security will fall somewhere within the unsecured creditors, because in most distressed situations secured creditors are clearly in-the-money and equity holders are clearly out-of-the-money. The period from 2008 to 2009 broke this pattern. In this era, it was frequently the *secured* creditors that held the fulcrum security and had a more active role in decision making. In large part, this development arose following a significant increase in second- and third-lien secured loans, which increased the number of overleveraged firms with senior debt when the distressed period began. Overcrowding at the secured end of the creditors' spectrum pushed the least secure of them back toward and even past the fulcrum midpoint. See Chapter 5 of this book for trends in second-lien debt issuance and the impact on leveraged buyouts.

Are creditors treated the same way under GAAP and under the Bankruptcy Code?

Not exactly. In general, the Bankruptcy Code has a broader definition of creditors and a different way of quantifying the debts owed to them.

Under both GAAP and the Bankruptcy Code, all of the liabilities on a company's balance sheet give rise to creditors. For example, accounts payable on the balance sheet turn vendors into creditors under the Bankruptcy Code, and long-term debt on the balance sheet turns lenders into creditors.

However, the Bankruptcy Code also considers liabilities that may be *off*-balance sheet. Furthermore, the way in which liabilities are quantified may differ significantly, for reasons that are detailed later in this chapter.

Therefore, a full analysis of who the company's creditors are, and how much they are owed, should involve all of the considerations detailed in this chapter rather than rely solely upon the company's latest balance sheet (which may be out of date anyway by the time a company becomes distressed). Indeed, it is common for a distressed company to have difficulty closing its books and generating accurate financial statements as it heads toward bankruptcy.

What are the key differences between pre- and post-petition creditors?

The date when a bankruptcy petition is filed is referred to as the *petition date*. This date is significant for creditors because those with claims that arose before the petition date will be subjected to the bankruptcy process to determine what recoveries they will receive and will have certain rights to participate in the reorganization process. Such creditors are called *pre-petition creditors*. On the petition date, all debts that are due in the future are accelerated to the present so that they may be addressed in the bankruptcy process. This is called *acceleration of debt*.

On the day *after* the petition date and beyond, the company continues doing business, and therefore continues incurring *new* liabilities to creditors— lenders, employees, vendors, and so on—in the course of its day-to-day operations. These creditors are called *post-petition creditors*; they are not subjected to the bankruptcy process and do not have rights to participate in the reorganization process.

Why would creditors agree to incur new debt with a bankrupt company?

The Bankruptcy Code gives post-petition creditors various incentives to entice them to work with the company during the bankruptcy process and beyond. For example, amounts paid to post-petition creditors are classified as *administrative expenses* and are paid in full as "actual, necessary costs and expenses of preserving the estate."[39] Clearly, it is in no one's interest to have the debtor lose its ability to conduct day-to-day operations because it cannot access credit. Reorganization would become impossible if the debtor's going-concern value were to dissipate, making liquidation inevitable.

What is a discharge?

A powerful component of a debtor's fresh start is receiving a *discharge* from its pre-petition debts and liabilities. As explained by the U.S. Courts:

> Section 1141(d)(1) generally provides that confirmation of a plan discharges a debtor from any debt that arose before the date of confirmation. After the plan is confirmed, the debtor is required to make plan payments and is bound by the provisions of the plan of reorganization. The confirmed plan creates new contractual rights, replacing or superseding pre-bankruptcy contracts.[40]

Accordingly, the bankruptcy process enables a debtor to discharge the claims of its creditors and begin anew. In exchange for extinguishing their pre-petition claims, creditors may receive partial or full recoveries in cash or in new post-petition claims (e.g., if the reorganized company issues new debt securities or assumes liability for other obligations). Once the bankruptcy case concludes, creditors are forever barred from reasserting their pre-petition claims against the debtor. Bankruptcy Code section 524 explains the effect of a discharge, and Bankruptcy Code section 523 describes the exceptions to a discharge.[41]

OVERVIEW OF CLAIMS AND ADMINISTRATIVE EXPENSES

What exactly is a claim?

The pre-petition amount that is due to a creditor from the debtor is called a *claim*. As discussed earlier in this book, creditors' claims can be secured or unsecured. In addition, creditors' claims can be

- Liquidated or contingent
- Matured or unmatured
- Legal or equitable
- Disputed or undisputed
- Allowed or disallowed

Each of these distinctions is discussed in greater detail later in this chapter.

What exactly are administrative expenses?

Administrative expenses are the post-petition costs and expenses of administering the bankruptcy case; they are paid in full before creditors receive recoveries on their pre-petition claims.[42] Such expenses include fees for attorneys, accountants, brokers, and consultants. Administrative expenses also include all of the costs of day-to-day operations in the ordinary course of business.

The Bankruptcy Abuse Prevention and Consumer Protection Act of 2005 (2005 BAPCPA) established a new category of administrative expenses. Vendors who delivered goods (but not those who provided services) to the debtor in the ordinary course of business within the 20 days prior to the petition date can recover the value of the goods as administrative expenses, which usually means payment in full.[43] Previously, creditors who had sold goods on credit terms to an insolvent debtor needed to consider filing a *reclamation claim* (i.e., a pre-petition claim), which remains a complicated process in bankruptcy.[44]

For administrative expenses that do not involve the ordinary course of business, an application must be submitted to, and approved by, the bankruptcy court. Potential buyers may sometimes find these applications useful because they typically provide details of the activities of attorneys, investment bankers, and turnaround consultants; such applications may also reveal plans to sell some or all of the company.

How do administrative expenses differ from claims?

Claims are pre-petition amounts that are due to third parties, while administrative expenses are post-petition amounts that are due to third parties. Administrative expenses receive priority payment, ahead of all claims.

What does *pari passu* mean?

Pari passu refers to claims or administrative expenses that have the same priority of payment and seniority. Therefore, pari passu claims should trade at the same levels. This Latin phrase is translated literally as "equal footstep" or "equal footing." Accordingly, it is typically used to mean "part and parcel," "hand in hand," "with equal force," "moving together," "fairly," and "without partiality."

What is a liquidated claim?

The term *liquidated claim* arises in contract law, and the meaning is generally the same when it is used in the Bankruptcy Code. A liquidated claim means that the claim is for payment of a sum certain, meaning an amount specified in the parties' agreement or an amount that can be precisely calculated based on the terms and conditions of a contract or as a matter of law. For example, a promissory note for $100 million and one month's unpaid interest at LIBOR plus 200 basis points would involve liquidated claims. (*LIBOR*, which stands for the London Interbank Offered Rate, is a commonly used reference point for short-term interest rates.)

Note that a liquidated claim has nothing to do with a liquidation, and the similarity of the terms is coincidental. Disputed claims may still be considered liquidated. Claims that are not liquidated may be referred to as unliquidated or contingent claims.

What is a contingent claim?

A *contingent claim* is a creditor's claim against the debtor for an amount that is uncertain as of the petition date. A future event needs to take place before the claim can be liquidated. For certain purposes, such as voting on a plan of reorganization, the bankruptcy court may estimate the amount of a contingent claim temporarily.[45]

What are matured versus unmatured claims?

Matured and unmatured claims typically involve pre-petition debt. If the debt involves a payment that came due pre-petition, then that payment is a *matured claim*. If the debt involves a payment that will come due post-petition, then that payment is an *unmatured claim*. An unmatured claim may be liquidated or contingent, depending upon the agreement.

In most cases, the issue of matured versus unmatured claims is insignificant. One noteworthy issue is that the Bankruptcy Code does not permit claims for unmatured interest. This has implications for original issue discount (OID) bonds, which are bonds that are issued at below par, such as zero coupon bonds. This interest is unmatured, so bondholders expecting to collect the remaining OID will be out of luck in a bankruptcy filing.[46]

What are legal versus equitable claims?

As mentioned earlier, the Bankruptcy Code broadly construes the concept of the bankruptcy estate as meaning all of the debtor's "legal and equitable" interests in any and all property as of the commencement of the bankruptcy case.[47] *Legal interests* emphasize statutory law; this term means that protection for the interests can be found in statutory law passed by state legislatures or by Congress. *Equitable interests* emphasize judge-made law; protection for these equitable interests is found in concepts of fairness expressed in legal precedents (common law).

What are disputed versus undisputed claims?

A *disputed claim* is any claim that is subject to legal or factual dispute. As mentioned, contingent claims may also be referred to as unliquidated. Contingent claims often become disputed claims because of the subjectivity of the assumptions used in calculating their estimated amounts. In essence, the creditor is deemed to be unable to provide a valid *proof of claim* (explained later in this chapter).

In large cases, a debtor may streamline the process of disputing claims by filing omnibus objections to address several claims, each of which is described using the same issue, such as that the claims[48]

- Duplicate other claims
- Have been filed in the wrong case
- Have been replaced by subsequently filed proofs of claim
- Have been transferred in accordance with Rule 3001(e)
- Were not filed in a timely manner
- Have been satisfied or released during the case in accordance with the Bankruptcy Code, the Bankruptcy Rules, or a court order
- Were presented in a form that does not comply with applicable rules, and the objection states that the objector is unable to determine the validity of the claim because of the noncompliance
- Are interests, rather than claims
- Assert priority in an amount that exceeds the maximum amount under section 507 of the Bankruptcy Code

Recent updates to the Bankruptcy Rules attempted to curb abuses by debtors filing omnibus claims and sought to minimize confusion among creditors with disputed claims.[49]

When do debtors usually resolve disputed claims?

Claims resolution usually occurs at the end of the bankruptcy process, after creditors have voted on the plan of reorganization and the company has exited from bankruptcy, either through a sale or through a stand-alone reorganization. During this period, the bankruptcy case continues to stay open to administer claims, including the payment of recoveries to creditors. When the claims resolution process is concluded and the proceeds of the bankruptcy process have been paid out, the bankruptcy case is closed.

What are insider claims?

Insider claims are claims against the company by officers, directors, control shareholders, general partners, and their relatives.[50] Such parties are typically considered to be equity holders, not creditors, so any claims that they may assert are subjected to extra scrutiny to ensure that they were negotiated fairly and objectively. In general, so-called claims filed by an insider for services provided to the company are disallowed under the Bankruptcy Code to the extent that such claims exceed the value of such services.[51]

Because of insiders' influence over the company's affairs, knowledge of confidential information regarding the business, and insights into the events that resulted in the bankruptcy filing, the Bankruptcy Code provides special treatment for insider claims. For example, the look-back period for voidable preferences is one year for insiders compared with 90 days for other creditors.[52] Also, the 2005 BAPCPA limited payments to insiders and any insider of an affiliate of the debtor, thereby restricting post-petition key employee retention programs (KERPs) that had previously facilitated lucrative compensation packages for executives of reorganizing companies.[53] Furthermore, the 2005 BAPCPA prohibited severance payments to insiders unless the severance program is generally applicable to all full-time employees and an insider's benefits are no more than ten times the average amount given to nonmanagement employees during the year in which the severance payment is made.[54]

When reviewing the proofs of claim on PACER and the liabilities on the balance sheet, a potential purchaser should pay special attention to insider claims. The bankruptcy court may ultimately *recharacterize* these insider claims as equity, meaning that they may not be due any recovery in the bankruptcy proceeding. (See Chapter 5 of this book for a discussion of recharacterization.) The negotiating dynamic for getting a plan of reorganization confirmed and a sale process completed may change significantly depending upon whether the court considers insider claims to be valid.

What is a proof of claim?

In order to receive a recovery in a company's bankruptcy proceeding, each creditor must fill out a *proof of claim* and file it with the bankruptcy court. Filing a proof of claim is *prima facie* evidence of the validity of the creditor's claim against the debtor's estate, in terms of both amount and basis.[55] The company must provide every creditor with proper notice of instructions and deadlines for filing claims. Failure to follow instructions and meet deadlines for filing can lead to a claim's becoming worthless, unless the creditor has an excuse that the bankruptcy court finds persuasive to permit a tardily filed proof of claim. Both the debtor and other creditors in the case can object to the proof of claim filed by a creditor on a variety of grounds; such claims are ultimately resolved by the bankruptcy court if the parties cannot reach agreement.

A debtor typically files schedules of assets and liabilities. If the debtor lists a creditor's claim on the schedule of liabilities, the creditor is not strictly required to provide a proof of that claim. However, out of an abundance of caution, a creditor should file its own proof of all claims to represent them from its perspective and to make sure that it does not inadvertently lose any of its rights to its claim.

A potential purchaser may want to review proofs of claim (and the schedule of liabilities), which are available via PACER. In particular, the federal judiciary's Case Management/Electronic Case Files (CM/ECF) project enables attorneys to file documents directly with the court over the Internet and enables courts to file, store, and manage their case files.[56] There are a few reasons for this.

- First, sometimes a potential purchaser of a debtor wishes to buy the debtor's claims. By buying the claims, the purchaser becomes a creditor, giving it some advantage as a buyer of the company. Conveniently, the proof of claim provides contact information for the creditors who might be interested in selling their claims.

- Second, if the purchaser discovers that resolving certain claim disputes may delay a sale process, it may want to review the related proofs of claim to independently evaluate the situation.
- Third, if the purchaser might assume any liabilities of the company in the sale, it might want to review the details in the proofs of claim to gain greater insight into the validity and amounts of such liabilities.
- Fourth, the purchaser may want to gain a deeper understanding of the number of creditors and the amount of claims with respect to voting on a plan of reorganization, which may affect the sale that the purchaser seeks.

Note that equity holders may file a *proof of interest*, rather than a proof of claim, which is reserved for creditors. However, if it is clear that the equity is out-of-the-money, equity holders may not bother.

What are allowed versus disallowed claims?

The inclusion of a claim in the company's schedule of liabilities and/or the filing of a proof of claim is sufficient for the bankruptcy court to deem a creditor's claim *allowed*, meaning that it will receive whatever recovery is provided in the plan of reorganization or liquidation, as the case may be. If the company or a third party properly objects to the creditor's claim, however, and the creditor's response is unpersuasive, the claim may be deemed disallowed by the bankruptcy court.

Is there any penalty for filing an untruthful proof of claim?

Yes. As explained on the proof of claim form: "Penalty for presenting fraudulent claim: Fine of up to $500,000 or imprisonment for up to 5 years, or both."[57]

How does the bankruptcy process determine the priority of payment to various creditors?

The entire Bankruptcy Code seeks to determine the priority of payment to various creditors, with the overarching goals of providing a fair and equitable distribution to creditors while also granting the debtor a fresh start. Even if a distressed company does not enter a bankruptcy process, creditors' behavior outside of bankruptcy is often heavily influenced by their expectations of what the priority of payment would be likely to be under the Bankruptcy Code.

In summary, the Bankruptcy Code provides for payment first of administrative expenses, then of secured claims, then of unsecured claims, and finally of equity interests. This is known as the *absolute priority rule*. There may be subdivisions among the various levels, such as first-lien and second-lien senior debt, tranches of subordinated debt, or preferred and common equity.

This priority of payment is often referred to as a "waterfall," where the distributable cash flows like water to fill the most senior bucket, then the next bucket, and so on until the water runs out.

After discharge from bankruptcy, a company can return to its normal operations. The quality of its "life after Chapter 11" will depend in part on how well it interacts with other players during the bankruptcy process. The remaining chapters in this section provide more detailed guidance regarding secured creditors, unsecured creditors, advisors, and other parties.

Endnotes

1. See 11 U.S.C. §101(13).
2. See 11 U.S.C. §341(a)(1).
3. See 11 U.S.C. §341(a)(7).
4. See 11 U.S.C. §§1101, 1107, 1108.
5. See 11 U.S.C. §1108.
6. See 11 U.S.C. §327.
7. See 11 U.S.C. §364.
8. See 11 U.S.C. §365.
9. See 11 U.S.C. §542.
10. See 11 U.S.C. §547.
11. See 11 U.S.C. §548.
12. See 11 U.S.C. §554.
13. See 11 U.S.C. §704(a)(5).
14. See 11 U.S.C. §506.
15. See 11 U.S.C. §553.
16. See Fed. R. Bankr. P. 7001, et seq.
17. See 11 U.S.C. §521(a).
18. See Fed. R. Bankr. P. 1007(c).

19. *Cash collateral* refers to cash and cash equivalents held by the debtor in bankruptcy subject to the liens of creditors.

20. See Dirk Jenter and Fadi Kanaan, "CEO Turnover and Relative Performance Evaluation"; http://papers.ssrn.com/sol3/papers.cfm?abstract_id=885531, last accessed September 11, 2010.

21. A rebuttable presumption is a legal concept that says that something will be considered true (the presumption) until it is proven untrue (rebutted). When a rebuttable presumption has been created, it shifts the burden of proof to the party that is rebutting. For a discussion that includes an example from bankruptcy law, see http://financial-dictionary.thefreedictionary.com/rebuttable+presumption, last accessed September 11, 2010.

22. See 11 U.S.C. §1104(a).

23. Ibid.

24. See 11 U.S.C. §1121(c)(1).

25. See 11 U.S.C. §1106.

26. See 11 U.S.C. §701.

27. See 11 U.S.C. §704.

28. See 11 U.S.C. §321.

29. See 11 U.S.C. §§704(a)(2), 1106(a)(1).

30. See 11 U.S.C. §§704(a)(8), 704(a)(11), 1106(a)(1).

31. See 11 U.S.C. §§704(a)(9), 1106(a)(1).

32. See 11 U.S.C. §323.

33. See 11 U.S.C. §321(b).

34. See 11 U.S.C. §322(b).

35. See 11 U.S.C. §321(c).

36. See Mark V. Bossi, "Are CROs More Powerful than Turnaround Consultants? Creditors Drive Trend toward New Title," Turnaround Management Association, October 1, 2006; available at http://www.turnaround.org/Publications/Articles.aspx?objectID=6588, last accessed May 1, 2010.

37. See, for example, Suzanne Hopgood and Michael W. Tankersley, *Board Leadership for the Company in Crisis* (Washington, D.C.: National Association of Corporate Directors, 2005).

38. REITs traditionally rely upon Section 3(c)(5)(C) of the 1940 Act, which excepts companies that are primarily engaged in "purchasing or otherwise acquiring mortgages and other liens on and interests in real estate" from becoming subject to regulation that affects mutual funds.

39. See 11 U.S.C. §503.

40. "Confirmation of a plan of reorganization discharges any type of debtor—corporation, partnership, or individual—from most types of pre-petition debts." However, "There are, of course, exceptions to the general rule that an order confirming a plan operates as a discharge." http://www.uscourts.gov/bankruptcycourts/bankruptcybasics/chapter11.html#discharge, last accessed September 11, 2010.

41. See 11 U.S.C. §§523, 524.
42. See 11 U.S.C. §§503(b), 507(a)(2).
43. See 11 U.S.C. §503(b)(9).
44. See 11 U.S.C. §546(c) and Section 2-703 of the UCC.
45. See 11 U.S.C. §502(c)(1).
46. See 11 U.S.C. §502(b)(2). Courts have held that unamortized OID is not allowable under section 502(b)(2), and that the proper method for calculating unamortized OID is the constant interest method. *In re Chateaugay Corp.*, 961 F.2d 378 (2d Cir. 1992).
47. See 11 U.S.C. §341(a)(1).
48. See Fed. R. Bankr. P. 3007(d).
49. See Fed. R. Bankr. P. 3007(c)–(e).
50. See 11 U.S.C. §101(31)(B)–(C).
51. See 11 U.S.C. §502(b)(4).
52. See 11 U.S.C. §547(b)(4)(B).
53. See 11 U.S.C. §503(c)(1).
54. See 11 U.S.C. §503(c)(2).
55. See Fed. R. Bankr. P. 3001(f).
56. See http://www.pacer.uscourts.gov/cmecf/, last accessed June 14, 2010.
57. See 18 U.S.C. §§152, 3571.

CHAPTER 5

Secured Creditors

If I owe you a pound, I have a problem; but if I owe you a million, the problem is yours.

—John Maynard Keynes

OVERVIEW OF SECURED CREDITORS

How does the perspective of secured creditors change when a debtor files for bankruptcy?

When a company is healthy, secured creditors generally remain unconcerned about how the collateral securing their loans is being used and where it is located; they are generally content to receive interest and principal payments. When a company moves into distressed territory, however, secured creditors understandably become anxious about these issues as they become increasingly worried about repayment.

On the one hand, apprehensive secured creditors need assurance that the value of their collateral will not suffer as a result of the debtor's continued poor business judgment, seizure of assets by other creditors, high administrative expenses involved in the bankruptcy process, or other threats. Ideally, the lenders would prefer to seize their collateral and transfer it to safe locations with trustworthy management. Therefore, the lenders tend to be more pessimistic regarding the debtor's ability to reorganize and prefer to limit the debtor's ability to use the collateralized property.

On the other hand, to increase the chances of repayment for all creditors, the struggling debtor needs breathing room and liquidity to reorganize its operations, restructure its balance sheet, and reconsider its strategic direction. Ideally, the debtor would prefer complete freedom to use its property (the collateral) without interference by, or accountability to, its creditors. Therefore, the debtor tends to be more optimistic regarding its ability to reorganize and prefers to limit the secured creditors' ability to control their collateral.This conflict over collateral goes to the heart of the relationship between borrowers and lenders and highlights the tension between the two sides' legal rights. Secured creditors are constitutionally entitled to protection of their interests, but only to the extent of the value of their bargain. They have a property right in their collateral that is protected by the Fifth Amendment of the U.S. Constitution, which states, in part, that "No person shall be . . . deprived of . . . property without due process of law." Conversely, under Article I, Section 8 of the Constitution, borrowers are constitutionally entitled to seek bankruptcy protection from creditors.

Especially on the petition date, there is so much confusion and disarray that it is extremely difficult to determine which side's legal rights should prevail. It is typically clear, however, that junior investors—like the equity holders and perhaps the unsecured lenders—are out-of-the-money. Therefore, the junior investors in the capital structure essentially have a free option to increase value for themselves without taking any additional risks; after all, they have already effectively lost their investments. Meanwhile, the senior investors in the capital structure bear all the risk of any further decline in the company's value, but they have no upside above and beyond the amount of their loans. This chapter will explore these and other issues in depth, beginning with an overview of the all-important topic of collateral, which is key to the value of any secured loan.

Who is a secured creditor under the Bankruptcy Code?

A *secured creditor* is one who has a claim secured by a lien on, or other security interest in, some or all of the debtor's property.[1]

Are there any other ways in which a creditor can have a secured claim?

Yes. A creditor's right of setoff may transform its unsecured claim into a secured claim. A *setoff* arises when the debtor owes an amount (A) to an unsecured creditor who owes an amount (B) to the debtor arising from separate and distinct transactions. (If the reciprocal obligations arise solely from one single integrated transaction, then the common law doctrine of *recoupment* applies instead. For the purposes of this discussion, the only distinction between a setoff and a recoupment is whether the amounts owed originated from the same transaction or from different transactions.) It is common sense for the parties to cancel out these debts to the extent that they overlap rather than formally expect the debtor to pay the creditor and then the creditor to return the same amount to the debtor. It seems reasonable for the party who owes more to simply pay the difference.

This situation changes when the debtor enters bankruptcy because the unsecured creditor may be due only a partial recovery in a Chapter 11 reorganization, or perhaps no recovery in a Chapter 7 liquidation. Therefore, setoff is a valuable concept for unsecured creditors because they may be able to receive full recovery for significant portions of their claims without incurring the delay and expense of the bankruptcy process. The Bankruptcy Code generally treats a creditor's setoff claim as a secured claim, giving that creditor priority over unsecured claims.[2] The Bankruptcy Code explicitly addresses this issue by determining that bankruptcy "does not affect any right of a creditor to offset a mutual debt owing by such creditor to the debtor that arose before the commencement of the case under this title against a claim of such creditor against the debtor that arose before the commencement of the case."[3] This resolution necessarily depends upon the creditor's claim being allowed and the creditor not having improperly acquired the claim from another creditor. The bankruptcy court can deny setoff if either of these assumptions is invalid.

The creditor may attempt to initiate the setoff either pre-petition or post-petition. In the pre-petition scenario, the bankruptcy court may unwind the setoff during the 90 days prior to the petition date if the creditor fails the *improvement in position test*. Under this test, the bankruptcy court will consider the amount (C) that the debtor owed the creditor immediately after the setoff and the amount (D) that the creditor owed the debtor immediately after the setoff. If $(A - B) > (C - D)$, then the creditor's position was improved, and the bankruptcy court may void the setoff in a similar fashion to a voidable preference claim. In the post-petition scenario, the creditor must request that the bankruptcy court provide relief from the automatic stay imposed by Bankruptcy Code section 362 before initiating setoff.[4] If the creditor engages in "self-help," there could be severe consequences; these may include penalties imposed by the bankruptcy court for violating the automatic stay.

LIENS

What exactly is a lien?

A *lien* (pronounced like "lean") is a legal term that refers to a security interest in one or more of a debtor's assets that has been granted by the debtor to a creditor to secure payment on a debt. It is a modification to the title of ownership of property that gives the lien holder some stated claim on the property. This modification does not entitle the creditor to possession of the assets as long as the debtor is paying off its debt. However, it may trigger a right for the creditor to take possession of the assets if the debtor defaults on the debt.

Can a borrower grant multiple liens on the same collateral?

Yes. Over the last few years, it has become increasingly common for debtors to grant second and even third liens, as well as first liens, on their assets to increase the amount of debt that they can raise and extend the advance rates on collateral. Essentially, the various creditors have different risk tolerances concerning the value of the assets that are being pledged as security for the debt. For example, a more conservative first-lien lender may advance $60 million on $100 million worth of assets, while a more aggressive second-lien lender may advance another $25 million on the same assets, and a risk-loving third-lien lender may advance another $10 million. The first-lien lender will typically charge a lower interest rate than the second-lien lender, and so on. If the lenders ever need to sell the asset to recover the amounts they lent to the borrower and the amount received is $95 million or greater, all of these lenders will receive full recoveries. However, if the amount received falls short, the third-lien lender will take any loss up to $10 million, then the second-lien lender will take a loss up to an additional $25 million, and finally, the first-lien lender will take the remainder of the loss.

Today's financial markets may involve multilien capital structures, including the following tranches of secured loans:

- Term B loans
- Tranche B financings

- Secondary collateralized institutional loans (SCILs)
- Last-out participations
- Senior stretch loans
- Senior secured notes
- Junior secured loans
- Tranche C financings

In essence, the extent to which a company can convince a lender to make these sorts of loans depends upon the company's ability to convince the lender that the company's enterprise value exceeds the aggregate amount of its secured loans. For this reason, third liens are uncommon and fourth liens may be only hypothetical for most businesses.

What are the key advantages of second-lien loans?

These innovations in the capital markets have provided powerful funding tools for financing leveraged buyouts, facilitating stock repurchases, refinancing more expensive debt, funding dividend recapitalizations, and providing "rescue financing" for corporate turnarounds—benefiting both borrowers and secured creditors. Currently, second-lien loans and the like have become widely accepted components of the risk/reward spectrum in the capital markets, as illustrated in Exhibit 5-1.

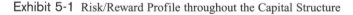

Exhibit 5-1 Risk/Reward Profile throughout the Capital Structure

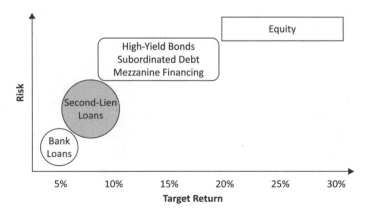

Making second-lien loans rather than providing mezzanine financing, such as bonds or subordinated notes, offers several key advantages for lenders if the borrower enters bankruptcy. Most significantly, second-lien loans receive priority recovery over all unsecured creditors, leapfrogging over vendors, unsecured bondholders, employees, retirees, plaintiffs, and governments. In complex situations involving underfunded pension plans, mass tort liability, and burdensome union contracts, this priority can be especially attractive. Like first-lien creditors, second-lien creditors may be entitled to *adequate protection* during the bankruptcy proceeding, including interest payments. (Adequate protection is defined and discussed in greater detail later in this chapter.) As secured creditors, second-lien lenders may have rights to approve post-petition debtor-in-possession (DIP) loans, object to the use of cash collateral, and approve 363 sales. Exhibit 5-2 explains the key differences between second-lien loans and mezzanine financing.

Second-Lien Loans	Mezzanine Financing
Secured	Unsecured
Less restrictive prepayment penalties	More restrictive prepayment penalties
More restrictive cap on first-lien debt	Less restrictive cap on first-lien debt
Tight restrictions on future second-lien debt	Fewer restrictions on future second-lien debt
Complex intercreditor agreement	No intercreditor agreement
No indenture	Indenture
No equity warrants	May include equity warrants
More favorable pricing for borrower	Less favorable pricing for borrower
Flexible terms	Standardized terms
Higher transaction costs	Lower transaction costs
Able to be syndicated	Able to be syndicated
Adequate protection may be available	Adequate protection unavailable
Difficult to be "crammed up"	Possible to be "crammed down"
Able to credit bid	Unable to credit bid

Exhibit 5-2 Second-Lien Loans versus Mezzanine Financing

When there are multiple liens involving the same collateral, how do secured creditors determine their respective rights?

As the capital markets have evolved to enable more complicated capital structures, secured creditors and their attorneys often negotiate an *intercreditor agreement*, entering into an advance arrangement regarding downside scenarios involving their common borrower, such as bankruptcy. Essentially, these customized contracts are an attempt by the creditors themselves to fill in the gaps in the Bankruptcy Code rather than allow a bankruptcy court to clarify vague and ambiguous issues for them. The law remains mixed on what aspects of intercreditor agreements are enforceable, what creditors' rights can be bargained away in advance, and which parts of the Bankruptcy Code can be superseded by mutual agreement. Therefore, issues involving intercreditor agreements generally require the advice of an experienced bankruptcy attorney as well as an experienced corporate lawyer.

A potential purchaser should review the intercreditor agreement in order to understand the arrangement among the creditors in the bankruptcy case, such as between the first- and second-lien creditors. By understanding how the creditors may have customized the proceedings, the potential purchaser can improve her understanding of a sales process by properly identifying the various parties' negotiating leverage, control over the case, and motivations.

Common intercreditor agreement provisions include[5]

- Mutual acknowledgment of, and agreement not to challenge, liens and relative lien priorities.
  - The relative priority among the parties remains effective even if the senior lien or claim is challenged effectively by the debtor or by third parties.
  - There are turnover provisions for noncomplying recoveries by second-lien creditors.
- Second-lien creditors being subject to a standstill, notwithstanding second-lien defaults.
  - The standstill may be limited to a specified time period (e.g., 90 to 180 days).
  - Second-lien creditors normally agree not to challenge the senior lender's exercise of its remedies against the collateral.

- ☐ In the event of a sale of the collateral, holders of second liens typically consent to release their liens when the holder of the first lien releases its liens.
- Second-lien creditors being subject to payment blockage if there are first-lien defaults.
  - ☐ A default, event of default, and/or acceleration of first-lien debt may be a trigger for payment blockage.
  - ☐ Payment blockage may be limited to a specified time period.
- Second-lien creditors consenting to possible future changes in first-lien documents.
  - ☐ The amount of covered first-lien debt may be capped.
  - ☐ Pricing and maturity changes may be subject to restrictions.
  - ☐ Second-lien creditors agree not to change the second-lien documents.
- An option in favor of second-lien creditors to buy first-lien debt at par.
  - ☐ The option is triggered by a remedies standstill or payment blockage.
  - ☐ Deadlines to exercise and close the option are specified.
- Certain post-petition bankruptcy provisions.
  - ☐ Prebankruptcy provisions remain applicable.
  - ☐ Second-lien creditors consent to DIP financing and priming lien by first-lien creditors (or to DIP financing to which first-lien creditors have consented), often up to a maximum amount.
  - ☐ Second-lien creditors consent to a use of cash collateral to which first-lien creditors have consented.
  - ☐ Second-lien creditors consent to all adequate protection afforded to first-lien creditors.
  - ☐ Second-lien creditors waive adequate protection rights, except rights to adequate protection liens junior to first-lien creditors' adequate protection liens.
  - ☐ Second-lien creditors consent to the exercise of remedies by first-lien creditors, and agree not to exercise their own remedies (including automatic stay relief).
  - ☐ Second-lien creditors consent to the sale of collateral if it is approved by the first-lien lenders and the bankruptcy court so long as all liens attach to the sale proceeds.

- ☐ The first lien is reinstated with respect to any claim arising from an avoidance recovery.
- ☐ Second-lien creditors agree that first-lien creditors control plan votes on second-lien claims.

Although intercreditor agreements are intended to resolve issues among the first- and second-lien creditors when they extend credit to the borrower (i.e., months or years before any bankruptcy filing), contentious intercreditor disputes inevitably arise during a company's bankruptcy proceeding. Disputes among creditors over such matters can, in effect, give rise to creditor claims against one another, in addition to their claims on the debtor's assets.

When such disputes arise, the bankruptcy court is not the proper forum for resolving them; the bankruptcy court does not have jurisdiction over intercreditor agreements and cannot modify them.

What is the difference between debt subordination and lien subordination in debt documents?

Debt subordination typically involves an agreement to turn over to senior debtholders everything received from the borrower from any source and payment blockage provisions for junior debtholders. *Lien subordination* typically involves an agreement to turn over to first-lien holders the sale proceeds from shared collateral; there is no payment blockage to second- and more junior lien holders. Lien subordination is a waiver of rights that is limited to collateral only, preserving the rights of unsecured creditors.

Antilayering covenants in a borrower's existing high-yield debt may restrict only debt subordination (e.g., subordinated "in right of payment") or may restrict lien subordination as well (e.g., subordinated "in any respect").

These concepts can be important to understanding the relative negotiating leverage of first-lien lenders, second-lien lenders, and bondholders, both in an out-of-court workout and in a bankruptcy proceeding.

What does it mean to perfect a lien?

To be valid, a lien—whether it be a first, second, or third lien—must be *perfected*. Lien perfection is a multistep legal process governed by either the Uniform Commercial Code (UCC) or state laws governing liens and mortgages.

Unless every step in the process is taken, the bankruptcy court may deem the lien defective and thus unenforceable. Lien perfection may vary by jurisdiction, but it typically involves a notice and claim of lien made under oath by the claimant and containing

- The name of the owner or reputed owner of the property concerned
- A description of the encumbered property
- A statement of the terms, time given, and conditions of the contract
- A statement of the lienor's demand

In general, the Bankruptcy Code respects nonbankruptcy law, such as state law, in determining whether a lien is proper and does not independently create liens for creditors. However, any new or additional liens granted with respect to past-due debt may be voided as preferences if they occurred within the 90 days before the petition date.[6]

What kinds of problems are most likely to be encountered in attempting to perfect liens on collateral?

If a lien is not properly perfected, it is defective, and this is likely to retroactively transform an alleged secured lender into an unsecured creditor from the date when the loan was not properly perfected (usually the beginning of the term). The reasons why a lien may be revealed to be defective include the following:

- Prior unsatisfied liens may be discovered. (For this reason, as well as for general due diligence considerations, it is prudent to begin a lien search as promptly as possible in all jurisdictions in which record filings affecting the collateral may have been made.)
- Liens on patents, trademarks and trade names, and copyright assignments require special federal filings, which may be time-consuming and require the services of specialized counsel.
- Collateral assignments of government contracts and receivables from the U.S. government require federal approval, which involves a potentially time-consuming process.
- UCC filings giving notice to the world of security interests must be made at state and, sometimes, local government offices

in the jurisdiction where the target and its assets are located. Filing requirements in Puerto Rico and Louisiana, the two non-UCC jurisdictions in the United States, are markedly different from, as well as more elaborate than, filing requirements in other U.S. jurisdictions.

■ Security interests in real estate and fixtures require separate documentation and recordation in the localities and states in which they are located. Lenders will often require title insurance and surveys, both of which involve considerable lead time.

■ Lenders will often want local counsel opinions as to the perfection and priority of liens, and obtaining these can be a major logistical task.

COLLATERAL

How does the Bankruptcy Code resolve the competing interests of the debtor and the creditors when it comes to collateral?

The Bankruptcy Code allows the debtor to continue to use the collateral that provides security for the lenders, but only so long as the parties agree that the lenders' interests are being protected. As explained by the U.S. courts:

> The debtor in possession may use, sell, or lease property of the estate in the ordinary course of its business, without prior approval, unless the court orders otherwise. 11 U.S.C. § 363(c). If the intended sale or use is outside the ordinary course of its business, the debtor must obtain permission from the court.
>
> A debtor in possession may not use "cash collateral" without the consent of the secured party or authorization by the court, which must first examine whether the interest of the secured party is adequately protected. 11 U.S.C. § 363. Section 363 defines "cash collateral" as cash, negotiable instruments, documents of title, securities, deposit accounts, or other cash equivalents, whenever acquired, in which the estate and an entity other than the estate have an interest. It includes the proceeds, products, offspring, rents, or profits of property and the fees, charges, accounts or payments for the use or occupancy of rooms and other public facilities in hotels, motels, or other lodging properties subject to a creditor's security interest.
>
> When "cash collateral" is used (spent), the secured creditors are entitled to receive additional protection under section 363 of the Bankruptcy Code.

The debtor in possession must file a motion requesting an order from the court authorizing the use of the cash collateral. Pending consent of the secured creditor or court authorization for the debtor in possession's use of cash collateral, the debtor in possession must segregate and account for all cash collateral in its possession. 11 U.S.C. § 363(c)(4). A party with an interest in property being used by the debtor may request that the court prohibit or condition this use to the extent necessary to provide "adequate protection" to the creditor.

Adequate protection may be required to protect the value of the creditor's interest in the property being used by the debtor in possession. This is especially important when there is a decrease in value of the property. The debtor may make periodic or lump sum cash payments, or provide an additional or replacement lien that will result in the creditor's property interest being adequately protected. 11 U.S.C. § 361.

When a chapter 11 debtor needs operating capital, it may be able to obtain it from a lender by giving the lender a court-approved "superpriority" over other unsecured creditors or a lien on property of the estate. 11 U.S.C. § 364.[7]

What happens if the collateral is insufficient to cover a debt?

In theory, the amount that a secured creditor lends is meant to be a fraction of the value of the assets owned by the borrower and available as collateral. However, a company's value can plummet precipitously when it enters financial distress, meaning that the senior lender's original calculation may have been significantly inaccurate. As of the petition date, if the amount of the senior lender's loan (including accrued interest and fees) exceeds the value of the collateral, the lender's secured claim is considered *undersecured*. If there is excess collateral value above and beyond the amount of the senior lender's loan, its secured claim is deemed *oversecured*. As the bankruptcy case proceeds and additional interest accrues (increasing the amount owed by the debtor to the lender), a secured lender's status may switch from oversecured to undersecured.

For example, if the senior lender believes that a company is worth $100 million, it might lend $25 million. A few years later, the company's performance declines, and the senior lender extends another $5 million of credit to help the company. However, the company's performance fails to improve, and it commences a bankruptcy proceeding with the senior lender due $30 million. If the company's assets are worth $20 million, the senior lender's claim is undersecured. If they are worth $40 million, the senior lender's claim is oversecured.

The notions of undersecured and oversecured collateral are often more art than science. Frequently, there is little clarity regarding the precise value of a company's assets during a bankruptcy proceeding. The Bankruptcy Code does not specify what standard should be used for calculating the value of the collateral involved with a secured lender's claim. Ultimately, it may take a sale of the company to determine the value with any precision. Therefore, various parties may introduce valuation experts if they want to dispute whether a secured creditor is under- or oversecured. If they did so, a potential purchaser should search for references on the bankruptcy docket to testimony and reports provided by these experts. If they did not, a potential purchaser can reasonably conclude that the various parties have reached consensus that the secured creditors are oversecured, and therefore that the value of the company is at least the amount of the secured debt. Either way, the purchaser can use this valuable information about the company to formulate a bid.

How does the bankruptcy court determine whether a secured claim is oversecured or undersecured?

Often the parties negotiate privately regarding whether a secured claim is oversecured or undersecured rather than incurring the time, expense, and risk of presenting such valuation issues to the bankruptcy court. The parties may argue that an appraised value, book value, original cost, replacement cost, or liquidation value is most relevant. The opinions of liquidators and appraisers are especially relevant. The answer usually requires a case-by-case analysis of the underlying assets and the current market environment. However, the Supreme Court has ruled that the replacement value of collateral is the best way to determine whether a claim is oversecured or undersecured in the context of Bankruptcy Code section 506(a).[8]

In arguing about whether a secured lender is oversecured or undersecured, parties need to be careful how they structure their arguments. For example, if they argue early in the case that a secured lender is undersecured with respect to adequate protection, their words may be used against them later in the case if they argue for a higher value for the plan of reorganization. An astute buyer can seize on the lower valuations given in arguing for adequate protection, and discount the higher valuations given later in the plan of reorganization.

Given how fluid the valuation of collateral can be, how can a secured creditor protect its rights to the value of its interests in the collateral while the debtor is using it?

Because secured creditors are constitutionally entitled to protection to the extent of the value of their bargain, the Bankruptcy Code includes the concept of *adequate protection* for secured creditors to the extent that their interest declines in value as a result of the debtor's actions.

Note, however, that only the secured creditor's interest is protected. If the creditor is undersecured, only the portion of its claim that is secured is protected, not the portion of its claim that is unsecured.

If a secured creditor is considered to be oversecured, the amount by which the value of the collateral exceeds the amount of the secured loan is called the *equity cushion*. A bankruptcy court may determine that the equity cushion itself is sufficient to provide adequate protection for a secured lender's interests. One bankruptcy court analyzed several other cases and concluded that an equity cushion of 20 percent or more constitutes adequate protection, while an equity cushion of less than 11 percent does not.[9] Equity cushions between 12 and 20 percent have divided the courts, making the outcome uncertain.

As a secured creditor's unpaid post-petition interest and other charges accrue, the amount of the equity cushion diminishes. While a secured creditor is entitled to adequate protection of its security interest, it is not entitled to protection of its equity cushion or the ratio of the value of the collateral to the amount of the debt.

How does the Bankruptcy Code define adequate protection?

While Bankruptcy Code section 361 does not explicitly define adequate protection, it authorizes three ways for the bankruptcy court to provide it:[10]

1. A cash payment or periodic cash payments
2. Additional or replacement liens
3. Other means of delivering equivalent value

These three methods are not exclusive, and the bankruptcy court may authorize other approaches on a case-by-case basis.

Bankruptcy Code section 361 refers to Bankruptcy Code sections 362 (automatic stay), 363 (use, sale, or lease of property), and 364 (obtaining credit) for determining whether or not a secured creditor is due adequate protection. A secured lender is entitled to seek adequate protection if it is denied relief from the automatic stay and is thereby unable to seize its collateral.[11] If a debtor is permitted to use, sell, or lease property that is encumbered by a secured lender's lien, the secured lender is entitled to seek adequate protection.[12] For example, a secured lender is entitled to seek adequate protection if a debtor encumbers property of the estate by creating a new lien that is senior to the creditor's lien on such property.[13]

Do the pre-petition secured creditors receive interest payments during the bankruptcy case?

It depends. If a secured creditor is entitled to adequate protection, the bankruptcy court is authorized to approve post-petition interest payments.[14] If there is a sufficient equity cushion, the bankruptcy court may determine that interest payments during the bankruptcy case are not warranted because the equity cushion itself provides adequate protection.

So long as it is oversecured, a pre-petition secured creditor is entitled to add post-petition interest and reasonable fees, costs, and charges during the bankruptcy proceeding to its claim if such amounts are not paid during the course of the bankruptcy proceeding.[15] Whether the interest rate is the pre-petition rate, the default rate, or another rate usually depends upon the terms of the credit agreement, the facts of the case, and relevant case law. The accrual of post-petition interest and other charges is limited to the amount of the equity cushion and will not cause the secured creditor to become undersecured.

Do the pre-petition secured creditors receive principal payments during the bankruptcy case?

No. Principal repayment schedules become irrelevant because all debts are accelerated as of the petition date and become immediately due and payable. The amount of principal that secured creditors will recover is eventually determined by the plan of reorganization.

Do first-lien lenders owe any duties to second-lien lenders if they seize collateral?

Upon seizing collateral, first-lien lenders have nearly complete control over that shared collateral until they are paid in full. Under the UCC, first-lien lenders have a duty to second-lien lenders to act in a commercially reasonable manner when disposing of the shared collateral. This duty cannot be waived. The first-lien lenders can determine which items of collateral to proceed against and in which order. They can also decide to whom collateral should be sold and whether the sale should be private or public. Meanwhile, second-lien lenders generally agree to a limited standstill period (e.g., 90 to 180 days), during which they will abstain from exercising any remedies against the shared collateral.

LOSING SECURED STATUS

Other than by being undersecured, can a creditor lose its secured status during a bankruptcy case?

Yes. If a secured creditor's lien is proven to be defective under relevant law (i.e., state law) because of lack of perfection or some other defect, the creditor may lose its secured status in bankruptcy and become an unsecured creditor. The Bankruptcy Code grants "strong-arm powers" to the debtor in possession (or the bankruptcy trustee, as the case may be) to avoid any unperfected liens placed on property of the debtor's estate, transforming the secured creditor into an unsecured creditor.[16]

Separately, a creditor can lose its secured status under several legal theories of *lender liability*, which promote lenders' fair treatment of borrowers. If lenders fail to treat borrowers fairly, they can be subject to litigation by borrowers involving a variety of legal claims, which can often become active in the bankruptcy context. However, while parties may often threaten a pre-petition secured lender with lender liability lawsuits in order to gain negotiating leverage, the burden of proof for lender liability is very high.

Two remedies for a finding of lender liability are explicitly authorized by the Bankruptcy Code: *equitable subordination* and *recharacterization*.[17] A secured creditor may lose its secured status during a bankruptcy case by being subjected to either of these extraordinary remedies. The Bankruptcy Court for the District of Delaware recently addressed these topics in the Radnor Holdings bankruptcy case, as illustrated by the following extract.

Bankruptcy Judge Peter Walsh observed that the Third Circuit Court of Appeals recently had occasion to address the factors that should be considered in evaluating a recharacterization claim in *Cohen v. KB Mezzanine Fund II (In re SubMicron Systems Corp.)*, 432 F.3d 448 (3d Cir. 2006). In addressing the issue of recharacterization of debt as equity, the Third Circuit in *SubMicron Systems* noted that such a remedy arises by virtue of the equitable authority of bankruptcy courts to ensure "that substance will not give way to form, that technical considerations will not prevent substantial justice from being done." The Third Circuit distinguished the remedy of recharacterization from the doctrine of equitable subordination. The focus of the recharacterization inquiry, according to the Third Circuit, "is whether a debt actually exists," or ". . . what is the proper characterization in the first instance of an investment." In contrast, equitable subordination is warranted "when equity demands that the payment priority of claims of an otherwise legitimate creditor be changed to fall behind those of other claimants."

In defining the recharacterization inquiry, the Court of Appeals in *SubMicron Systems* observed that "[n]o mechanistic scorecard suffices." Instead, the issues "devolve to an overarching inquiry: the characterization as debt or equity is a court's attempt to discern whether the parties called an instrument one thing when in fact they intended it as something else. That intent may be inferred from what the parties say in their contracts, from what they do through their actions, and from the economic reality of the surrounding circumstances. Answers lie in facts that confer context case-by-case."[18]

How can a claim become subject to equitable subordination or recharacterization?

In *equitable subordination*, the bankruptcy court exerts its power as a court of equity to reprioritize the recovery that a creditor receives vis-à-vis that received by other creditors (or, in the case of equity holders, the recovery that one equity holder receives vis-à-vis that received by other equity holders).

This usually happens because the court finds that it is more fair, or equitable, to put a particular lender further back in line, often because of misconduct on the part of that lender.[19] For example, a claim that a creditor asserts is secured can be deemed unsecured, stripping its liens and putting it on an equal footing (or *pari passu*) with other unsecured claims.[20] As a practical matter, this development can mean that a creditor that is expecting to receive nearly full recovery may wind up with reduced or no recovery. Another example would be one unsecured creditor's claim being equitably subordinated to receive recoveries only after all other unsecured creditors' claims and, thereby, no longer rank *pari passu*.[21]

In contrast, in a *recharacterization*, a court focuses not on the (mis) conduct of the lender, but rather on the instrument itself. Recharacterization may achieve a result similar to that of equitable subordination, but it takes a different route to get there. The court literally recharacterizes debt as equity. As a practical matter, whether a creditor goes to the back of the line among unsecured creditors or becomes part of the equity holders may make no difference if both positions receive no recovery.

Who is likely to press for equitable subordination or recharacterization?

Following the dramatic rise in second-lien loans, as discussed earlier in this chapter, unsecured creditors face a much longer line of secured creditors ahead of them in today's bankruptcy cases than there historically has been. Indeed, in many current bankruptcy cases, unsecured creditors receive no recoveries whatsoever. One strategy that unsecured creditors can use to level the playing field is to argue that some debt—such as a second- or third-lien loan—is only nominally secured and is, in fact, only a disguised equity contribution by the owner of the company.[22]

The Radnor Holdings case provides a recent—albeit unsuccessful— example of unsecured creditors asserting such claims and how the Bankruptcy Court for the District of Delaware reacted.

> One such situation came in a decision handed down on November 16, 2006, in the Chapter 11 cases of Radnor Holdings Corp. in Delaware.[23] When Radnor began to have financial problems, hedge fund Tennenbaum Capital Partners, along with two of its affiliates, got involved. They made a $25-million preferred stock investment in Radnor, loaned Radnor $95 million to refinance existing secured debt, and provided Radnor with an additional secured loan of $23.5 million. Tennenbaum also designated one of the four members of Radnor's board of directors, pursuant to its Investor's Rights Agreement, and retained the rights to increase that representation if certain levels of EBITDA were not met and to veto certain employment agreements and transactions with affiliates. Tennenbaum obtained these protections even though, at all times, it held less than 20 percent of the equity of Radnor.

In its complaint, the Creditors' Committee (appointed to represent the interests of Radnor's general unsecured creditors) accused Tennenbaum of having entered into the loans with no expectation of Radnor's being able to repay them, but rather as a means to acquire Radnor—a so-called "loan to own" strategy. In the Creditors' Committee's view, Tennenbaum insisted on terms for the secured loan that it knew Radnor could not meet and that would ultimately cause the loan to go into default. In its lawsuit, the Creditors' Committee sought to: (i) recharacterize Tennenbaum's secured loans to Radnor as equity, or, as an alternative, to equitably subordinate Tennenbaum's secured claims to the claims of the general unsecured creditors; (ii) prohibit Tennenbaum from using its $128 million in secured claims to make a credit bid on the sale of Radnor's assets; and (iii) recover as preferences monies Radnor had paid to Tennenbaum more than 90 days but less than one year before Radnor's bankruptcy filing, on the basis that Tennenbaum was an "insider" of Radnor.

Fortunately for Tennenbaum, at the end of the lengthy trial, Judge Walsh found that the Creditors' Committee had not proven its case or that existing statutes or case law precluded it from succeeding. The Bankruptcy Court held against the Creditors' Committee and in favor of Tennenbaum on all counts, a result that is likely to continue to cause secured creditors and boards of directors to look kindly on Delaware as a venue of choice for bankruptcy cases.[24]

What factors will the bankruptcy court consider in making the decision to equitably subordinate a creditor's claim?

Because equitable subordination is an extraordinary action, bankruptcy courts examine the facts and circumstances surrounding creditors' behavior carefully. It is difficult to create specific guidelines for determining when to apply equitable subordination because, once they were set, parties would simply become more creative and devious in concocting schemes to circumvent them. Therefore, bankruptcy courts must stay flexible in this area so that they can react to the latest developments among businesses that result in unjust and inequitable outcomes. This may be frustrating to businesspeople who believe that the law should provide clear rules for courts to apply objectively. However, bankruptcy courts are created to be courts of equity as well as courts of law, and one of the fundamental tenets of bankruptcy law is to provide a fair and equitable recovery to all creditors.

Equitable subordination is, therefore, an important and flexible tool for dealing with certain types of issues in a bankruptcy proceeding. However, it should be used sparingly and as a last resort, after other legal tools within the Bankruptcy Code have been ineffective.

In general, bankruptcy courts will consider three broad factors in making decisions about equitable subordination: (1) whether there was inequitable conduct on the part of the creditor, (2) if so, whether the inequitable conduct provided the creditor with an unfair advantage or otherwise harmed other creditors, and (3) whether equitable subordination would be consistent with other aspects of the Bankruptcy Code.

In particular, bankruptcy courts will exercise higher scrutiny of insiders, such as management and private equity owners. Insiders can use their influence and control over the company to provide unfair advantages, show favoritism, and otherwise create inequitable results that a bankruptcy court may find warrant an extraordinary remedy like equitable subordination.

If a potential purchaser encounters a situation in which equitable subordination may be involved, it is strongly recommended that he consult a bankruptcy attorney to evaluate the details of the case. Negotiating the sale of the company may be a way out of arguing thorny equitable subordination issues.

Recent noteworthy bankruptcy cases involving equitable subordination include[25]

- *Adelphia.* The creditors' committee brought equitable subordination claims against both those lenders who had acted as agents under various credit facilities and lenders who had purchased the debt at any time in any of the credit facilities. The asserted claims stemmed from the lenders' alleged dealings with Adelphia's former management, against whom Adelphia had brought suit for looting the company. Notably, the plan of reorganization provided that unsecured creditors would be paid in full in cash with interest. The district court determined that, given that the creditors received full payment with interest under the plan, (1) the creditors would not benefit from the lawsuit, and therefore the creditors' committee did not have standing to bring it as a threshold matter, and (2) the equitable subordination claims should be dismissed because the lenders would be paid in full regardless of whether their claims were secured or unsecured.[26]

- *Elrod Holdings.* The bankruptcy court ruled that a secured creditor has standing to seek equitable subordination of another creditor's claim so long as the injury underlying the subordination is particularized to the creditor seeking subordination (e.g., is not an injury suffered by all creditors).[27]

- *Kreisler.* Two individual Chapter 7 debtors formed a corporation to purchase a secured claim against their own estates. The resulting secured claim, if allowed, would have eliminated any distribution to unsecured creditors. The bankruptcy court viewed the debtors' actions as misconduct and equitably subordinated the purchased claim, and the district court affirmed. The Seventh Circuit Court of Appeals reversed, however, noting that while the debtors' actions may have amounted to misconduct, they did not harm other creditors, who would receive the same recoveries (i.e., none) regardless of whether the original secured creditor or the debtors' corporation owned the secured claim.[28]

- *Schlotzsky's.* The Fifth Circuit Court of Appeals held that the critical factor in the application of equitable subordination was that a claim should be subordinated only to the extent necessary to offset the harm that the debtor or its creditors have suffered as a result of the inequitable conduct. According to the Fifth Circuit, subordination of the insiders' secured claims was inappropriate because the bankruptcy trustee had failed to show that the defendant insiders' loans to the debtor harmed either the debtor or the general creditors. The court also rejected the trustee's "deepening insolvency" argument on the facts and as a matter of law.[29] (Chapter 10 of this book discusses the theory of deepening insolvency in greater detail.)

- *Winstar Communications.* The Third Circuit Court of Appeals reversed the lower courts on the issue of subordinating a lender's unsecured claim to the claims of certain equity interests, reasoning that the Bankruptcy Code does not permit the subordination of creditors' claims to equity interests.[30]

Although secured creditors may have held the fulcrum securities in many bankruptcy cases during the recession, in 2008–2009, leaving unsecured creditors with minimal recoveries, we next turn to unsecured creditors who experienced a resurgence in bankruptcy cases during 2010.

Endnotes

1. See 11 U.S.C. §506.
2. See 11 U.S.C. §506(a)(1).
3. See 11 U.S.C. §553(a).
4. See 11 U.S.C. §362(a)(7).
5. See Harold S. Novikoff, "Common Intercreditor Agreement Provisions," Wachtell, Lipton, Rosen & Katz, April 2006; available at http://www.abiworld .org/committees/newsletters/financebank/vol3num3/SiblingRivalrieII.pdf, last accessed April 14, 2010. See also Model First Lien/Second Lien Intercreditor Agreement Task Force, "Model Intercreditor Agreement; available at http:// www.abanet.org/dch/committee.cfm?com=CL190029, last accessed April 13, 2010.
6. See 11 U.S.C. §547(b).
7. http://www.uscourts.gov/bankruptcycourts/bankruptcybasics/chapter11.html#cash, last accessed April 13, 2010.
8. See *Associate Commercial Corp. v. Rash*, 520 U.S. 953 (1997).
9. See *In re McKilips*, 81 B.R. 545 (Bankr. ND Ill. 1987).
10. See 11 U.S.C. §361. The precise wording of the third item is as follows: "Granting such other relief . . . , as will result in the realization by such entity of the indubitable equivalent of such entity's interest in such property."
11. See 11 U.S.C. §362(d)(1).
12. See 11 U.S.C. §363(e).
13. See 11 U.S.C. §364(d)(1)(B).
14. See 11 U.S.C. §361.
15. See 11 U.S.C. §506(b).
16. See 11 U.S.C. §§544, 545, 546.
17. See 11 U.S.C. §510(c).
18. Leon R. Barson, "*Radnor Holdings*: Delaware Bankruptcy Court Rejects Creditors' Committee's Effort to Recharacterize Secured Creditor's Claims as Equity," *Pepper Hamilton Bankruptcy Update*, March 12, 2007; available at http://www.pepperlaw .com/publications_update.aspx?ArticleKey=867, last accessed April 13, 2010.
19. See, for example, *Citicorp Venture Capital, Ltd. v. Comm. of Creditors Holding Unsecured Claims*, 160 F.3d 982, 986-87 (3d Cir. 1998); and *Bayer Corp. v. MascoTech, Inc. (In re Autostyle Plastics, Inc.)*, 269 F.3d 726, 749 (6th Cir. 2001).
20. See 11 U.S.C. §510(c)(2).
21. Specifically, Bankruptcy Code section 510(c) provides: "after notice and a hearing, the court may (1) under principles of equitable subordination, subordinate for purposes of distribution all or part of an allowed claim to all or part of another allowed claim or all or part of an allowed interest to all or part of another allowed interest; or (2) order that any lien securing such a subordinated claim be transferred to the estate." See 11 U.S.C. §510(c).
22. Michael Klein and Ronald R. Sussman, "Recharacterization Battles Likely in Next Round of Bankruptcies," Turnaround Management Association, October 20, 2008;

available at http://www.turnaround.org/Publications/Articles.aspx?objectID=9859, last accessed April 13, 2010.

23. *Official Comm. of Unsecured Creditors of Radnor Holdings Corp. v. Tennenbaum Capital Partners, LLC* (*In re Radnor Holdings Corp.*), Adversary Proceeding No. 06-50909, Chapter 11 Case No. 06-10894 (Bankr. Del. filed November 16, 2006).

24. Mark Berman, "Lessons for Hedge Funds Investing in Distressed Debt," *Nixon Peabody Private Equity Newsletter*, January 22, 2007; available at http://www .nixonpeabody.com/publications_detail3.asp?ID=1676, last accessed August 19, 2010.

25. See "Update: Lender Liability Theories, Trends and Defenses," ABA Section of Business Law Spring Meeting, April 16, 2009; available at http://www.abanet.org/ buslaw/committees/CL190000pub/materials/2009/spring/lender-liabillity.pdf, last accessed May 14, 2010.

26. See *Adelphia Recovery Trust v. Bank of Am., N.A.*, 390 B.R. 80 (S.D.N.Y. June 18, 2008).

27. See *Elway Co., LLP v. Miller* (*In re Elrod Holdings Corp.*), 392 B.R. 110 (Bankr. D. Del. August 7, 2008).

28. See *In re Kreisler*, 546 F.3d 863 (7th Cir. 2008).

29. See *Wooley v. Faulkner* (*In re SI Restructuring, Inc.*), 532 F.3d 355 (5th Cir. June 20, 2008).

30. See *In re Winstar Comm. Inc.*, 554 F.3d 382 (3d Cir. 2009).

Unsecured Creditors

Creditors have better memories than debtors.

—Benjamin Franklin

OVERVIEW OF UNSECURED CREDITORS

How has the function of unsecured creditors changed in recent years?

Chapter 6 outlines the way unsecured creditors typically operate during the bankruptcy process. As with much in the financial industry, this general framework was faced with considerable and previously unseen pressures during the recent economic downturn. Accordingly, this discussion includes some perspective on how the historical function of unsecured creditors has evolved in recent years—particularly following the dramatic rise of second-lien financings in the middle to end of the last decade.

Chapter 6 also introduces the official committee of unsecured creditors. This committee, which has been called the "watchdog" of the bankruptcy process, can play an integral part in shaping the course of a particular case. That is, the creditors' committee has the unique role of advising the court any time a debtor seeks court approval to enter into an agreement that is outside the ordinary course of business or to dispose of any assets. The committee is thus a key driving force in determining the direction and success of a debtor's bankruptcy case, often affecting the likelihood of the debtor's reorganizing or liquidating.

Conceptually, what function do the unsecured creditors have in the bankruptcy process?

In theory, after the secured creditors have been paid, the balance of a distressed company's value is supposed to go to the unsecured creditors: the equity holders gambled on the company's upside and lost; the secured creditors lent conservatively and are covered by their collateral; and the unsecured creditors were supposed to have taken a balanced risk/reward position somewhere in the middle. Upon the distressed company's reorganization, the unsecured creditors were expected to become the new owners of the company and, therefore would have a key role in shaping how the company emerged from bankruptcy.

The Bankruptcy Code implicitly assumes this theoretical debtor-creditor framework by creating an official committee of unsecured creditors to be the opponent to the debtor in the reorganization of the distressed company.

The *official committee of unsecured creditors* (sometimes simply called the *creditors' committee* or *UCC*) represents a wide variety of unsecured creditors who may have had very different dealings with the company prepetition, but who now all have in common the fact that the debtor owes them money and they have no security interests or priority of payment. Acknowledging that bankruptcy involves an extensive legal process, the Bankruptcy Code essentially mimics the plaintiff-defendant configuration in other U.S. courts, with the debtor on one side and the creditors' committee on the other.

Throughout the bankruptcy process, the creditors' committee is the primary critic of the debtor's efforts to reorganize and will typically negotiate the terms of the plan of reorganization with the debtor. Generally, the debtor will have the exclusive right to propose a plan of reorganization, but the unsecured creditors will have the right to vote on it—producing a balance of power in the bankruptcy proceeding that theoretically will lead to the optimal resolution for the company.

How has this framework changed in recent years?

The system just described worked well until the dramatic rise in second-lien financing in the middle of the last decade. Essentially, the investors in second-lien debt sought to receive economic benefits similar to those of bonds but recoveries ahead of trade and other unsecured creditors in a downside scenario. This significant development in the financial markets defied the original expectations of Congress when it originally enacted the Bankruptcy Code. However, Congress has not yet amended the Bankruptcy Code to respond to this new configuration of creditors.

In the economic downturn of 2008–2009, the increase in secured debt (particularly second-lien financings) resulted in unsecured creditors frequently being out-of-the-money. Therefore, the fulcrum security was often among the secured creditors, not the unsecured creditors. With nothing to gain in a reorganization, unsecured creditors did not have as much power to negotiate or as much reason to have a voice. However, for those unsecured creditors who used their negotiating leverage to bide their time until 2010, their perseverance was rewarded many times over as valuations returned to prior levels. Once the fulcrum security moved from the secured debt to the unsecured claims, the balance of power shifted in favor of the official committee.

While an official committee of unsecured creditors still exists in such cases, its role is diminished to attempts to squeeze small recoveries for its constituents. For example, preference claims are typically assets of the debtor upon which secured creditors cannot have a lien, providing a potential for slight recoveries to unsecured creditors after the payment of attorneys' fees.

When the creditors' committee plays a diminished role in bankruptcy proceedings, is it safe to assume that the committee plays a similarly diminished role in distressed M&A?

Not necessarily. A distressed purchaser should still seek to befriend the official committee of unsecured creditors and its advisors because they may be able to assist or delay the sale process.

Because of the authority granted to it by the Bankruptcy Code, the creditors' committee can object to a debtor's motions to sell assets, motions to establish bidding procedures, and other motions that are necessary to complete a sale—even if it appears clear that the unsecured creditors are out-of-the-money. In addition, the creditors' committee may be an important source of current information about the company, its assets, and its performance. Moreover, certain unsecured creditors may be important parties that the potential purchaser will need to work with after the sale is complete; key among these are vendors, employees, and landlords. Furthermore, if the potential purchaser seeks to replace management after the sale is complete, the debtor may be unfriendly to the purchaser, whereas the creditors' committee may be a strong ally.

For these reasons and others, a potential purchaser may want to give serious consideration to providing some recovery to unsecured creditors—even if they otherwise would not warrant it.

CLAIMS OF UNSECURED CREDITORS

Who are the typical holders of unsecured claims?

Unsecured creditors may include

- Holders of bonds, debentures, subordinated notes, and other types of unsecured securities
- Vendors who are awaiting payment after shipping goods or providing services to the debtor; such creditors are often referred to as "the trade"
- Employees who are due unpaid wages
- Landlords who entered into leases that have been rejected by the debtor but have future rental periods outstanding
- Plaintiffs who have been awarded damages from the debtor
- Utilities that have provided unbilled services to the debtor
- Counterparties with open swaps, futures, or other trades with the debtor, assuming that such parties are in-the-money as of the petition date
- Governments that are due unpaid, nonpriority taxes from the debtor

Do all unsecured creditors hold claims that are *pari passu*?

Although they all rank below secured creditors, there may be some sequence of payments among the unsecured creditors (assuming that the unsecured creditors receive any recovery).

If there are multiple tranches of debt, the noteholders may have agreed that certain holders will receive payment before others. For example, a company may have issued senior subordinated notes for first-priority payment or junior subordinated notes for last-priority payment among the noteholders.

The Bankruptcy Code includes several special rules for priority payments to certain types of unsecured creditors.[1] However, many of these rules address issues in consumer bankruptcies, not business bankruptcies.

What is a critical vendor?

A company often has certain suppliers who are essential to its operations. When a company becomes distressed, even before it files for bankruptcy, its vendors may become aware of the situation and begin restricting the supplies they ship in advance of payment. For instance, vendors might conclude that their customer is experiencing distress because a pattern of late payments develops. When a situation becomes extreme, vendors may refuse to ship additional supplies until past due bills are paid, or may demand cash-on-delivery (COD) payment terms. If the company is cut off by a vendor, it may be able to simply source supplies from a competing vendor that may be unaware of the company's distress and may not perform an adequate credit check. However, there are some circumstances in which the company relies on a particular vendor and no other vendor can serve as a substitute. In these circumstances, such a vendor is known as a *critical vendor*.

Where do critical vendors fall among the continuum of creditors in a bankruptcy process?

Critical vendors have strong leverage in negotiating their recoveries in a bankruptcy proceeding because they can simply refuse to provide the additional supplies that the company needs if it is to continue operating. Therefore, most bankruptcy courts allow companies to pay critical vendors' pre-petition unsecured claims in full toward the beginning of the case. As a result, critical vendors get paid not only before other unsecured creditors, but also before secured creditors. Moreover, critical vendors are paid in full, whereas other creditors may ultimately receive partial recoveries.

Where in the Bankruptcy Code might one find a framework for evaluating whether a supplier is a critical vendor?

There is no provision in the Bankruptcy Code that explicitly addresses critical vendors. Instead, bankruptcy courts routinely use their equitable powers to grant such relief.[2] Even so, the concept of critical vendors is necessarily designed to be narrow. If all of the trade could receive payment in full, a company probably would never have entered the bankruptcy process in the first place.

Whether a particular vendor is, in fact, critical is determined by the *doctrine of necessity*. Under this doctrine, the critical vendor payments must allow for reorganization and provide a greater recovery to the remaining creditors than they could expect without such payments. Without critical vendor payments, therefore, reorganization will fail, and the debtor and its estate will suffer substantial harm. One bankruptcy court established a three-part test for applying the doctrine of necessity:[3]

1. The debtor must have a critical need to deal with the specific creditor.
2. Unless the debtor deals with the creditor, the debtor risks
   a. The probability of harm, or
   b. Loss of some economic benefit to the estate's going-concern value that is disproportionate to the payment
3. There is no practical or legal solution other than payment of the claim.

In the Kmart bankruptcy case, however, the debtor took the concept to an absurd extreme by seeking to pay more than 2,300 suppliers in full as critical vendors at the beginning of the case, with payments totaling more than $300 million! When the bankruptcy court approved the debtor's motion, one creditor objected so strenuously that it decided to appeal. On appeal, the district court agreed with the bankruptcy court, but, upon further appeal, the Seventh Circuit Court of Appeals overruled the lower courts and ordered the so-called critical vendors to return the payments that they had received from the debtor.[4] The appellate court determined that creditors that could be adversely affected were not given proper notice before the bankruptcy court approved the debtor's critical vendor motion. In addition, the appellate court was concerned that the bankruptcy court had approved the debtor's critical vendor motion under the doctrine of necessity without sufficiently reviewing operational, financial, or other evidence. The debtor was then forced to sue each of the critical vendors to demand return of the payments. These lawsuits created additional complexity for the debtor, increased its legal fees significantly, and irritated the very suppliers with whom the company was trying to maintain positive relationships.

Some commentators believe that the Kmart case significantly narrowed the circumstances in which the notion of critical vendor payments can apply.

The *Kmart* ruling was not an outright rejection of the critical vendor concept, but it does make it much more difficult to apply. In addition to the [bankruptcy court's equitable powers] limitation, *Kmart* suggests compliance with heightened procedural and evidentiary standards is necessary before any payment is deemed critical. At least in the Seventh Circuit, the bankruptcy court should determine whether (i) discrimination among unsecured creditors is the only way to facilitate reorganization and (ii) the disfavored creditors are at least as well off as they would have been had the critical vendor payments never occurred. . . .

The result of the evolving case law is that critical vendor treatment is more difficult to achieve, but possible. Increased evidentiary standards or a longer notice period might cause some vendors to refuse to work with the debtor. A more likely result is that the creditors will still do business with the debtor and the higher burden of proof will shake out those "critical" vendors that were only looking to improve their position over other similarly situated creditors.[5]

Do the pre-petition unsecured creditors receive interest payments during the bankruptcy case?

No. Unlike pre-petition secured creditors, who may be entitled to interest payments during the bankruptcy proceeding as adequate protection under Bankruptcy Code section 506(b), pre-petition unsecured creditors are not entitled to such treatment. However, there are rare circumstances known as *solvent debtor* cases in which equity holders receive recoveries and unsecured creditors recover 100 percent of the face amount of their claims. In solvent debtor cases, unsecured creditors may demand that they be paid the interest that would have accrued during the bankruptcy proceeding as part of their claims. In other words, their claims would be increased by the amount of post-petition interest because they cannot receive more than 100 percent recoveries. As a practical matter, however, the amount of cash interest that can be paid to unsecured creditors in a plan of reorganization depends upon the amount of liquidity raised through the exit financing.

The form of recovery received by unsecured creditors is irrelevant to whether they are entitled to receive post-petition interest. If they receive all cash, cash and new notes, cash plus equity, and so on, the issue is whether the plan's stated amount of their recovery exceeds 100 percent of their claims.

In solvent debtor cases, what rate is used to calculate post-petition interest for unsecured creditors?

If a plan of reorganization provides for post-petition interest to be paid to unsecured creditors, the plan proponent must then determine what rate of interest should be used. There are three main choices: contract rate, default rate, and statutory rate.

The first choice is the agreed-upon rate in the contract, such as a note agreement or vendor agreement. Since the parties initially bargained for this contract rate, it may be fair to use it for calculating post-petition interest. However, it may not be equitable to use rates of interest that may vary widely in the different agreements for each individual unsecured creditor. Furthermore, many unsecured creditors' claims may not be based on agreements with a stated rate of interest.

The second choice is the default rate in the contract. Many agreements will increase the contract rate upon a default, such as an additional 2 percentage points. The parties agreed to this increased rate, and it may seem fair that the bankruptcy court should honor this agreement. As a practical matter, in many situations, if the bankruptcy court does not honor this agreement, then there may be no scenario when the creditor ever gets paid default interest, rendering the entire section of the agreement moot. The same issues of equitable treatment that arise when applying contract rates are also present when using default rates.

The third choice is the statutory rate determined in the relevant jurisdiction. The key advantage of using the statutory rate is that all unsecured creditors are treated equitably using the same rate for calculating post-petition interest. However, it may be unfair to deprive some creditors of the benefit of their bargain to receive a contract or default rate, which is typically much higher and theoretically represents the risk-reward profile determined by the financial markets at the time of the initial agreement.

Until Congress amends the Bankruptcy Code to address the proper rate for calculating post-petition interest in solvent debtor cases, there is likely to be significant variation from jurisdiction to jurisdiction and among bankruptcy courts.

What is an example of a situation in which pre-petition unsecured creditors were, in fact, paid interest?

In the bankruptcy case of Berry-Hill Galleries, which began in December 2005 and ended in March 2007 before the Bankruptcy Court for the Southern District of New York, the unsecured creditors received full recoveries of the face amount of their claims plus, on average, an additional 5 percent for interest. The solvent debtor was a fourth-generation family-run art gallery with assets that included Early American fine art and real estate on the Upper East Side of Manhattan. It filed a voluntary bankruptcy petition when its senior lender refused to extend its loan past the maturity date and litigation made refinancing with a new lender impossible.

Accordingly, the Berry-Hill Galleries case was a situation that involved *illiquidity* but not *insolvency*. The company had total assets worth more than its total liabilities, but pending litigation and an uncooperative senior lender meant that it could not raise additional capital to fund its day-to-day operations. Therefore, unsecured creditors believed that they would receive full recovery if the company were liquidated. As a result, the official committee of unsecured creditors refused to negotiate a discounted recovery in the company's plan of reorganization and represented to the debtor that unsecured creditors would vote only for a plan in which they received at least 100 percent recoveries. However, unsecured creditors could receive such recoveries in cash only if exit financing provided liquidity to cover the debtor-in-possession (DIP) loan, outstanding administrative expenses for attorneys and other professionals, court costs, and then sufficient amounts for unsecured creditors.

Raising such financing proved very difficult. Ultimately, the official committee of unsecured creditors and the exit lender agreed to a loan amount where (1) the exit lender was comfortable with the collateral coverage, and (2) the unsecured creditors agreed to vote for a plan that provided full recovery plus, on average, approximately 5 percent for interest. In an unusual turn of events, the family received 100 percent of the equity in the reorganized company.

Other recent bankruptcy cases in which unsecured creditors received recoveries of 100 percent of the face amount of their claims plus postpetition interest include Adelphia, Chemtura, General Growth Properties, and Six Flags.

Do the pre-petition unsecured creditors receive principal payments during the bankruptcy case?

No. The principles of adequate protection, described in Chapter 5 of this book, do not apply to unsecured creditors.

Are there any other amounts to which unsecured creditors may be entitled?

Yes. Sometimes agreements involving notes and bonds contain make-whole provisions or call protection. These concepts are discussed in Chapter 14 of this book. In solvent debtor cases, these concepts may become relevant because noteholders, bondholders, and other unsecured creditors are receiving more than the face amount of their claims. In addition to post-petition interest, these creditors may be entitled to make-whole or non-call payments. Ordinarily, the two concepts are mutually exclusive. Whether certain unsecured creditors are entitled to such payments is fact-intensive and a qualified attorney can provide advice on the proper interpretation of the applicable legal agreements and case law. The Bankruptcy Code does not directly address make-whole provisions or call protection, but Section 502(b)(2) prohibits the payment of unmatured interest. (See Chapter 4 of this book for an overview of matured versus unmatured interest.)

SPECIAL SITUATIONS INVOLVING UNSECURED CLAIMS

Are there any other types of unsecured claims?

Yes. The Bankruptcy Code provides special provisions for extraordinary situations involving unsecured claims. These are summarized in Exhibit 6-1.

Each of these complex situations is beyond the scope of this book—in fact, properly addressing each probably requires a separate book—and definitely requires the advice of a seasoned bankruptcy professional. The following questions will address some fundamental concepts concerning these unsecured claims.

What happens to the pension plan of a debtor when the company files bankruptcy? Does it automatically terminate?

No. A *plan termination* is a separate event under ERISA law that may need to be addressed in a debtor's bankruptcy filing. In fact, many companies emerge from bankruptcy with their pension plans intact.

Exhibit 6-1 Special Provisions for Unsecured Claims

Special Situation	Bankruptcy Code	Key Cases
Terminating retiree benefit plans (pensions)	Sections 523(a)(18) and 1114	■ Bastian Co. ■ Delta Air Lines ■ Fruehauf Trailer ■ Kaiser Aluminum ■ Oneida ■ Philip Services ■ Resol Manufacturing ■ WCI Steel
Rejecting collective bargaining agreements (union contracts)	Section 1113	■ Allied Holdings ■ Bildisco & Bildisco ■ Bruno's Supermarkets ■ Delphi ■ Horsehead Industries ■ Ionosphere Clubs ■ Mesaba Airlines ■ United Air Lines
Resolving mass tort claims	Section 524(g)	■ A.H. Robins (Dalkon Shield) ■ Babcock & Wilcox (asbestos) ■ Combustion Engineering (asbestos) ■ Dow Corning (breast implants) ■ Eagle-Picher (asbestos) ■ Johns-Manville (asbestos) ■ National Gypsum (asbestos) ■ Owens Corning (asbestos) ■ UNR Industries (asbestos)
Cleaning up environmental contamination and toxic torts	Sections 523(a)(7) and 554(a)	■ *In re Chateaugay Corp. v. LTV Corp. v. LTV Steel Co.*, 944 F.2d 997 (2d Cir. 1991) ■ *In re McCrory Corporation*, 188 B.R. 763 (S.D.N.Y. 1995) ■ *Midlantic National Bank v. N.J. Dept. of Environmental Protection*, 474 U.S. 494, 106 S.Ct. 755 (1986) ■ *Ohio v. Kovacs*, 469 U.S. 274, 105 S.Ct. 705 (1985) ■ *Torwico Electronics, et al v. N.J. Dept. of Environmental Protection*, 8 F.3d 146 (3d Cir. 1993)

If the debtor, known as a *plan sponsor* in pension terminology, files for bankruptcy protection (whether Chapter 7 liquidation or Chapter 11 reorganization) before the pension plan ends, and is still in bankruptcy when the pension plan ends, a federal government agency called the Pension Benefit Guaranty Corporation (PBGC) (see Chapter 7 of this book for further details) uses the bankruptcy petition date instead of the termination date for the plan to determine the guaranteed pension benefit amount, which becomes an unsecured claim in the bankruptcy case. Bankruptcy Code section 1114 addresses the termination of insurance benefits to retired employees.[6] In general, the debtor cannot modify or terminate a pension plan unilaterally, but must negotiate in good faith with the plan's representative.

If a pension plan terminates, the debtor and each member of its *controlled group* are jointly and severally liable for the pension plan's unfunded benefit liabilities, any unpaid contributions, and unpaid premiums. A debtor's controlled group includes businesses under common control, such as a parent and its 80 percent-owned subsidiaries.

In 2006, as part of the Deficit Reduction Act of 2005, Congress amended ERISA to require that a termination premium be paid to the PBGC when a restructuring debtor terminates an underfunded pension plan either in or out of bankruptcy.[7] Few bankruptcy cases have interpreted this relatively new law.[8]

How may an employer terminate a pension plan?

There are three ways to terminate a plan: standard, distress, and involuntary. First, the employer can end the plan in a *standard termination*—but only after showing the PBGC that the plan has enough money to pay all benefits owed to participants. The plan must either purchase an annuity from an insurance company (which will provide each employee with lifetime benefits upon retirement) or, if the specific plan allows, issue one lump-sum payment that covers each employee's entire benefit. Before purchasing such an annuity, the plan administrator must give employees an advance notice that identifies the insurance company (or companies) that the employer may select to provide the annuity. The PBGC's guarantee ends when the employer purchases an annuity or gives the employees lump-sum payments.

If the plan is not fully funded, an employer who is in financial distress may apply for a *distress termination*. To do so, however, the employer must prove to a bankruptcy court or to the PBGC that the employer cannot remain in business unless the plan is terminated. If the application is granted, the PBGC will take over the plan as trustee and pay plan benefits, up to the legal limits, using the plan assets and PBGC guarantee funds. There are four types of distress terminations under ERISA: liquidation in bankruptcy,[9] reorganization in bankruptcy,[10] business continuation,[11] and unnecessary burden.[12]

In an *involuntary termination*, the PBGC may terminate the pension plan under certain conditions, since termination is a right created by ERISA law, not bankruptcy law.[13] In summary, these conditions include (1) the pension plan's not meeting the PBGC's funding standards, (2) the pension plan will be unable to pay benefits when they come due, and (3) the PBGC's long-term exposure is expected to increase unreasonably.

What are the key considerations for a debtor that is considering whether to reject a union contract in a bankruptcy case?

The key cases listed in Exhibit 6-1 provide some important guidance for a debtor who is seeking to assume, reject, or modify a union contract in a bankruptcy proceeding. In general, when Congress enacted Bankruptcy Code section 1113, it sought to encourage debtors and unions to reach mutually acceptable agreements while the existing collective bargaining agreement remained in effect.[14] Therefore, a debtor cannot unilaterally terminate a union contract. Instead, Bankruptcy Code section 1113 requires the debtor to make a good faith effort to negotiate with the union's authorized representative, including a reasonable opportunity to confer, before rejecting a collective bargaining agreement. During negotiations, the debtor may propose only necessary modifications to the contract and must provide the union with adequate information to enable it to evaluate the proposal. If the parties are unable to reach agreement and the debtor seeks to reject the collective bargaining agreement, the debtor must demonstrate to the bankruptcy court that rejection is necessary for the debtor's reorganization.

Under Bankruptcy Code section 1113, a bankruptcy court may approve a debtor's motion to terminate a collective bargaining agreement if the debtor followed the procedures just explained, the union (or its authorized representative) refused to accept the proposed modification without good cause, and the balance of the equities clearly favors rejection of the collective bargaining agreement. As a middle ground, the bankruptcy court is authorized to provide interim relief by temporarily modifying a collective bargaining agreement if doing so is essential to the continuation of the business or necessary to avoid irreparable damage to the estate.[15]

What are the limitations on discharging a debtor's liability for toxic torts?

The five cases listed in Exhibit 6-1 regarding the treatment of environmental cleanup and toxic torts in bankruptcy are the key rulings on this topic. Generally, a debtor's environmental liabilities arise when the debtor is a Potentially Responsible Party (PRP) under the Comprehensive Environmental Response, Compensation and Liability Act, 42 U.S.C. §9601 *et seq.* (CERCLA, also known as Superfund). In summary, debtors have attempted unsuccessfully to use the bankruptcy process to abandon contaminated property under Bankruptcy Code section 554(a), which states, "After notice and hearing, the [debtor in possession] may abandon any property of the estate that is burdensome to the estate or that is of inconsequential value and benefit to the estate."[16] Instead, the broad exclusion to a debtor's discharge contained in Bankruptcy Code section 523(a)(7), which states in relevant part that debts are not dischargeable to the extent that they are for a "fine, penalty, or forfeiture payable to and for the benefit of a governmental unit," generally includes a debtor's environmental liabilities.[17]

A leading environmental and litigation attorney recently summarized the takeaways from the five key cases involving environmental claims in bankruptcy as follows:

> Very often, the knowledge that you have a problem with contaminated property occurs in such a manner that advance planning is not possible. It is difficult to plan for contingencies you had no reason to foresee. But to the extent you have the ability to plan ahead, and in the midst of the many complex technical and legal issues you must deal with, the possibility of some party filing for bankruptcy should be part of your thinking.
>
> Simplifying the findings of these decisions is difficult, but the following seem to be possible outcomes when contaminated property is addressed in bankruptcy:

- If the remediation obligation is reduced to a monetary amount, it will be discharged as a debt. Though this relieves the debtor of the immediate financial obligation, it leaves the property contaminated and future liability for remediation obligations still possible.
- If the value of the property exceeds its clean-up costs, the trustee can sell the property and the buyer, who presumably bought it at a discount, is responsible for its remediation.
- If the cost of remediation exceeds the property's value, and the condition of the property does not threaten public health or the environment, the trustee can abandon the property and the debtor is left with the property and the remediation obligation post-bankruptcy.
- If the property presents a hazard, the trustee may not abandon it without taking some action to render it safe. Presumably the costs of that action are administrative expenses, which may or may not receive priority.
- If the state cleans up the property, as is likely to be the situation in many cases, it will probably put a lien on the property to recover its costs, and that recovery could depend on whether the property can be sold for more than the cost of the remediation.

The best a debtor who owns contaminated property probably can do is to have the cost of remediation become a debt that is discharged by the bankruptcy court. The debtor most likely will lose the property, but also lose the debt. The worst the debtor can do is to be left post-bankruptcy with both the property and a remediation cost obligation that exceeds the value of the property. A middle ground would be where concern that an environmental debt could be discharged if bankruptcy is filed leads to settlement discussions among PRPs, allowing the debtor to resolve its obligation for a negotiated figure. If the debtor PRP pays a reduced share, the shares of other PRPs would increase, but that would also be the result if the decision was made in the context of bankruptcy.[18]

THE ROLE OF CREDITORS' COMMITTEES

How is the official committee of unsecured creditors formed, and how does it function?

The Bankruptcy Code makes the establishment of the creditors' committee mandatory. The primary purpose of the creditors' committee is to represent the interests of all general unsecured creditors and to maximize their recoveries.

According to the official explanation by the U.S. courts:

> The committee is appointed by the U.S. trustee and ordinarily consists of unsecured creditors who hold the seven largest unsecured claims against the debtor. 11 U.S.C. § 1102. Among other things, the committee: consults with the debtor in possession on administration of the case; investigates the debtor's conduct and operation of the business; and participates in formulating a plan. 11 U.S.C. § 1103. A creditors' committee may, with the court's approval, hire an attorney or other professionals to assist in the performance of the committee's duties. A creditors' committee can be an important safeguard to the proper management of the business by the debtor in possession.[19]

Service on a creditors' committee is entirely voluntary. At the request of any party involved in the bankruptcy case, the bankruptcy court may order a change in the membership of an official committee of unsecured creditors to ensure adequate representation of the unsecured creditors.[20] A change may be necessary, for example, if claims have been traded during the course of the bankruptcy case.

What are the advantages and disadvantages of serving on a creditors' committee?

Serving on a creditors' committee involves significant responsibility. The typical committee may meet several times a month, usually via a telephone conference call to minimize disruption.

On the one hand, the advantages of serving on a creditors' committee may include

- Expressing opinions collectively, which can be more effective than individually
- Influencing the decisions of the debtor and the bankruptcy court
- Pooling administrative costs, which are then reimbursed by the debtor's estate
- Minimizing the overall costs of attorneys and financial advisors for the creditors
- Having access to confidential information and case developments

- Finding opportunities to network with other individuals involved in the same industry
- Strengthening the relationship with the debtor after it reorganizes

On the other hand, the disadvantages may include

- Making a significant time commitment
- Acting as a fiduciary to the unsecured creditors as a whole
- Maintaining confidentiality of information
- Being prohibited from claims trading
- Harming the relationship with the debtor if the reorganization becomes contentious

What is the role of the chairperson of an official committee of unsecured creditors?

The creditors' committee elects one of its members as chairperson. Often, the chairperson represents the largest unsecured claimant or has important experience with the bankruptcy process. The chairperson does not have any special votes or authority to bind the committee; the creditors' committee typically enacts bylaws that specify the duties of the chairperson and any other officers, such as a vice chairperson and secretary.

The duties of a chairperson might include

1. Convening (or directing counsel to convene) meetings of the creditors' committee, or authorizing the creditors' committee to convene meetings as necessary
2. Presiding at the meetings of the creditors' committee
3. Directing counsel to have agendas prepared for the meetings of the creditors' committee
4. Appointing appropriate subcommittees
5. Serving as an ex officio member of all subcommittees to which the chairperson is not appointed as a member
6. Performing such other duties as may be delegated to the chairperson by the creditors' committee that are not inconsistent with the bylaws

Although a potential purchaser might attempt to make contact with the chairperson of a creditors' committee, from a practical standpoint, it is usually preferable to begin with the creditors' committee's law firm or financial advisor. Typically, individual members of a creditors' committee dislike speaking with third parties.

What authority does the official committee of unsecured creditors possess?

Bankruptcy Code section 1103(c) provides the tools with which the creditors' committee works. It provides that the creditors' committee may[21]

1. Consult with the bankruptcy trustee or debtor in possession concerning the administration of the case
2. Investigate the acts, conduct, assets, liabilities, and financial condition of the debtor, the operation of the debtor's business and the desirability of the continuance of such business, and any other matter relevant to the case or to the formulation of a plan
3. Participate in the formulation of a plan, advise those represented by the committee of the committee's determinations concerning any plan formulated, and collect and file with the court acceptances or rejections of a plan
4. Request the appointment of a trustee or examiner under section 1104 of this title
5. Perform such other services as are in the interest of those represented

Bankruptcy Code section 1103(c)(5) is intended to be a flexible catchall clause that bankruptcy courts can interpret on a case-by-case basis to enable the creditors' committee to represent the interests of the unsecured creditors. Separately, the Bankruptcy Code explicitly gives the creditors' committee authority to be heard by the bankruptcy court on any issue.[22] As mentioned earlier in this chapter, it is often said that the creditors' committee serves as the watchdog for the bankruptcy case because it has these powers to represent its constituents.

The limits on the flexibility of Bankruptcy Code section 1103(c)(5) are often tested by creditors' committees. A common objection is the amount of fees and expenses incurred by the creditors' committee to combat other constituents in the bankruptcy case—particularly when it is clear that the unsecured creditors are out-of-the-money. In such a scenario, the bankruptcy court may place greater emphasis on strenuous objections by the debtor and secured creditors rather than force them to pay for the frivolous and wasteful activities of the creditors' committee. Indeed, attacking the debtor and secured creditors in a desperate effort to gain negotiating leverage and extract value for the unsecured creditors may backfire if the bankruptcy court subsequently denies the fees and expenses of the creditors' committee's advisors.

Who advises the official committee of unsecured creditors?

If the bankruptcy court approves, the creditors' committee may retain a law firm, financial advisor, and other consultants to represent it, pursuant to Bankruptcy Code section 1103(a).[23] These advisors' fees and expenses are paid by the debtor's estate, which theoretically means that the unsecured creditors are indirectly paying for the creditors' committee from their future recoveries.

The advisors to the creditors' committee typically spend most of their time reviewing the documents filed by the debtor and summarizing them for the creditors' committee. They also spend time negotiating with the debtor's advisors over various aspects of the bankruptcy proceeding.

Does the official committee of unsecured creditors have a right to retain advisors at the estate's expense?

Yes. The creditors' committee submits the expenses for its advisors to the bankruptcy court for direct payment from the debtor's estate. Neither the members serving on the creditors' committee nor the creditors themselves pay these expenses directly. However, individual creditors may decide to retain their own counsel and advisors to represent them, and the debtor's estate typically does not pay for these expenses.

What is a 341 meeting?

The creditors' committee forms in the first few weeks following the petition date. The U.S. trustee holds a meeting of the creditors pursuant to

Bankruptcy Code section 341.[24] This meeting, often called the *341 meeting* or *formation meeting*, is where the U.S. trustee chooses which creditors will serve on the creditors' committee. Also, the U.S. trustee conducts a brief examination of the debtor's management, including the debtor's financial predicament, the impetus for the bankruptcy filing, management's turnaround capabilities, the future prospects for the business, and the strategy for reorganizing the company. Individual creditors may participate in this inquiry. The date, time, and location of the 341 meeting are typically available on the bankruptcy docket. While this meeting may occur at or near the courthouse, the bankruptcy court does not preside over the 341 meeting; in fact, the Bankruptcy Code prohibits the bankruptcy court from even attending the 341 meeting.[25] In a *prepackaged bankruptcy*, which is discussed more fully in Chapter 12 of this book, the parties may request that the bankruptcy court order the U.S. trustee not to convene the 341 meeting because the debtor is filing a plan of reorganization for which the debtor has already solicited creditors' acceptances.[26]

A potential purchaser may want to attend the 341 meeting because she can gather valuable and insightful information in the hallways from the various parties who attend—particularly early in the case, when many motions may not yet have been filed on the bankruptcy docket. Another reason for a potential purchaser to attend the 341 meeting is to let the parties know that she is interested in buying the company and wants to receive information about a sale process.

Making parties aware of the potential purchaser's interest early is especially important if the purchaser wants to become a *stalking horse bidder* (see the discussion of 363 sales in Chapter 13 of this book).

Who reviews and opposes the debtor's motions before the formation of the official committee of unsecured creditors?

The U.S. trustee (see Chapter 7 of this book) reviews and may oppose the debtor's motions before the formation of the creditors' committee. In addition, the bankruptcy court itself will review the debtor's motions with heightened scrutiny during this period, acknowledging that the creditors' committee does not yet exist.

May the official committee of unsecured creditors propose a plan of reorganization?

Yes. The creditors' committee may propose a plan of reorganization once the debtor's *exclusivity period* has expired. Separately, individual creditors may also propose a plan of reorganization at their own expense. See Chapter 12 of this book for a full discussion of plans of reorganization and exclusivity periods.

May the official committee of unsecured creditors propose a sale of the company?

It depends. If the creditors' committee is proposing a plan of reorganization for creditors to vote on, it may include a sale process in the plan. However, the creditors' committee does not have the explicit authority to propose a 363 sale because the language of Bankruptcy Code section 363 refers only to the trustee and, pursuant to Bankruptcy Code section 1107, the debtor in possession.[27] If the creditors' committee seeks a sale of the company, it may be able to use its negotiating leverage on unrelated topics to achieve its objectives.

May the official committee of unsecured creditors be a bidder during an auction for a sale of the company?

No. The function of the creditors' committee does not include becoming a bidder at an auction for a sale of all or part of the company. However, members of the creditors' committee are free to become bidders and may use their insights into the bankruptcy proceeding to develop a bidding strategy.

The next chapter addresses the remaining key players in a bankruptcy proceeding who may advise parties such as the creditors' committee.

Endnotes

1. See 11 U.S.C. §507.
2. See 11 U.S.C. §105.
3. See *In re Co-Serv, L.L.C.*, 273 B.R. 487, 498 (Bankr. N.D. Tex. 2003).
4. See *In re Kmart Corp.*, 359 F.3d 866 (7th Cir. 2004).
5. Gregory R. Schaaf, "Are There Any Critical Vendors Left?" Greenebaum Doll & McDonald PLLC, 2005; available at http://library.findlaw.com/2005/Feb/6/133644.html, last accessed April 19, 2010.

6. See 11 U.S.C. §1114.

7. See ERISA §4006(a)(7)(B), 29 U.S.C. §1306(a)(7)(B).

8. See, for example, *Pension Benefit Guaranty Corporation v. Oneida, Ltd.*, 562 F.3d 154 (2d Cir. April 8, 2009), where the Second Circuit Court of Appeals reversed a ruling by the Bankruptcy Court for the Southern District of New York characterizing certain "termination premiums" owed to the PBGC as contingent, pre-petition claims that were dischargeable in bankruptcy.

9. See 29 U.S.C. §1341(c)(2)(B)(i).

10. See 29 U.S.C. §1341(c)(2)(B)(ii).

11. See 29 U.S.C. §1341(c)(2)(B)(iii)(I).

12. See 29 U.S.C. §1341(c)(2)(B)(iii)(II).

13. See 29 U.S.C. §1342.

14. See 11 U.S.C. §1113.

15. See 11 U.S.C. §1113(e).

16. See 11 U.S.C. §554(a).

17. See 11 U.S.C. §523(a)(7).

18. Diane W. Whitney, "Bankruptcy and Contaminated Property," *For the Defense*, January 2010; available at http://www.dri.org/(S(nexbt5555cpoaoqwkyctil55))/articles/Toxic/FTD-1001-Whitney.pdf, last accessed August 21, 2010.

19. U.S. Courts, "Reorganization under the Bankruptcy Code"; available at http://www.uscourts.gov/bankruptcycourts/bankruptcybasics/chapter11 .html#committee, last accessed April 19, 2010.

20. See 11 U.S.C. §1102(a)(4).

21. See 11 U.S.C. §1103(c).

22. See 11 U.S.C. §1109(b).

23. See 11 U.S.C. §1103(a).

24. See 11 U.S.C. §341(a).

25. See 11 U.S.C. §341(c).

26. See 11 U.S.C. §341(e).

27. See 11 U.S.C. §§363, 1107.

CHAPTER 7

Advisors and Other Parties

Most of the important things in the world have been accomplished by people who have kept on trying when there seemed to be no hope at all.

—Dale Carnegie, author of How to Win Friends
and Influence People

OVERVIEW OF ADVISORS AND OTHER PARTIES INVOLVED IN THE BANKRUPTCY PROCESS

What types of advisors and other parties are also involved in the bankruptcy process?

In nearly every business bankruptcy, multiple advisors play important and significant roles. As in most legal proceedings, the debtor and creditors are represented by attorneys. Over the years, a broader cast of advisors to deal with the increasing complexities of cases has become commonplace: financial advisors (also known as restructuring advisors), turnaround consultants, accountants, and others. Chapter 6 discusses the official committee of unsecured creditors, but there may also be an unofficial committee of such creditors, and there may also be a formal committee of equity holders. Finally there are a number of administrative parties—a U.S. trustee, an examiner, and a claims agent, to name a few—that may also be part of the process. This chapter describes the roles of these parties in greater detail.

As in any profession, there is a range of talent among advisors. We recommend taking the selection of advisors seriously. Reputation is important, as is specific experience with the issues at hand. The following bankruptcy advisors from the Turnaround Management Association's (TMA's) Turnaround, Restructuring and Distressed Investing Industry Hall of Fame are examples of excellence:

- Bankruptcy attorneys
    - John (Jack) Wm. Butler, Jr., Skadden, Arps, Slate, Meagher & Flom
    - Harvey Miller, Weil, Gotshal & Manges

- Turnaround consultants
  - □ Jay Alix, AlixPartners
  - □ Dominic Dinapoli, FTI Consulting
- Financial advisors
  - □ Henry Miller, Miller Buckfire
  - □ William Repko, Evercore Partners

Why do debtors and creditors use advisors during the bankruptcy process?

Executives generally become familiar with many legal concepts during the ordinary course of business; their experience typically includes contract law, employment law, securities law, litigation, and other business-related topics. Fortunately, few executives are exposed to bankruptcy law even once—clearly they do not experience it with the frequency necessary to develop an informed perspective. Furthermore, nearly all management training on business strategy and tactics that executives receive implicitly assumes that a company has adequate liquidity.

Therefore, when dealing with the unfamiliar territory of bankruptcy law, insolvency, and illiquidity, management understandably relies especially heavily on its advisors. Indeed, in many instances, the bankruptcy advisors' roles go beyond dispensing advice and include making decisions—especially when the business questions become intertwined with complex and technical legal issues. Like most areas of the law, bankruptcy law is continually evolving with each ruling by bankruptcy courts and each change in the capital markets, so advisors are constantly updating their skills. While it is impossible to find an advisor who has mastered every aspect of every part of the bankruptcy process, it is important to choose advisors who are not training themselves at their client's expense.

A debtor-side advisor's role may include in effect acting as a therapist for executives. After all, executives often have no one else to confide in. Also, they are already fatigued as a result of the turmoil and stress that resulted in the bankruptcy. They often cannot confide their confusion, admit their mistakes, question their judgment, and ask questions of their boards of directors, their fellow executives, their direct reports, or even their families. Meanwhile, they are probably wondering about their job security and perhaps feeling guilty for leading the company down a path that caused others to lose theirs.

Likewise, an advisor to a creditors' committee may find itself representing committee members who are not very familiar with the bankruptcy process. Committee members may be representing large institutions and have little or no personal incentives to achieve a specific outcome. Moreover, such individuals usually need to give priority to the responsibilities that they have in their regular jobs and are not as focused on the bankruptcy case as their advisors are. Furthermore, the various members of the creditors' committee may have conflicting interests, so that the advisors have to serve as referee. The advisors to the creditors' committee often have to lead the committee members through complex legal and business analyses to make important decisions under tight time frames.

What role, if any, do bankruptcy courts play in overseeing advisors?

Courts serve two primary functions in overseeing advisors: ruling on conflicts of interest and approving fees and expenses.

Bankruptcy courts pay careful attention to advisors' actual and potential conflicts of interest and whether an advisor may have an interest that is adverse to that of its client. Courts enforce these rules strictly, and disclosure should be broad and inclusive. Because the reorganization process results from negotiations both between the debtor and the creditors and among the creditors themselves, it is critical that advisors represent their clients objectively and not be influenced by relationships with other parties. Especially in large bankruptcy cases, clearing conflicts among the wide cast of creditors involved can be very challenging. This is one reason why some advisors (other than attorneys, as described later) operate boutique firms rather than affiliate with large institutions with a broad base of clients. Advisors may limit their practices to the debtor side or the creditor side to further limit the potential for conflicts, while others represent a wide variety of parties. If a pre-petition advisor is owed accrued fees as of the petition date, the advisor may waive such pre-petition fees to avoid the disqualifying conflict of becoming its own client's creditor.

Prior to the 2005 BAPCPA, financial advisors and their attorneys were prohibited from representing a debtor post-petition if the financial advisory firm had served pre-petition as investment bankers for a security of the debtor, such as for a bond issuance. Congress had intended this restriction to ensure that a debtor's advisors would be neutral and would not be interested in protecting their own interests. If a debtor's advisors needed to reexamine prior transactions, conflicts could arise if the same firm that advised a company pre-petition was hired to scrutinize and critique that advice after the company collapsed. Although the SEC objected to changing the pre-BAPCPA rule, lobbyists for the securities industry succeeded in convincing Congress to amend the Bankruptcy Code to remove this provision.

How do the parties retain advisors in bankruptcy?

The parties retain their advisors by filing retention applications for approval by the bankruptcy court, after notice and a hearing, including approval of each advisor's lack of conflicts, qualifications, and compensation. A retention application is accompanied by a sworn affidavit by an officer of the advisory firm. Bankruptcy Rule 2014 requires that the contents of a retention application include the following elements:[1]

1. Specific facts showing the necessity of employing the advisor
2. The name of the person to be employed
3. The reasons for the selection
4. The professional services to be rendered
5. Any proposed arrangement for compensation
6. All of the person's connections with the debtor, the creditors, any other party in interest, their respective attorneys and accountants, the U.S. trustee, or any person employed in the Office of the U.S. Trustee

The bankruptcy court strictly construes these requirements. It is the responsibility of the professional, not the bankruptcy court, to make sure that all relevant connections have been fully disclosed.

Bankruptcy Code section 327 provides for the employment of professional advisors for the debtor,[2] while Bankruptcy Code section 1103 provides for the employment of such advisors for the creditors' committee.[3] Note that bankruptcy courts construe the word *accountants* broadly to include financial advisors, investment bankers, and other finance professionals.

The retention applications and accompanying affidavits can sometimes be useful for potential buyers. There is important contact information for the advisors. Also, the description of the scope of the advisors' role may indicate the likelihood that all or part of the company will be put up for sale, rather than reorganized.

What criteria will a court use when considering an advisor's retention application?

Bankruptcy court approval of a professional's retention application is contingent upon finding that the applicant passes a two-part test: (1) the professional must be disinterested, and (2) the professional must not hold an interest adverse to the debtor's estate. These determinations are fact-specific, and the bankruptcy court emphasizes that the applicant must make full disclosure. A failure to fully disclose the facts may be grounds for denial of the application and disqualification of the professional.

Bankruptcy Code section 101(14) defines a *disinterested person* as a person who:[4]

1. Is not a creditor, equity holder, or insider
2. Is not, and was not within two years before the petition date, a director, officer, or employee of the debtor
3. Does not have an interest materially adverse to the interest of the estate or of any class of creditors or equity holders by reason of any direct or indirect relationship to, connection with, or interest in the debtor for any other reason

While Bankruptcy Code section 327(c) requires the absence of an actual conflict of interest, the statute does not define an actual conflict of interest.[5] In practice, whether a court precludes a professional's representation depends upon a detailed consideration of the relevant circumstances, including both actual and potential conflicts of interest. Even the appearance of impropriety can be grounds for disqualification of a professional. Under certain circumstances, a client can formally waive a conflict of interest to overcome grounds for disqualification.

Are advisors barred from starting work on an engagement until they gain bankruptcy court approval?

No. As a practical matter, the process of submitting and approving retention applications involves bureaucracy. Because time is of the essence for companies that are in distress, it is important and encouraged that advisors begin work as soon as possible, without worrying that they will not be paid.

Accordingly, a bankruptcy court may retroactively approve the retention of an advisor—an action called *nunc pro tunc* (a Latin expression meaning "now for then")—because the advisor usually has already begun its engagement prior to approval. However, if a bankruptcy court denies an advisor's retention application, the advisor forfeits any accrued fees for work performed while waiting for the decision.

How do bankruptcy advisors get paid?

The Bankruptcy Code provides for compensation of advisors for the debtor[6] and the creditors' committee[7] by the debtor's estate, while the senior lenders' credit agreements usually provide for reasonable fees and expenses for attorneys and other advisors to be added to the secured loan balance. Individual creditors may retain their own advisors, but at their own expense. Such costs may not be added to the amounts of their claims.

Advisors for both the debtor and the creditors' committee are paid by the estate as administrative expenses. After being retained, each advisor files monthly fee applications with the bankruptcy court. The bankruptcy court holds a hearing to approve each fee application, after which the debtor can pay the advisor. Because the debtor in possession (DIP) lender and possibly certain pre-petition senior lenders have a security interest in the debtor's assets, they need to approve the amount of cash that the estate uses to pay the advisors to the debtor and the creditors' committee. The amount of the DIP loan that the credit agreement states can be used to pay for these advisors is referred to as the *administrative expense carveout*.

Providing bankruptcy advice can be a highly lucrative business. As comedian Robin Williams quipped, "*Carpe per diem*—seize the check!" Bankruptcy attorneys generally receive a premium hourly rate because of their expertise. Restructuring advisors—such as investment bankers—typically receive monthly fees plus success fees. In general, debtor-side advisors receive significantly higher compensation than creditor-side advisors because the creditor-side advisors' role is often limited to reviewing and objecting to the work product of the debtor-side advisors. As a rule of thumb, the compensation that debtor-side advisors will receive is three times the amounts paid to creditor-side advisors.

Professor Lynn LoPucki of the University of California at Los Angeles (UCLA) has been monitoring the amounts that advisors get paid in numerous bankruptcy cases. He created a calculator for estimating the total amount of professionals' fees in a case based upon certain assumptions, such as the amount of assets in the debtor's estate (see lopucki.law.ucla.edu/feecalculator .asp for further details). In addition, Professor LoPucki and fellow UCLA Professor Joseph W. Doherty are the authors of articles that criticize the amount of fees charged by bankruptcy professionals and warn of abuse in the system.[8] See Chapter 2 for more information on how much a bankruptcy may cost.

How do bankruptcy advisors and prospective clients typically find each other?

There is a relatively small community of bankruptcy advisors. Because they do not (they hope) receive repeat business from their clients, bankruptcy advisors typically get their clients through referrals. Sometimes advisors are able to align with investors in distressed debt who serve on creditors' committees, but they will still need to get a majority of the votes of all the committee members. Organizations such as the Turnaround Management Association (www.turnaround.org), the American Bankruptcy Institute (www.abiworld.org), and the Association of Insolvency & Restructuring Advisors (www.airacira.org) allow advisors to network and gain referrals for their next cases. For example, the American Bankruptcy Institute has more than 5,000 dues-paying members who refer to themselves as "insolvency professionals," including experts on consumer and business bankruptcies.

What about from the prospective buyer's perspective? What governing principles should a buyer keep in mind when dealing with debtor- or creditor-side advisors?

When a buyer is considering a particular distressed business, it should identify all of the advisors for the debtor(s), the official committee of unsecured creditors, and the senior lenders. The names and contact information of these advisors can be obtained from the bankruptcy docket online via PACER from their retention applications and accompanying affidavits. Then the buyer can determine if his interests are more closely aligned with those of the debtor or those of its creditors.

If a buyer wants to become a repeat purchaser of distressed businesses, she can benefit from forming relationships with multiple bankruptcy advisors to build credibility and trust. Given the urgency involved in the bankruptcy process, a buyer's credibility with the various advisors can be very important. In general, advisors are looking for sophisticated buyers who understand the intricacies of the distressed sale process, have substantial financial resources, and have proven ability to close a deal. Because the bankruptcy advisory field is a relatively small club, a buyer must manage its reputation carefully. Buyers should be concerned that their behavior in one case is likely to affect their image when negotiating subsequent transactions.

THE ROLE OF BANKRUPTCY LAWYERS

How is a bankruptcy lawyer different from a corporate lawyer?

A bankruptcy attorney is a specialist whose practice is a blend of corporate law and litigation. Bankruptcy is a niche within corporate law, and most corporate attorneys are only generally familiar with bankruptcy law. Corporate lawyers typically do not have a thorough understanding of the latest legal precedents and the nuances of the various issues that arise in bankruptcy. Moreover, corporate lawyers typically do not appear in court and are inexperienced in litigation practices and procedures.

Unfortunately, some corporate attorneys will tell existing or potential clients that they can handle their bankruptcy issues. It is strongly recommended that parties, such as a potential purchaser, who are going to get involved in a company's out-of-court workout or bankruptcy case engage a seasoned bankruptcy attorney.

What is the role of local counsel?

Most jurisdictions require the lead counsel for a bankruptcy case to be an attorney who is licensed in that jurisdiction. Because bankruptcy courts are federal, not state, courts, attorneys must be admitted to the proper federal jurisdiction. For example, if a case is filed in the Southern District of New York, the lead counsel must be admitted to practice in the Southern District of New York. These rules are designed to protect the franchises of the local law firms. For jurisdictions like the Southern District of New York, there are many law firms in Manhattan with lawyers who have been properly admitted. However, jurisdictions like the District of Delaware, which is a popular venue for bankruptcy cases because many companies are incorporated in Delaware and there is ample bankruptcy law precedent, are typically populated by law firms that do not have the resources and expertise to handle a complex bankruptcy case. Therefore, the lead firm must partner with a local counsel to administer a bankruptcy case in such jurisdictions.

The local counsel's role typically involves making routine appearances before the bankruptcy court and handling the filings with the bankruptcy court. The offices of the local counsel might be used for depositions, negotiations, and conferences. Depending on the experience and resources of the law firm and the individual attorney, a local counsel's role may become more expansive. Although law firms take steps to avoid duplication of costs, costs for communications (and miscommunications) and coordination between law firms inevitably accumulate.

National law firms such as Skadden, Arps, Slate, Meagher & Flom, LLP sometimes maintain their own offices in places like Wilmington, Delaware, to avoid the need for and expense of local counsel. Other law firms establish mutually beneficial relationships with multiple local counsel in places like Delaware for reciprocal referrals. It is common for a lead law firm to be opposed to a particular local counsel in one case and allied with the same local counsel in another case. As a result, the relationships among firms are often very close.

In Delaware, popular local counsel include

- McCarter & English, LLP
- Morris, Nichols, Arsht & Tunnell LLP
- Pachulski Stang Ziehl & Jones LLP
- Pepper Hamilton LLP
- Richards, Layton & Finger PA
- Young Conaway Stargatt & Taylor LLP

Typically, the heading of each bankruptcy docket will list the local counsel for both the debtor and the creditors' committee. To find the lead counsel, a potential purchaser will need to look at the retention applications listed on the bankruptcy docket. Most of the time, a potential purchaser will want to have direct communication with the lead counsel regarding the sales process. However, establishing a dialogue with a local counsel can sometimes be beneficial, especially if the potential purchaser thinks that the local counsel will share rumors regarding the developments in bankruptcy cases in progress and the expectations for upcoming bankruptcy cases.

So, are attorneys who are not licensed in a particular jurisdiction precluded from appearing altogether?

No, provided that the attorney has filed, and the court has approved, a *pro hac vice* application. The Latin phrase *pro hac vice* translates as "for this occasion" or "for this event." It is a legal term that refers to an attorney who is allowed to participate in a particular case even though he has not been admitted to practice in the jurisdiction of the case. Attorneys who have not been admitted to practice in the jurisdiction must submit applications to the bankruptcy court, specifically requesting that they be admitted *pro hac vice*. Without this permission, these attorneys cannot appear before the bankruptcy court for argument or trial.

Pro hac vice applications are usually approved quickly and involve minimal delay. Local counsel, if available, can appear in court for the client during the approval period for the lead counsel's *pro hac vice* applications.

What is the role of a special counsel?

When a company has industry-specific or company-specific complexities, such as being in a regulated industry or having a complicated structure, the debtor will retain special counsel to deal with these limited issues. While the debtor's law firm may employ leading bankruptcy experts, it may not possess the appropriate resources or expertise in other areas. Often, the debtor will employ its pre-petition corporate counsel as a special counsel in the bankruptcy case because those lawyers are most familiar with the complex nonbankruptcy areas, such as environmental, union, pension, and litigation issues.

Bankruptcy courts usually apply a three-part test regarding whether an application to employ special counsel should be approved:

1. Whether appointment is in the best interests of the debtor's estate
2. Whether counsel holds an adverse interest to the debtor's estate with respect to the matter for which the attorney may be employed
3. Whether the special purpose is so broad that it encompasses nearly the entire bankruptcy case

In general, bankruptcy courts are predisposed to rule against special counsel in order to avoid increasing overall fees and other administrative expenses unnecessarily. If the debtor gets to employ special counsel, the creditors' committee may feel that it also needs to employ its own special counsel with similar expertise, and so on.

Who are the leading business bankruptcy law firms?

As attorneys change firms, law firms merge, and bankruptcy cases conclude, the list of leading bankruptcy law firms is constantly in flux. Publications like *The Deal* (see pipeline.thedeal.com for details) track the top law firms by active cases (for those firms that self-report) and prepare lists at regular intervals. Within each industry and jurisdiction, there are usually specific firms that have the best reputations, so it is worth investigating referrals, checking references, and asking questions. Also, some firms are more experienced at advising debtors, others focus on creditors' committees, and some work with individual creditors. Exhibit 7-1 contains a representative list of leading bankruptcy law firms, which is by no means exhaustive. The increasing complexity of bankruptcy cases has nearly ended the era of boutique bankruptcy law firms, and today's bankruptcy practices exist within firms whose practices span nearly all forms of corporate, securities, litigation, employment, pension, environmental, tax, and intellectual property legal work.

How much do bankruptcy lawyers get paid?

While it is difficult to draw broad conclusions, the trend clearly has been toward higher fees, with the most sought-after bankruptcy lawyers commanding fees in excess of $1,000 per hour. Particularly in the era of U.S.

Exhibit 7-1 Representative Law Firms Serving as Lead Counsel for Bankruptcies

Lead Counsel for Bankruptcies
Akin Gump Strauss Hauer & Feld LLP
Bingham McCutchen LLP
Blank Rome LLP
Bryan Cave LLP
Cadwalader, Wickersham & Taft LLP
Duane Morris LLP
Greenberg Traurig LLP
Holland & Knight LLP
Jones Day
King & Spalding LLP
Kirkland & Ellis LLP
Klee, Tuchin, Bogdanoff & Stern LLP
Kramer Levin Naftalis & Frankel LLP
Latham & Watkins LLP
LeBoeuf, Lamb, Greene & MacRae LLP
Lowenstein Sandler PC
Morgan, Lewis & Bockius LLP
Pachulski Stang Ziehl & Jones LLP
Reed Smith LLP
Saul Ewing LLP
Skadden, Arps, Slate, Meagher & Flom LLP
Weil, Gotshal & Manges LLP
White & Case LLP
Winstead PC

government-led bailouts, this has created some public relations challenges for the bankruptcy advisory industry as a whole (and not just attorneys), as evidenced by the discussion in Chapter 2 of this book about fees and expenses in the Lehman Brothers case exceeding $1 billion.

Such challenges aside, the precise amount that bankruptcy lawyers are paid is generally subject to negotiation with the potential client on the front end, and then (at least on the debtor's side) subject to court approval on the back end. Fees might differ depending on which constituency the attorney is representing (e.g., the creditor side or the debtor side), the size of the assignment (e.g., the total pre-petition funded debt), the level of complexity (e.g., the number of creditors and the expected level of contentiousness), and supply/demand factors for bankruptcy lawyers at that given time.

Exhibit 7-2 ranks bankruptcy lawyers' hourly fees, first from the standpoint of debtor's counsel and then from the perspective of creditor's counsel. Generally, debtor-side work commands higher fees because, as noted previously, the creditor-side role consists mostly of reviewing and objecting to the work product of the debtor-side attorneys.

Exhibit 7-2 Ranking of Bankruptcy Lawyers' Hourly Fees

Debtor's Counsel

	Firm	Case	Year	Hourly Fee
1	Jones Day	Chrysler LLC	2009	$1,175
2	Paul, Weiss	Samsonite Company	2009	$1,025
3	Kirkland & Ellis	Atrium Corp.	2010	$995
4	Gibson, Dunn & Crutcher	Building Materials	2009	$995
5	Simpson Thacher & Bartlett	Qimonda Richmond	2009	$980
6	Kirkland & Ellis	Dura Automotive	2006	$975
7	Paul, Weiss	Progressive Moulded	2008	$975
8	Kirkland & Ellis	Majestic Star Casino	2009	$965
9	Kirkland & Ellis	Lear Corp.	2009	$965
10	Kirkland & Ellis	DBSD North America	2009	$965

Creditors' Committee Counsel

	Firm	Case	Year	Hourly Fee
1	Cooley Godward Kronish	Linens Holding Co.	2008	$780
2	Akin Gump Strauss Hauer & Feld	Pegasus Satellite	2004	$775
3	Cooley Godward Kronish	Shoe Pavilion Inc.	2008	$760
4	Bingham McCutchen	NRG Energy Inc.	2003	$750
5	Bingham McCutchen	Parmalat Finanziaria	2003	$750
6	Cooley Godward Kronish	Shoe Pavilion Inc.	2008	$750
7	Bingham McCutchen	Outboard Marine	2000	$750
8	Bingham McCutchen	EOTT Energy Partners	2002	$750
9	Bingham McCutchen	Teleglobe Inc.	2002	$750
10	Bingham McCutchen	Global TeleSystems Inc.	2002	$750

Source: pipeline.thedeal.com.

THE ROLE OF FINANCIAL ADVISORS

Do all debtors have financial advisors?

No. Not all debtors formally engage financial advisors to provide investment banking services, such as capital raising and divestitures, and the
Bankruptcy Code does not require that a financial advisor be retained.
However, in more complex cases, financial advisors are typically involved
to perform complicated financial analyses, manage sale processes, and participate in creditor negotiations. If the debtor does not select a financial
advisor, it may rely upon its chief financial officer and other internal
resources to carry out the fund-raising and sale processes. Alternatively, the
debtor may expect its attorneys and crisis managers to take on the role of
financial advisor because they are already familiar with the company's
assets, operations, and industry.

The DIP lender may influence the debtor's decision on whether to
have separate financial advisors, crisis managers, accountants, and so on,
by minimizing the size of the administrative expense carveout.

How does a restructuring advisor differ from a traditional investment banker?

All of the legal, financial, accounting, tax, diligence, and valuation issues
discussed in this book make the job of a restructuring advisor significantly
more challenging than that of a traditional investment banker. There are
many disciplines—such as bankruptcy law—that a restructuring advisor
must master in addition to understanding traditional investment banking
areas, such as M&A. While traditional investment bankers rarely interact
with courts, restructuring advisors often submit sworn affidavits, may serve
as expert witnesses, and regularly file applications for fees and expense
reimbursement with the bankruptcy court.

Restructuring advisors are functional experts and industry general-
ists, whereas traditional investment bankers typically develop deep industry expertise. Financial advisors for troubled companies must exhibit a high
degree of creativity because their deals tend to vary so broadly, with diverse
facts and issues.

With respect to clients, traditional investment bankers usually work
with management teams that have ample resources to answer financial,

accounting, operational, and other questions about the company's past and future performance. On the other hand, restructuring advisors often need to fill in the gaps themselves. Whereas most traditional investment banking assignments last weeks or months, a restructuring advisor may work on a variety of issues within the same bankruptcy case for years.

Regarding compensation, restructuring advisors typically receive monthly fees to cover overhead expenses, whereas traditional investment bankers nearly always do not. Both types of financial advisors typically receive success fees for meeting the objectives of the deal.

Who are the leading restructuring advisory firms?

Over the past decade, there has been a proliferation of firms providing restructuring advisory services. Following the changes in conflict-of-interest rules in the 2005 BAPCPA, an increasing number of investment banks have sought to add restructuring groups as countercyclical hedges to their traditional businesses. Similar to tracking business bankruptcy law firms, publications like *The Deal* track the top restructuring advisory firms by active cases (for those firms that self-report). Exhibit 7-3 contains a representative list of restructuring advisors; however, it is by no means exhaustive.

What does a typical engagement for a financial advisor entail?

This will depend largely upon whether the advisor is working for one of the creditors' committees, the debtor, or some other constituent and whether the assignment involves an out-of-court workout or a Chapter 11 reorganization. As described previously, creditor-side work often focuses more on reviewing and objecting to the work product of the debtor-side advisors. To illustrate common engagement terms, the following list summarizes the services that financial advisor Houlihan Lokey agreed to perform on behalf of the unsecured creditors' committee for the Thermadyne Holdings case in 2002:

- Evaluate the assets and liabilities of the debtors and their subsidiaries
- Analyze and review the financial and operating statements of the debtors

- Evaluate all aspects of any debtor financing or exit financing in connection with any plan
- Provide valuation or other financial analyses as the committee may require
- Assess the financial issues and options concerning a sale of the debtor or reorganization plan
- Prepare, analyze, and explain any plan to the committee.
- Provide testimony

Exhibit 7-3 Representative Restructuring Advisors

Restructuring Advisors
BDO Capital Advisors
Blackstone Group
Brown Gibbons Lang & Company
Carl Marks & Co.
Conway Del Genio Gries & Co.
Duff & Phelps
Evercore Partners
Gleacher & Company
Gordian Group
Greenhill & Co.
Houlihan, Lokey, Howard & Zukin
Imperial Capital
Jefferies & Co.
KPMG Corporate Finance
Lazard
Loughlin Meghji & Company
Macquarie Capital
Mesirow Financial
Miller Buckfire & Co.
Moelis & Co.
Navigant Capital Advisors
Perella Weinberg Partners
Peter J. Solomon Co.
Rothschild
SSG Capital Advisors

In addition to drafting the documents in the previous list, debtor-side work may also involve capital-raising activities, whether in the form of DIP, unsecured, equity, or other financing. Typically, these services will involve a success fee that is linked to the amount of capital raised—similar to capital raising or M&A in the context of a going concern.

How are financial advisors paid during a bankruptcy engagement?

Whereas bankruptcy lawyers are paid by the hour, investment banks offering restructuring services are typically paid a monthly retainer plus a success fee. For the very largest cases, the monthly retainer may range from $175,000 on the low end to as much as $400,000 on the high end. Success fees also vary greatly; one analysis contained in the bankruptcy pleadings for General Growth Properties shows success fees in 30 transactions from 2001 to 2010 ranging from $6 million on the low end to $30 million on the high end. (See Exhibit 7-4.) As a general guideline, the parties may target financial advisory fees in a range of 0.10 to 0.20 percent of the debtor's total pre-petition funded debt. Capital raising would typically involve an additional layer of fees. Here, again, though, there will be many exceptions and outliers.

THE ROLE OF TURNAROUND CONSULTANTS

How do turnaround consultants differ from traditional management consultants?

One way to think about this question is to view turnaround consultants (sometimes also referred to as *crisis management* consultants) as a subset of the broader universe of management consultants. As a general rule, traditional management consulting will focus on high-level corporate strategy. For instance, a traditional print publisher might hire a management consultant to develop a strategy for entering or expanding its presence in electronic media. Another example might be an emerging-growth business that brings in an operational or IT consultant with expertise in just-in-time inventory management for tactical help in

Exhibit 7-4 Selected Debtor-Side Investment Banking Fees for Cases from April 2001 to January 2010 with Debt above $3 Billion

Bankruptcy Case	Petition Date	Average Monthly Fee	Success Fee ($MM)	Est. Total Fees ($MM)	Pre-Petition Debt ($BN)	Est. Total Fees as % of Pre-Petition Debt
General Motors	06/01/09	$400,000	$30.0	$36.2	$74.4	0.05%
CIT Group	11/01/08	$350,000	$30.0	$34.9	$62.3	0.06%
Lehman Brothers	09/15/08	$400,000	$17.5	$24.7	$613.0	0.00%
Lyondell Chemical	01/06/09	$350,000	$18.5	$22.1	$24.0	0.09%
XO Communications	06/07/02	$250,000	$20.0	$20.5	$6.7	0.31%
SemGroup	07/22/08	$300,000	$15.0	$20.4	$3.1	0.66%
WorldCom	07/21/02	$300,000	$15.0	$20.4	$30.8	0.07%
Pacific Gas & Electric Co.	04/06/01	$225,000	$20.0	$20.0	$13.4	0.15%
Delphi Corp.	10/08/05	$250,000	$15.0	$19.5	$5.4	0.36%
Conseco, Inc.	12/17/02	$250,000	$16.0	$19.0	$5.1	0.37%
Calpine	12/20/05	$250,000	$14.0	$18.5	$17.2	0.11%
Nortel Networks	01/14/09	$250,000	$15.0	$18.0	$4.6	0.39%
Charter Communications	03/27/09	$250,000	$16.0	$17.5	$21.8	0.08%
Tribune Company	12/08/08	$200,000	$14.0	$17.0	$13.0	0.13%
UAL Corp.	12/09/02	$217,000	$15.0	$16.4	$16.8	0.10%
AbitibiBowater Inc.	04/16/09	$308,000	$10.0	$16.3	$6.7	0.24%
US Airways (2002)	08/11/02	$250,000	$16.0	$16.0	$7.8	0.20%
Williams Communications	04/22/02	$200,000	$12.0	$15.6	$5.6	0.28%
Enron	12/02/01	$281,000	$10.0	$15.1	$9.2	0.16%
R.H. Donnelley Corp.	05/28/09	$200,000	$13.0	$14.6	$10.0	0.15%
Extended Stay	06/15/09	$200,000	$13.0	$14.2	$7.4	0.19%
Delta Air Lines	09/14/05	$200,000	$10.5	$14.1	$17.0	0.08%
Kmart	01/22/02	$225,000	$12.5	$13.5	$4.7	0.29%
Lear Corporation	07/07/09	$250,000	$10.9	$13.1	$3.5	0.37%
Adelphia	06/25/02	$225,000	$13.0	$13.0	$16.3	0.08%
Capmark Financial Group	10/25/09	$250,000	$12.5	$12.5	$8.9	0.14%
Mirant Corp.	07/14/03	$225,000	$7.0	$11.1	$8.6	0.13%
Idearc Inc.	03/31/09	$300,000	$9.0	$10.2	$9.3	0.11%
Smurfit-Stone	01/26/09	$250,000	$9.0	$10.0	$4.1	0.24%
US Airways (2004)	09/12/04	$175,000	$6.0	$7.6	$6.1	0.12%

Source: General Growth Properties' bankruptcy pleadings.

improving its inventory-control system. Other companies may engage a management consulting firm to assist with integrating the operations of a recent acquisition.

Turnaround consulting continues along this continuum toward increased operational consulting. (See Exhibit 7-5.) As a general rule, turnaround consultants become actively involved in their clients' businesses, often taking on a very limited number of assignments at any given time. Such consultants' roles frequently involve stepping in as interim management (e.g., chief restructuring officer), thereby bringing a fresh perspective as well as experience in distressed situations. The turnaround consultant

Exhibit 7-5 The Management Consulting Continuum

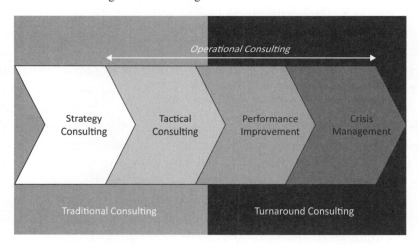

will also often be charged with rapidly reining in expenses and stemming cash outflow, including taking over control of certain vendor relationships. Finally, many turnaround consultants will often lead an overhaul of the company's balance sheet, including engaging in active dialogues with banks and other creditors, working out loans, raising capital, or even selling the business.

Another way in which traditional consultants differ from turnaround consultants may be how they are viewed by corporate management. That is, a skeptic might argue that some managers bring in traditional management consultants to evaluate a problem as an insurance policy ("Well, I agree that this strategy didn't work, but it was the consultant's idea"), whereas many managers might not have the humility to admit that the business has deteriorated to such an extent that a turnaround consultant is needed.

Who are the leading turnaround consultants?

The pioneer in turnaround consulting is Jay Alix, founder of AlixPartners and, later, the distressed private equity firm Questor. Based in Detroit, Michigan, since 1981, Alix recognized that the automotive industry needed a special type of consulting that was not being offered by traditional consulting firms, such as McKinsey & Co., Boston Consulting Group, Bain

Consulting, and Booz Allen Hamilton. The turnaround consulting industry then grew as a practice area of the leading accounting firms, who saw the opportunity to expand their services to troubled clients. Over the last decade, a complex maze of mergers, acquisitions, initial public offerings, defections, and recruitment has created a robust industry of independently branded turnaround consulting firms. Today, there are two tiers of turnaround consulting firms: firms that supply legions of consultants for mega-cases—like General Motors or Lehman Brothers—and firms that provide smaller teams of primarily senior-level talent to focus on turnarounds and workouts for middle-market companies. Firms in each tier will often compete in the other's markets.

In addition, the crisis management industry is populated by numerous "single-shingle" consultants who have developed a strong network of relationships among bankruptcy attorneys, lenders' workout groups, and boards of directors. Usually, these individuals have developed their strong reputations through outstanding performance on a challenging case. By maintaining low overhead and offering only senior-level expertise, these consultants offer a discreet, effective, reasonably priced alternative to hiring branded turnaround consulting firms, which may produce undesired publicity.

Exhibit 7-6 contains a table of representative crisis management firms in each tier. Publications like *The Deal* also track the top firms by active cases (for firms that self-report) and prepare lists at regular intervals. Many of these firms will also provide financial advisory work for troubled clients if the debtor does not want to engage a separate restructuring advisor. Some of them have other financial advisory practice areas that generally do not involve bankruptcy work, enabling them to serve their clients long after a bankruptcy case concludes. FTI Consulting, for instance, also offers economic consulting, litigation consulting, strategic communications, and technology consulting, among other areas.

How could the selection of a turnaround consultant trigger lender liability?

Lenders are supposed to be passive participants who do not manage the day-to-day operations of the borrower. When the borrower defaults on its loan or otherwise becomes distressed, however, lenders understandably

Exhibit 7-6 Leading Turnaround Consulting and Crisis Management Firms

Turnaround Consulting and Crisis Management	
Tier I—Megacases	**Tier II—Middle Market**
AlixPartners	Alliance Management
Alvarez & Marsal	Bridge Associates
Capstone Advisory Group	Buccino & Associates
FTI Consulting	Conway MacKenzie & Dunleavy
Kroll Zolfo Cooper	CRG Partners
Mesirow Financial	Donlin Recano
	GlassRatner
	Grant Thornton
	Huron Consulting Group
	Marotta Gund Budd & Dzera
	MorrisAnderson & Associates
	NachmanHays
	Qorval
	Traxi
	XRoads Solutions

become concerned. A lender may seek to have the borrower retain a turn-around consultant to assist the borrower's management in improving performance and addressing the issues that are causing the distress.

The borrower, on the other hand, may consider the turnaround consultant to be a spy for the lender, helping the lender improve its situation in a bankruptcy or liquidation. Moreover, the borrower's management may be in denial regarding its predicament and may resist the lender's efforts to involve a turnaround consultant. Furthermore, the borrower's management may be optimistic about its financial forecast and its ability to generate improved revenue, earnings, and cash flow. If the lender pushes too hard, it may risk lender liability because it is becoming active in deciding how the company is managing its day-to-day operations.

In such circumstances, it has become a standard practice for the lender to recommend three turnaround consultants and for the borrower to choose one from the lender's list.

What does a typical engagement for a turnaround consultant entail?

One of the most common services that a turnaround consultant provides is creating and updating a 13-week cash flow forecast for the company. Depending upon the nature of the company's distress, a turnaround consultant may also provide one or more of the following types of services:

- Production
  - Lean manufacturing
  - Six Sigma strategies
  - Plant consolidation
- Supply chain
  - Inventory reduction
  - Vendor streamlining
  - Asia outsourcing
- Marketing
  - Stock-keeping unit (SKU) rationalization
  - Pricing reevaluation
  - Product revitalization
- Customer service
  - New customer acquisition
  - CRM software installation
  - Billing and collections fixes
- Human resources
  - Compensation realignment
  - Benefits cost savings
  - Union negotiations
- Financial restructuring
  - Liquidity management
  - Standard cost updating
  - Working capital reduction

THE ROLE OF THE U.S. TRUSTEE

What is the role of a U.S. trustee during a bankruptcy proceeding?

As stated in the U.S. Trustee Program mission statement: "The [U.S. Trustee Program] Mission is to promote integrity and efficiency in the nation's bankruptcy system by enforcing bankruptcy laws, providing oversight of private trustees, and maintaining operational excellence."[9] To further the public interest in the just, speedy, and economical resolution of cases filed under the Bankruptcy Code, U.S. trustees monitor the conduct of the parties in bankruptcy cases, oversee related administrative functions, and act to ensure compliance with applicable laws and procedures.

As explained by the U.S. courts:

> The U.S. trustee plays a major role in monitoring the progress of a chapter 11 case and supervising its administration. The U.S. trustee is responsible for monitoring the debtor in possession's operation of the business and the submission of operating reports and fees. Additionally, the U.S. trustee monitors applications for compensation and reimbursement by professionals, plans and disclosure statements filed with the court, and creditors' committees. The U.S. trustee conducts a meeting of the creditors, often referred to as the "section 341 meeting," in a chapter 11 case. 11 U.S.C. § 341. The U.S. trustee and creditors may question the debtor under oath at the section 341 meeting concerning the debtor's acts, conduct, property, and the administration of the case.
>
> The U.S. trustee also imposes certain requirements on the debtor in possession concerning matters such as reporting its monthly income and operating expenses, establishing new bank accounts, and paying current employee withholding and other taxes. Should a debtor in possession fail to comply with the reporting requirements of the U.S. trustee or orders of the bankruptcy court, or fail to take the appropriate steps to bring the case to confirmation, the U.S. trustee may file a motion with the court to have the debtor's chapter 11 case converted to another chapter of the Bankruptcy Code or to have the case dismissed.
>
> In North Carolina and Alabama, bankruptcy administrators perform similar functions that U.S. trustees perform in the remaining forty-eight states. The bankruptcy administrator program is administered by the Administrative Office of the United States Courts, while the U.S. trustee program is administered by the Department of Justice. For purposes of this publication, references to U.S. trustees are also applicable to bankruptcy administrators.[10]

How does a bankruptcy trustee differ from a U.S. trustee?

Although both roles contain the word *trustee*, the two concepts are very different. As described in Chapter 4 of this book, a bankruptcy trustee takes control of the debtor's estate, usurping the role of the debtor in possession. The bankruptcy trustee manages the day-to-day operations of the company and negotiates all aspects of the bankruptcy process, including a plan of reorganization or liquidation. On the other hand, a U.S. trustee is involved in the legal administration of a bankruptcy case and does not get involved in the business.

Where is the U.S. Trustee Program located within the federal government?

The U.S. Trustee Program is a component of the Department of Justice. The attorney general appoints U.S. trustees and assistant U.S. trustees. The Executive Office for U.S. Trustees in Washington, D.C., provides general policy and legal guidance, oversees the program's substantive operations, and handles administrative functions. The director of the Executive Office, whose authority is derived from the attorney general, oversees a staff composed of the Offices of the Director, General Counsel, Administration, Review & Oversight, and Research & Planning. The Executive Office also provides administrative and management support to individual U.S. trustee offices in their implementation of federal bankruptcy laws. When identifying and investigating bankruptcy fraud and abuse, U.S. trustees may coordinate with U.S. attorneys, the Federal Bureau of Investigation, and other law enforcement agencies.

Where can I find information about the U.S. Trustee Program?

Visit www.justice.gov/ust or call (202) 307-1399.

How are U.S. trustees paid?

U.S. trustees are paid from the debtor's estate. By law, the debtor in possession must pay a quarterly fee to the U.S. trustee until the case is converted or dismissed.[11] The amount of the quarterly fee, which may range from $250 to $10,000, depends on the amount of the debtor's disbursements during each quarter.

If all of the parties (e.g., debtors, lenders, creditors' committees, management, and equity holders) agree on a certain matter, can a U.S. trustee nevertheless object?

Yes. In fact, objecting in such circumstances is one of the most important functions of the U.S. trustee program. If all of the parties have conspired to corrupt the integrity of the bankruptcy process in order to build consensus, it is the duty of the U.S. trustee to object and urge the bankruptcy court to deny the relief sought.

THE ROLE OF THE EXAMINER

What is the role of a bankruptcy examiner in a Chapter 11 proceeding?

Under Bankruptcy Code section 1106(a)(3), an examiner who is appointed in a Chapter 11 bankruptcy case is obligated to "investigate the acts, conduct, assets, liabilities, and financial condition of the debtor, the operation of the debtor's business and the desirability of the continuance of such business, and any other matter relevant to the case or to the formulation of a plan," unless ordered otherwise. Bankruptcy Code section 1106(a)(4) states that the examiner must, among other things, "file a statement of any investigation conducted . . . including any fact ascertained pertaining to fraud, dishonesty, incompetence, misconduct, mismanagement, or irregularity in the management of the affairs of the debtor, or to a cause of action available to the estate." If the bankruptcy examiner's report includes such facts, this can help claimants recover funds by suing the individuals or institutions involved, so that claimants against a bankrupt entity are not limited to the assets of the entity, but can look for deep pockets elsewhere.

How common are examiners in bankruptcy cases?

The appointment of an examiner by the bankruptcy court is an extraordinary event. Unless there are serious issues that warrant the introduction of a new participant, there is no need to increase the costs of administering the debtor's estate. After all, the bankruptcy court itself and the U.S. trustee are already neutral, objective participants in the bankruptcy proceeding.

In addition, the adversarial process between the debtor and the creditors should result in one side or the other evaluating all relevant aspects of the case. The need for an examiner arises when circumstances compel the parties to seek a time-consuming analysis that requires the expertise of an outside specialist. Usually, there are issues involving the "elephant in the room" that no one wants to discuss—perhaps because of conflicts of interest. Other times, the issues involve criminal or dysfunctional aspects of the bankruptcy process that require more serious attention.

If a potential purchaser encounters a case in which an examiner has been appointed or may be appointed, this could be a warning sign that the case is in disarray, mired in gridlock, or otherwise in a procedural bind. The purchaser should be wary of wasting time on these cases because decisions on a sale process could be significantly delayed, and it may not be clear who will ultimately make the decisions. On the other hand, sometimes the confusion can work to the purchaser's advantage, especially if it chases away other potential bidders.

Jenner & Block's examiner report on Lehman Brothers is a timely (albeit extreme) example of a case in which an examiner's report was necessary. The document, which runs thousands of pages, took more than a year to complete and cost more than $30 million. As discussed in Chapter 3 of this book, the Lehman Brothers bankruptcy filing is widely identified as being the final catalyst that drove the largest global contraction since the Great Depression. While the report, written by court-appointed examiner Anton Valukas (chairman of Jenner & Block), is probably best remembered for its depictions of risk-control abuses at Lehman, the report also dedicated more than 300 pages to balance sheet manipulation, accusing Lehman of using accounting methods to move assets off its books.

While an exhaustive discussion of such accounting methods is beyond the scope of this book, the following attempts to summarize one of the (multiple) headline issues succinctly:

- Major financial institutions regularly engage in transactions in the so-called repo market. This market, in effect, is a source of short-term liquidity; the financial institution sells an asset and simultaneously agrees to buy it back in a few days. The proceeds, which typically go to fund daily operations, are thus outstanding for only a few days in most cases. Typical repo transactions are disclosed as cash flows from financing activities; the assets stay on the balance sheet, as does the corresponding debt obligation.

- According to the examiner's report, Lehman regularly engaged in transactions that firm insiders dubbed *Repo 105* structures. In such transactions, the assets sold represented 105 percent or more of the cash that the firm received in return. This had a distinct advantage over a typical repo transaction: accounting rules allowed the transactions to be treated as "sales" instead of financings. As a result, the assets left Lehman's balance sheet and the Repo 105 transaction reduced the amount of debt that the firm showed to investors. Reportedly, Lehman's own global financial controller told the examiner that "the only purpose or motive for the transactions was reduction in balance sheet" and "there was no substance to the transactions."

Another extreme example of circumstances warranting an examiner's report was the WorldCom bankruptcy. Chapter 3 of this book discusses this case, which essentially led to the Sarbanes-Oxley Act of 2002, in greater detail.

THE ROLE OF THE INFORMAL COMMITTEE OF CREDITORS

Certain creditors may decide to form a suballiance within their own official committee in order to organize for negotiations with other parties, share the expenses of advisors, and facilitate communications about the case. Such committees are called "informal" or "ad hoc" committees because they are not given official authority under the Bankruptcy Code the way the official committee of unsecured creditors and the official committee of equity holders are. The Bankruptcy Code gives the bankruptcy court the authority to appoint additional committees of creditors upon request by a party in interest.[12]

A common situation in which an informal committee is formed is when secured noteholders or second-lien creditors band together to address the issues resulting from their being situated between secured lenders and unsecured creditors. Plaintiffs in mass litigation may also find benefits in forming an informal committee when the defendant enters bankruptcy.

How do creditors form an informal committee?

Usually, law firms will facilitate the formation of informal committees in the hopes of being retained to represent them. Sometimes, a lead creditor will assemble other creditors. Often, the formation of an informal committee will occur prior to the debtor's entering bankruptcy so that the creditors can engage in out-of-court negotiations.

Who serves on an informal committee?

While the Bankruptcy Code specifies that official committees have seven members, there are no rules for informal committees. As a result, the represented creditors may decide on their own structure.

What are the duties of an informal committee?

When forming an informal committee, represented creditors may decide to establish bylaws similar to those used by an official committee of unsecured creditors. However, because informal committees exist outside of the Bankruptcy Code, they have no statutory duties to perform.

What authority does an informal committee possess?

Because it represents creditors who are interested parties in the debtor's case, the informal committee usually has the authority to object to the debtor's motions and to make its own motions to the bankruptcy court. The informal committee's bylaws may give it the authority to bind the represented creditors in negotiations with the debtor and other creditors.

Who advises an informal committee?

The informal committee typically engages a law firm, sometimes hires a financial advisor, and perhaps employs other advisors. Because the creditors that the committee represents are probably responsible for the fees and expenses involved, the informal committee understandably wishes to keep its costs low.

Does an informal committee have the right to retain advisors at the estate's expense?

While the informal committee probably does not have a right to be reimbursed for its advisors' fees and expenses, the creditors represented by the informal committee may be able to negotiate for such reimbursement in exchange for their votes on a plan of reorganization or other matters. It is often unclear whether the informal committee will be reimbursed until after the costs have been incurred.

THE ROLE OF THE OFFICIAL COMMITTEE OF EQUITY HOLDERS

Can shareholders get a committee to represent their interests in a reorganization plan under Chapter 11?

Upon request, the U.S. trustee may appoint a shareholders' committee. If one is not appointed, the bankruptcy court may order its appointment if shareholders may have a real interest in the case.

Also, as long as the company is not hopelessly insolvent, shareholders can ask the bankruptcy court to appoint an equity committee that would extend the focus of the court beyond the creditors.[13] This is a rare practice—one attorney specializing in it said that he found only six examples out of hundreds he researched—but it does happen.[14] However, the rise in so-called solvent debtors in 2010 has resulted in an increase in the number of equity committees. The goal of such a committee and its advisors would be to obtain as much value as possible in a plan of reorganization or liquidation.

Finally, there are many ways in which shareholders can petition the bankruptcy court to protect their rights. For example, the Official Committee of Equity Security Holders in the Chapter 11 reorganization of Adelphia Communications actively pursued multiple legal initiatives, including to terminate the debtor's exclusivity period, to force the company to hold a shareholders' meeting to elect directors, to encourage a sale of the company's cable assets, to object to the proposed deal protections to be granted to a proposed buyer, to join the creditors' committee's lawsuit against the company's pre-petition commercial banks and lenders and assert new claims, and to appeal the confirmation of the plan of reorganization.

How is an official committee of equity holders formed?

While the Bankruptcy Code makes the formation of an official committee of unsecured creditors by the U.S. trustee mandatory, the formation of an official committee of equity holders is optional for the U.S. trustee.[15] If the U.S. trustee decides to form an official committee of equity holders, the bankruptcy court must approve the decision.

Alternatively, any interested party may request the appointment of an official committee of equity holders if it is necessary to represent the interests of equity holders at any point in the bankruptcy proceeding.[16] If the bankruptcy court approves the request, it will direct the U.S. trustee to appoint the committee.

Upon the request of a party in interest, the bankruptcy court may order a change in the membership of an official committee of equity holders to ensure adequate representation of the equity holders.[17] A change may be necessary, for example, if some holders have sold shares during the course of the bankruptcy case.

According to Bankruptcy Code section 1102(b)(2), the U.S. trustee forms the official committee of equity holders by selecting the seven largest equity holders that are willing to serve.[18]

What are the factors that the bankruptcy court will consider with regard to the formation of an official committee of equity holders?

In general, equity holders that are seeking to form an official committee face a heavy burden of proof. The formation of an official committee of equity holders is extraordinary relief that should be granted as the rare exception. After all, if the equity holders are clearly in-the-money, the company should have been able to avoid a bankruptcy as a threshold matter. The bankruptcy process is supposed to involve insolvency, which necessarily means that the equity holders are out-of-the-money. Therefore, the overarching concern when appointing an official committee of equity holders is whether the equity holders are looking to pursue a free option that wastes precious assets of the debtor's estate or whether they have legitimate interests to protect.

The bankruptcy court will review a motion to appoint an official committee of equity holders to determine whether (1) there is a substantial likelihood that the equity holders will receive a meaningful distribution in the case, and (2) the equity holders are unable to represent their interests without an official committee. Equity holders must provide persuasive evidence that there is a substantial likelihood that they will be in-the-money; mere speculation is inadequate. If the official committee of unsecured creditors is already serving as an effective advocate for junior investors and sufficiently challenging the debtor's reorganization process, the bankruptcy court may find that the interests of equity holders are adequately represented.

The bankruptcy court may also consider the timing of the request to appoint an official committee of equity holders. A request made early in the case may impose expenses that are too onerous, especially given that the company has just recently determined that bankruptcy is its best option. A request made late in the case may interfere with negotiations between the debtor and the creditors. During the course of a bankruptcy case, however, the company's operations may improve significantly, the capital markets may become more favorable, and/or damaging factors may be resolved to such a degree that equity holders may become convinced that their investment once again has value. Indeed, overly optimistic arguments by the unsecured creditors might motivate the equity holders to believe that they should resume advocating for themselves.

A potential purchaser should be wary of getting in the middle of a dispute over whether an official committee of equity holders should be formed because the purchaser's bid may become fodder for a court battle between unsecured creditors and equity holders. Letters of intent and verbal indications of value may become the subject of scrutiny by various parties. The potential purchaser may even end up having to testify before the bankruptcy court regarding the valuation of the company. Ultimately, the argument between the unsecured creditors and the equity holders may result in a consensual plan of reorganization rather than a sale, disappointing the potential purchaser and wasting her time.

Does the official committee of equity holders have a right to retain advisors at the estate's expense?

Yes. The official committee of equity holders has a right to retain a law firm and perhaps other advisors, pursuant to Bankruptcy Code section 1103.[19] The expense of these professionals is borne by the debtor's estate. Therefore, if the equity holders are, in fact, out-of-the-money, it is a particularly onerous burden for the creditors to have to pay for frivolous services out of their partial recoveries.

THE ROLE OF CLAIMS AGENTS

What is the role of a claims agent in a bankruptcy case?

Acknowledging that the technological and administrative complexities of managing large bankruptcy cases are beyond the budgets and capabilities of the bankruptcy court clerks and staff, bankruptcy courts will typically approve a debtor's request to employ a claims agent.

A claims agent may be employed to deal with

- Claims management, including Internet access to general claim schedule information, proofs of claim, and case data
- Noticing and communication, including high-speed duplication and mailing services to ensure timely and accurate preparation of first-day orders, notices of 341 meetings, bar date notices, claims, motions, and exhibits
- Balloting and solicitation for plans of reorganization
- Disbursement of proceeds to creditors, including calculating cash and security payments by class and establishing reserves for disputed claims
- Virtual data rooms, including information for potential lenders and purchasers

What are some examples of firms that serve as claims agents?

There are many companies that provide claims agent services. The following firms are listed as approved agents by the Bankruptcy Court for the Southern District of New York (see www.nysb.uscourts.gov/claimsagents.html):

- Administar Services Group (www.administarllc.com)
- BMC Group (www.bmcgroup.com)
- CPT Group (www.cptgroup.com)

- Delaware Claims Agency (www.delawareclaimsagency.com)
- Donlin, Recano & Company (www.donlinrecano.com)
- Epiq Systems (www.epiqbankruptcysolutions.com)
- J.P. Morgan Trust Company (www.jpmorgan.com/visit/settlement)
- Kurtzman Carson Consultants (www.kccllc.com)
- Logan & Company (www.loganandco.com)
- Phase Eleven Consultants (www.phaseeleven.com)
- Poorman-Douglas Corporation (www.poorman-douglas.com)
- Omni Management Group (www.omnimgt.com)
- The Altman Group (www.altmangroup.com)
- The Garden City Group (www.gardencitygroup.com)
- XRoads Case Management Services (www.xroadscms.com)

How do claims agents get paid?

A claims agent's fees and expenses are borne by the debtor's estate.

THE ROLE OF LIQUIDATORS AND APPRAISERS

What are the roles of liquidators and appraisers in a bankruptcy case?

Liquidators, who often also provide appraisal services, play a valuable role in the bankruptcy case by disposing of unwanted assets, generating much-needed liquidity for the insolvent company. Unwanted assets may include excess inventory, underperforming stores, obsolete machinery, extraneous fixtures, unused trademarks or patents, uncollected accounts receivable, nonperforming loans, and other such items. Liquidating these unwanted assets may be critical for salvaging the company's remaining business, which may become viable once underperforming operations are discontinued. Disposition services may range from offering guaranteed asset value recoveries to marketing and managing asset auctions to acting as a liquidation consultant. Liquidators' clients are primarily drawn from the retail, financial, and manufacturing industries.

In retail bankruptcies, such as those of Linens 'n Things and Circuit City, liquidators play an especially important role by promptly and efficiently converting store inventories into cash. These situations are known as going-out-of-business (GOB) sales, and the liquidator's efforts may produce the bulk of the proceeds that are available for creditors' recoveries. Indeed, the initial estimates of the appraised value that can be generated from GOB sales may trigger controversy among the parties if it appears that the secured lenders are undersecured. Seasoned liquidators have nearly perfected the formula for maximizing recoveries through GOB sales with increasing discounts as the weeks go by. Moreover, they optimize the staffing levels in each store and spur sales with effective advertising techniques. Furthermore, experienced liquidators sometimes bring in *new* merchandise to increase sales volume during GOB sales by taking advantage of heightened advertising and peak consumer traffic.

A potential buyer of the remainder of a distressed company should pay close attention to the opinions of liquidators and appraisers concerning the company and the industry. Often, the Web sites of liquidators contain real-time information about assets that are for sale.

What are some examples of leading liquidators?

While there are many regional firms across the country that can dispose of certain assets, firms that specialize in large bankruptcy liquidations include Gordon Brothers Group (www.gordonbrothers.com), Great American Group (www.greatamerican.com), Hilco (www.hilcotrading.com), Maynards Industries (www.maynards.com), and SB Capital Group (www.sbcapitalgroup.com). In addition to these generalist liquidators, several firms specialize in disposing of real estate and unexpired leases, including the real estate group at KPMG Corporate Finance (www.kpmg.com) and DJM Realty (www.djmrealty.com). Furthermore, there are Web-only auction sites, such as eBay, that can be used for liquidating individual items.

How do liquidators and appraisers get paid?

If they are working for a fee, such as when creating an appraisal report, liquidators and appraisers may be paid directly by the debtor, subject to bankruptcy court approval. As mentioned previously, however, many liquidators are willing to pay the debtor's estate—instead of being paid—a guaranteed minimum value for the disposable assets and then profit from the spread between this amount and the ultimate selling price. In other cases, the liquidator and the estate may split the upside from an auction or arrange a commission schedule.

THE ROLE OF GOVERNMENT AGENCIES

Will the SEC protect investors in a bankruptcy?

Generally, the SEC's role is limited, but it will include the following:

- Reviewing the disclosure document to determine whether the company is giving investors and creditors certain information that they need to know
- Ensuring that stockholders are represented by an official committee, if this is appropriate

Although the SEC does not negotiate the economic terms of reorganization plans, it may take a position on important legal issues that will affect the rights of public investors in other bankruptcy cases as well. For example, the SEC might step in if it believes that the company's officers and directors are using the bankruptcy laws to shield themselves from lawsuits for securities fraud.[20]

How does the FDIC participate in the financial distress of financial institutions?

There is a long string of distressed acquisitions related to banks seized by the FDIC (www.fdic.gov). Nonperforming loans plagued banks during the recent financial downturn well into 2010, spurring fire sales—FDIC-assisted transactions have ranged from small local transactions, such as the Bank of Upson (Thomaston, Georgia) assuming the deposits of Century Security Bank (Duluth, Georgia) in March 2010,[21] to multibillion-dollar mergers. Big bank examples include BB&T's purchase of Colonial BancGroup ($25.5 billion in total assets, in August 2009),[22] IMB Management's takeover of IndyMac ($23.5 billion, in March 2009),[23] and BBVA Compass's acquisition of Guaranty Bank ($12.0 billion, in August 2009).[24] From the buyer's perspective, FDIC-assisted deals remove most of the credit uncertainty as a result of favorable loss-sharing agreements.[25]

The rising wave of potential bank failures undoubtedly contributed to the FDIC's decision in August 2009 to adopt new rules that allow and encourage private equity firms to buy failed banks.[26] Under the new rules, private equity firms are required to hold on to failed banks for at least three years; investors are required to maintain high-quality capital—commonly called "Tier 1 common equity"—equal to 10 percent of the bank's overall assets (compared to the 15 percent Tier 1 leverage requirement that the FDIC previously sought); and private equity-owned banks are restricted from extending credit to their investors and some affiliates.[27]

However, the FDIC subsequently narrowed the potential involvement of private equity in the takeover of failed banks when, in the November 6, 2009, press release announcing the FDIC-assisted sale of United Commercial Bank (San Francisco, California) to East West Bancorp (Pasadena, California), the agency disclosed that it "encourages private equity participation in failed bank acquisitions through private investment in established holding companies."[28]

What is the PBGC?

The *Pension Benefit Guaranty Corporation* (PBGC; www.pbgc.gov) is a federal corporation created by the Employee Retirement Income Security Act (ERISA).[29] It currently protects the pensions of more than 44 million American workers and retirees in more than 29,000 private single-employer and multiemployer defined-benefit pension plans. The PBGC receives no funds from general tax revenues; its operations are financed by insurance premiums set by Congress and paid by sponsors of defined-benefit plans, investment income, assets from pension plans entrusted to the PBGC, and recoveries from the companies that were formerly responsible for the plans.

What other regulatory agencies are typically involved in distressed M&A transactions?

Antitrust regulators, specifically the Federal Trade Commission and the Department of Justice, might become involved depending on the circumstances. Chapter 10 of this book discusses the role of antitrust in distressed M&A, with a particular focus on the so-called failing firm defense.

Other, industry-specific regulators might also be involved, depending on the specific sector at issue. Certain highly regulated industries, such as financial services, will encounter an unusually large number. For instance, a banking deal might involve the FDIC, the Office of the Comptroller of the Currency (OCC), the U.S. Department of Treasury, and the Office of Thrift Supervision (OTS), among others, depending upon the size and complexity of the transaction and other factors surrounding it. As discussed in Chapter 2, The Wall Street Reform and Consumer Protection Act of 2010, known as the Dodd-Frank Act, is changing the regulatory framework for financial institutions and setting new guidelines for bankruptcy of financial institutions.

All of these players participate in various aspects of the distressed M&A process, including the financing, valuation, due diligence, accounting, tax, and legal issues that are discussed in the next section.

Endnotes

1. See Fed. R. Bankr. P. 2014.
2. See 11 U.S.C. §327.
3. See 11 U.S.C. §1103.
4. See 11 U.S.C. §101(14).
5. See 11 U.S.C. §327(c).
6. See 11 U.S.C. §§327, 328, 329, 330.
7. See 11 U.S.C. §§328, 330, 1103(a).
8. See Lynn LoPucki and Joseph W. Doherty, "Professional Overcharging in Large Bankruptcy Reorganization Cases," *Journal of Empirical Legal Studies* 5, (2008), p. 983; "Rise of the Financial Advisors: An Empirical Study of the Division of Professional Fees in Large Bankruptcies," *American Bankruptcy Law Journal* 82 (2008), pp. 141–174; and "The Determinants of Professional Fees in Large Bankruptcy Reorganization Cases," *Journal of Empirical Legal Studies* 1, (2004), pp. 111–142.
9. Department of Justice, U.S. Trustee Program, "Strategic Plan & Mission"; available at http://www.justice.gov/ust/eo/ust_org/mission.htm, last accessed April 22, 2010.
10. U.S. Courts, "Reorganization under the Bankruptcy Code"; available at http://www.uscourts.gov/bankruptcycourts/bankruptcybasics/chapter11. html#trustee, last accessed August 30, 2010.
11. See 28 U.S.C. §1930(a)(6).
12. See 11 U.S.C. §1102(a)(2).
13. Ibid.
14. The source for this material on shareholders' committees is Jonathan Rosenthal of Saybrook Capital, Santa Monica, advisor to both Kmart and Adelphia. He cautions, in an article posted on both the Turnaround Management Association Web site (tma.org) and BusinessWeek Online (bwonline.com): "Having an equity panel doesn't guarantee shareholders a better shake, but at least they

have a fighting chance. . . . Once you gain official status, you have a very different standing in the courtroom. The judge will listen to you, and the company is obligated to pay for your legal and financial advisers."

15. See 11 U.S.C. §1102(a)(1).
16. See 11 U.S.C. §1102(a)(2).
17. See 11 U.S.C. §1102(a)(4).
18. See 11 U.S.C. §1102(b)(2).
19. See 11 U.S.C. §1103.
20. See http://www.sec.gov/answers/bankrup.htm, last accessed August 30, 2010.
21. See http://www.fdic.gov/bank/individual/failed/cent-security.html, last accessed August 30, 2010.
22. Eric Dash, "BB&T Takes Over Failing Colonial BancGroup," *New York Times*, August 14, 2009; available at http://www.nytimes.com/2009/08/15/business/15bank.html, last accessed May 17, 2010.
23. See http://www.fdic.gov/bank/individual/failed/IndyMac.html, last accessed August 30, 2010.
24. PR Newswire, "BBVA Compass Acquires the Banking Operations of Guaranty Bank," August 21, 2009; available at http://www.prnewswire.com/news-releases/bbva-compass-acquires-the-banking-operations-of-guaranty-bank-62282437.html, last accessed August 30, 2010.
25. The FDIC Web site has an excellent Q&A resource for loss sharing. See http://www.fdic.gov/bank/individual/failed/lossshare/index.html, last accessed May 17, 2010.
26. Russell J. Bruemmer et al., "FDIC Releases Final Policy Statement Governing Private Equity Investments in Failed Banks," WilmerHale, August 27, 2009; available at http://www.wilmerhale.com/publications/whPubsDetail.aspx?publication=9242, last accessed May 17, 2010.
27. Ibid.
28. See http://www.fdic.gov/news/news/press/2009/pr09201c.html, last accessed August 30, 2010.
29. The discussion that follows is drawn largely from the PBGC Web site (www.pbgc.gov). Like those of other federal regulatory agencies, this site provides an excellent primer of the basic terminology and principles necessary for understanding this complex area.

Avoiding Common Pitfalls

Astute maneuvering to avoid thorny tax, accounting, and legal pitfalls will lead to above-average investment returns. In distressed situations, the answers are rarely obvious and, as they say, the devil is in the details. In order to determine the optimal strategy for distressed M&A, buyers and sellers must navigate through many tactical issues before they can arrive at their goal of ownership or sale. These undertakings may be intricate, time-consuming, and mind-numbing, but within them lies opportunity for those who persevere and think creatively. While nearly all of the topics discussed in this chapter require the advice of seasoned professionals, the client cannot leave these professionals on autopilot. In most distressed situations, the tax, accounting, and legal issues are intertwined with financial, operational, and industry challenges. Even the best legal and accounting professionals are typically not equipped to think cross-functionally to this extent and may not even have all the information about the company's situation that they need if they are to do so.

Therefore, project leaders must actively police the intersection to coordinate the input from accountants and lawyers with reports from management, consultants, and investment bankers to arrive at a robust analysis. This means that the project leaders must be prepared to scrutinize, monitor, and challenge the detailed findings and conclusions of legal and accounting professionals, rather than simply accepting their initial responses. Project leaders should take care to select legal and accounting professionals who are skilled in the unusual exceptions, caveats, and unwritten rules that often complicate distressed situations. Accordingly, a company's existing outside experts may move outside of their comfort zones without realizing it, leaving their clients without meaningful answers or clear solutions. See Chapter 7 of this book for a discussion of advisors who specialize in distressed situations.

A favorable deal structure typically involves carefully crafting a comprehensive strategy that balances all of the data and opinions from various experts. The process is often iterative and involves going back and forth among various aspects of the deal until an equilibrium of sort is reached. This challenge often conjures up the image of wrestling with a water balloon— when you finally have one portion under control, another part pops out. With patience and out-of-the-box thinking, however, there may indeed be a narrow path out of the chaos facing a distressed company.

To prepare distressed M&A project leaders for these complexities, this pivotal section of our book tackles two distinct clusters of accounting issues: first, the world of workouts, with its emphasis on troubled debt restructuring, debt extinguishments, and loan modifications; and second, bankruptcy, including the ins and outs of net operating losses and so-called fresh start reporting. As this overview demonstrates, no two distressed situations are exactly alike but there are key lessons from past examples that can be applied to future predicaments. The section ends with a broad overview of legal risk in distressed M&A, focusing on fiduciary duties, antitrust law, and fraudulent transfers in the context of distressed transactions, including both out-of-court workouts and bankruptcies.

CHAPTER 8

Accounting for Workouts: TDRs, Extinguishments, and Modifications

The hardest thing in the world to understand is the income tax.

—*Albert Einstein*

INTRODUCTION TO ACCOUNTING FOR DISTRESSED COMPANIES

When during the distressed M&A process should buyers sharpen their focus on accounting and tax issues?

If the mere mention of FASB or IRS rules causes your eyes to glaze over, fear not—even Einstein was bewildered by the complexity of accounting and tax regulations. Nevertheless, navigating such regulations is an essential step in nearly every distressed acquisition. Some elements, such as the preservation of net operating losses and other tax attributes, are highly sensitive to the structure of the transaction, meaning that a change in structure can materially change the return profile of a particular opportunity. As a result, we urge deal makers to consider accounting and tax factors as early in the restructuring process as possible—despite the fact that some rules can seem highly technical (if not downright arcane).

In general, there are three primary inflection points during the restructuring continuum that can potentially affect a company's book and tax accounting. These inflection points are[1]

- Restructuring debt in an out-of-court workout
- Filing a petition under Chapter 11 of the Bankruptcy Code
- Emerging from a bankruptcy process via either a 363 sale or a stand-alone plan of reorganization

After providing some basic accounting and tax definitions, this chapter summarizes some of the financial reporting and income tax consequences of out-of-court workouts, including troubled debt restructurings. Then, Chapter 9 describes some of the accounting and tax issues that frequently arise during a bankruptcy process. This discussion addresses the preservation of net operating losses and provides an overview of fresh start reporting, a process that every restructured business must undertake, but on which there is surprisingly very little literature.

> *Caveat 1*: Tax laws and accounting principles affecting distressed M&A are often in a state of flux, changing at a pace that ranges from glacial reform to lightning speed.
>
> *Caveat 2*: Always consult with qualified tax and accounting professionals.

DEFINING TAX BASIS

What is basis?

The *basis* in an asset is the value at which the taxpayer carries the asset on its balance sheet for tax purposes. An asset's initial basis is subsequently increased by capital expenditures (i.e., improvements and betterments) and decreased by depreciation, amortization, and other charges, becoming the taxpayer's *adjusted basis* in the asset. The adjusted basis in the asset represents, in effect, the remaining cost of the asset that may be recovered either through depreciation deductions or through proceeds from a sale. Upon such sale, the difference between the sale proceeds and the adjusted basis is the gain or loss for tax purposes.

Which is more beneficial to the owner of an asset, a high tax basis or a low tax basis?

A high tax basis in an asset is almost always more beneficial to its owner than a low tax basis because it can reduce tax liabilities. The higher the basis, the greater the depreciation or amortization deductions (if allowable), and the smaller the gain (or the greater the loss) on the subsequent disposition of the asset.

How does tax basis influence acquisition structure for traditional M&A?

The purchase of a company as a going concern should generally be structured so as to maximize the tax basis of the assets acquired.

When a purchaser acquires the assets of a going concern directly, and the acquired corporation is subject to tax on the sale or exchange of the assets, the basis of the assets for the purchaser is their cost. This is called *cost* or *stepped-up basis*. When a purchaser acquires the assets of a going concern indirectly, through the purchase of the stock of that entity, the basis of the assets in the possession of the target is generally not affected. This is called *carryover basis* because the basis of an asset in the acquired corporation "carries over" despite the change of stock ownership.

If a purchaser's prospective cost basis for the assets of the acquired corporation exceeds its prospective carryover basis, an asset acquisition or step-up transaction is generally more beneficial to the purchaser than a stock acquisition. If a purchaser's prospective carryover basis exceeds its prospective cost basis in the assets of the acquired corporation, a stock acquisition is generally more beneficial to the purchaser than an asset, or cost-basis, acquisition. This is summarized in Exhibit 8-1.

The primary exceptions to these preferences are situations in which (1) the purchaser would acquire beneficial tax attributes—net operating losses, tax credits, or accounting methods—in a carryover-basis transaction that would be lost in a step-up transaction (this is often the case in a distressed scenario), and (2) the value of such tax attributes to the purchaser

Exhibit 8-1 Tax Basis in Asset versus Stock Acquisitions

Transaction Type	Seller	Purchaser	When Preferred
Asset (direct purchase)	Subject to tax on sale of its assets	Stepped-up basis = purchase price	When a purchaser's stepped-up basis would exceed its carryover basis
Stock (indirect purchase)	Not subject to tax on sale of its assets	Carryover basis = seller's adjusted cost basis	When a purchaser's carryover basis would exceed its stepped-up basis

exceeds the value of the stepped-up basis in the acquired corporation's assets that it would have obtained in a cost-basis transaction.

The seller (especially if it is not a publicly held company) may have offsetting concerns about the tax (and legal) attributes of a taxable or tax-free purchase and an asset versus a stock sale. For instance, depending on a number of factors (e.g., corporate structure, tax basis, net operating losses, and so on), the seller may potentially face unfavorable tax consequences by selling assets instead of stock. Likewise, if the seller disposes of selected assets but retains certain liabilities that the buyer did not want to assume, the seller may still be on the hook for those liabilities. Differences such as these are likely to become part of the negotiation of the terms of the deal and reflected in the purchase price.

The tax and legal treatment of going-concern acquisitions is discussed at length in *The Art of M&A Structuring: Techniques for Mitigating Financial, Tax, and Legal Risk*—a companion book in *The Art of M&A* series.

How do considerations regarding basis change in the context of distressed M&A?

When the target has significant unrealized tax losses resulting from high-basis, low-value assets, the acquirer is likely to have a strong interest in *preserving the tax attributes* of the debtor. This can be a highly critical step in structuring a distressed acquisition; in fact, these unrealized losses are often among the debtor's most valuable assets because they potentially can be used to shield future income of the reorganized entity from income taxes.

In contrast, the acquirer may place a lower priority on preserving the tax attributes of the debtor when the target does not have significant built-in tax losses, or when such losses would be partially or fully eliminated because of the Internal Revenue Code's (IRC's) loss limitation rules (e.g., a Section 382 limitation, as discussed in Chapter 9).

What determines whether an acquirer will be able to preserve the tax attributes of the debtor?

This is an issue that is subject to numerous statutory, regulatory, and judicial requirements, many of which are addressed throughout this chapter and the next. Typically, the key issue is whether the reorganization is structured as a tax-free or a taxable transaction. The different treatment of basis in tax-free versus taxable distressed acquisitions is similar to the tax treatment of basis in stock versus asset deals in traditional M&A. The general rule is that tax-free transactions result in a carryover basis and preserve the tax attributes of the debtor, whereas taxable transactions lead to a stepped-up basis and do not preserve such attributes.

All else equal, a tax-free structure that preserves the tax attributes of the debtor may be possible if (1) the historical creditors are receptive to exchanging their claims for either debt or equity in the distressed entity, or (2) the assets of the debtor are transferred to a third-party acquirer and the creditors receive equity in the third-party acquirer in settlement of their claims.

A taxable transaction is a more likely outcome where (1) the creditors do not wish to continue to hold an interest (whether in the form of debt or equity) in the debtor after the transaction, (2) a third-party acquirer does not wish to use stock to fund the transaction, or (3) the tax attributes will be subject to significant loss limitations or are otherwise not economically attractive.

ACCOUNTING AND TAX CONSEQUENCES OF RESTRUCTURING DEBT OUTSIDE OF BANKRUPTCY

What are the most common accounting and tax issues that can arise in an out-of-court restructuring?

As described earlier in this text, an out-of-court restructuring can take many different forms; these may include a modification of credit terms, a debt-for-debt swap, a debt-for-equity swap, or an outright debt extinguishment, among other alternatives. The recurring tax/accounting issue among these, as well as in the majority of out-of-court restructurings, is whether such transactions create income to the company.

From an accounting perspective, when does an out-of-court debt restructuring create income?

The general rule from an accounting standpoint is that an extinguishment of debt generates an accounting gain (or loss) for the issuing company.

However, the specific treatment depends upon the structure, facts, and circumstances of a particular restructuring. As noted earlier, such out-of-court restructurings can take many forms. Broadly speaking, three forms are most common:

1. An *asset swap*, pursuant to which the lender settles the loan in full or in part in exchange for a particular asset. The borrower books two potential gains or losses: (a) a gain or loss upon disposition of the asset, based on the difference between the carrying amount and the fair value of that asset, and (b) a gain upon the debt restructuring, based on the difference between the carrying amount of the debt and the fair value of the asset tendered.

2. A *debt-for-equity swap*, pursuant to which the lender converts the loan to equity of the borrower. As a general rule, the borrower will typically realize a gain if the creditor accepts equity that is worth less than the total amount of debt due.

3. A *modification of debt terms*, or a *debt-for-debt swap*, pursuant to which the borrower and the lender formally agree to new lending terms—whether in the form of a straight modification or via the issuance of a new debt instrument. The accounting treatment of a transaction such as this hinges on several factors, the first of which is whether the transaction qualifies as a *troubled debt restructuring*, or *TDR* (a subset of the broader universe of modified loans).

    (a) In the event that the transaction qualifies as a troubled debt restructuring, the debtor must book a gain in the year of extinguishment—but only to the extent that the gross cash flows of the new debt instrument are less than the carrying amount of the old debt instrument (that is, whether total cash payments under the new agreement are less than the carrying amount of the debt). Exhibit 8-2 contains an illustration of this scenario.

    (b) If, on the other hand, the gross cash flows of the new instrument are expected to exceed the previous instrument's carrying amount, the debtor has no restructuring gain or loss to book. Instead, the debtor accrues the difference between the original instrument's carrying amount and the new restructured cash payments as interest expense, over the life of the new payment schedule. Exhibit 8-3 illustrates an example.

Exhibit 8-2 TDR Accounting: Debtor Books a Gain

3 (a). Modification of Debt Terms

Initial facts: Assume that the debtor (D) has borrowed $60 million from a creditor (C) at a stated annual interest rate of 12 percent. The loan has two years remaining on it. Because of financial problems, D missed the interest payment from this past year. As illustrated here, the carrying value of the loan is currently $67.2 million.

Loan amount	$60,000,000
Annual interest rate	12%
Annual interest payment	$7,200,000
Carrying value:	
Loan principal	$60,000,000
Missed interest payment	7,200,000
Carrying value	$67,200,000

Modification Scenario 1: C agrees to a workout of the loan with D, pursuant to which C agrees to (a) waive the $7.2 million of accrued interest, (b) cut the remaining two interest payments to $3 million each from $7.2 million each, and (c) reduce the maturity value of the loan to $45 million from $60 million. As illustrated here, the gross cash flows of the new loan are $51 million.

First interest payment	$3,000,000
Second interest payment	3,000,000
New maturity value	45,000,000
Future cash flows	$51,000,000

As a result, the debtor has a gain of $16.2 million, the difference between the original loan's carrying value of $67.2 million and the new instrument's future cash flows of $51.0 million.

Carrying value	$67,200,000
Less: Future cash flows	(51,000,000)
Gain to debtor	$16,200,000

Exhibit 8-3 TDR Accounting: Debtor Books No Gain *(Continues)*

Modification Scenario 2: Assume the same initial facts as in Exhibit 8-2. Instead of the facts in Restructuring Scenario 1, however, C agrees to simply accept $75 million in two years in settlement for the entire loan. Because the gross cash flows of the new instrument, $75 million, are greater than the carrying value of the existing loan, $67.2 million, D does not book any gain or loss on the day of the workout.

However, D must still calculate the effective interest rate on the new loan and book noncash interest expense in each year that the loan remains outstanding. The new effective interest rate is calculated (essentially, an internal rate of return, or IRR, calculation) as 5.64 percent.

Carrying value (Yr 0)	$67,200,000
Interest payment (Yr 1)	-
Interest payment (Yr 2)	-
Settlement value (Yr 2)	75,000,000
New effective interest rate	**5.64%**

In each of the remaining two years of the loan, D books interest expense. The first-year expense accrual is $3.8 million, while the second-year accrual is $4.0 million. This is illustrated as follows:

Year 1 Interest Expense	
Carrying value	$67,200,000
New effective interest rate	5.64%
Year 1 Interest Expense	$3,792,957

Year 2 Interest Expense	
Carrying value	$70,992,957
New effective interest rate	5.64%
Year 2 Interest Expense	$4,007,043

Finally, we note that the carrying value of the loan must increase each year by the amount of interest expense that was only an accrual and not paid in cash. In this case, the loan became zero coupon. As a result, the carrying value accretes up to the redemption value over the remaining two years of the loan. This is illustrated here:

Exhibit 8-3 TDR Accounting: Debtor Books No Gain *(Continued)*

Carrying value (Yr 0)		$67,200,000
Interest accrual (Yr 1)	$3,792,957	
Carrying value (Yr 1)		70,992,957
Interest accrual (Yr 2)	4,007,043	
Carrying value (Yr 2)		75,000,000

How does a transaction qualify as a troubled debt restructuring?

In order for a modification to qualify as a troubled debt restructuring, the creditor must grant a concession to the debtor that the creditor would not consider other than for economic or legal reasons related to the borrower's financial difficulties.[2] The following are examples of concessions that would be significant enough to qualify under this definition:

1. A reduction in the stated absolute or contingent interest rate for the remaining original life of the debt
2. An extension of the maturity date at a favorable interest rate
3. A reduction in the absolute or contingent face or maturity amount of the debt
4. A reduction in the absolute or contingent amount of accrued interest

Accordingly, not all loan modifications will qualify as troubled debt restructurings. For instance, assume that a debtor with good credit and adequate collateral value wants to restructure an asset-backed loan to take advantage of lower rates that are being offered in the marketplace. This concession in rates is not the result of the borrower's financial difficulties, and so it would not be considered a troubled debt restructuring.

What if the transaction does not meet the criteria for a troubled debt restructuring? What are the accounting ramifications?

If the transaction does not qualify as a troubled debt restructuring, the next question is whether the new instrument has "substantially different terms" from the previous debt instrument.

If the two instruments do, in fact, have substantially different terms, the transaction is likely to be considered a debt extinguishment for accounting purposes, giving rise to an accounting gain or loss for the borrower. This has the following carryover effects:

- The new debt instrument should initially be recorded at fair value. That amount should be used to determine the debt extinguishment gain or loss to be recognized and the effective rate of the new instrument.
- Fees paid by the debtor to the creditor are to be associated with the extinguishment of the old debt instrument and included in determining the debt extinguishment gain or loss to be recognized.
- Costs incurred with third parties that are directly related to the exchange or modification (e.g., legal fees) are to be associated with the new debt instrument and amortized over the term of the new debt instrument using the interest-rate method in a manner similar to debt issue costs.

If the instruments do not have substantially different terms, the transaction will probably be considered a loan modification. In this situation,

- There is no extinguishment of debt and no immediate gain or loss for accounting purposes. The borrower must calculate a new effective interest rate based on the carrying amount of the original debt and the revised cash flows. The carrying amount is adjusted for an increase (but not a decrease) in the fair value of an embedded conversion option (calculated as the difference between the fair value of the embedded conversion option immediately before and after the modification or exchange) resulting from the modification, as well as the revised cash flows.
- Fees paid by the debtor to the creditor are to be associated with the replacement or modified debt extinguishment and, along with any existing unamortized premium or discount, amortized as an adjustment of interest expense over the remaining term of the replacement or modified debt instrument using the interest method.

Exhibit 8-4 Decision Tree: Workout Accounting

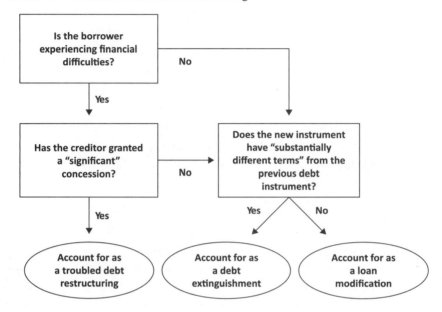

■ Costs incurred with third parties that are directly related to the exchange or modification should be expensed as incurred.

Exhibit 8-4 contains a flowchart that walks through the key decision points in determining whether a particular debt-for-debt swap should be accounted for as a TDR, debt extinguishment, or a loan modification.

What determines whether a nontroubled debt restructuring involves a new instrument with "substantially different terms" from the previous instrument?

Any of the following three conditions would fall within the definition of *substantially different terms*:

1. The present value (PV) of the cash flows under the terms of the new debt instrument is at least 10 percent different from the present value of the remaining cash flows under the terms of the original instrument.

2. A modification or an exchange that affects the terms of an embedded conversion option, from which the change in the fair value of the embedded conversion option (calculated as the difference between the fair value of the embedded conversion option immediately before and after the modification or exchange) is at least 10 percent of the carrying amount of the original debt instrument immediately prior to the modification or exchange.

3. A modification or an exchange of debt instruments that adds a substantive conversion option or eliminates a conversion option that was substantive at the date of the modification or exchange.

Exhibit 8-5 contains a sample analysis of a particular situation.

Exhibit 8-5 Sample Analysis of Loan Workout *(Continues)*

Facts: D borrows $10 million from C on January 1, 2011, with a stated interest rate of 13 percent and a 10-year term. Following an extended period of declining interest rates, during which time D has achieved its internal plan, D and C agree on January 1, 20x5, to lower the rate to 10 percent, and C increases the size of the loan to $15 million. The original 10-year term remains unchanged.

Question 1: Is this a TDR?

Per Exhibit 8-4, the borrower is not experiencing financial difficulties. As a result, the transaction is not a TDR, but rather either a loan modification or a debt extinguishment. Question 2 hits on the key determining factor for which of these two the workout is.

Question 2: Does the new instrument have "substantially different terms" from the original instrument?

The answer to this question depends on whether the PV of the future cash flows under the terms of the new debt instrument is at least 10 percent different from the PV of the future cash flows under the terms of the original instrument. This analysis is summarized here:

The present value of cash flows in this case changed 15.8 percent, which exceeds the 10 percent threshold. As a result, the new instrument does, in fact, have "substantially different terms" from the original loan. Debt extinguishment, not loan modification, accounting would be appropriate.

Exhibit 8-5 Sample Analysis of Loan Workout *(Continued)*

Original principal:	$10,000,000	New principal:	$15,000,000
Original interest rate:	13%	New interest rate:	10%
Discount rate (same as interest rate):	13%	Discount rate (original interest rate):	13%
Remaining term (yrs):	5.0	Remaining term (yrs):	5.0

PV of original loan	$10,000,000	PV of principal on modified loan	$8,141,399
		PV of interest on modified loan	5,275,847
		Less: Add'l principal on modified loan	(5,000,000)
Less: PV of modified loan	(8,417,246) ◄———	Present value of modified loan	$8,417,246
Change in PV of cash flows, $	$1,582,754		
Change in PV of cash flows, %	15.8%		

What about changes to a borrower's revolving credit facility? How does that affect the borrower's financial reporting?

An out-of-court workout frequently may also involve changes to a borrower's revolving credit facility. The accounting impact of a transaction such as this will depend on the *borrowing capacity* of the new facility compared to that of the old facility. The borrowing capacity is the product of the remaining term and the maximum credit available.

If the borrowing capacity of the new facility is greater than or equal to that of the previous facility, the borrower should defer fees paid to the creditor, third-party costs, and unamortized costs from the previous facility and amortize them over the term of the new facility.

In contrast, if the borrowing capacity of the new facility is less than that of the previous facility, the borrower should make two adjustments: (1) defer fees paid to the creditor and third-party costs, and amortize them over the term of the new facility, and (2) expense unamortized costs from the previous facility in proportion to the decrease in borrowing capacity, and amortize the remaining deferred costs over the new facility's term.

What about income tax consequences? Under what circumstances does a debt restructuring generate taxable income?

While the terminology used here differs modestly from that used in bankruptcy accounting guidance, the same general principle applies: a taxable event occurs, in the form of *cancellation of debt (COD) income*, when an issuer settles debt at a discount to its face value.

What is COD income, and how is it treated in an out-of-court workout scenario?

As a general rule, the cancellation of indebtedness by a creditor for less than the amount owed results in taxable COD income to the debtor. This rule originated in the Supreme Court case of *United States v. Kirby Lumber*,[3] and was subsequently codified in Section 61(a)(12) of the IRC. There are several exceptions to this rule, codified in Section 108(a) of the IRC, under which COD income is not taxed. These exceptions, which are particularly relevant in the case of insolvency or a formal bankruptcy filing, are outlined in greater detail in Chapter 9.

Out-of-court workouts frequently do not qualify for one of these exceptions (unless the debtor is insolvent). Creditors rarely agree to simply reduce the amount owed in an out-of-court debt restructuring;[4] most transactions involve a discounted debt buyback, an equity-for-debt swap, a debt-for-debt exchange, or a modification of debt terms. The tax treatment of each of these alternatives usually depends on the facts and circumstances of the specific case. However, the legal test is whether the exchange or modification is treated as the issuance of a new instrument (whether debt, equity, or a blend thereof) in exchange for the existing debt instrument.

The following is a broad framework for high-level consideration:

1. *Does the transaction involve an exchange or modification of privately held debt?* The IRC generally does not tax such transactions. In most cases, so long as the outstanding loan balance is not reduced and the interest rate payable on the modified debt is at least equal to the Applicable Federal Rate (AFR)[5] at the time of modification, no COD income will result from the debt modification, even if the modification is otherwise significant.

2. *Does the transaction involve a modification of debt that is publicly traded for tax purposes, but without a "significant" change in terms?* If so, the IRC generally treats such transactions in the same manner as privately held debt.

3. *Does the transaction involve an exchange of debt that is publicly traded for tax purposes (whether debt-for-debt or debt-for-equity)?* If so, the transaction generally gives rise to taxable COD income to the issuing corporation in the amount by which the fair market value of such debt exceeds its tax basis.

4. *Does the transaction involve an exchange of publicly traded debt for equity, including a sweetener to induce conversion?* In such circumstances, the company may net the value of this sweetener against the COD income, thereby lowering the amount of taxable income that the transaction creates—provided, however, that the transaction does not result in a retirement premium.

Note that a transaction that qualifies, under the rules just given, as a debt exchange for tax purposes should also be evaluated for potential limitations on the deductibility of interest on the new instrument. Tax deductibility of interest on the new instrument will generally be subject to limitations in three situations:

1. The new instrument is deemed to be *equity for tax purposes.* A new instrument is more likely to be considered debt the more it satisfies a number of conditions, including whether the new instrument has a fixed maturity date that is not extended too far into the future, whether the obligation to repay the debt is unconditional, whether the creditor has reasonable remedies upon default, and so on.

2. The new instrument is issued with significant *original issue discount* (OID), which is the excess of a debt instrument's stated redemption price at maturity over its issue price, and triggers the other requirements of an *applicable high-yield discount obligation* (AHYDO). In particular, any zero coupon bond or payment-in-kind debt instrument with a maturity greater than five years must be analyzed for AHYDO attributes. If the debt instrument is classified as an AHYDO,[6] a portion of the applicable interest deduction may be deferred until the interest is actually paid in cash, and a portion may be disqualified permanently—even if it is eventually paid.

3. The new instrument is a *disqualified debt instrument.* This generally arises when a "substantial amount" of the interest or principal of the new instrument is payable in, or determined with reference

to the value of, the equity of the debtor (or a related party). This scenario can arise in the context of a convertible debenture or similar instrument. Where conversion is optional (whether at the issuer or the holder's option), the instrument is considered to be disqualified debt only if the option is "substantially certain" to be exercised. The threshold for "substantially certain" is unsettled; however, it would probably be considered a reasonable reporting position that an out-of-the-money convert does not trigger this threshold. The situation with an at-the-money convert is less clear, but it also probably is not an issue because of the high threshold implied by the "substantially certain" terminology. In the event that the new instrument is, in fact, disqualified debt, none of the interest is deductible—even if it is paid.

What is a "significant modification" of debt terms?

Treasury Regulation §1.1001-3(c)(1)(i) defines a *modification* as "any alteration, including any deletion or addition, in whole or in part, of a legal right or obligation of the issuer or a holder of a debt instrument, whether the alteration is evidenced by an express agreement (oral or written), conduct of the parties, or otherwise." Carved out of this definition are changes in rights or obligations that automatically occur pursuant to the original terms of the instrument. In addition, a simple forbearance of interest falls outside the definition of modification, as long as the period is limited to two years and the parties make no other changes in the debt instrument.

Whether a modification is *significant* hinges on whether the parties' legal rights and obligations are altered to a degree that is "economically significant." To this end, merely adding, deleting, or altering customary accounting or financial covenants generally does not constitute a significant modification.

In contrast, changes that generally would be considered economically significant, and thus a significant modification, would include the following:[7]

1. A change in the instrument's yield, other than a *de minimis* change. When the debt instrument is fixed rate, is variable rate, or follows an alternative payment schedule, the *de minimis* threshold is the greater of changes in annual yield of 25 basis

points or 5 percent of the annual yield of the unmodified instrument. Contingent payment debt instruments cannot use this de minimis exception.

2. A *material deferral* of scheduled payments. The term *material* is subject to a facts and circumstances test. Nonetheless, as a safe harbor threshold, a debtor can generally assume that a deferral is not material if the deferral period does not exceed the lesser of five years or 50 percent of the original term of the debt instrument.

3. A *change in the obligor or the security*. The substitution of an obligor is considered a significant modification, unless the underlying debt is nonrecourse.

4. A *change in payment expectations* (e.g., changing priority or collateral, changing from recourse to nonrecourse or vice versa, and so on).

5. A *change in the nature of the debt instrument*. This includes the scenario in which the debt is converted into an instrument that is no longer debt for tax purposes.

When is debt considered publicly traded for tax purposes?

Debt is *publicly traded for tax purposes* if, at any time 30 days before or after the issue date, it[8]

- Is traded on a registered national securities exchange, interdealer quotation system, or certain foreign exchanges
- Is traded on a designated contract market or interbank market
- "[A]ppears on a system of general circulation . . . that provides a reasonable basis to determine fair market value by disseminating either recent price quotations (including rates, yields, or other pricing information) of one or more identified brokers, dealers, or traders or actual prices (including rates, yields, or other pricing information) of recent sales transactions (a quotation medium)"[9]
- Is a debt instrument for which price quotations are readily available from dealers, brokers, or traders

If a debt exchange or modification does give rise to COD income that is not subject to any IRC exception, is it taxed all at once?

Assuming that the transaction gives rise to COD income, and that neither the insolvency nor the bankruptcy exceptions of Section 108 apply, recent legislation might still help. The American Recovery and Reinvestment Act of 2009 contains a provision, subject to certain criteria, by which such a debtor may defer recognizing taxable COD income that was created during 2009 and 2010. Depending on the year in which the income was generated, the debtor may fully defer the income for either four or five years, and then recognize the income ratably over the subsequent five years. (Unlike other provisions of the American Recovery and Reinvestment Act discussed later in this chapter, this COD provision is not limited to small businesses.)

What if the debtor settles a secured liability by transferring the asset to the creditor?

Restructurings—whether via an out-of-court workout or as part of a formal bankruptcy process—often involve selling or transferring assets. All else equal, such dispositions are taxable events, and a taxpayer normally realizes a Section 1001 gain if it transfers property and the amount realized exceeds the asset's tax basis.

During a restructuring process, the debtor will sometimes transfer an asset to a secured creditor in full or partial satisfaction of the debt. A transfer such as this still constitutes a taxable event and is treated as a sale of the asset, even if cash does not change hands. For the purposes of calculating the Section 1001 gain, the debtor's adjusted basis in the asset is relatively straightforward; it is no different from the basis that would be used if the debtor had simply sold the asset for cash. In contrast, the amount realized (or, thought of a little differently, the purchase price for tax purposes) depends on whether the secured debt was nonrecourse or recourse.

If the debt is nonrecourse, the purchase price is the face value of the secured debt at the time of the transfer. Accordingly, the debtor recognizes a gain or loss equal to the difference between the amount of the debt discharged and the debtor's adjusted tax basis in the property immediately before the transfer. The entire gain or loss falls within Section 1001 and no COD income arises, and the current market value of the asset is not factored into the analysis.

If the debt is recourse, both COD income and Section 1001 gain or loss can be realized on the transfer via a two-part analysis. The precise tax treatment depends on whether the disposition is in full or partial satisfaction of the secured debt.

1. First, the debtor is treated as having made a taxable disposition of the asset. The debtor records a Section 1001 gain or loss equal to the difference between the fair market value of the asset and the debtor's adjusted tax basis in that asset.
2. Second, any additional amount of canceled debt is COD income. That is, if the value of the property is less than the recourse liability, the parties can either retain the excess liability as a continuing debt obligation or forgive this amount. If the remainder of the debt is forgiven, the amount forgiven will constitute COD income, and will be deemed ordinary income, *unless* the bankruptcy exception applies to the situation.

Exhibit 8-6 illustrates one example.

Exhibit 8-6 Illustration of Asset Transfer Taxation *(Continues)*

Assume that a debtor (D) owns a piece of machinery called an Autobot, with a current fair market value of $75 million and a tax basis of $45 million. D had mortgaged the Autobot several years ago, when times were better, for $100 million from a creditor (C). D is in the process of negotiating an out-of-court restructuring with creditors, and it has transferred the Autobot to C in full satisfaction of the $100 million loan.

- *Scenario 1: Nonrecourse Loan.* If C loaned $100 million to D on a nonrecourse basis, with the sole collateral being the value of the Autobot, D would have a Section 1001 gain of $55 million. The amount realized is $100 million (or the face value of the debt) less D's tax basis in the equipment of $45 million.
- *Scenario 2: Recourse Loan.* If C's loan to D was recourse to other assets of the company, D would still have a $55 million gain. However, the character of that income would be split between a $30 million Section 1001 gain (fair market value of $75 million less $45 million tax basis) and $25 million of COD income (face value of debt less fair market value of Autobot).

Exhibit 8-6 Illustration of Asset Transfer Taxation *(Continued)*

($ in millions)

Fair market value of Autobot	$75
Tax basis of Autobot	$45
Face value of secured debt	$100

Scenario I: Nonrecourse		Scenario 2: Recourse	
Amount realized by debtor	$100	Amount realized by debtor	$75
Note: Face value of		*Note: Fair market value*	
secured debt		*of Autobot*	
Tax basis in hands of debtor	(45)	Tax basis in hands of debtor	(45)
Section 1001 gain/(loss)	$55	Section 1001 gain/(loss)	$30
		Excess debt forgiven	
		Face value of debt	$100
		Fair market value of Autobot	(75)
		COD income	$25

As this discussion shows, workouts offer many options for companies that opt to deal with their problems themselves. The next chapter will explore the accounting issues involved in the alternative solution of a Chapter 11 reorganization.

Endnotes

1. The accounting and tax implications of Chapter 7 liquidations are outside the scope of this text. However, a companion book in this series, *The Art of M&A Structuring: Techniques for Mitigating Financial, Tax, and Legal Risk*, covers the tax impact of liquidating distributions.
2. For the purposes of evaluating whether a borrower is in sufficient "financial difficulty," the lender may consider several factors. These include whether the borrower (1) is currently in default on any of its debt, (2) either has filed or soon will file for bankruptcy, (3) cannot otherwise obtain funds from sources other than the existing creditors at an effective interest rate equal to the current market interest rate for similar debt for a nontroubled debtor, (4) has projected cash flows that are likely to be insufficient to cover debt maturities, (5) has outstanding securities that have been delisted, or (6) has limited access to capital because of deteriorating creditworthiness.

3. 284 U.S. 1 (1931).
4. It is rare for an out-of-court workout to involve an outright debt extinguishment if the debtor is solvent.
5. This rate is published monthly and is available at http://www.irs.gov/app/picklist/list/federalRates.html, last accessed March 18, 2010.
6. Section 163(i) of the IRC defines AHYDO as any debt instrument issued by a corporation with (a) a maturity date of more than five years from the date of issue; (b) a yield to maturity that equals or exceeds the Applicable Federal Rate plus 5 percent; and (c) significant OID features. A debt instrument is issued with significant OID if the aggregate amount included in gross income for periods before the close of any accrual period ending after five years from the date of issue exceeds the sum of (1) the aggregate amount of interest to be paid under the instrument before the close of that accrual period, and (2) the product of the issue price of the instrument and its yield to maturity. An additional formula determines the amount of the interest deduction that is permanently disqualified. For the deduction to be disqualified, the debt instrument's yield to maturity must exceed the Applicable Federal Rate plus 6 percent—the higher the disqualified yield, the greater the disqualified interest deduction.
7. Note that the debtor may not make multiple changes that individually would qualify for one of the exceptions enumerated in the text.
8. Treasury Regulation §1.1273-2(f).
9. Ibid.

CHAPTER 9

Accounting for Bankruptcy: NOLS and Fresh Start Reporting

I have no use for bodyguards, but I have very specific use for two highly trained certified public accountants.

—*Elvis Presley*

INTRODUCTION TO BANKRUPTCY ACCOUNTING

What are the key tax and accounting issues to focus on when a company enters Chapter 11?

While there are many tax and accounting issues that arise, two issues are of particular importance when a company files for Chapter 11: (1) the preservation of net operating loss carryforwards (which are often sizable for bankrupt companies), and (2) the implementation of fresh start reporting (which takes effect upon emergence from bankruptcy). While these issues are highly complex, it is very important to understand them. As a result, most of Chapter 9 focuses on these two issues.

Where does the FASB provide accounting guidance for companies in Chapter 11?

The FASB's Accounting Standards Codification (ASC 852), "Reorganizations," provides accounting and financial reporting guidance for nongovernment business entities that are in Chapter 11 reorganization (and thus expect to continue as going concerns), or that have emerged from Chapter 11 under court-approved plans for reorganization.[1]

According to ASC 852, a Chapter 11 filing, while a significant event, does not ordinarily affect or change a particular company's application of GAAP. That is, the company generally continues to book income in the same manner as a business outside the jurisdiction of the bankruptcy court.

However, the needs of financial statement users change. This, in turn, triggers the need to implement some changes in the company's financial reporting practices. On a conceptual level, the recurring theme in these changes is to distinguish transactions and events that are directly associated with the reorganization from those that are related to the ongoing operations of the business. As a result, GAAP continues to apply, provided that it does not conflict with the guidance in ASC 852.

What accounting changes typically take effect immediately upon a company's bankruptcy filing?

The most significant accounting change that takes effect immediately upon a company's bankruptcy filing is that the company must distinguish between pre-petition liabilities that are *subject to compromise* (liabilities that were incurred before a Chapter 11 filing or became known after the filing and are either unsecured or undersecured) and those that are not subject to compromise, as well as post-petition liabilities. As noted earlier in this book, the automatic stay provisions of the Bankruptcy Code preclude pre-petition creditors from seizing the company's assets without permission from the U.S. bankruptcy court. By the same token, the debtor cannot pay pre-petition obligations without the court's approval. In many cases, such pre-petition liabilities will not be paid until the debtor emerges from bankruptcy. Post-petition liabilities, in contrast, should be paid in the ordinary course of business.

What about pre-petition tax liabilities? How are they treated upon a company's Chapter 11 bankruptcy filing?

With limited exceptions, the taxing authorities are treated like other creditors during bankruptcy. Tax obligations related to pre-petition income generally rank senior to most other unsecured claims, but are subordinate to secured claims (unless the taxing authority perfected a tax lien against the company before it filed for bankruptcy). Also like other creditors, the taxing authorities must file proofs of claim for unpaid pre-petition taxes. This frequently increases the likelihood of a tax audit. (As the saying goes, when it rains it pours!)

One wrinkle related to pre-petition tax liabilities that may arise involves trust fund taxes. A *trust fund tax* is money that a business withholds from third parties and holds in trust until it is paid to the U.S. Treasury or some other taxing authority. A prime example is money withheld from employee wages (e.g., income tax, social security, and Medicare taxes). Congress has established large penalties for delays in turning over such employment taxes to the Treasury. In addition, under federal (and most state) tax laws, certain individuals—such as officers, directors, and employees that have the authority to sign a company's tax returns—can be held personally liable for trust fund taxes if the company does not pay them in full. It is therefore standard practice for a bankruptcy court to approve motions to pay pre-petition trust fund taxes, particularly as such monies are typically not company property and thus are not part of the debtor's estate.

What about accrued interest on pre-petition debt? Is that deductible for troubled loans or after a company files Chapter 11?

This question—i.e., whether a borrower who is experiencing financial hardship may deduct accrued interest on debt that it may not be able to repay—is an issue that has bedeviled the courts, the IRS, and taxpayers for many years.[2] A bankruptcy court decision early in the last decade, *In re Dow Corning Corp.*,[3] along with the IRS's Chief Counsel Advice (CCA) 200801039 (1/4/08), at least creates a defensible reporting position. Still, the New York City Bar has recently recommended that the normal rules of accrual for interest and original issue discounts (OID) should no longer apply once a debtor has filed for bankruptcy, and that the debtor in such circumstances should generally be required to convert to the cash method of accounting.[4] As a result, this is a topic on which it may be particularly important to keep in touch with legal developments.

Ultimately, the facts and circumstances of any given situation will greatly influence whether the debtor may deduct interest, and the lender must accrue interest income, on pre-petition debt. In a nutshell, however, a borrower generally may continue to deduct accrued interest on pre-petition debt so long as there is an unconditional obligation to pay the interest (i.e., the liability may not be subject to a substantial contingency), although such deductions have been denied in situations in which insolvency, bankruptcy, or other factors indicate with certainty (or suggest with near certainty) that the interest will not be paid.[5] Lenders, on the other hand, generally must accrue interest income until that interest is of "doubtful collectability."[6]

What is the initial impact from a tax standpoint when a company files for Chapter 11?

The tax regulations continue to treat the business as the same tax entity, and its tax year does not change. Similarly, the company's historical tax attributes are unchanged (for the time being); this means that tax loss carryforwards remain available during the bankruptcy process. Also, the company typically remains a member of a consolidated group, provided it was treated as such before bankruptcy.

Two issues do, however, come to the forefront: (1) preserving the debtor's tax attributes, especially its loss carryovers and carrybacks, and (2) avoiding cancellation of debt (COD) income. Each of these is discussed in greater detail later in this chapter.

What are loss carryovers and carrybacks?

If a corporate taxpayer has an excess of tax deductions over its taxable income in a given year, this excess becomes a *net operating loss* (NOL) of that taxpayer. Section 172 of the Internal Revenue Code (IRC) allows such a taxpayer, also known as a *loss corporation*, to use its NOL to offset taxable income in subsequent years (a carryover or carryforward) or to offset taxable income in earlier years (a carryback) by filing an amended tax return. For most taxpayers, an NOL may be carried back for up to two taxable years and may be carried forward for up to 20 years.

In 2009, Congress passed two laws that temporarily modified these carryback and carryforward periods:

- First, the American Recovery and Reinvestment Act of 2009 allows a corporation with average annual gross receipts of less than $15 million to elect to carry back an NOL generated in a tax year ending in 2008 for up to five years.
- Second, the Worker, Homeownership and Business Assistance Act of 2009 allows all businesses [except recipients of funds from the Troubled Asset Relief Program (TARP)] to carry back NOLs that arise in either 2008 or 2009 (but not from both years) for up to five years. If an election is made to carry back an NOL for the full five years, it can be used to offset only up to 50 percent of the fifth preceding year's taxable income.[7]

Under other provisions of the IRC, certain additional types of tax losses or tax credits that are unusable in a given year may be carried forward or carried back to other tax years. Examples of such deductions or credits include capital losses, excess foreign tax credits, and investment credits. In some circumstances, loss limitation provisions apply to the use of NOLs and unrealized built-in losses (i.e., the tax basis exceeds the asset's fair market value) that a loss corporation sells during the five-year period following an ownership change. Generally, IRC regulations covering a company's ability to utilize NOL carryovers apply to these other items as well. For purposes of simplicity, all these items tend to be grouped together with loss carry-overs. This is a practice that we will follow in the discussion here.

As an aside, the issue of maintaining NOLs during Chapter 11 is essentially limited to C corporations. This is because most other business entities—such as S corporations and limited liability companies (LLCs), among others—are pass-through entities for tax purposes;[8] there are no NOLs at the company level to preserve. Instead, the concept of NOLs for a pass-through entity is handled at the shareholder/member level. For instance, in the case of an S corporation, each shareholder must treat any loss or deduction that exceeds his stock and debt basis as a suspended (disallowed) loss. This suspended loss carries forward indefinitely until it can be applied toward future earned income passed through by the S corporation.

What role do loss carryovers play in distressed transactions?

NOLs and other favorable tax attributes can increase after-tax cash flow, and thus offer significant value—whether the loss corporation remains an independent company or is sold upon emergence—provided that the favorable tax attributes survive bankruptcy. In some cases [and subject to the separate return limitation year (SRLY) rules and other limitations described later in this chapter], a prospective buyer may even have the opportunity to utilize the carryover losses to offset tax liability generated by the buyer's own operations. However, over the course of many years, Congress and the IRS have imposed various limitations on the use of loss carryovers by persons other than those who owned the entity at the time that the loss was generated. For example, after a substantial ownership change (as defined later in this chapter), the NOLs are deductible only up to a certain limit, called a Section 382 limitation.

What is a Section 382 limitation, and how is it calculated?

Under a *Section 382 limitation*, the general ability of the *new loss corporation* (or the postbankruptcy company) to use pre-petition NOLs is limited annually to an amount equal to the company's equity market value (i.e., not book value) immediately prior to an ownership change multiplied by the IRS's long-term tax-exempt rate. (This long-term tax-exempt rate is based on the rate that is in effect during the month of the ownership change, and is then locked in. That is, the NOL limitation does not reset every month as the IRS releases the most recent long-term tax-exempt rate in monthly letter rulings. This process is described in greater detail later in this chapter.)

In evaluating these requirements, three issues must be analyzed: (1) whether an ownership change occurred for the purposes of Section 382 of the IRC; (2) what the debtor's equity value is; and (3) what the current long-term tax-exempt rate is.

Even after the acquirer has passed all of these tests, it must still meet a *continuity of business enterprise* requirement in order to overcome the Section 382 limitation and utilize the new loss corporation's NOLs. Continuity of business enterprise means the continuation of a significant business of the acquired corporation or the continued use of a significant portion of the corporation's business assets for two years after the ownership change. These rules have achieved a level of complexity that is extreme even by the standard of the tax laws generally.

Finally, the preservation of NOLs is markedly more difficult in a workout scenario than it is in a bankruptcy scenario. This is because loss corporations reorganizing through a formal bankruptcy process under Title 11 of the United States Code benefit from two statutory carveouts from Section 382 limitations. These carveouts, called the insolvency and bankruptcy exceptions, are described in greater detail later in this chapter.

Can you provide a numerical example of a Section 382 limitation?

Exhibit 9-1 illustrates what an NOL limitation under Section 382 might look like in practice. In this example, we assume that Company X has filed for Chapter 11 bankruptcy with $150 million of pre-petition NOLs. Assuming that an ownership change occurs under Section 382 (discussed in the next section) that values the company at $100 million, Company X's ability to use these $150 million in pre-petition NOLs after emerging is limited to $4.03 million annually (calculated as $100 million of equity value multiplied by the current long-term tax-exempt rate of 4.03 percent). Even if the company were able to use the full 20-year carryforward described earlier, this would yield an aggregate NOL of $80.6 million, with the company effectively losing $69.4 million of future income offsets. The net impact in

Exhibit 9-1 Illustration of NOL Limitation under Section 382

Value of NOLs before bankruptcy		$150,000,000
Company's equity value upon emergence	$100,000,000	
Long-term tax-exempt rate in month of ownership change	4.03%	
Annual NOL limitation	$4,030,000	
Carryforward period, in years	20	
Maximum allowable NOL		80,600,000
Amount of NOLs "lost"		$69,400,000

this particular example is that the cash value of the NOL is cut nearly in half. While the exact numerical outcome will differ based on the facts and circumstances of a particular situation, an ownership change, as defined by Section 382, will often erode a substantial amount of the cash value of such NOLs.

When has an ownership change occurred for purposes of Section 382?

As with most tax matters, the test for determining whether an ownership change for the purposes of Section 382 has occurred is relatively technical.

An *ownership change* occurs for a loss corporation if, immediately after the close of the testing date, the percentage of the stock of the corporation owned by one or more 5 percent shareholders has increased by more than 50 percentage points over the lowest percentage of stock owned by such shareholders at any time during the prior three years (also known as the *testing period*).[9] For the purposes of measuring the testing period, a "year" is considered a rolling 365-day period (or a 366-day period in the case of a leap year).

The *testing date* is essentially any point during the bankruptcy process at which there has been an owner shift. An *owner shift*, in turn, occurs whenever there is a change in the percentage of stock owned by a 5 percent shareholder. Certain groups of shareholders who, individually, are not 5 percent shareholders might nonetheless trigger this test if they acquired their shares in a single offering or exchange transaction.

Because only those 5 percent shareholders whose percentages of stock ownership have increased are taken into account, a 5 percent shareholder is disregarded if her percentage of stock ownership, immediately after the close of the testing date, has either *decreased* or *stayed the same* compared to her lowest percentage ownership interest on any previous date during the testing period. Also, for the purposes of the 5 percent test, all less than 5 percent shareholders (i.e., the public at large) are considered a single 5 percent shareholder.

Importantly, if creditors have the right to convert their debt to equity upon a future raising of equity capital by the debtor, such creditors' pro forma interest will be included in the ownership change test. Similarly, the parties generally cannot circumvent the test by selling a call option instead of equity; certain stock options are deemed to have been exercised if their exercise would trigger a Section 382 ownership change.

That does sound relatively technical. Can you provide some examples of ownership changes for the purposes of Section 382?

Here are a few examples:

- *Example of an ownership change via a single transaction.* A and B each own 40 percent of the outstanding stock of Loss Corporation. The remaining 20 percent of Loss Corporation stock is owned by 100 unrelated individuals, none of whom owns as much as 5 percent of Loss Corporation stock.

    On September 13, 2010, C purchases all of the Loss Corporation stock that A and B own. C is now an 80 percent shareholder of Loss Corporation. An ownership change has occurred because C's percentage ownership has increased to 80 percent from 0 percent (his lowest ownership stake during the three-year testing period). This 80-percentage-point increase exceeds the 50-percentage-point threshold discussed earlier.

- *Example of an ownership change via multiple transactions.* There are 100 shares of Loss Corporation issued and outstanding. A, B, and C own 50, 25, and 25 shares, respectively.

    On January 1, 2011, A sells 30 shares of Loss Corporation stock to B. A now owns 20 shares, while B now owns 55 shares. In percentage terms, B's ownership stake has thus increased by 30 points—to 55 percent from 25 percent. This transaction, in isolation, does not exceed the 50-percentage-point threshold.

    Then, on January 1, 2012, C sells his entire interest in Loss Corporation to A, who now owns 45 shares. A's percentage ownership has thus increased by 25 points—to 45 percent from 20 percent.

    While A's transaction in 2012, in isolation, does not exceed the 50-percentage-point threshold, both B (in 2011) and A (in 2012) are considered 5 percent shareholders. Collectively, A's and B's ownership stake has increased by 55 percentage points during the testing period. The fact that A decreased his percentage ownership in the first transaction is irrelevant; the test is measured from his *lowest* ownership stake during the three-year testing period. This 55-point increase exceeds the 50-percentage-point threshold discussed earlier.

- *Example of no ownership change because of the three-year testing period limitation.* A owns all 100 outstanding shares of Loss Corporation stock. A sells 40 shares to B on January 1, 2010. B's percentage ownership has thus increased by 40 points—to 40 percent from 0 percent. This does not trigger the 50-percentage-point threshold.

  Then, on July 1, 2013, A sells 20 shares to C. In isolation, C's purchase increases his ownership stake by only 20 percentage points and thus does not meet the 50-point test. Moreover, C's transaction cannot be aggregated with B's purchase, because B's acquisition occurred more than three years prior, or outside the testing period.

Are there any structuring techniques that can preserve a loss corporation's NOLs in these scenarios?

In certain circumstances, the parties can avoid triggering a Section 382 loss limitation if the transaction involves straight preferred stock. Nonetheless, there are still substantial limitations on the type of preferred stock that can qualify. Among other limitations, the preferred stock generally may not

- Have voting rights (except if dividends fall into arrears)
- Significantly participate in corporate growth
- Have redemption or liquidation rights that exceed the issue price of the shares (except for a reasonable redemption or liquidation premium)
- Be convertible into common stock

The challenge for this structuring alternative, however, is that some investors may find such limitations unappealing—particularly for the perceived risk/reward of allocating capital to a distressed company. That is, the type of preferred shares that would qualify would have little or no control over the loss corporation, and generally would not participate in any equity upside if the company does, in fact, restructure successfully.

Isn't an ownership change typical during a Chapter 11 bankruptcy process? Doesn't this create a structural bias against the retention of NOLs for companies that are undergoing a restructuring?

For all practical matters, a change in the equity ownership of a loss corporation is particularly common in the bankruptcy context; this is because the shareholders who held the stock prior to the bankruptcy typically will be different from those who hold it following the bankruptcy. However, companies reorganizing under the Bankruptcy Code are offered at least some modest statutory relief. (Notably, this relief is available only to loss corporations in formal bankruptcy, not to those that are undergoing an out-of-court workout.)

Under Section 382(l)(5) of the IRC, an ownership change that occurs during a formal bankruptcy process will not create a Section 382 limitation if the loss corporation's historical shareholders and/or creditors prior to the ownership change receive more than 50 percent of the total voting power and value of the stock of the newly reorganized corporation pursuant to the bankruptcy plan of reorganization. Stock that is transferred to creditors counts toward this 50 percent requirement only if it is transferred with respect to *old and cold* indebtedness—that is, if the indebtedness (1) was held by the creditor for at least 18 months before the date of the filing of the Title 11 case[10] or (2) arose in the ordinary course of the trade or business of the old corporation and is held by the person who at all times held a beneficial interest in that debt. This last rule prevents debtor corporations that have a significant portion of their outstanding debt acquired by vulture funds within 18 months of the bankruptcy petition date from making use of the Section 382(l)(5) protection.

This statutory relief from Section 382(l)(5) is violated—and the NOLs are lost in their entirety—if there is an actual ownership change within two years of the loss corporation's emergence from bankruptcy.

Because of the strong need to preserve an asset such as a significant NOL, the loss corporation may request the court to approve severe restrictions on the transfer of stock within the two-year period following emergence from bankruptcy. However, in practice, this often proves to be too restrictive for many large companies that are undergoing Chapter 11 reorganization.

Even if the statutory relief isn't violated through a subsequent ownership change, the loss corporation's NOLs will still be limited in two circumstances:

1. To the extent that Section 382(l)(5) applies to the transfer of stock to the old creditors, the NOL carryovers of the loss corporation may still be reduced by 50 percent of the COD income not taken into account by virtue of the stock-for-debt exception of Section 108(e)(10)(B) of the IRC. COD income is described in greater detail later in this chapter.
2. Also, the NOLs are reduced for certain interest payments made within the past three years to creditors that become shareholders of the debtor corporation and certain amounts related to the cancellation of debt. In the case of a highly levered company, this NOL reduction may result in a significant reduction of the debtor's pre-petition losses.

A loss corporation in bankruptcy that has an ownership change can elect not to apply the foregoing rules and instead allow the normal Section 382 limitation rules to apply. If the loss corporation makes this election, the value of the corporation for purposes of determining the Section 382 limitation is allowed to reflect the increase in value resulting from the surrender or cancellation of creditors' claims in the bankruptcy proceeding.

How is the loss corporation's equity value calculated?

For the purposes of a Section 382 limitation analysis, the equity value of the loss corporation is the fair market value (FMV) of its outstanding equity *immediately prior to the ownership change*. Included in a loss corporation's equity value is the value of all preferred stock (including straight preferred stock that does not count in the ownership change test described earlier).

Excluded from the equity value calculation (and thus making the loss limitation stricter) are the following:

- Nonbusiness assets, particularly assets held for investment (even cash raised from the divestiture of business assets), if one-third or more of the loss corporation's assets are nonbusiness. In this situation, the indebtedness related to such assets is an offsetting entry.
- The value of recent capital infusions (known as the *antistuffing rule*). For the purposes of determining a Section 382 loss limitation, the regulations deem any capital infusions within two years of the ownership change as "recent." Exceptions include capital infusions made upon the formation of the company, before losses arose, or to meet basic operating expenses.

Absent a formal valuation, it is reasonable to use the price of publicly traded shares to estimate the value of a publicly traded corporation. For a company that is not publicly traded, the price of the stock in the transaction that triggers the ownership change may be used to determine a value for the corporation.

Intuitively, distressed companies would seem to have low equity values. If the value of a loss corporation's NOLs is limited by its equity value immediately prior to an ownership change, doesn't this create an enormous barrier to the preservation of NOLs for a distressed company?

All else equal, the answer is yes—in a distressed company scenario, the equity value of the loss corporation is, by definition, likely to be very low. As a result, the Section 382 loss limitation in such circumstances is likely to be unusually low—meaning that most of the cash value of the NOLs is likely to be lost.

Fortunately, as with the definition of "ownership changes," there is some statutory relief in the application of "equity value" for companies that are undergoing a formal bankruptcy process. (Again, this relief is not available to loss corporations that are undergoing an out-of-court workout.)

Under Section 382(l)(6) of the IRC, a loss corporation may essentially value itself after all the debt cancellation of bankruptcy has occurred. This should result in a significantly higher equity value for purposes of calculating the loss corporation's Section 382 limitation; this, in turn, should increase the amount of NOLs that can be used to offset future taxable income. Still, the above-referenced limitations on nonbusiness assets and capital infusions still apply.

How is the long-term tax-exempt rate calculated?

As noted earlier, the long-term tax-exempt rate is used to compute the annual Section 382 limitation on NOLs following any change in ownership. This rate, which changes monthly, is equal to the highest rate published by the IRS in regularly scheduled revenue rulings for that month and the prior two months. (For example, the rate for September 2010 was 3.86 percent.) The current rate is also readily available at selected Web sites.[11]

How is COD income treated in the bankruptcy scenario?

As a general rule, the cancellation of indebtedness by a creditor for less than the amount owed results in taxable COD income to the debtor. This rule, which originated in the Supreme Court case of *United States v. Kirby Lumber*,[12] was subsequently codified in Section 61(a)(12) of the IRC.

Section 108(a) of the IRC contains several exceptions to this rule.[13] Assuming that the taxpayer meets the requirements of one of the following exceptions, the debtor generally does not recognize COD income:

- The discharge of indebtedness occurs during a formal bankruptcy case. The exclusion for Title 11 bankruptcies takes precedence over any other exclusion under Section 108 of the IRC. Moreover, unlike other exclusions (notably, the insolvency exclusion described next), there is no dollar limit associated with the bankruptcy exclusion.
- The discharge of indebtedness occurs when the taxpayer is insolvent. The IRC excludes from COD income any debt discharge up to the amount of the taxpayer's insolvency. Any

such discharge that exceeds this insolvency amount is deemed taxable COD income.

- The indebtedness discharged is qualified farm indebtedness.
- The indebtedness discharged is qualified real property business indebtedness.

Nevertheless, there is a trade-off involved: to the extent that the debtor does not recognize COD income because of the bankruptcy or insolvency exclusions just covered, the debtor must either reduce its basis in depreciable property under Section 108(b)(5) of the IRC or reduce tax attributes in an amount equal to the unrecognized COD income.[14] From a practical perspective, this trade-off between current-year COD income and the consequent reduction in tax attributes means that the bankruptcy and insolvency exclusions are more akin to a *deferral* than to a *permanent forgiveness* of tax.[15]

Section 108 of the IRC also contains a prioritized list of tax attributes to be reduced, the first (and, for purposes of this text, the most important) of which is NOLs. The first NOL subject to reduction is a loss generated in the taxable year of the discharge. This is followed by NOL carryovers in the order in which they arose. In both cases, the reduction is on a dollar-for-dollar basis and is made prior to any Section 382 limitation. Accordingly, companies that trigger a Section 382 limitation are affected less by the COD rules, as their NOLs have already been discounted substantially.

After NOLs, the additional tax attributes to be reduced, in order, are general business credits, alternative minimum tax credits, capital loss carryovers, basis of assets, passive activity losses and credits, and foreign tax credits, with a long tail of additional attributes to follow. Capital loss carryovers and basis of assets are reduced dollar for dollar, while the other tax attributes just listed are reduced 33⅓ cents on the dollar.

If COD income exceeds the tax attributes that are available for reduction, the analysis shifts to whether the debtor is the parent or a member of a consolidated tax group. If the answer is no, the COD income has no further tax impact. If the answer is yes, and if the excludable COD exceeds the attribute reduction at the reorganized entity, the consolidated attributes across the group become subject to reduction. Such reduction is limited to so-called outside attributes (e.g., NOLs and credit carryovers) of other members of the group and does not include their inside attributes (depreciable property).

Where the debtor is a pass-through entity, special rules may apply:

- If the debtor is an S corporation, the exclusions are applied at the S-corporation level and are available only if the S corporation is in bankruptcy or insolvent.
- If the debtor is a partnership or an LLC, the exclusions are applied at the partner/member level. Generally, this means that even if the debtor partnership/LLC is bankrupt or insolvent, the partnership/LLC's COD income will pass through to its partners/members. Only those partners/members that are bankrupt or insolvent can take advantage of the exclusions and avoid recognizing COD income.

How does the IRC define insolvency?

As noted throughout this book, the term *insolvency* has different meanings in different contexts. (Chapter 1 of this book contains a more detailed discussion of how various regulatory authorities have differing definitions of the term *insolvency*.) For the purposes of Section 108 of the IRC, insolvency means an excess of liabilities over the fair market value of assets. The value of such assets is measured on a going-concern basis, and it generally includes intangible assets such as trademarks, goodwill, and so on.[16] A reasonable reserve should probably be accrued for contingent liabilities, although the rules are not always consistent on this point.[17]

Another question that arises periodically in determining whether a debtor is insolvent is whether a nonrecourse liability can be included in the calculation. For this purpose, the amount of the liability that may be included in this calculation is limited to the excess amount of the nonrecourse liability over the fair market value of the property that secures the liability—provided the nonrecourse liability is discharged in the transaction that triggered the COD income.

The issues of whether or not the taxpayer is insolvent and the amount by which the taxpayer is insolvent are determined on the basis of the taxpayer's assets and liabilities immediately before the discharge of debt. As a practical matter, these calculations can be subjective and ripe for challenge by the IRS. Although documentation of internal valuation analyses may suffice, it is advisable that the taxpayer obtain third-party appraisals to support its reporting position.

For example, a loss corporation would be insolvent if it had assets of $40 million but liabilities of $100 million. In this scenario, cancellation of

$20 million of debt would not give rise to COD income, all else equal, because the amount of the cancellation does not exceed $60 million, or the amount by which the loss corporation is insolvent. However, if we modify the scenario so that $65 million of debt was canceled, the loss corporation would have COD income of $5 million—the amount by which the canceled debt exceeds the corporation's insolvency just prior to such cancellation.

ACCOUNTING AND TAX CONSEQUENCES OF EMERGING FROM A CHAPTER 11 BANKRUPTCY

What accounting and tax issues are most common when a company emerges from Chapter 11 bankruptcy?

Fresh start accounting (also called *fresh start reporting*) is inevitably a front-and-center issue for nearly any company as it concludes the formal reorganization process. Fresh start accounting refers to a balance sheet overhaul that some companies must undertake upon emerging from bankruptcy, provided they meet certain criteria outlined here. The concept behind this process is to allow companies to present their assets, liabilities, and equity as a "new entity" on the day the company emerges from Chapter 11 bankruptcy protection.

A company that adopts fresh start accounting essentially "hits the reset button"—i.e., the basis of the company's assets and liabilities for book purposes is restated from historical balances to fair value. In this way, the exercise is similar to applying purchase accounting to a corporate target in the M&A context.

When should a company adopt fresh start accounting?

Whether a company must adopt fresh start accounting is governed by ASC 852. A company must adopt fresh start accounting if it meets both of the following criteria:

1. *Insolvent immediately before emerging.* The reorganization value (defined below) of the emerging entity immediately prior to confirmation of its plan of reorganization must be less than the total amount of all post-petition liabilities plus all allowed pre-petition liabilities. Another way of thinking about this requirement is that the emerging entity must be balance sheet insolvent immediately before emerging.

2. *Significant ownership change.* The pre-petition voting shareholders immediately before confirmation must receive less than 50 percent of the voting shares in the new entity (i.e., they must no longer have control). The loss of control must be substantive, not temporary; the new controlling interest must not revert to the shareholders that existed immediately before the plan was filed or confirmed. For this reason, fresh start accounting is more common for publicly traded companies than for private businesses, as the latter often do not involve a significant ownership change upon plan confirmation.

Both of these standards help to ensure that a company will not file for Chapter 11 bankruptcy protection for the sole purpose of adopting fresh start accounting to write up the value of its assets to fair value. When both standards are met, the reconstituted company is deemed to be sufficiently distinct from the old entity to conclude that a fresh start basis of accounting for the company's assets and liabilities is appropriate.

In the event that the emerging entity does not meet both of these criteria, it does not qualify for fresh start accounting and must continue to apply U.S. GAAP without modification to the book bases of its assets and its liabilities. Nevertheless, the company should still state, at present value, the liabilities compromised by the confirmed plan.

What is a company's reorganization value?

Reorganization value (which, for the purposes of fresh start accounting, is different from equity value for the purposes of a Section 382 limitation) is the valuation that the bankruptcy court ascribes to the *assets* of the reconstituted entity immediately prior to the court's approval of the company's plan of reorganization. As a general rule, the entity's reorganization value is the price that a willing buyer would pay for the emerging entity's assets (including the expected net realizable value of those assets that will be disposed of before reconstitution occurs), *before* considering liabilities. Post-petition liabilities and allowed claims and interest are satisfied by the reorganization value.

The best starting point is a discounted cash flow analysis of the pro forma projections from the court-approved plan of reorganization (POR).

Nevertheless, this valuation process is perhaps best described as price discovery—it's as much about negotiation and litigation as it is about raw analyses. It is also important to keep in mind that the company's valuation will often change a number of times as the parties gradually inch toward an agreed-upon POR. To this end, it is important that the emerging entity update its fresh start accounting to reflect the final version of these valuation analyses.

What is the process by which a company should implement fresh start accounting?

The process of implementing fresh start accounting is complex, even by bankruptcy standards. At a high level, the process involves allocating the reorganization value of the reconstituted entity to its identifiable assets (both tangible and intangible) and liabilities based on their "fair value" at the time of plan approval. This process follows the procedures specified by FASB ASC 805, "Business Combinations."[18] If the reorganization value exceeds the aggregate tangible or identified intangible assets of the emerging entity, this excess should be reported as goodwill on the company's new balance sheet.

What is fair value, and how should it be allocated to assets and liabilities in the context of fresh start accounting?

Fair value is defined as "the amount at which an asset (or liability) could be bought (or incurred) or sold (or settled) in a current transaction between willing parties, that is, other than in a forced or liquidation sale." Independent appraisals may be used in determining the fair value of some assets and liabilities. Subsequent sales of assets might also provide evidence of values.

The following are general guidelines for assigning amounts to certain individual assets and liabilities:

- Present value, determined at a court-approved discount rate, of receivables (net of estimated allowances for uncollectibility); accounts payable and other claims payable; and other liabilities, such as warranties, vacation pay, deferred compensation,

unfavorable leases, contracts and commitments, and plant closing expenses incident to the reorganization.

- Current replacement cost of raw materials inventories and plant
  and equipment, adjusted to their remaining economic lives.
- Net realizable value of marketable securities and property and
  equipment to be sold or to be used temporarily.
- Finished goods and merchandise at estimated selling prices
  less the sum of (1) the cost of disposal and (2) a reasonable
  profit allowance for the selling effort of the reconstituted entity.
- Work-in-process inventory at estimated selling prices of finished goods less the sum of (1) the cost to complete, (2) the
  cost of disposal, and (3) a reasonable profit allowance for the
  completing and selling effort of the emerging entity based on
  profit for similar finished goods.

The excess of the reorganization value over the fair value amounts
assigned to the tangible assets, the financial assets, and the identifiable assets
is evidence of an unidentified intangible asset or assets, or goodwill.

In implementing fair value allocation process, what are some of the most common issues that arise?

In planning for implementation, there are certain issues that are particularly
important to keep in mind:

- *What is the "highest and best use" of the asset?* Fair value is
  dictated not by the intended use of the asset by the parties at
  hand, but rather by its likely use by other market participants.
  One example might be a trademark that the reconstituted entity
  owns but does not currently use (this issue proliferates
  throughout the financial services industry, where corporate
  acquirers have "retired" legendary names such as DLJ, Kidder
  Peabody, and Salomon Brothers, among many others). The
  "highest and best use" of that mark by market participants, not
  by the emerging company, determines its fair value.
- *What is the principal market for the asset or liability?* As a general rule, the principal market is the most active market in which
  an entity would sell an asset or transfer a liability—typically the

market in which the reconstituted entity normally conducts business. If there is no principal market, the focus shifts to the most advantageous market. Transaction costs are often a key determinant of which market for the asset or liability is most advantageous.

- *Does the fair value measurement properly reflect the "exit price," not the "entry price"?* The definition of fair value centers on the exit price—the gross price (i.e., before transaction costs) that would be received for selling the asset or paid for transferring the liability. This stands in contrast to the entry price—the price that would be paid to acquire the asset or received to assume the liability. This issue is particularly relevant for asset or liability classes in which there is a measurable bid-ask spread.

When must an emerging entity recognize an intangible asset?

As noted earlier, the excess of the reorganization value over the fair value amounts assigned to various tangible assets is evidence of an unidentified intangible asset or assets.

In this situation, the issue that typically arises is whether the company should recognize this excess value as a specific intangible asset or as more broadly defined goodwill. As a general rule, an intangible asset must be recognized as an asset apart from goodwill if (1) it arises from a contractual or legal right, or (2) it is separable. If an asset does not meet one of these two criteria, the asset must be included in the amount initially recorded as goodwill.

An intangible asset is considered *separable* if the emerging entity is able to separate or divide it from the broader organization and subsequently sell, license, rent, exchange, or otherwise transfer the asset to another entity. Thus, a contractual or legal right might give rise to an intangible asset even if it cannot be separated and/or sold, while a separable asset likewise represents an intangible asset regardless of the reconstituted entity's intent to subsequently sell the asset. Examples include

- *An acquired customer list.* While it is not a contractual right, the list is separable and thus represents an intangible asset. However, a "walk-in" customer base is not an intangible asset because it is not separable.

- *An acquired patent that expires in 15 years.* Regardless of the entity's intent to sell or otherwise dispose of it, the patent represents a legal right and thus is an intangible asset.
- *Technology that cannot be patented.* While this is not based on a contractual or legal right, the technology is separable and thus represents an intangible asset.
- *An employee's five-year noncompete agreement.* The agreement is based on a contractual right and thus is an intangible asset. However, an "at-will" employee workforce is generally not considered an intangible asset unless the employees are subject to some form of employment agreement.

Unlike tangible assets, intangible assets do not typically have a "principal" or "active" market. How, then, should an intangible asset's fair value be determined?

The ideal fair value of an asset is based on a quoted market price in an active market. However, this scenario typically exists only when the asset is a commodity; intangible assets are rarely fungible, even if they are separable. Alternatively, the emerging entity should consider using one of three methods:

1. *Income approach.* This is the most commonly used approach and involves a discounted cash flow (DCF) analysis of the asset's expected future cash flows. As in other DCF analyses, the present value to which the cash flow is discounted is particularly sensitive to the choice of discount rate.
2. *Cost approach.* This method estimates the asset's value at its replacement cost. This approach is not very effective when the asset at issue is unique or highly proprietary, as it might not be easily replicated at a reasonable or otherwise appropriate cost.
3. *Market approach.* This third and final approach looks to the purchase prices of comparable assets in other arms-length transactions. This type of analysis is common in M&A, for instance, which frequently incorporates analyses of comparable companies or comparable transactions in the valuation process. However, the market approach is more difficult to apply to the

valuation of intangible assets because no market for the asset exists or the prices are not widely reported.

What disclosures about the fresh start accounting process are required?

The emerging entity's disclosure statement should include certain information related to the fresh start accounting process. This information, which typically appears in the footnotes to the pro forma balance sheet, includes the following:

- Adjustments to the historical amounts of individual assets and liabilities
- The amount of debt forgiveness
- The amount of prior retained earnings or deficit eliminated
- The assumptions and measurement techniques used in determining reorganization value, including discount rate, tax rate, forecast period, and so on

The balance sheet itself should be presented in a four-column format with information that bridges the carrying values from the predecessor to the successor company. These columns give predecessor company data, effects of the plan of reorganization, effects from the adoption of fresh start accounting, and successor company data. By the same token, the reconstituted company should segregate data from the successor periods in its income and cash flow statements (as well as related footnotes).

What does a fresh start balance sheet look like in a company's financial statements?

The discussion that follows illustrates various disclosures by Lear Corporation, an auto parts supplier that filed for bankruptcy on July 7, 2009. The bankruptcy court subsequently approved Lear's plan of reorganization on November 7, 2009, which became the effective date for the company's adoption of fresh start accounting. Exhibit 9-2 contains the four-column balance sheet as of that date:

Exhibit 9-2 Sample Fresh Start Balance Sheet ($ millions)

	Predecessor November 7, 2009	Reorganization Adjustments[1]	Fresh-start Adjustments[9]	Successor November 7, 2009
Assets				
Current Assets:				
Cash and cash equivalents	$1,493.9	$(239.5)[2]	$–	$1,254.4
Accounts receivable	1,836.6	–	–	1,836.6
Inventories	471.8	–	9.1	480.9
Other	338.7	–	6.7	345.4
Total current assets	4,141.0	(239.5)	15.8	3,917.3
Long-Term Assets:				
Property, plant and equipment, net	1,072.3	–	(4.7)	1,067.6
Goodwill, net	1,203.7	–	(582.3)	621.4[8]
Other	518.0	(20.2)[3]	161.6	659.4
Total long-term assets	2,794.0	(20.2)	(425.4)	2,348.4
	$6,935.0	$(259.7)	$(409.6)	$6,265.7
Liabilities and Equity (Deficit)				
Current Liabilities:				
Short-term borrowings	$30.4	–	$–	$30.4
Debtor-in-possession term loan	500.0	(500.0)[2]	–	–
Accounts payable and drafts	1,565.6	–	–	1,565.6
Accrued liabilities	884.7	(1.8)[2]	17.5	900.4

Current portion of long-term debt	4.2	–	–	4.2
Total current liabilities	2,984.9	(501.8)	17.5	2,500.6
Long-Term Liabilities:				
Long-term debt	8.2	925.0[2][4]	–	933.2
Other	679.7	–	(37.7)	642.0
Total long-term liabilities	687.9	925.0	(37.7)	1,575.2
Liabilities Subject to Compromise	3,635.6	(3,635.6)[4]	–	–
Equity (Deficit):				
Successor Series A Preferred Stock	–	450.0[2][4]	–	450.0
Successor Common Stock	–	0.4[4][7]	–	0.4
Successor additional paid-in capital	–	1,635.8[4][7]	–	1,635.8
Predecessor Common Stock	0.8	(0.8)[5]	–	–
Predecessor additional paid-in capital	1,373.3	(1,373.3)[5]	–	–
Predecessor Common Stock held in treasury	(170.0)	170.0[5]	–	–
Retained deficit	(1,565.9)	2,070.6[6]	(504.7)	–
Accumulated other comprehensive loss	(60.8)	–	60.8	–
Lear Corporation stockholders' equity (deficit)	(422.6)	2,952.7	(443.9)	2,086.2
Noncontrolling interests	49.2	–	54.5	103.7
Equity (deficit)	(373.4)	2,952.7	(389.4)	2,189.9
	$6,935.0	$(259.7)	$(409.6)	$6,265.7

The following summarizes some of the key footnote disclosures from the fresh start balance sheet in Exhibit 9-2. Where appropriate, we have included some commentary elaborating on, or others supplementing, this footnote disclosure.

- *Footnotes 1–7: Effects of the plan of reorganization.* This series of footnotes summarizes the net outflow of cash resulting from approval of the plan of reorganization, as well as the corresponding impact on capitalized debt issuance costs and other capitalization line items.

1. Represents amounts recorded as of the Effective Date for the consummation of the Plan, including the settlement of liabilities subject to compromise, the satisfaction of the DIP Agreement, the incurrence of new indebtedness and related cash payments, the issuances of Series A Preferred Stock and Common Stock and the cancellation of Predecessor Common Stock.
2. This adjustment reflects net cash payments recorded as of the Effective Date, including both the initial and delayed draw funding under the First Lien Facility and the Excess Cash Paydown.

Borrowings under First Lien Facility	$ 375.0
Less: Debt issuance costs	(12.7)
First Lien Facility—net proceeds	362.3
Prepayment of Second Lien Facility	(50.0)
Prepayment of Series A Preferred Stock	(50.0)
Repayment of DIP Agreement, principal and accrued interest	(501.8)
Net cash payments	$ (239.5)

3. This adjustment reflects the write-off of $32.9 million of unamortized debt issuance costs related to the satisfaction of the DIP Agreement, offset by the capitalization of debt issuance costs related to the First Lien Facility (see (2) above).

4. This adjustment reflects the settlement of liabilities subject to compromise (see "—Liabilities Subject to Compromise" below).

Settlement of liabilities subject to compromise	$ (3,635.6)
Issuance of Successor Series A Preferred Stock (a)	500.0
Issuance of Successor Common Stock and Warrants (b)	1,636.2
Issuance of Second Lien Facility (a)	600.0
Gain on settlement of liabilities subject to compromise	$ (899.4)

(a) Prior to the Excess Cash Paydown.
(b) See (7) below for a reconciliation of the reorganization value to the value of Successor Common Stock (including additional paid-in-capital).

5. This adjustment reflects the cancellation of the Predecessor Common Stock.

6. This adjustment reflects the cumulative impact of the reorganization adjustments discussed above.

Gain on settlement of liabilities subject to compromise	$ (899.4)
Cancellation of Predecessor Common Stock (see (5) above)	(1,204.1)
Write-off of unamortized debt issuance costs (see (3) above)	32.9
	$ (2,070.6)

7. A reconciliation of the reorganization value to the value of Successor Common Stock as of the Effective Date is shown below:

Reorganization value	$3,054.0
Less: First Lien Facility	(375.0)
Second Lien Facility (c)	(550.0)
Other debt	(42.8)
Series A Preferred Stock (c)	(450.0)
Reorganization value of Successor Common Stock and Warrants	1,636.2

Less: Fair value of Warrants (d)	305.9
Reorganization value of Successor Common Stock	$1,330.3
Shares outstanding as of November 7, 2009	34,117,386
Per share value (e)	$38.99

(c) After giving effect to the Excess Cash Paydown.
(d) For further information on the fair value of Warrants, see Note 13, "Capital Stock."
(e) The per share value of $38.99 was used to record the issuance of the Successor Common Stock.

- *Footnote 8: Successor goodwill.* This footnote illustrates how the carrying value of the successor's goodwill is calculated. That is, a goodwill account of $621 million is created to reflect the amount by which the reorganization value of $6.265 billion exceeds the fair value of the successor's assets of $5.644 billion. (This resulted in a goodwill write-down of approximately $900 million from the predecessor company's carrying balance.)

8. A reconciliation of the reorganization value of the Successor assets and goodwill is shown below:

Reorganization value	$3,054.0
Plus: Liabilities (excluding debt and after giving effect to fresh start accounting adjustments)	3,108.0
Fair value of noncontrolling interests	103.7
Reorganization value of Successor assets	6,265.7
Less: Successor assets (excluding goodwill and after giving effect to fresh start accounting adjustments)	5,644.3
Reorganization value of Successor assets in excess of fair value—Successor goodwill	$621.4

- *Footnote 9: Fresh start adjustments.* This lengthy footnote summarizes the fresh start adjustments made to individual asset and nondebt liability line items on the emerging entity's balance sheet. Key fair value adjustments to Lear's balance sheet include the following:

- *Customer/technology intangible assets*: An increase in value of $162 million. The annual amortization expense related to Lear's intangible assets was $22 million.
- *Fixed assets*: A reduction in value of $5 million. This included a $14 million reduction in the value of Lear's land and buildings and a $9 million increase in the value of the company's machinery and equipment.
- *Finished goods inventory*: A write-up of $9 million.
- *Equity investments (nonconsolidated joint ventures)*: An increase of $9 million.
- *Noncontrolling interests (consolidated joint ventures)*: An increase of $55 million.

9. Represents the adjustment of assets and liabilities to fair value, or other measurement as specified by ASC 805, in conjunction with the adoption of fresh start accounting. Significant adjustments are summarized below.

Elimination of Predecessor goodwill	$ 1,203.7
Successor goodwill (see (8) above)	(621.4)
Elimination of Predecessor intangible assets	29.0
Successor intangible asset adjustment (f)	(191.0)
Defined benefit plans adjustment (g)	(55.0)
Inventory adjustment (h)	(9.1)
Property, plant and equipment adjustment (i)	4.7
Investments in nonconsolidated affiliates adjustment (j)	(8.7)
Noncontrolling interests adjustment (j)	54.5
Elimination of Predecessor accumulated other comprehensive loss and other adjustments	120.0
Pretax loss on fresh start accounting adjustments	526.7
Tax benefit related to fresh start accounting adjustments (k)	(22.0)
Net loss on fresh start accounting adjustments	$504.7

(f) Intangible assets—This adjustment reflects the fair value of intangible assets determined as of the Effective Date. For further information on the valuation of intangible assets, see Note 4, "Summary of Significant Accounting Policies."

(g) Defined benefit plans—This adjustment primarily reflects differences in assumptions, such as the expected return on plan assets and the weighted average discount rate related to the payment of benefit obligations, between the prior measurement date of December 31, 2008, and the Effective Date. For additional information on the Company's defined benefit plans, see Note 12, "Pension and Other Postretirement Benefits."

(h) Inventory—This amount adjusts inventory to fair value as of the Effective Date. Raw materials were valued at current replacement cost, work-in-process was valued at estimated finished goods selling price less estimated disposal costs, completion costs and a reasonable profit allowance for selling effort. Finished goods were valued at estimated selling price less estimated disposal costs and a reasonable profit allowance for selling effort.

(i) Property, plant and equipment—This amount adjusts property, plant and equipment to fair value as of the Effective Date, giving consideration to the highest and best use of the assets. Fair value estimates were based on independent appraisals. Key assumptions used in the appraisals were based on a combination of income, market and cost approaches, as appropriate.

(j) Investments in nonconsolidated affiliates and noncontrolling interests—These amounts adjust investments in non-consolidated affiliates and noncontrolling interests to their estimated fair values. Estimated fair values were based on internal and external valuations using customary valuation methodologies, including comparable earnings multiples, discounted cash flows and negotiated transaction values.

(k) Tax benefit—This amount reflects the tax benefits related to the write-off of goodwill and other comprehensive loss, partially offset by the tax expense related to the intangible asset and property, plant and equipment fair value adjustments.

Additional disclosure of segregated data for the predecessor and successor companies should appear in subsequent financial statements that include historical results from the bankruptcy period. The following disclosure is excerpted from Lear Corporation's fourth-quarter earnings release on February 5, 2010:

Fresh-Start Accounting

In connection with the Company's emergence from Chapter 11 bankruptcy proceedings on November 9, 2009, and the application of fresh-start reporting on November 7, 2009, in accordance with ASC Topic 852, "Reorganizations," the results for the two-month period ended December 31, 2009 (references to the Company for such period, the "Successor") and the results for the one-month and ten-month periods ended November 7, 2009 (references to the Company for such periods, the "Predecessor") are presented separately. This presentation is required by GAAP, as the Successor is considered to be a new entity for financial reporting purposes, and the results of the Successor reflect the application of fresh-start reporting. Accordingly, the Company's financial statements after November 7, 2009, are not comparable to its financial statements for any period prior to its emergence from Chapter 11. For illustrative purposes in this earnings release, the Company has combined the Successor and Predecessor results to derive combined results for the three- and twelve-month periods ended December 31, 2009. However, because of various adjustments to the consolidated financial statements in connection with the application of fresh-start reporting, including asset valuation adjustments, liability adjustments and recognition of cancellation of indebtedness income, the results of operations for the Successor are not comparable to those of the Predecessor. The financial information accompanying this earnings release provides the Successor and Predecessor GAAP results for the applicable periods, along with the combined results described above.

Exhibit 9-3 is the income statement presentation that accompanied Lear's fourth-quarter report. This presentation illustrates how Lear segregated and reported its 2009 financial results in two columns: preemergence financial results are presented as "predecessor" (including the impact of Chapter 11 reorganization, such as the extinguishment of debt and fresh start accounting), while postemergence financial results are presented as "successor."

This concludes our discussion of accounting issues in distressed M&A. The next chapter will present another set of process issues—namely, key areas of legal exposure in bankruptcy and how to mitigate them.

Exhibit 9-3 Sample Income Statement from a Post-bankruptcy Earnings Report ($ millions)

Lear Corporation and Subsidiaries
Condensed Consolidated Statements of Operations
(In millions, except per share amounts)

	Two Month Period Ended	Ten Month Period Ended	Twelve Month Period Ended	
	Successor December 31, 2009	Predecessor November 7, 2009	Combined December 31, 2009	Predecessor December 31, 2008
Net sales	$1,580.9	$8,158.7	$9,739.6	$13,570.5
Cost of sales	1,508.1	7,871.3	9,379.4	12,822.9
Selling, general and administrative expenses	71.2	376.7	447.9	511.5
Amortization of intangible assets	4.5	4.1	8.6	5.3
Goodwill impairment charges	–	319.0	319.0	530.0
Interest expense	11.1	151.4	162.5	190.3
Other expense, net	17.9	47.3	65.2	89.1
Reorganization items and fresh start accounting adjustments, net	–	(1,474.8)	(1,474.8)	–
Consolidated income (loss) before income taxes	(31.9)	863.7	831.8	(578.6)
Income taxes	(24.2)	29.2	5.0	85.8
Consolidated net income (loss)	(7.7)	834.5	826.8	(664.4)
Net income (loss) attributable to noncontrolling interests	(3.9)	16.2	12.3	25.5
Net income (loss) attributable to Lear	$(3.8)	$818.3	$814.5	$(689.9)
Basic net income (loss) per share	$(0.11)	$10.56		$(8.93)
Diluted net income (loss) per share	$(0.11)	$10.55		$(8.93)
Weighted average number of shares outstanding				
Basic	34.5	77.5		77.2
Diluted	34.5	77.6		77.2

Endnotes

1. Prior to FASB's adoption of the new codification rules, fresh start accounting was governed by AICPA Statement of Position 90-7, "Financial Reporting by Entities in Reorganization Under the Bankruptcy Code" (SOP 90-7). While SOP 90-7 is no longer authoritative, it remains instructive in many circumstances. SOP 90-7, adopted in November 1990, was the first specific accounting guidance for what basis companies should adopt upon emerging from bankruptcy. Until SOP 90-7, there often was an inconsistent application of the accounting standards following reorganizations. See Edward E. Nusbaum and Judith Weiss, "Preconfirmation Contingencies in Fresh-Start Reporting and an Update on Disclosure of Risks and Uncertainties," *Journal of Corporate Accounting and Finance.* Summer 1994, p. 575.

2. See, for example, New York City Bar, Committee on Taxation of Business Entities, "New York City Bar Report Regarding Proposals for Accounting Treatment on Non-Performing Loans," July 23, 2008; available at http://www.nycbar.org/pdf/report/ABCNY%20CityBar_%20Distressed_debt.pdf, last accessed April 25, 2010 (hereinafter "New York City NPL Tax Proposal").

3. 270 B.R. 393 (Bankr. E.D. Mich. 2001).

4. See New York City NPL Tax Proposal, note 2, p. 13.

5. Accrued but unpaid interest that was not deducted at the time may be deducted if it is paid at a later date.

6. New York City NPL Tax Proposal, note 2, p. 20. The New York City NPL Tax Proposal contains an excellent synopsis of the various conflicting case law, as well as recommendations for creating a more uniform legal approach.

7. For an excellent discussion of the Worker, Homeownership and Business Assistance Act of 2009, see Janet Pegg, "Turning NOLs into Cash," UBS, November 5, 2009.

8. *Pass-through entities* are structures that permit one level—rather than two levels—of taxation. There are four types of pass-through entities: (1) a partnership, both general and limited, (2) an LLC, (3) an S corporation, and (4) a C corporation that files a consolidated income tax return with its corporate parent. The earnings of C corporations are subject to double taxation, but the consolidated return provisions generally permit the earnings of subsidiary members of the consolidated return group to be taxed to the ultimate parent only. The earnings of an S corporation, with certain exceptions, are subject to taxation only at the shareholder level. The earnings of a partnership are also subject to a single tax, but only to the extent that such earnings are allocated to noncorporate partners (unless the partner is an S corporation). Partnership earnings that are allocated to corporate partners are subject to double taxation, just as though the income were earned directly by the corporations.

9. A worthless stock deduction counts toward this calculation and can inadvertently trigger an ownership change.

10. The debtor generally has a duty of inquiry to determine whether debt has been held for the required period, subject to a *de minimis* rule. In some cases, the debtor may seek an injunction to preclude trading in certain of its debt securities once the bankruptcy reorganization process is under way. This may help preserve the availability of the bankruptcy exemption for use upon emergence.
11. See, for example, http://pmstax.com/afr/exemptAFR.shtml, last accessed August 24, 2010, and http://www.rothcpa.com/archives/005713.php, last accessed March 2, 2010.
12. 284 U.S. 1 (1931).
13. The Mortgage Forgiveness Debt Relief Act of 2007 (Pub. Law 110-142) created a new exclusion under Sections 108(a)(1)(E) and 108(h) of the IRC for discharged qualified principal residence indebtedness. This exclusion applies to qualified principal residence indebtedness that is discharged on or after January 1, 2007, and before January 1, 2010 (subsequently extended to January 1, 2013). However, this exclusion is related to personal bankruptcy; as a result, it is outside the scope of this text.
14. However, the debtor cannot apply either the bankruptcy or the insolvency exclusion a second time on the same debt if the debtor subsequently files for bankruptcy a second time.
15. If the emerging entity subsequently sells substantially all of its assets, liquidates, or otherwise ceases to conduct business, any COD income that was deferred under these exclusions is pulled forward.
16. Because the IRC definition of insolvency includes the concepts of both fair market value and intangible assets, the insolvency test can prove to be particularly difficult in real-world applications.
17. According to one precedent, a contingent liability may be included in the insolvency determination only to the extent that the issuer is able to "prove by a preponderance of the evidence that he or she will be called upon to pay [the] obligation claimed to be a liability." D. B. Merkel, CA-9, 99-2 USTC ¶ 50,848, 192 F.3d 844, *aff'g* 109 T.C. 463, Dec. 52,423 (1997).
18. ASC 805 was formerly known as Financial Accounting Standard (FAS) No. 141R, "Business Combinations."

CHAPTER 10

Mitigating Legal Risks in Distressed M&A: Fiduciary Duties, Antitrust, and Fraudulent Transfers

> Wisdom too often never comes, and so one ought not to reject it merely because it comes too late.
>
> *—Felix Frankfurter, U.S. Supreme Court Justice*

OVERVIEW OF LEGAL RISK IN DISTRESSED ACQUISITIONS

What are the critical legal risks to keep in mind during the distressed M&A process?

When a company is experiencing financial and operational pressures, the last thing the buyer or seller needs is legal headaches. Yet this is precisely what may have to be faced if myriad legal issues are not addressed properly and proactively. When a company is already in a precarious condition, mishandled legal issues can accelerate the death spiral and make liquidation inevitable. The legal aspects of transactions can contain hidden minefields; deal makers must avoid detonation of these mines at all costs. Because it may still be possible to find creative solutions even late in a company's distress, it is important to keep Justice Frankfurter's point in mind. Indeed, astute legal maneuvering can transform a dire situation into a worthwhile investment opportunity.

The legal process permeates the restructuring process, and thus is worthy of a treatise in itself. Chapter 10 zeros in on three areas of legal risk that are of particular importance when buying, selling, or financing a distressed business: (1) directors' duties, (2) antitrust considerations, and (3) fraudulent transfer issues. This chapter summarizes the key principles for each of these three areas, and then addresses unusual legal considerations in distressed transactions. For a general overview of each of these three areas, please refer to *The Art of M&A*—Chapter 10 for directors' duties,[1] Chapter 2 for antitrust,[2] and Chapter 4 for fraudulent transfers.[3]

DUTIES OF CARE, LOYALTY, AND GOOD FAITH IN M&A

How do the fiduciary duties of loyalty, care, and good faith under state law apply in M&A?

In both traditional and distressed M&A, directors and officers must serve the company's interests, not their own, in approving a transaction; they must exercise care in making the decision to buy or sell; and they must act in good faith to fulfill their responsibilities. Evolving case law illuminates the meanings of these three concepts over time.

To elaborate, a director owes a *duty of loyalty* to act in the best interests of the company and its shareholders, for which he is a fiduciary. As such, the director is prohibited from entering into a transaction that is tainted by fraud or bad faith. If it appears that a director has a personal interest in a particular transaction, a court often will shift the burden of proof to the director to show that the transaction is fair and that it serves the best interests of the company and its shareholders.

A director also owes a *duty of care* (or *due care*), which involves acting on behalf of the company's stockholders by making informed decisions. This means that a director should obtain all reasonably available information that is required to make an intelligent decision and evaluate all relevant circumstances—including arguably whether a company has a workable system for reporting and compliance, as implied in the famous *Caremark* case.[4]

Finally, a director owes a *duty of good faith,* which is a very broad concept that underlies the other two duties. In a 2005 case involving Disney before the Delaware Chancery Court, later upheld by the Delaware Supreme Court, Chancellor William Chandler wrote, "The good faith required of a corporate fiduciary includes not simply the duties of care and loyalty, in the narrow sense that I have discussed them above, but all actions required by a true faithfulness and devotion to the interests of the corporation and its shareholders."[5]

In certain circumstances, a board's actions in carrying out its duties may face heightened scrutiny. For example, directors should proceed with extreme caution when approving a transaction that contemplates a change of control, occurs as the company is approaching insolvency, or involves bankruptcy. These situations are explored more deeply later in this chapter.

If directors and officers meet their fiduciary duties of care, loyalty, and good faith, their business decisions, even if flawed in hindsight, are generally protected from lawsuits under nonbankruptcy law under a judicial concept called the *business judgment rule.*

What is the business judgment rule?

The business judgment rule is a judicial doctrine applied by courts in cases where shareholders have sued directors for violating their fiduciary duties to the company. In a nutshell, the business judgment rule protects directors from liability if they act in a manner consistent with their duties of care, loyalty, and good faith.

The public policy rationale behind the rule is that the decisions of officers and directors should not be subject to attack by the courts with the benefit of hindsight. The rule thus presumes "that in making a business decision, the directors of a corporation acted on an informed basis, in good faith and in the honest belief that their actions are in the best interests of the company."[6] Accordingly, many courts generally will protect a director from mere errors of judgment or lack of prudence if the director, in making a business decision, acts in good faith, short of gross negligence.[7] As a general rule, this line of thinking carries over to a director's reliance on the reports of management[8] or on an expert opinion.[9]

Even where a director has not exercised the proper measure of care, she will be held personally liable only for corporate losses suffered as the direct and proximate result of her breach of duty. That is, injury to the company and causation must still be shown.[10] So-called acts of others are also a hot-button issue: a director is liable for the wrongful acts of other officers and directors only if she participated therein, was negligent in failing to discover the misconduct, or was negligent in appointing the wrongdoer.[11]

Nuances of legal interpretation have made fiduciary duties and the business judgment rule complex. The leading legal treatise on the topic is more than 6,000 pages long![12] Most major law firms offer very good guidance on these concepts and the latest cases involving them.

Under what circumstances might some courts find a director personally liable, despite the business judgment rule?

Most courts broadly conclude that a director cannot invoke the business judgment rule if he has failed to be reasonably diligent—i.e., if the director knew, or should have known, that he did not have sufficient facts to make a judgment, yet failed to make reasonable efforts to investigate further.[13] On the other hand, some courts, most notably in *Smith v. Van Gorkom*, have stated that the more narrow "*gross* negligence is . . . the proper standard for determining whether a business judgment reached by a board of directors was an informed one."[14]

Also, a director generally cannot invoke the business judgment rule if he causes the company to engage in acts that are illegal or contrary to public policy. A director is typically liable for any loss sustained by the corporation because of such acts, even if they were undertaken for the benefit of the company.[15]

Are there any legal strategies that corporate directors can adopt in order to further insulate themselves from a business judgment rule attack?

After the seminal *Van Gorkom* case, Delaware legislators enacted a provision in the state's General Corporation Law that permits an exculpatory clause for directors in a corporation's certificate of incorporation.[16] This provision enables the limitation, or outright elimination, of directors' personal liability for money damages to the company for breaches of fiduciary duties. Accordingly, in circumstances in which a plaintiff overcomes the business judgment rule by, for example, proving directors' gross negligence, such directors may nevertheless be exculpated for their breach.

Still, there are three general situations in which an exculpatory clause will not protect directors: (1) a breach of the duty of loyalty, (2) an act or omission that is not in good faith, and (3) intentional misconduct, a knowing violation of the law, or a transaction in which the director derives an improper personal benefit, among other circumstances.

Separately, an individual director may seek to avoid being held personally liable for acts of the entire board by recording her dissent in the minutes of a meeting of the board. However, in some circumstances, she may have to pursue other means, such as threatening a lawsuit.

Finally, directors should double-check the status, coverage, and exceptions to the company's directors and officers insurance policies (D&O insurance) to understand how they are protected from personal liability for their decisions.

What about officers and other managers? How does the business judgment rule apply to their decisions?

Alas, Delaware legislators were not as protective of corporate officers as they were of directors—at least in the context of creating the above-mentioned exculpatory provision. As noted by the Delaware courts in a recent 2009 case, "Although legislatively possible, there currently is no statutory provision authorizing comparable exculpation of corporate officers."[17] Corporate officers and other managers may still receive protection from personal liability through D&O insurance.

What should be considered when a shareholder is selling a large block of stock?

One of the most important considerations for a shareholder who is selling a large block of stock is the duty of due care that the shareholder may have to exercise, depending on the circumstances. This may include reasonable investigation of the potential purchaser: the courts have imposed liability on a controlling stockholder in circumstances in which such stockholder could reasonably foresee that the person acquiring the shares would engage in activities that would clearly be damaging to the corporation, such as looting, fraud, or gross mismanagement of the corporation. (By "person" here and for the rest of this chapter, we include corporations.) In planning a sale, a potential seller should fully investigate the potential purchaser's motive, resources, reputation, track record, conflicts of interest, and any other material items that are relevant to the transaction and the corporation.

A second consideration is the duty of loyalty that a controlling stock-holder owes to the minority stockholders. This duty generally arises when a controlling stockholder is selling shares at a premium. For example, if a corporation owns a large quantity of a product that is in short supply and could be sold at above-market rates, a controlling stockholder may have a fiduciary obligation to refrain from selling shares at a premium on the theory that the shareholder's receipt of the premium would constitute a misappropriation of a corporate opportunity (that is, the stockholder would be appropriating a certain amount of the corporate goodwill).

In addition, a few courts have imposed a requirement of "equal oppor-tunity" on a controlling stockholder. This requires a controlling stockholder to offer all of the other stockholders an opportunity to sell the same propor-tion of their shares as the controlling stockholder. Many courts have refused to apply this unwieldy principle.[19]

Accordingly, if a block purchase is challenged, the courts will review the particular facts surrounding the purchase to determine its fairness.

What is a recent M&A case involving the fiduciary duty of loyalty owed to shareholders of a public company?

In the case of *Oliver v. Boston University* (2006),[18] the Delaware Court of Chancery awarded $4.8 million, plus interest, to plaintiff shareholders for damages suffered from alleged breach of the fiduciary duty of loyalty before and during a merger.

The defendant, Boston University (BU), was the controlling share-holder of Seragen, and the plaintiffs were a group of former minority stock-holders of Seragen's common stock. The plaintiffs challenged certain transactions that occurred before Seragen was acquired by Ligan Pharma-ceuticals, such as a large stock offering that diluted the value of the existing equity. They also challenged the process used to allocate merger proceeds. The plaintiffs contended that BU breached its fiduciary duties to them by approving various financial transactions that were not fair to all sharehold-ers as a matter of price and process.

What about the duty of good faith? Are there any recent court decisions involving that?

In *Emerging Communications*, the court found that nine directors had breached their fiduciary duties to minority shareholders by approving a particular merger. Nevertheless, the court found that four of the directors were shielded from liability by the company's exculpation provision (in its indemnification agreement with directors and officers). This was because the plaintiffs had failed to present "a prima facie case of bad faith or disloyalty that [those] directors would be called upon to negate or disprove."[20] In other words, as one expert put it in a comprehensive article on the duty of good faith, "a breach of fiduciary duty will not automatically create a presumption of bad faith or disloyalty that the defendant must disprove. Rather, the court will presume that the breach was exclusively the product of a lack of due care until the plaintiffs produce evidence to the contrary."[21]

FIDUCIARY DUTIES IN DISTRESSED M&A

How do directors' duties change as the company approaches insolvency?

At a minimum, when a company is approaching insolvency, but remains outside of bankruptcy, there are more competing interests for directors to balance. While case law has created uncertainty regarding this topic, the historical rule has been that directors' duties change when insolvency is a concern. Notably, in *Credit Lyonnais*, an influential 1991 case, the Delaware Chancery Court suggested that directors' duties may shift from exclusively maximizing shareholder value to maximizing the value of the corporate enterprise when a company is in the so-called *zone of insolvency*.[22] In other words, when a company is approaching insolvency, the focus of directors' fiduciary duties changes from maximizing shareholder value to maximizing creditors' recoveries.

Therefore, the duties of care and loyalty described previously that are typically owed to stockholders come to be owed to creditors. An added twist in any complex transaction is the law of trusts, also called the corporate *trust fund doctrine*. In general, this doctrine provides that, once a company is insolvent, its assets are to be managed as though they were held in trust for the benefit of its creditors. Under this doctrine, directors and officers of a financially distressed company should avoid intermingling funds and other assets among affiliated companies or within the same company if different groups of creditors may have different claims on the assets. According to basic trust law principles, a fiduciary may not mingle assets in a way that weakens the claims against any of those assets. While directors' decisions as fiduciaries are generally protected by the business judgment rule discussed earlier, some legal experts say that the business judgment rule may not apply to board decisions made outside of court-supervised proceedings, such as bankruptcy.[23]

More recent Delaware case law appears to be gradually chipping away at, or at least narrowing, the *Credit Lyonnais* standard. For instance, in a 2004 decision, the Delaware Chancery Court held that directors may pursue the course of action that they believe is in the best interests of the firm and its stockholders, provided such directors honor *legal obligations* owed to the firm's creditors. In *Production Resources Group, L.L.C. v. NCT Group, Inc.*,[24] the court decided that because there was no fraud, officers and directors were protected against the fiduciary claims of creditors by the business judgment rule, which protects directors' decisions made in good faith with due care, even if the decisions turn out to have negative consequences.[25]

The Supreme Court of Delaware took an even stronger stance in *Gheewalla*. In this 1997 decision, the court held that directors' focus does not change in the zone of insolvency: such directors "must continue to discharge their fiduciary duties to the corporation and its shareholders by exercising their business judgment in the best interest of the corporation *for the benefit of its shareholders*."[26] The *Gheewalla* decision is also notable for underscoring that creditors' rights do not give rise to a direct claim, but rather give rise to a derivative action—at least in Delaware: "The creditors of a Delaware corporation that is either insolvent or in the zone of insolvency have no right, as a matter of law, to assert direct claims for breach of fiduciary duty against the corporation's directors."[27] This is because creditors have a different standing from shareholders: creditors already have sufficient protection from contract, implied duties of good faith and fair dealing, bankruptcy law, and the law of fraud and fraudulent conveyances, as well as other forms of creditors' rights.[28] Upon a corporation's insolvency, such creditors may nonetheless assert derivative actions.[29] Other states have left the door open for direct claims.[30] Clearly, the legal discussion in this area is still evolving.

Directors should proceed with extreme caution because their action or inaction could trigger legal liability. For example, in *In re Buckhead America Corp.*,[31] directors were held to have breached their fiduciary duties to creditors when they authorized a transaction whereby the subsidiary would incur $175 million in long-term debt to acquire the parent company's stock at a time when the company was insolvent or "operating within the vicinity of insolvency." Similarly, in *Brandt v. Hicks, Muse*, the bankruptcy court held that "the rights of creditors become paramount" and a trustee may not bring an action against the directors on behalf of the corporation where a transaction leaves the corporation insolvent or on the brink of insolvency with an unreasonably small amount of capital.[32]

We strongly recommend consulting legal counsel under these circumstances, which may also affect directors' duties under federal securities laws. It's currently unclear whether the expansion of the board's fiduciary duties may, in itself, be a material event requiring an SEC filing. On the one hand, such events rarely happen without the concurrent rising risk of a default on a material loan agreement, which clearly would require public disclosure. On the other hand, premature disclosure of the board's expanded duties could actually *harm* the board's ability to maximize enterprise value.

What exactly is the zone of insolvency, and when is a corporation in it?

Conflicting case law has created much uncertainty surrounding the so-called zone of insolvency, and, indeed, some professionals question whether it really exists. The concept of the zone of insolvency refers to the period where a company is approaching actual insolvency, meaning that the company is probably still solvent, but insolvency is a serious concern. If the company ultimately enters bankruptcy, then it seems safe to conclude that it probably was insolvent for a period of time beforehand, which is why voidable preference and fraudulent transfer claims consider the debtor's solvency in the pre-petition period. This concept produces legal theories that there may be liability for causing *deepening insolvency* for a company, which is discussed later in this chapter. However, if a company avoids bankruptcy by arranging so-called rescue financing, by completing a distressed sale of some or all of the business, or by experiencing fortuitous improvements in cash flow (e.g., from unexpected new business, a surprise victory in litigation, or a government bailout), concerns over its solvency will become moot.

For the purposes of this book, we will address these topics by assuming that there is no meaningful difference between actual insolvency and the zone of insolvency. As discussed in Chapter 1 of this book, the insolvency tests include (1) the balance sheet test, (2) the equity test, and (3) the unreasonably small amount of capital test.

From a practical (and cynical) perspective, if a board of directors has to ask whether a business is in the zone of insolvency, the company may already be there. Under these circumstances, it seems prudent to prepare for the worst rather than hope for the best.

It is important to note that insolvency, which implies long-term balance sheet issues, differs from illiquidity, which involves near-term cash flow challenges. Directors, officers, and creditors should consider the following to understand the company's predicament:

- What are the financial covenants in the company's credit agreements, and has the company already breached any of these financial covenants?
- What are the implications of the company's 13-week cash flow forecast, including the possibility of breaching financial covenants?
- Are there near-term refinancing solutions that can solve or prevent a liquidity crisis?
- Will lenders consent to forbearance agreements to give the company time to work through issues?
- Can payment terms with vendors be "stretched" or "termed out" to reduce working capital needs?
- What are the implications of the aging reports for accounts receivable or accounts payable?
- Are vendors refusing to ship new supplies or demanding payment upon delivery?
- Does the book value of the company's assets reflect the current market value?
- Are there any off-balance sheet liabilities to consider?
- Do appraisals of the company's assets need to be updated?
- Is the sum of the parts of the company worth more than the whole?
- Are there surplus or extraneous assets that can be liquidated quickly?
- Are there any lines of business that are unprofitable (or generating suboptimal profits) and should be discontinued or sold?

- Will the company's attempts to raise prices be offset by volume declines?
- What are the implications of the company's latest backlog of orders?
- How can overhead be reduced, SKUs be rationalized, and operations be made more efficient to improve cash flow?

Can actions that hasten a company's insolvency trigger legal liability?

Possibly. Multiple federal circuit courts in recent years have addressed the still-developing concept of *deepening insolvency*, which refers to harm to a debtor's corporate property from the fraudulent expansion of corporate debt and prolonging of a corporation's life outside of bankruptcy.[33] Those who have claims on the property can sue directors and officers of the insolvent company based on allegations of injury if such harm could have been "averted, and the value within an insolvent corporation salvaged, if the corporation [had been] dissolved in a timely manner, rather than kept afloat with spurious debt."[34]

In the limited case law that has followed from this concept, the judicial line of thinking appears to suggest that the theory of deepening insolvency is likely to apply only in circumstances that also involve fraudulent conduct—not merely negligence.[35] The following are examples of scenarios in which courts recognized deepening insolvency claims:[36]

- Directors used fraudulent financial statements to increase capital and shareholder investments, deepening the company's insolvency and causing bankruptcy.
- The parent company and directors continued to operate an insolvent company by fraudulently concealing the company's insolvency.
- The company negligently prepared and/or the company's auditors negligently approved financial statements that caused the corporation to incur unmanageable debts and file for bankruptcy.
- The company's advisors negligently prepared valuation reports that induced the corporation to continue to make corporate acquisitions and borrow additional funds, which resulted in financial deterioration.

Moreover, a growing number of decisions have held that deepening insolvency is not a separate cause of action, but rather a claim in conjunction with a claim of self-dealing or fraud.[37] For instance, one Ohio court suggested that deepening insolvency is redundant with some states' traditional causes of action,[38] while a New York decision suggested that the concept might be a theory of damages.[39] In all likelihood, this theory will be the subject of continued legal evolution.

What actions should a director consider if he believes that the business may be insolvent or approaching insolvency?

At a minimum, the director should verify and update the company's D&O insurance, which is an expense of the company but benefits the company's directors and officers personally. Separately, the board may consider retaining its own counsel to advise it on its fiduciary duties. Also, a director may want to carefully consider whether to resign from the board.

Many boards and board committees already retain their own counsel to work on matters of governance, so it seems appropriate for directors to retain independent counsel to advise on insolvency. Indeed, many governance guidelines and committee charters explicitly encourage this practice.[40] Such retention of independent counsel by the board for representation in the matter of a distressed company is typically necessary only when the interests of the board and those of the company are in conflict. If the interests are aligned, then it may be more efficient and economical for both the board and the company to rely on advice from the same attorney. If the interests may diverge, however, the company's counsel may advise that the board retain independent counsel and perhaps that individual directors consider obtaining their own attorneys. Of course, if an individual director ever feels uncomfortable, she may benefit from independent advice, which may involve an independent expense.

With regard to resigning from the board outright, a director may attempt to avoid tarnishing his reputation by being associated with a bankrupt company (although it may already be too late for that). Also, resigning from the board will eliminate the time-intensive, high-pressure, highly publicized responsibilities of directing the company through the bankruptcy process.

Furthermore, the director may feel fatigued and unwilling to learn the many peculiar topics discussed throughout this book that affect companies in distress.

One might argue that the director's own interests are better served by sticking it out rather than resigning. The director can rehabilitate her reputation by orchestrating a successful Chapter 11 reorganization, 363 sale process, or operational turnaround, which would be much more respectable than throwing in the towel. Because most plans of reorganization confirmed by bankruptcy courts provide for nondebtor releases that cover the directors, officers, and bankruptcy professionals of a debtor as well as official committees and their members, personal liability can be minimized.[41] Such releases are typically accompanied by protection by permanent injunction—the functional equivalent of a discharge granted to debtors—although there are legal limits in bankruptcy law to their breadth.[42]

After the bankruptcy case begins, if the company enters into a DIP loan, which is discussed in detail in Chapter 14 of this book, any change of control, which is defined to include a new majority of the board, is likely to be an event of default. Therefore, it is best for directors to decide whether or not to resign from the board prior to authorizing the filing of a voluntary bankruptcy petition.

If a director remains on the board of a company that enters bankruptcy, then the rates for the D&O insurance to cover that director on any company's board in the future may increase. Generally speaking, if a director of Company A discloses that he served on the board of bankrupt Company B, D&O insurance rates for Company A are likely to increase with respect to that director. However, the D&O policy questionnaire for Company A gives the director an opportunity to explain the circumstances of the bankruptcy of Company B. If the director served on the board of Company B prior to and leading up to its bankruptcy filing, this may increase the premium rates of both Company A and Company B. On the other hand, if the director was appointed to Company B's board during or after its bankruptcy, this fact may mitigate against increased premium rates for the director at both Company A and Company B. Clearly, directors dealing with these issues should double-check the exact wording of the D&O insurance policies in question.

SECTION 3: Avoiding Common Pitfalls

What is a board's role when a bankruptcy trustee is appointed?

If the bankruptcy court appoints a bankruptcy trustee, the bankruptcy trustee replaces the board of directors and assumes control of the debtor's business. See Chapter 4 of this book for details on bankruptcy trustees.

ANTITRUST CONSIDERATIONS IN DISTRESSED TRANSACTIONS

How does the antitrust analysis of distressed transactions differ from that of transactions involving going concerns?

Acquisitions proposed in the context of bankruptcy still must follow the merger guidelines involved in antitrust law. Like all M&A transactions, distressed transactions are governed by Section 7 of the Clayton Act, which is enforced by the Federal Trade Commission (FTC) and the Antitrust Division of the Department of Justice (DOJ). The parties to a proposed distressed transaction must furnish certain information about themselves and the deal to the FTC and the DOJ under the Hart-Scott-Rodino Antitrust Improvements Act of 1976, if applicable, before the transaction is allowed to go forward. There are two key differences in these requirements when transactions involve a distressed company: the timing of the review and the *failing firm defense*.

How does the timing of the antitrust review differ in a distressed scenario?

Ultimately, antitrust law's goal of keeping markets competitive is no less important during times of hardship—whether it be economywide or company-specific—than during times of prosperity. A bankruptcy filing does not affect the scope of the antitrust review, and a bankruptcy court does not have the authority to overrule or circumvent antitrust regulators; however, a bankruptcy can affect the speed with which the FTC and the DOJ conduct an antitrust review. Because of the urgency of a dire situation, there is less time to engage the relevant agency in the substance of the proposed transaction and to evaluate the assets involved. Accordingly, the substantive process for antitrust review generally should not be different—just faster.

What are the history and public policy rationale of the failing firm defense?

The rationale for the *failing firm defense*, also known as the *failing company doctrine*, is explained in the horizontal merger guidelines jointly issued by the FTC and DOJ as follows:

> [A] merger is not likely to create or enhance market power or to facilitate its exercise, if imminent failure . . . of one of the merging firms would cause the assets of that firm to exit the relevant market. In such circumstances, post-merger performance in the relevant market may be no worse than market performance had the merger been blocked and the assets left the market.[43]

The failing firm defense traces its roots back to a 1917 circuit court decision.[44] The Supreme Court first accepted the failing firm defense in *International Shoe* in 1930[45] and further articulated it in *Citizen Publishing* in 1969.[46] In a nutshell, the failing firm defense exempts an otherwise anticompetitive merger from antitrust challenge when the only alternative for a failing company is elimination from the relevant market.

In *International Shoe*, the Court reversed an FTC ruling against a proposed merger for two reasons: (1) that the two companies operated in separate markets and thus that their combination was unlikely to substantially lessen competition, and (2) that the acquired company faced financial ruin. In supporting the concept of the failing firm defense, the *International Shoe* Court emphasized the adverse impact of a bankruptcy of the acquired company on various constituencies (including shareholders, creditors, employees, and so on), as well as the viewpoint that competition would not be substantially lessened if a corporation that would otherwise fail were acquired by a competitor.

Thus, in *International Shoe*, the Court seemingly grounded the defense in the avoidance of the social costs of liquidation, specifically harm to shareholders of the failing firm and the communities in which its operations were located. This emphasis on social costs was not repeated in the Court's subsequent *Citizen Publishing* decision. In this case, the Court found that the situation did not meet the requirements for the failing firm defense. There was no proof that Citizen's owners were thinking of liquidating the newspaper, and the acquiring company was not the only available purchaser.

The emphasis on social costs has been repudiated by many as mistaken, in that the social costs of liquidation do not necessarily exceed the social costs of alternative dispositions. Nonetheless, the proverbial pendulum may be swinging back to the *International Shoe* approach. *International Shoe*'s Depression-era consideration of social costs does seem to be in step with contemporary economic policy, forged out of economic crisis.

As described later in this chapter, the legal threshold to proffer a failing firm defense successfully is very high. From a practical standpoint, therefore, the defense is not used often.

What are the legal elements of the failing firm defense?

When defending against an alleged antitrust violation in federal court, this affirmative defense must be alleged in the defendant's answer to the complaint, and the defendant bears the burden of proof. Out of an abundance of caution, defendants should present evidence to satisfy both (1) the requirements under the guidelines explained by the FTC and the DOJ and (2) the conditions established by case law.

There are four requirements in the horizontal merger guidelines jointly issued by the FTC and DOJ that must be met in asserting the failing firm defense for an alleged antitrust violation:

1. The allegedly failing firm must be unable to meet its financial obligations in the near future.
2. The firm must be unable to reorganize successfully under Chapter 11 of the Bankruptcy Code.
3. Unsuccessful good faith efforts to elicit reasonable alternative offers to acquire the failing firm's assets must have been made.[47]
4. Absent the acquisition, the firm's assets would exit the market.

Courts have articulated the standard slightly differently, requiring two conditions:

1. The acquired firm must be in a failing condition. This means that it faces "the grave probability of business failure,"[48] such as when it is in, or is about to enter, bankruptcy or receivership.[49]

2. The acquired company must have had no other reasonable alternatives to the proposed merger that are less detrimental to competition.[50]

How does the antitrust law concept of "failing condition" differ from insolvency?

While this may sound like a paradox, not all insolvent companies are in a failing condition, legally speaking. For the purposes of the failing firm defense under antitrust law, not only must the firm face financial distress in the short term, but its fundamental ability to compete effectively over the long run must be in doubt. To this end, if a company is overleveraged, needs a new business strategy, or should upgrade its management, it is unlikely to meet the standard for being in a failing condition. Instead, the failing condition standard focuses on whether the company has valuable assets that are capable of supporting its continued existence as a going concern. As a leading antitrust regulator recently explained, "Accounting losses do not necessarily correspond to true economic losses from ongoing operations, especially for firms that have taken on substantial debt."[51]

The failing condition standard appears to be more closely aligned with the feasibility requirement for a plan of reorganization in bankruptcy, which is discussed in Chapter 12 of this book, or the proof required to convert a Chapter 11 reorganization to a Chapter 7 liquidation, rather than the concept of insolvency.

Is the defense available when divesting a failing division of an otherwise healthy company?

Generally, yes. The horizontal merger guidelines jointly issued by the FTC and the DOJ include a defense for divesting failing divisions of otherwise healthy companies in violation of antitrust laws.[52] Courts have generally recognized this defense.[53] The requirements are as follows:

1. Upon applying appropriate cost allocation rules, the division must have a negative cash flow on an operating basis.
2. Absent the divestiture, the assets of the division would exit the relevant market in the near future (e.g., via liquidation, abandonment,

or discontinuation). Because of the ability of the parent firm to manipulate the accounting for costs, revenues, and intracompany transactions for antitrust purposes, the FTC or the DOJ will require clear evidence beyond management's alleged plans for the failing division.

3. The parent has made unsuccessful good faith efforts to elicit reasonable alternative offers of acquisition of the assets of the failing firm that would both keep its tangible and intangible assets in the relevant market and pose a less severe danger to competition than does the proposed merger. Note that this requirement is the same as the third requirement for the failing firm defense explained earlier.

It is difficult to determine the amount of capital that the parent company may allocate to the failing division to support its future operations and fund turnaround strategies. Therefore, the FTC and the DOJ will consider evidence regarding whether a third-party lender or investor (i.e., a party with no incentive to pursue an anticompetitive merger with the prospective acquirer) would provide capital for the failing division to pursue a turnaround.

How frequently is the failing firm defense invoked successfully?

Because the requirements are strict and can rarely be fully satisfied, the failing firm defense has been upheld in only a few court decisions since 1930,[54] and in no Supreme Court cases since *International Shoe*. Moreover, in light of the strict legal standard, there have been few mergers in which this defense has been proffered and in which either the FTC or the DOJ has accepted it after investigation.

Some commentators have suggested that the current failing firm defense is analytically superfluous. That is, any firm that met the defense's strict requirements probably would not raise competitive concerns under competitive effects analysis in the FTC/DOJ's guidelines as a threshold matter. Others suggest that the rigidity of the failing firm doctrine should be somewhat loosened. Such commentators point to economic thinking that indicates that it is generally preferable to allow a merger rather than have assets exit the market because output is reduced when assets exit. Finally, more recent discussion has centered on whether it would be appropriate to relax the requirements of the failing firm defense in distressed economic situations. To this end, while a deep economic recession does not affect the broader antitrust analysis, it might be one relevant factor to consider in evaluating the overall competitive environment.[55]

What if a merger target is weakened instead of failing? What impact does that have on the antitrust analysis?

Financial weakness cannot be the primary justification for permitting a merger; in fact, the court of appeals in *Kaiser Aluminum* dubbed it "probably the weakest ground of all for justifying a merger."[56] Interestingly, although Kaiser Aluminum remained viable for over two decades following this 1981 decision, it ultimately filed a voluntary bankruptcy petition in 2002. The reader can draw his own conclusions as to which side was correct in 1981, given this outcome.

Because antitrust analysis is forward-looking, if a firm is "flailing"—rather than failing—the merger is unlikely to be anticompetitive. That is, the merger may not substantially lessen future competition in the industry if the flailing firm is unable to be an effective competitor on its own anyway.[57] The competitive landscape would remain approximately the same regardless of whether the merger is completed. Thus, courts typically consider the financial weakness of a firm "as one relevant factor among many" to be considered when determining whether the merger will substantially lessen competition.[58]

FRAUDULENT TRANSFERS GENERALLY

What, exactly, are fraudulent conveyance laws, and what attributes of an M&A deal can cause a company to run afoul of them?

Fraudulent conveyance laws—also called fraudulent transfer laws—stem originally from English common law. Dating back to 1571 in the Statute of Elizabeth laws (after Queen Elizabeth I),[59] fraudulent conveyance laws are now enshrined in the Bankruptcy Code, the Uniform Fraudulent Conveyance Act (UFCA), and the Uniform Fraudulent Transfer Act (UFTA). All states have adopted fraudulent conveyance laws based either on the uniform acts or on common law.

Under the Bankruptcy Code and comparable provisions of state law, a transfer of property (such as a lien given by the acquired company on its assets or a note secured by that lien), may be deemed "fraudulent" under certain conditions, enabling interested parties to avoid a transfer or to sue over it.[60]

A court may find fraud if the debtor transfers property with an actual intent to hinder, delay, or defraud creditors. For instance, suppose a company with $50 million of unsecured debts and unencumbered property worth $2 million gifted such property to the CEO's daughter—with the implicit understanding that the debtor could continue to use the property in the future—immediately prior to filing a voluntary bankruptcy petition.[61] Basic tenets of equity and fairness would support the view that a bankruptcy court should not permit such a transaction.

Nonetheless, few situations (one would hope) would be so egregious, making "actual intent" a difficult standard to meet in many cases. Accordingly, a court may more typically also find fraud if an acquirer of the property receives "less than reasonably equivalent value"[62] in exchange *and* one of the following three conditions exists:

1. The company was *insolvent* at the time of such transfer or became insolvent as a result of the transfer.
2. The company was left with *unreasonably small capital* as a result of the transfer.
3. The company incurred or intended to incur debts beyond its *ability to pay*.

Still, "less than reasonably equivalent value" is a somewhat ambiguous term and is not defined in the Bankruptcy Code. Under the relevant case law, the term does not necessarily refer to market value.[63] Instead, it may be as simple as the price *actually paid for property in a foreclosure*,[64] as long as state foreclosure laws (pertaining to notice of intent to foreclose and other such issues) are otherwise respected. State foreclosure laws, by the way, are basically the law of mortgages (because any foreclosure essentially ends a mortgage agreement). In the United States, mortgage law is mainly governed by state and common law. When a mortgage is a negotiable instrument, it is governed by Article 3 of the Uniform Commercial Code (UCC), which covers negotiable instruments. Legal treatment of a mortgage depends in part on the identity of the entity holding the mortgage (the mortgagee). Thus, although mortgage law is handled at the state and common law level, as noted, institutions that are chartered by the federal government may nevertheless fall under federal law.[65]

In addition, the meaning of the term *insolvent* differs among jurisdictions, largely depending on whether the jurisdiction has adopted the UFCA or the UFTA (defined earlier). The federal definition, dictated by the Bankruptcy Code, uses a simple balance sheet test and excludes both fraudulently transferred property and exempt property from the fair value of the debtor's property. Contingent assets, such as rights to contribution and subrogation, must be valued for purposes of determining solvency under the federal rules. However, to value the contingent asset or liability correctly, it is necessary to discount it by the probability that the contingency will occur and the asset will be realized or the liability will become real.[66]

The UFCA's approach is more complex, defining a person as insolvent "when the present fair salable value of his assets is less than the amount that will be required to pay his probable liability on his existing debts as they become absolute and matured."[67] *Present fair salable value* means the value that can be obtained if the assets are sold with reasonable promptness in an existing (not theoretical) market. Accordingly, a debtor could have assets in excess of its liabilities (and thus be solvent under the Bankruptcy Code), but be insolvent under the UFCA's definition if the assets were longer-term and illiquid while the liabilities were shorter term.

The UFTA defines a person as insolvent when the sum of its liabilities exceeds the sum of its assets "at a fair valuation." While this balance sheet test is more closely aligned with the Bankruptcy Code's approach than the UFCA's framework, the UFTA does not define "a fair valuation." However, the UFTA does create a rebuttable presumption that a person is insolvent if she generally has not been paying debts as they become due. This is significant because a debtor that is not a timely payer of maturing debts in effect has the burden of proof of demonstrating solvency under the UFTA. Since fraudulent transfer laws consider insolvency only on the actual date that such transfer was made (not before and not after), proving insolvency at a precise moment of time can be particularly burdensome; nonetheless, creditors in UFTA jurisdictions may have a means around this requirement.

Would a court be likely to find a fraudulent transfer when a debtor repaid only selected creditors prior to filing for bankruptcy?

Not necessarily. First of all, a debtor's preference for one creditor over others is not a *prima facie* indication of fraud. Fraudulent conveyance laws are not particularly focused on the *allocation* of a debtor's estate, but rather that *some* deserving creditor is being repaid from the debtor's reachable assets.

Second, provided the debtor does not receive less than reasonably equivalent value, as described earlier, the transaction would generally fall outside the fraudulent transfer construct. One primary exception, however, would be where the transferee is deemed an *insider* to the debtor and the insider had reasonable cause to be aware of the debtor's insolvency.

Who can sue under fraudulent conveyance laws?

Under Section 1107(a) of the Bankruptcy Code, generally only the trustee or debtor in possession has the "avoiding power" and the right to commence an action alleging a fraudulent conveyance. However, courts have, in special circumstances, made exceptions:

> A creditor or creditors' committee may have derivative standing to initiate an avoidance action where: 1) a demand has been made upon the statutorily authorized party to take action; 2) the demand is declined; 3) a colorable claim that would benefit the estate if successful exists, based on a cost-benefit analysis performed by the court; and 4) the inaction is an abuse of discretion ("unjustified") in light of the debtor-in-possession's duties in a chapter 11 case.[68]

A prime example of this scenario might be where the debtor's estate lacks sufficient funds to bring the action itself. Finally, an individual debtor may have standing in limited cases, such as when the trustee does not initiate an action and the property would have been exempt.

Who can be sued or be forced to give up funds if a company goes bankrupt after it is acquired?

Courts may impose penalties on any party who knew that the loan proceeds would be paid to the target's original shareholders while debt was being imposed on the target's assets.[69]

- *The entity that emerges from bankruptcy* may be liable for the full amount of the conveyance (the purchase price of the company).
- *Target shareholders* might have to refund the purchase price for their stock.

- *Lenders* who were in the know might have to subordinate their claims to the claims of other creditors, or be asked to refund any loan payments that they received.
- *Professionals* advising the transaction might have to refund their fees, or be sued for negligence.

Can a pledge of collateral, or a note or guaranty, be a fraudulent conveyance, even though there is no intent to defraud anyone?

Yes. Although fraudulent *conveyance* is the term of art, the legal principle also applies to liens and obligations. Both the Bankruptcy Code and comparable provisions of state law permit the voiding of a lien or obligation as "fraudulent" without the requirement of bad faith or intent. These laws may, in effect, be utilized to protect the interests of general creditors of acquired companies when the transactions financed by the banks have the effect of depriving the acquired company of the means to pay its debts to its general creditors, whether those transactions are actually intended to have this effect or not.

What are upstreaming and cross-streaming, and why are they bad?

Upstreaming occurs when a subsidiary provides collateral to secure a borrowing by its parent. *Cross-streaming* occurs when collateral is provided by one subsidiary to secure borrowing by a sister subsidiary. Both are undesirable under the law because the donor entity—the one providing the collateral or the guaranty—is not getting "reasonably equivalent value," which is going instead to its affiliate.[70] Thus, one of the triggers (although not the only one) for fraudulent conveyance is tripped. In addition, each subsidiary is typically asked to guarantee all the senior debt of its parent, yet the assets of the subsidiary represent only a fraction of the total acquisition. The result is that each subsidiary, taken by itself, cannot repay the full acquisition debt and may be rendered insolvent if the guarantee is called against it alone. This illogical result would be avoided if the test of solvency took into account that all the subsidiaries would share in meeting the guarantee obligation.

Some cases give support for this conclusion, but unfortunately, the law is not clear enough to eliminate the risk.

By contrast, *downstreaming* poses no particular danger to creditors. Downstreaming occurs when a parent makes guarantees and pledges to support borrowing by a subsidiary.

Are there ways to solve upstreaming and cross-streaming problems?

Yes. If the transaction passes each of the three additional tests—(1) no insolvency, (2) not unreasonably small capital, and (3) ability to pay debts—there is no fraudulent conveyance. However, to guard against the risk of flunking one of the tests, two kinds of additional solutions can be explored: (1) merging the entity providing the collateral or guaranty with the borrower before the acquisition is consummated, or (2) dividing up the loan into two or more distinct credit facilities, each collateralized by (and commensurate with) the particular borrower's collateral. If the latter course is used, care should be taken to avoid having the loan proceeds simply pass through one of the borrowers into the hands of another borrower or affiliated entity. The loan proceeds can be used to pay off bona fide intercorporate debt, but if the cash flow among the borrowing entities indicates that the separate loans are shams, the transaction runs the risk of being collapsed in a bankruptcy proceeding. In such a case, the liens and guaranties could be voided.

Are upstream or cross-stream guaranties that are limited to the net worth of the guarantor fraudulent conveyances?

No. Indeed, limiting the guaranty (and the lien collateralizing it) to the amount of the guarantor's net worth at the time of delivery of the guaranty can provide an ingenious way to ensure that the guarantor is not rendered insolvent by delivery of the guaranty and consequently should eliminate any fraudulent conveyance problem. However, the guarantor must have the requisite net worth in the bankruptcy sense, not just net worth under generally accepted accounting principles (GAAP), in addition to being able to pay its debts and not having an unreasonably small amount of capital. Net worth guaranties have yet to be tested in a bankruptcy proceeding, and although they appear to be conceptually sound, there are no certain predictions on what the courts will say.

What impact did the 2005 BAPCPA have on Section 548 of the Bankruptcy Code?

The Bankruptcy Abuse Prevention and Consumer Protection Act of 2005 (2005 BAPCPA) had three primary impacts on federal fraudulent conveyance laws:

1. For cases filed on or after April 20, 2006, the amendments extended the reachback period to two years, from the previous one year.
2. For cases filed on or after April 20, 2005, the amendments empowered the trustee to avoid an insider transfer made pursuant to an employment contract if the transfer was made outside the ordinary course of business and the debtor received less than reasonably equivalent value. Proof of insolvency is not required.
3. The amendments also permit the trustee to avoid transfers made within 10 years before commencement of the case if the debtor makes a transfer to a self-settled trust of which it is a beneficiary with actual intent to hinder, delay, or defraud the creditor.

Suppose that through sophisticated structuring, a transaction gives the appearance of providing adequate consideration. Won't a court respect that at face value?

No. The courts are smarter than that. They have developed something called the *step-transaction* doctrine to see through such tricks. This doctrine developed out of common law but is now enshrined in U.S. tax law. Decisions citing this doctrine vary greatly, but the applicability of the step-transaction doctrine (i.e., the collapsibility of the structure containing the steps) depends on the following four factors:

1. *The degree of interdependence of the steps.* The higher the degree of interdependence, the more likely it is that the steps may be collapsed.
2. *The extent of any binding commitments.* The fewer the binding commitments, the more collapsible the structure.
3. *The elapsed time between the various steps.* The shorter the time, the more collapsible the structure.

4. *The end result or intention of the parties.* The more the structure appears to have been engineered for a specific outcome, the more likely it is to be collapsed.[71]

Will accounting firms give solvency opinions?

No. Such opinions were given from time to time in the past to provide reassurance to lenders. After adverse outcomes on some such opinions in early 1988, the American Institute of Certified Public Accountants (AICPA) prohibited all accounting firms from rendering solvency letters, and they are unlikely to reappear soon. Some appraisers or valuation consultants will give such opinions, however.

Will law firms give opinions that fraudulent conveyance laws have not been violated?

Almost never. Law firms generally refuse to give fraudulent conveyance opinions, largely because they cannot evaluate the question of solvency, and because lawyers have traditionally refused to predict what actions a bankruptcy court may take under a set of unforeseeable circumstances. Lenders usually understand and accept this reluctance, although some skirmishing on this point sometimes occurs at the closing.

The "Samex" Case: Illustrating the Vulnerability of the Bankruptcy Process to Fraud and the Relative Finality of Acquisition Decisions Made in Bankruptcy Court

The following case is based on actual events as alleged in correspondence from a bidder to the unsecured creditors committee of a manufacturing company located in the Midwest. The information given is true, but the names of the parties are fictitious.

Two manufacturing companies, Retool and NewThink, attempted to buy an insolvent entity, Samex, located in another state. When Samex filed for bankruptcy, its CEO announced the board's decision to sell the company. The sale would be structured as an asset sale, and substantially all the assets of the company would be sold.

The three largest stockholders of Samex were also three of the company's largest creditors, with both secured and unsecured debt. Less than two years before, these same stockholders had crafted a reverse merger that allowed them to take over the majority interest in Samex. These stockholder/creditors then controlled the board with three out of the five seats, allowing them to orchestrate this decision. They formed an investment group called TET, which made a first ("stalking horse") bid, purportedly intended to be part of a court-approved process for soliciting "competitive" bids. The bidders claimed that their bid price, at a minimum, would match the amount of all the secured debts of the company, which were senior to their own debt.

The TET bid was structured to be partly in cash and partly in notes. The TET bidders said that the cash portion would be capped at $20 million, the estimated amount of the company's current senior secured debt. They said that the notes portion was worth $12 million, an amount representing what Samex already owed to TET. (The TET credit was junior only to Samex's bank and other lenders, principally leasing companies.) This was supposed to be a lowball bid to attract additional bids. The unsecured creditors' committee of the board, believing that other bids would be forthcoming, approved the bid.

Therefore, the CEO of Samex stated that the target price was $32 million. The deal was structured so as to give a cap on a purchase price, rather than a purchase price. Here is the actual agreement language (disguising the name of the commercial bank holding the senior debt):

> The cash consideration to be paid by Buyer to Seller for the Assets (the "Purchase Price") shall be the sum of (a) the amount required to pay the secured debt of Senex Bank as of Closing plus (b) $750,000 plus (c) any Cure and Closing Costs (as hereinafter defined) plus (d) any other liabilities specifically assumed by Buyer as part of the Approval Order plus (e) the Stay Bonuses (as hereinafter defined) less (f) the Closing Date Cash (as defined in Section 1.2). Notwithstanding the foregoing, if the Purchase Price exceeds the Purchase Price Cap (hereinafter defined) or the Cure and Closing Costs exceed $2,500,000, then the Buyer shall be entitled to elect not to pay the Purchase Price and refrain from consummating the Closing. Buyer shall be entitled to participate in any discussions regarding the Cure

and Closing Costs. For the purposes of this Agreement, "Cure and Closing Costs" shall mean the aggregate of (i) any amount(s) required to cure a default under any contract, lease or license listed in Exhibits A to C hereof or any Discretionary Agreement, (ii) any purchase option(s) on assets not owned by Seller and used in connection with the Business, (iii) any amount(s) required to pay a third-party to extinguish a lien upon any of the Assets or assets not owned by Seller and used in connection with the Business, (iv) any fees due and owing by the Seller that would be permitted under the Debtor Professional Fee Carveout (as defined in the DIP Financing Facility), (v) any fees due and owing by the Seller that would be permitted under the Committee Professional Fee Carveout (as defined in the DIP Financing Facility), (vi) quarterly fees due and owing by the Seller to the Office of United States Trustee, (vii) any winding up fees incurred by the Seller not to exceed $50,000. For the purposes hereof, the "Stay Bonuses" shall mean the aggregate amount necessary to pay each of the employees listed on Schedule 2.1.1 hereto an amount equal to (x) one-half of the annual salary that such employee is currently receiving from Seller and as listed on Schedule 2.1.1 (such annual salary with respect to each such employee, his or her "Annual Salary") for each such employee that is not offered a full-time position with the Buyer, and (y) one-twelfth of such employee's Annual Salary, for each such employee that is offered a full-time position with the Buyer. The "Purchase Price Cap" shall mean (a) Twenty Million and No/100 Dollars ($20,000,000) subject to adjustment as set forth in Section 2.1.2 below plus (b) any cure costs for Discretionary Agreements that Buyer elects to assume plus (c) any other liabilities specifically assumed by Buyer as part of the Approval Order less (d) the Closing Date Cash.

The competing bidders had the impression that $32 million was an actual bid, and so tried to match it, even though it was actually high for an asset sale. Each of these bidders had a strategic reason for wanting to purchase the company. That is, they had new technologies that could be leveraged to increase the worth of Samex's assets into something that could justify the $32 million price. Although they lowered their bids slightly during the bidding process, they wound up bidding more than TET, the insider group.

Previously, the TET group, through the company's bankruptcy filings, had convinced the bankruptcy court to allow an investment banking company selected by the TET group to monitor and supervise the competitive bidding process. This investment banking company succeeded in disqualifying all other bidders through a process that it defined and controlled, and that was not subject to oversight review by the courts.

In the end, following the recommendation of the investment banking firm, the court approved the bid from the insider "stalking horse" group, the only remaining bid on the table. The inside bidders wound up paying less than $20 million, because a decision of the bankruptcy court forced a lowering of the amount of senior debt owed to Senex Bank, the senior lender.

Shareholders in a Samex subsidiary called RIF attempted to challenge the transaction. After acquiring RIF for stock and holding it as a wholly owned subsidiary, Samex put RIF into bankruptcy when RIF was operating at near breakeven. The Samex shares owned by the sellers of RIF lost virtually all of their value as a result of the bankruptcy filing. The RIF sellers have alleged that the acquisition of RIF and the subsequent bankruptcy filing indicated a pattern of fraud by TET for the purpose of obtaining control of RIF (via Samex) at bargain rates. Specifically, the RIF sellers alleged that the insider group from TET used the bankruptcy process to take over Samex (and, via Samex, RIF), eliminating the shareholders of RIF and weakening the claims of the shareholders of Samex, giving almost nothing to all other creditors, and using the assets of Samex to finance RIF's purchase.

An attorney in a major law firm specializing in litigation against directors and officers, when presented with this same pattern of facts, declined to take on the case, stating, "My conclusion is that any claims related to the acquisition in the bankruptcy proceedings are probably barred as a result of the Court's approval of the transaction. Thus, it is not a case that we would be willing to prosecute."

The competing bidders, unsecured creditors, and minority investors in Samex all believe that they could have been better served through a truly independent bidding process. At this time, however, it appears that the decision of the bankruptcy court, because of its legal status as such, is final.[72]

This cautionary case concludes our discussion of the legal aspects of distressed M&A. The next and final section of our book examines M&A issues from a strategic perspective.

Endnotes

1. For more on directors' fiduciary duties, see Stanley F. Reed, Alexandra R. Lajoux, and H. Peter Nesvold, *The Art of M&A: A Merger/Acquisition/Buyout Guide*, Chapter 10 (New York: McGraw-Hill, 2010).

2. For more on antitrust basics, see Stanley F. Reed, Alexandra R. Lajoux, and H. Peter Nesvold, *The Art of M&A: A Merger/Acquisition/Buyout Guide*, Chapter 2 (New York: McGraw-Hill, 2010). For an extensive discussion of current antitrust law, see Alexandra R. Lajoux and Charles Elson, *The Art of M&A Due Diligence: Navigating Critical Steps and Uncovering Crucial Data*, Chapter 8 (New York: McGraw-Hill, 2010).

3. For more on fraudulent transfers, see Stanley F. Reed, Alexandra R. Lajoux, and H. Peter Nesvold, *The Art of M&A: A Merger/Acquisition/Buyout Guide*, Chapter 4 (New York: McGraw-Hill, 2010).

4. *In re Caremark Int'l Inc. Derivative Litigation,* 698 A.2d 959 (Del. Ch. 1996). This section, and some other parts of this chapter, incorporates some materials from Stanley Foster Reed, Alexandra Reed Lajoux, and H. Peter Nesvold, *The Art of M&A: A Merger/Acquisition/Buyout Guide* (New York: McGraw-Hill, 2007).

5. This 2005 case was upheld in the Delaware Supreme Court in 2006. *In re The Walt Disney Company Derivative Litigation,* No. 411, 2005 (Del. June 8, 2006).

6. *Aronson v. Lewis,* 473 A.2d 805, 812 (Del. 1984), *overruled in part on other grounds by Brehm v. Eisner,* 746 A.2d 244 (Del. 2000).

7. See *Shlensky v. Wrigley,* 237 N.E.2d 776 (Ill. 1968).

8. See, for example, Cal. Corp. Code §309(b).

9. Ibid.

10. This judicial precedent has a particularly long lineage in the context of corporate law. See, for example, *Barnes v. Andrews,* 298 F. 614 (S.D.N.Y. 1924).

11. See, for example, *Francis v. United Jersey Bank,* 432 A.2d 814 (N.J. 1981).

12. Nancy E. Barton, Dennis J. Block, and Stephen A. Radin, *The Business Judgment Rule: Fiduciary Duties of Corporate Directors,* 6th ed. (New York: Aspen Publishing, 2009)—a 6,000-page book.

13. See, for example, *Francis v. United Jersey Bank,* 432 A.2d 814 (N.J. 1981).

14. 488 A.2d 858, 873 (Del. 1985) (emphasis added), *overruled in part on other grounds by Gantler v. Stephens,* No. Civ. A. 2392, 2009 WL 188828, at *13 n.54 (Del. Jan. 27, 2009).

15. See, for example, *Miller v. American Telephone & Telegraph Co.,* 507 F.2d 759 (3d Cir. 1974).

16. See 8 Delaware Section 102(b)(7).
17. *Gantler v. Stephens*, No. Civ. A. 2392, 2009 WL 188828, at *9 n.37 (Del. Jan. 27, 2009).
18. 2006 Del. Ch. LEXIS 210 (Del. Ch., Dec. 8, 2006).
19. Anupam Chander, "Minorities, Shareholder and Otherwise," *Yale Law Journal*, vol. 112 (October 2003).
20. *In re Emerging Communications, Inc. S'holders Litig.*, 2004 WL 1305745 (Del. Ch. 2004).
21. The duty of good faith is especially complex. For an excellent article discussing this duty, see Zachary S. Klughaupt, "Good Faith in the World of Delaware Corporate Litigation: A Strategic Perspective on Recent Developments in Fiduciary Duty Law," *FDCC Quarterly*, the official journal of the Federation of Defense and Corporate Counsel, Spring 2006; available at http://findarticles.com/p/articles/mi_qa4023/is_200604/ai_n16522834/pg_10, last accessed August 30, 2010.
22. *Credit Lyonnais Bank Nederland, N.V. v. Pathe Communications Corp.*, No. Civ. A. 12150, 1991 WL 277613, at *34 (Del. Ch. Dec. 30, 1991).
23. See Martin J. Bienstock and Robert L. Messineo, "When Financial Trouble Comes: A Guide for Directors," *Director's Monthly*, September 2001, pp. 1–8.
24. 863 A.2d 772 (Del. Ch. Nov. 17, 2004).
25. *Production Resources Group, L.L.C. v. NCT Group, Inc.*, 863 A.2d 772, 787 (Del. Ch. 2004). The *Production Resources* decision "reversed a trend among some courts and commentators of imposing a new set of fiduciary duties on directors in favor of creditors of insolvent corporations or those in the zone of insolvency," according to an article by Cooley Godward. "New Delaware Decision Clarifies the Duties of and Protections Afforded to Directors of Insolvent Companies," Cooley Godward LLP, March 22, 2005.
26. *North American Catholic Educational Programming Foundation, Inc. v. Gheewalla*, 930 A.2d 92, 101 (Del. 2007) (emphasis added).
27. 930 A.2d at 103.
28. Ibid. at 99.
29. Ibid. at 101–102.
30. See, for example, *In re Dulgerian*, 388 B.R. 142 (Bankr. E.D. Pa. 2008) (recognizing a directors' duty to creditors under Pennsylvania law when a debtor is insolvent); and *Medlin v. Wells Fargo Bank, N.A. (In re I.G. Services, Ltd.)*, Nos. 99-53170-C, 99-53171-C, ADV 04-5041-C, 2008 WL 783551, at *2-3 (Bankr. W.D. Tex. Mar. 19, 2008) (finding a direct claim for breach of fiduciary duty arising out of a broker/dealer relationship).
31. 178 B.R. 956, 968 (D. Del. 1994).
32. *Brandt v. Hicks, Muse & Co., Inc. (In re Healthco Int'l Inc.)*, 208 B.R. 288, 300 (Bankr. D. Mass 1997).
33. *Official Committee of Unsecured Creditors v. R.F. Lafferty & Co., Inc.*, 267 F.3d 340 (3d Cir. 2001).

34. Courts have found proper cause of action and have ordered compensation in these circumstances. Ibid. at 350.
35. See, for example, *Fehribach v. Ernst & Young LLP*, 493 F.3d 905, 908 (7th Cir. 2007) (the theory of deepening insolvency might apply in a case where management conspired with an outsider such as an auditor and concealed "the corporation's perilous state, which if disclosed earlier would have enabled the corporation to survive in reorganized form"); *In re CitX Corp., Inc.*, 448 F.3d 672, 677 (3d Cir. 2006) (deepening insolvency claims require fraudulent conduct, not merely negligence); and *In re Global Service Group, LLC*, 316 B.R. 451, 458 (Bankr. S.D.N.Y. 2004) ("one seeking to recover for 'deepening insolvency' must show that the defendant prolonged the company's life in breach of a separate duty, or committed an actionable tort that contributed to the continued operation of a corporation and its increased debt").
36. See "Directors' Duties in the Zone of Insolvency," March 8, 2007, Foley & Lardner LLP; available at http://www.foley.com/files/tbl_s31Publications/FileUpload137/4010/DirectorsDutiesZoneInsolvency.pdf, last accessed June 15, 2010.
37. See, for example, *In re SI Restructuring, Inc.*, 532 F.3d 355 (5th Cir. 2008); and *In re The Brown Schools*, 386 B.R. 37 (Bankr. D. Del. 2008).
38. *In re Amcast Industrial Corp.*, 365 B.R. 91, 119 (Bankr. S.D. Ohio 2007).
39. *In re Global Service Group, LLC*, 316 B.R. at 458.
40. As a typical example, the corporate governance guidelines for Aetna state, "Board members have full access to Company management. In addition, the Board and any of its Committees have the authority to retain counsel and other independent experts or consultants, as they may deem necessary, without consulting or obtaining the approval of any officer of the Company in advance." Also, the charter for the Nominating and Corporate Governance Committee of Aetna states, "The Committee shall have the resources and authority appropriate to discharge its responsibilities, including the authority to retain counsel and other experts or consultants." http://www.aetna.com/investors-aetna/governance/nominating_cgcc.html, last accessed August 30, 2010.
41. See Wendell H. Adair, Jr., and Kristopher M. Hansen, "The Discharge of Non-Debtor Parties in Bankruptcy," *Journal of Corporate Renewal*, Turnaround Management Association, May 1, 2000; http://www.turnaround.org/Publications/Articles.aspx?objectID=1324, last accessed June 6, 2010.
42. See 11 U.S.C. §524(e).
43. See Section 5.0 of the Horizontal Merger Guidelines at http://www.justice.gov/atr/public/guidelines, last accessed June 6, 2010.
44. *American Press Ass'n v. United States*, 245 F. 91 (7th Cir. 1917).
45. *Int'l Shoe v. FTC*, 280 U.S. 291, 50 S. Ct. 89 (1930).
46. *Citizen Publ'g Co. v. United States*, 394 U.S. 131, 89 S. Ct., 927 (1969).
47. See Section 5.1, n. 39 of the Horizontal Merger Guidelines at http://www.justice.gov/atr/public/guidelines, last accessed June 6, 2010. "Any offer to purchase the assets of the failing firm for a price above the liquidation value of those assets—the highest valued use outside the relevant market or equivalent offer to

purchase the stock of the failing firm—will be regarded as a reasonable alternative offer."

48. *Citizen Publ'g Co.*, 394 U.S. at 137, *quoting Int'l Shoe*, 280 U.S. at 302.
49. See *United States v. Greater Buffalo Press, Inc.*, 402 U.S. 549, 555 (1971); *Citizen Publ'g Co.*, 394 U.S. at 137–138; *Int'l Shoe*, 280 U.S. at 302.
50. See *Citizen Publ'g Co.*, 394 U.S. at 137.
51. Remarks of Carl Shapiro, Deputy Assistant Attorney General for Economics, Antitrust Division, U.S. Department of Justice, Prepared for Delivery to ABA Antitrust Symposium, Competition as Public Policy, *Competition Policy in Distressed Industries*, May 13, 2009 ("Shapiro Remarks"), p. 21.
52. See Section 5.2 of the Horizontal Merger Guidelines at http://www.justice.gov/atr/public/guidelines, last accessed June 6, 2010.
53. See, for example, *FTC v. Great Lakes Chem. Corp.*, 528 F. Supp. 84, 96 (N.D. Ill. 1981); and *United States v. Reed Roller Bit Co.*, 274 F. Supp. 573, 584 n.1 (W.D. Okla. 1967).
54. See, for example, *Int'l Shoe v. FTC*, 280 U.S. 291 (1930); *California v. Sutter Health Sys.*, 130 F. Supp. 2d 1109 (N.D. Cal. 2001); *Reilly v. Hearst Corp.*, 107 F. Supp. 2d 1192 (N.D. Cal. 2000); *United States v. Culbro Corp.*, 504 F. Supp. 661 (S.D.N.Y. 1981); *FTC v. Great Lakes Chem. Corp.*, 528 F. Supp. 84 (N.D. Ill. 1981); *United States v. M.P.M., Inc.*, 397 F. Supp. 78 (D. Colo. 1975); *Granader v. Public Bank*, 281 F. Supp. 120 (E.D. Mich. 1967); and *United States v. Md. & Va. Milk Producers Ass'n, Inc.*, 167 F. Supp. 799 (D.D.C. 1958).
55. In fact, in a 2009 roundtable, FTC chairman Jon Leibowiz stated that his agency would vigorously enforce the antitrust laws in merger cases, despite the economic crisis. American Bar Association, *Roundtable Conference with Enforcement Officials* 16, Washington, D.C. (2009); available at http://www.abanet.org/antitrust/at-source/09/04/Apr09-EnforcerRT4-29f.pdf, last accessed August 30, 2010.
56. *Kaiser Aluminum & Chem. Corp. v. FTC*, 652 F.2d 1324, 1339 (7th Cir. 1981).
57. See, for example, *United States v. Gen. Dynamics Corp.*, 415 U.S. 450 (1974).
58. *FTC v. Arch Coal, Inc.*, 329 F. Supp. 2d 109, 157 (D.D.C. 2004).
59. The Statute of 13 Elizabeth provides that "covinous and fraudulent feoffments, gifts, grants, alienations, conveyances, bonds, suits judgments and executions, as well of lands and of tenements as of goods and chattels, . . . devised and contrived of malice, fraud, covin, collusion or guile, to the end, purpose and intent, to delay, hinder or defraud creditors and others . . . shall be utterly void, frustrate and of no effect."
60. See generally M. Cook, "Fraudulent Transfer Liability Under the Bankruptcy Code," *Houston Law Review* 17 (1980), p. 263.
61. Some legal historians might recognize this basic fact pattern as the general scenario behind the *Twyne's Case* (1601), which is believed to be the first decision to create the "badges of fraud" test—i.e., that a conveyance will be deemed fraudulent if it meets the following five-pronged test: (1) the conveyance constitutes all of the debtor's assets; (2) the debtor continues to possess the property and/or treats it as such debtor's own; (3) the conveyance is made during a

pending suit; (4) the conveyance is secret; and (5) the transferee accepts the property in trust for the debtor.

62. This concept of "reasonably equivalent value" is noteworthy in that it breaks from traditional notions of contract law theory and considers the adequacy of consideration—i.e., absent fraud, the proverbial peppercorn may be sufficient to constitute legally binding consideration.

63. See *BFP v. Resolution Trust Corporation*, 511 U.S. 531 (1994) (holding that a "reasonably equivalent value" for foreclosed real property is the price in fact received at the foreclosure sale, so long as all the requirements of the state's foreclosure law have been complied with).

64. See, for example, ibid. Foreclosures also include tax sales. *Kojima v. Grandote Int'l LLC (In re Grandote Country Club Co. Ltd.)*, 252 F.3d 1146, 1152 (10th Cir. 2001) ("[T]he decisive factor in determining whether a transfer pursuant to a tax sale constitutes 'reasonably equivalent value' is a state's procedure for tax sales, in particular, statutes requiring that tax sales take place publicly under a competitive bidding procedure.").

65. The Office of Thrift Supervision, an office in the Department of the Treasury, regulates federally chartered savings associations. The Comptroller of the Currency charters and regulates national banks. Federal credit unions are chartered and regulated by the National Credit Union Administration.

66. See, for example, *Federal Deposit Ins. Corp. v. Bell*, 106 F.3d 258 (8th Cir. 1997).

67. UFCA §2(1).

68. *Canadian Pa. Forest Prod. Ltd. vs. J.D. Irving, Ltd. (In re Gibson Group, Inc.)*, 66 F.3d 1436, 1446 (6th Cir. 1995).

69. This list is a paraphrase of one found in Martin D. Ginsberg and Jack S. Lewis, *Mergers, Acquisitions, and Buyouts: A Transactional Analysis of the Governing Tax, Legal, and Accounting Considerations* (New York: Panel Publishers/Aspen Publishers, 2005), Sec. 1506.2.

70. See, for example, *Central Nat'l Bank v. Coleman (In re B-F Bldg. Corp.)*, 312 F.2d 691, 694 (6th Cir. 1963) ("In the usual case . . . the payment of another's debt is held to be a transfer without fair consideration").

71. See Robert W. Wood, "Sale vs. Reorganization: Eye of the Beholder," *M&A Tax Report* 10, no. 12, July 2002, p. 5.

72. See Kurt A. Mayr, "Unlocking the Lockup: The Renewal of Plan Support Agreements under New Section 1125(g) of the Bankruptcy Code," *Journal of Bankruptcy Law and Practice*, December 2006. This article explains that plan support lockup agreements "memorialize the material terms of a restructuring proposal (often simply a term sheet) that has been agreed upon between a debtor and one or more of its major stakeholders." It also says that lockups are "an essential tool in out-of-court workouts and so-called 'prenegotiated' or 'prearranged' Chapter 11 cases."

Deal Structures That Work

It is always darkest before the dawn. Likewise, "distress" and "strategy" may seem as different as night and day, but they form a continuum: getting out of distress requires strategy; conversely, any wise strategy must involve taking calculated risks.

This section of our book can help buyers and sellers think and act strategically when they are designing a deal structure for distressed M&A. Once all parties have an idea of the value of the company that is to be bought, the viability of and difficulties with different potential structures become clearer. Indeed, because the various approaches discussed in this section may exist as parallel paths until a final decision is made, buyers and sellers should contemplate the pros and cons of each approach under the most realistic scenarios.

- Chapter 11 of this book describes how to value distressed companies by triangulating the results obtained from a variety of
  valuation techniques. Valuation underlies all the deal structures
  described in this section; indeed, it is often the key factor in
  choosing which structure is ultimately consummated.
- The Bankruptcy Code's famed Chapter 11 is all about refram-
  ing the future; the next chapter of this book, Chapter 12, shows
  how. In this chapter, we cover stand-alone plans, prepackaged
  plans, and prearranged plans.
- Chapter 13 covers Section 363 sales and loan-to-own transactions. As Chapter 13 explains, Section 363 sales are considered
  asset sales; they do not usually convey the seller's liabilities
  to the buyer. A loan-to-own transaction generally refers to the

purchase of debt with the goal of converting the debt to equity
and owning the underlying assets or the broader business.

■ We conclude with Chapter 14, offering financial hope. The
chapter first addresses the multiple alternatives that may be
available to a distressed company to refinance its troubled debt
and increase its scarce liquidity, then focuses on obtaining
debtor-in-possession (DIP) loans after entering bankruptcy.
Moving from the "sunset" of bankruptcy to the "sunrise" of a
new start, this final chapter explains how to obtain exit financing for a company in the context of a plan of reorganization or
a 363 sale, giving lessons that extend beyond to any situation
in which one company's financial need becomes another's
financing opportunity, leading to greater prosperity for all.

CHAPTER 11

Principles of Distressed Company Valuation

For every complex problem there is a simple solution that is wrong.

—George Bernard Shaw, Irish critic and playwright

OVERVIEW OF DISTRESSED COMPANY VALUATION

When does the concept of valuation arise in bankruptcy?

Although there is no explicit explanation of valuation in the Bankruptcy Code and bankruptcy courts do not typically decide a company's worth, valuation permeates the entire bankruptcy process. The following are only a handful of the seemingly countless instances in which valuation can be a critical factor in a bankruptcy case:

- Whether a company is even insolvent to begin with
- Whether a pre-petition transfer constitutes a fraudulent conveyance
- Whether there is a sufficient equity cushion to provide adequate protection for a secured lender
- Whether a plan of reorganization passes the best interests of creditors test
- Whether a bankruptcy case should be converted from Chapter 11 to Chapter 7 (or vice versa)
- Determining which creditors get to vote on a plan of reorganization (or whether they are deemed to have accepted or rejected the plan)
- Whether a plan of reorganization is feasible

Given how prevalent valuation is throughout bankruptcy, it may come as little surprise that this is frequently the most disputed element of the process. Sometimes the subjective views of various groups can legitimately differ. Other times, however, valuation can be manipulated to arrive at a desired outcome, especially when the stakes are high and the pressure is higher. As one group of academic researchers explained:

> Valuation errors in Chapter 11 have significant wealth consequences. Under-estimating value benefits claimants who receive shares or stock options. The estimated value also affects the allocation of assets and relative payouts. Underestimating value increases the proportional claim of senior claimants because of relative priority. Therefore senior claimants have incentives to underestimate cash flows to increase their recovery in Chapter 11 proceedings. . . . Estimated values are also lower when management receives stock or options under the plan of reorganization, creating a windfall for managers. Finally, estimated values are lower when firms sell new equity securities to a third-party investor under the plan of reorganization. Collectively, our findings suggest valuations are used "strategically" in a negotiation to promote a desired bargaining outcome.[1]

Why doesn't the bankruptcy court determine a company's valuation?

Rather than focusing on defining how to value a debtor's assets, Congress created a bankruptcy process involving the Bankruptcy Code, the Bankruptcy Rules, and the bankruptcy courts to foster a democratic negotiation in which the parties are supposed to determine valuation consensually. Valuation methodologies and issues may change over time and may differ for assets in various situations, but lawmakers needed to design a timeless process that would apply to all debtors' circumstances. Therefore, as discussed throughout this book, Congress established a flexible process that is designed to provide debtors with a fresh start and creditors with fair and equitable recoveries.

Accordingly, bankruptcy courts do not typically determine the value of assets, although they may hear arguments that involve valuation as part of other issues. During these decisions, the bankruptcy courts will need to evaluate the persuasiveness of the evidence submitted, the credibility of the expert witnesses provided, the logic of the various arguments, and any relevant case law precedents. While prior case law may provide broad guidelines for valuation, the details of valuation usually differ so dramatically from case to case that it is unusual for prior case law to be directly relevant. Commonly, many bankruptcy judges will avoid making a valuation determination by making in-court statements or delivering rulings that are designed to get the parties to reach consensus on valuation issues. Many times, after the parties recommit to negotiations at the bankruptcy judge's stern urging, they find a framework for compromise.

This system makes sense because, after all, bankruptcy judges are not usually educated in finance. Most bankruptcy judges' backgrounds involve law school and practicing law, neither of which typically provides extensive training in valuation.

How does valuation in bankruptcy differ from traditional valuation methodologies?

The bankruptcy process itself—in a vacuum—actually has *no* impact on the valuation process. The tail does not wag the dog! That is, the bankruptcy process employs traditional out-of-court valuation methodologies when evaluating the worth of a particular asset or enterprise.

Still, two important issues do arise when considering valuation in a *distressed* scenario, whether in an out-of-court workout or in Chapter 11 bankruptcy. First, the value of any business, at its core, is the intersection between the highest price that a willing buyer will pay and the lowest price that a willing seller will accept.[2] However, this traditional notion of valuation assumes an efficient market—one in which a seller has many potential options and there are multiple prospective buyers. But how can you say that a bankrupt seller is a *willing* seller? Similarly, the universe of prospective buyers is narrower in the bankruptcy context, as many acquirers perceive stepping into a distressed business as having disproportionate risk.

As the U.S. Supreme Court has highlighted, this challenge is further underscored when valuation is being contemplated during a debtor's period of exclusivity for proposing a plan of reorganization: "Under a plan granting an exclusive right, making no provision for competing bids or competing plans, any determination that the price was top dollar would necessarily be made by a judge in bankruptcy court, whereas the best way to determine value is exposure to a market."[3]

Without a full stable of prospective buyers, how can you say that even an auction process with open bidding (such as in a 363 sale) reflects the view of an efficient market?[4] (In fact, it is precisely such market inefficiencies that create outsized opportunities for buyers to buy assets at bargain prices.) When it comes to a distressed entity, both the buyer and its lender will tend to be conservative in setting values. This is because, generally speaking, the market for a distressed entity sale is a buyer's market, and the market for a distressed entity loan is a lender's market.

A second issue that arises in distressed situations is that a company that is in the midst of financial or operational duress probably faces a much broader range of future financial outcomes than many going concerns. This deepens the need for extensive scenario analysis when valuing a business that is in bankruptcy: What will this company look like if next year's GDP growth is 3 percent, 1 percent, or negative? How will this company perform if it cannot refinance its high-cost exit financing within two or three years, whether because of its own operational lapses, an industry downturn, or another marketwide credit seizure? If the company has starved R&D in recent years in order to address more urgent financial pressures, is the company's brand now "damaged goods," and what is the range of assumed success rates for future product launches?

Such factors can introduce even more subjectivity than what one might ordinarily expect in going-concern valuation. This, in turn, can complicate the notion of a business's "worth" and understandably open the door to many potential disagreements and disputes.

As a result, the "debate" at hand is not the valuation of a company in bankruptcy per se, but rather the valuation of a company in distress. The discussion that follows attempts to balance these considerations by presenting traditional valuation methodologies with a distressed "overlay."

How can the buyer of a distressed company minimize the purchase price?

Most sellers have multiple objectives, including price, speed, and certainty of closing. Thus, a buyer need not necessarily offer the highest price in order to gain the contract. It can also offer the seller noncash incentives for the deal, such as the following:

- "We can close faster."
- "We have a good track record in obtaining financing and closing similar transactions."

- "We can offer a substantial deposit on signing the acquisition agreement."
- "We can work well with you and your management."

Other incentives that can make a deal attractive include good terms for management, such as shares in the company, favorable employment contracts, profit-sharing plans, and the like. When the transaction involves the sale of a privately owned company, there is no limit to the value and utility of such social considerations. In the sale or merger of a public company, however, it is good to exercise caution. Such considerations may give the appearance of self-dealing at the expense of shareholders. Even companies that have maintained a strong reputation for ethics can be tarred by this brush.[5]

One of the most delicate questions in buying (or buying out) a company is whether to obtain a lower price by assuming substantially greater risks or accepting significant defects in the candidate. Such risks or defects can loom very large in the eyes of the acquisition lenders, and the timing of negotiations does not always permit them to be checked out with a lender before signing the contract. Here is a cardinal rule: negotiate and sign *fast* when the price is right. The willingness to close can bring a lower price. (Some of the most spectacularly successful deals have been achieved when a buyer saw that management and a lender could live with a minor flaw that the seller thought was major.)

Another way to lower the purchase price is to buy only some of the assets or divisions of a company, or to buy all of them with a firm plan for postmerger sell-offs in mind.

So what are the basic methods of corporate valuation?

When valuing a company, the first question to be asked is whether the company is to be sold as a going concern or its assets are to be sold pursuant to a liquidation. In a liquidation, valuation is based on the value of the company's individual assets, meaning that the value of the sum of the parts exceeds that of the whole. Liquidation value typically refers to orderly liquidation value (net of any liquidating costs), not irrational "fire sale" prices. In theory, liquidation value should be a floor on corporate valuation.

There are many methods for calculating going-concern valuation. Any reputable guide to valuation will recommend using multiple methods, and then determining a median value based on the results.[6] To summarize, the basic methods (to be considered in combination—never in isolation) are as follows:

- Valuation based on what others have paid for a similar company
- Valuation based on expected future cash flows discounted to the present
- Valuation based on company earnings
- Valuation based on the market price of the company's equity and debt securities
- Valuation based on a particular combination of the above (hybrid approach)

PRINCIPLES OF ASSET VALUATION

What are the basic principles of asset valuation?

As stated in the discussion on asset-based lending (see Chapter 14 of this book), an asset, most simply, is a present economic resource to which an entity has a present right or other privileged access.[7] Assets can be tangible or intangible, but asset-based financiers tend to prefer tangible, or "hard," assets.[8] Asset-based valuations will typically yield the lowest valuation estimate for a particular business. This is because the process generally looks only at the aggregate value of the individual assets that a business owns, rather than evaluating the enterprise as a going concern.

The branch of valuation that focuses on assets, whether tangible or intangible, is known as appraisal, and appraisers follow a code of practice with 10 detailed standards—from real property appraisal to business appraisal.[9]

The most important principle (1.1, and restated throughout the standards) is that in developing an appraisal, an appraiser must "be aware of, understand, and correctly apply the recognized approaches, methods, and procedures that are necessary to produce a credible appraisal."

For example, in valuing a real property asset, there are three basic approaches: sale (what it would cost to buy it today, also called market value), cost (what it would cost you to build it now, also called replacement cost), and income (what kind of funds it is generating through rental or otherwise). Appraisers have standards for each.[10] The American Society of Appraisers offers a number of standards (see Exhibit 11-1).[11]

Exhibit 11-1 The Asset-Based Approach to Valuation

I. The asset-based approach is a general way of determining a value indication of a business, business ownership interest, security, or intangible asset using one or more methods based on the value of the assets net of liabilities.

II. In business valuation, the asset-based approach may be analogous to the cost approach of other appraisal disciplines.

III. Assets, liabilities, and equity relate to a business that is an operating company, a holding company, or a combination thereof (a mixed business).

   A. An operating company is a business that conducts an economic activity by generating and selling, or trading in a product or service.

   B. A holding company is a business that derives its revenues from a return on its assets, which may include operating companies and/or other businesses.

   C. The asset-based approach should be considered in valuations conducted at the enterprise level and involving:

     1. An investment or real estate holding company

     2. A business appraised on a basis other than as a going concern

Valuations of particular ownership interests in an enterprise may or may not require the use of the asset-based approach.

IV. The asset-based approach should not be the sole appraisal approach used in assignments relating to operating companies appraised as going concerns unless this approach is customarily used by sellers and buyers. In such cases, the appraiser must support the selection of this approach.

Source: American Society of Appraisers, ASA Business Valuation Standards, BVS-III.

What are some ratios based on assets, and what do they measure?

There are three kinds of asset ratios: those measuring efficiency, liquidity, and leverage.[12]

Efficiency Indicators Using Assets

These numbers say something about how the business is being managed.

- The *accounting rate of return (ARR)* shows the undiscounted average earnings after taxes and depreciation divided by the average book value of the investment during its life. The rule then accepts projects with an accounting return greater than a specified cutoff rate.[13]
- The *return on assets (ROA)* shows how successfully management is using the company's resources compared to others in its industry. To calculate ROA, divide net profit before taxes by total assets. An ROA of 1 says that for every dollar invested in assets, the company makes $1 in profit. ROA can vary greatly from industry to industry; those with a lot of "bookable" assets, such as plants, equipment, and inventory (all recorded or "booked" on the balance sheet as assets) will have a relatively low ROA, while service companies will have a high ROA because they require minimal bookable assets to operate.
- The *DuPont formula for return on equity (ROE)* shows how much cash is created from the existing equity base. The formula starts with net income divided by sales, but it also adds two more multipliers, namely, sales divided by total assets and total assets divided by stockholders' equity, with the final result being net income divided by stockholders' equity. If the return on equity is 15 percent, then 15 cents of net income are created for each dollar that was originally invested as equity.[14]
- *Inventory turnover* tells an investor how quickly a company is selling its goods—an important ratio for companies that sell a tangible product (not for service companies). It is calculated by dividing total purchases by average inventory.
- The *average collection period* (also known as *days' sales outstanding*) helps managers and investors alike to assess the quality of accounts receivable and to predict cash flows (expected time to collect). It is calculated by dividing net accounts receivable by total sales for the past four quarters and multiplying by 365.

Liquidity Indicators Using Assets

These numbers measure liquidity.

- The *quick ratio* (also called the *acid test ratio*) measures the strength of a company's short-term liquidity. The ratio is calculated by dividing current assets (minus inventory) by current liabilities (except current portion of long-term debts). In the going-concern context, one ideally looks for a ratio of about 1.0×. If it is lower, this may mean that the company is flirting with insolvency (i.e., it may have problems paying its bills as they come due). Conversely, a ratio higher than 1.0× could mean that the company's capital is not being used efficiently enough (for example, is the company collecting its receivables too slowly?). Companies with a quick ratio above 1.0× are usually proud of the fact, although such companies are "putting gold under the mattress," so to speak.
- The *current ratio* (also called the *working capital ratio*) quantifies a company's intermediate-term liquidity. The ratio is calculated by dividing a company's current assets (including cash, inventory, and accounts receivable) by current liabilities (including drawdowns on line of credit balances, long-term debt falling due within 30 days, and accounts payable). While it is good to have a high current ratio, too high a ratio can indicate that the company is carrying too much inventory.

Leverage Indicators Using Assets

These numbers assess the long-term solvency of a company.

- The *debt/equity ratio* quantifies how much leverage a company has relative to its book value. The ratio is calculated as total liabilities divided by shareholders' equity, or as total interest-bearing, long-term debt divided by shareholders' equity. The meaning of the debt/equity ratio depends on the industry in which the company operates. For example, capital-intensive industries such as auto manufacturing tend to have a debt/equity ratio above 2.0×, while personal computer companies

have a debt/equity ratio of under 0.5×. High debt/equity ratios
(above 0.75×, according to U.S. federal banking standards) make
a company "highly leveraged." So does a transaction that doubles
liabilities, even if it only brings the debt/equity ratio to 0.50×.

- The *debt/total assets ratio* shows the proportion of a company's
assets that are financed through debt. The ratio is measured as
total liabilities divided by total assets. If the ratio is at 0.5×, it
shows that the company balances debt and equity as its source
of funding. If it is greater than 0.5×, most of the company's
assets are financed through debt. If it is less than 0.5×, most of
the company's assets are financed through equity.

PRINCIPLES OF CASH FLOW-BASED VALUATION

What is cash flow-based valuation?

In many ways, cash flow-based valuation is the granddaddy of all valuation
techniques. This is because, at the end of the day, all valuation measures
are directly or indirectly focused on answering the same question: how
much cash do I expect this business to generate during the relevant measurement period?

It is also worth underscoring that cash flow-based valuation—as well
as other measures such as EV/EBITDA and P/E, which are described later—
should reflect forward-looking earnings projections, not historical results.
This is particularly critical in the context of a distressed acquisition, as trailing financial results fail to account for the often significant operational
turnaround that is expected.[15] Indeed, it has been a basic valuation principle
for over 60 years that projected, not trailing, earnings should be considered
when a company anticipates significant improvement in the near term.[16] It
is also worth noting the wisdom of management guru Peter Drucker: "Erro-
neous assumptions can be disastrous." In other words, when making assumptions about future cash flows, remember—garbage in, garbage out.

How are a company's cash flows reported
to users of financial statements?

The *cash flow statement* (also known as the *funds flow statement* or *statement of cash flows*) shows the sources and uses of cash. (In fact, *sources*

and uses statement was the old name for this statement before it rose to prominence in the 1970s.) One challenge with cash flow analysis is the fact that companies use two different techniques for reporting it: the *direct method* and the *indirect method.*

The direct method of preparing the cash flow statement is probably the easier to understand of the two, because it depicts an actual process. Little or no interpretation is involved: cash is cash. However, relatively few companies use the method because Accounting Standards Codification (ASC) 230 [previously known as Statement of Financial Accounting Standard (SFAS) 95] requires a supplementary report similar to that prepared using the indirect method if a company elects to use the direct method. The indirect method, in contrast, uses a company's net income as a starting point, and then adjusts for noncash accruals.

Statements prepared using either method are typically divided into three components.

Operating Cash Flow

Also called *working capital* or *free cash flow from operations*, the source of this cash flow is internal operations. The basic formula for calculating operating cash flow under the direct method is

Receipts from the sale of goods and/or services
Minus: Payments to suppliers for goods and/or services
Minus: Payments to employees or on behalf of employees
<u>Minus: Cash taxes paid</u>
Equals: cash flow from operations

The basic formula for calculating operating cash flow under the indirect method is

Net income
Plus or minus: Adjustments to reconcile net income to net cash provided by operating activities
  Changes in working capital (accounts receivable/payable, inventories, etc.)
  Depreciation and amortization
  Changes in tax accruals
  <u>Noncash gains or losses from disposal of assets</u>
Equals: cash flow from operations

Investing Cash Flow

This is also generated internally, but it is from nonoperating activities. Examples include cash invested in plant and equipment or other fixed assets and cash generated from the sale of such assets; nonrecurring gains or losses (windfalls or catastrophes); or other sources of cash outside of normal operations.

The formula for calculating investing cash flow is as follows:

> Cash received from investments (e.g., dividend payments, sale of property)
> Minus: funds paid to make investments (e.g., buying stock or property)
> Equals: cash flow from investing activities

Some firms define "free cash flow" as operating cash flow minus investing cash flow.

Financing Cash Flow

Financing cash flow is the cash from and back to external financing sources, such as lenders, investors, and shareholders. A new loan, the repayment of a loan, the issuance of stock, and the payment of a dividend are some of the activities that would be included in this section of the cash flow statement.

The formula for cash flow from financing activities is as follows:

> Cash received from issuing stock or debt
> Minus: cash paid as dividends and for the reacquisition of debt or stock
> Equals: cash flow from financing activities

OK, I see how cash flows are calculated. But how does this translate into a company's valuation?

Looking at current cash flow statements can prepare the investor to see what is happening to a company's cash at present. But what about the future? This requires a *discounted cash flow (DCF) analysis*.

A DCF analysis involves discounting multiple future years of free cash flows to the present and adding the present value of a terminal enterprise value. As one commentator notes, "Terminal value is '[t]ypically the most significant factor in determining the [DCF analysis's] value.'"[17] Cases in which a bankruptcy court approved DCF analyses as the exclusive method for determining enterprise value include *In re Peregrine Systems, Inc.*[18] and *In re Zenith Electronics Corporation.*[19]

Here are the basic steps in a DCF analysis:

1. Set aside the value of all assets—current and fixed—that are not used in the business to produce the estimated future earnings stream that is to be discounted.
2. Estimate future sales year by year over a preselected time horizon. (This would be the period of time that the investor intends to hold the investment before selling it.)
3. Estimate the gross margins year by year, including depreciation expenses.
4. Estimate earnings before interest and taxes (EBIT) year by year.
5. Subtract cash interest and estimated cash taxes year by year.
6. Compute and subtract the average marginal incremental working capital costs required to put on each additional dollar of sales year by year (reverse for downsizing).
7. Compute and subtract the average marginal incremental fixed capital costs of putting on each additional dollar of sales year by year (reverse for asset sales).
8. Add back depreciation (reverse for recaptures).
9. Compute the residual value of the company after the end of the horizon period by capitalizing the last year's projected earnings at the reciprocal of the selected discount rate.
10. Discount all values, including residual value, to present value, using a risk-adjusted cost of capital for the discount rate.[20]
11. Add back all set-aside values (step 1) for current and fixed assets that are not used to produce revenues. The total will be the present value (PV) of the business based on its anticipated future cash flows.[21]
12. If the investor does not want to forecast cash flows out to infinity (clearly, a daunting task!), a preferable approach would be to model cash flows for some reasonable period until the business has stabilized (five to seven years is usually the most practical), and then calculate a terminal value. Be careful to go out far enough before calculating the terminal value, which is a measure of steady-state cash flows in perpetuity. Then this terminal value is similarly discounted back to the present, along with the cash flows during the agreed-upon measurement period.

13. From this, the investor can calculate the net present value (NPV) of the opportunity by comparing the company's PV to the cash outlay required.

This is only one approach. A number of professors of finance have developed spreadsheets for calculating DCF.[22]

The DCF analysis just given seems to presume that a company is currently generating positive free cash flow. But many bankrupt or distressed companies arrived at such states specifically because they *are not* generating cash. What then?

This is the need that restructuring advisors serve—i.e., to model the turn-around to show how cash flow should improve as a result of various initiatives. Clearly, reducing the debt load eliminates interest expense and increases cash flow. Consolidating plants, reducing headcount, rationalizing stock-keeping units (SKUs), and other such activities will cost money at first, but then lead to recurring improvements to earnings before interest, taxes, depreciation, and amortization (EBITDA) and cash flow. This is where M&A may come into play as well—selling off part of the business and reorganizing around the remainder may result in sufficient debt pay-down and increased cash flow, for example.

Therefore, DCF is often the only way to value a distressed company because it gets down to intricate detail over multiple years. Other valuation measures, such as comparable companies (described later in this chapter), look at one period, which may be distorted by the distress.

What are the downside issues with using DCF as a valuation methodology?

One issue with DCF analyses is that the terminal value may be too large a portion of the total value (e.g., 90 percent). If the terminal value is too large in proportion to the overall value, then the DCF analysis may be meaningless because the interim cash flows that the DCF is supposed to be valuing have become insufficiently relevant. In particular, the higher the perpetuity growth rate discounted into the analysis, the higher the terminal value. For instance, in the recent *Spansion* decision,[23] one financial advisor arrived at its terminal value by applying a perpetuity growth-rate range of negative 2.5 percent to positive 2.5 percent, which has the midpoint of 0 percent growth. This advisor testified that this 0 percent perpetuity growth rate assumed that the debtors' market share would grow, even though its specific market would shrink. In contrast, a second financial advisor applied a perpetuity growth rate range of 0 percent to 3 percent, with a midpoint of 1.5 percent. In this case, the court held that a perpetuity growth rate of 1.5 percent appeared to be at odds with the industry projections of negative growth rates for the debtor's products.

Another flaw in the DCF approach is that it is enormously sensitive to the discount rate that is used. Because the discount rate can be influenced by many subjective factors, the valuation method is criticized at times as being ripe for manipulation. For instance, one of the first steps in calculating a discount rate is selecting a peer group of comparable publicly traded companies to establish "beta," a component of the weighted average cost of capital (WACC) calculation. Which companies are, or are not, included in this peer group is entirely the decision of the individual conducting the analysis. (Factors to consider when choosing public "comps" for valuation purposes are discussed later in this chapter.) Indeed, this was also a key argument in the recent *Spansion* decision.

All in all, the different valuation inputs used by the respective financial advisors in the *Spansion* case had the impact of more than doubling the DCF valuation!

But to both of these criticisms, we suggest the words of Winston Churchill as a fitting analogy to the dilemma: "Democracy is the worst form of government except for all those others that have been tried." Because it focuses only on cash flow and disregards accounting-based forms of earnings, we believe DCF is a superior valuation methodology. However, any party proffering a DCF-based valuation is well advised to be able to defend all the assumptions reflected in the model.

What are some ratios based on cash flow, and what do they measure?

- The *operating cash flow ratio* (OCF)[24] measures a company's ability to generate the resources required to meet its current liabilities. It is calculated as cash flow from operations divided by current liabilities. If the ratio falls below 1.00, then the company is not generating enough cash to meet its current commitments and may be deemed insolvent.

- *Cash current debt coverage* (CCD) is a ratio that can be used to measure a company's ability to repay its current debt. CCD is calculated as follows: (cash flow from operations minus cash dividends) divided by current interest-bearing debt. The numerator is the same as retained operating cash flow.

PRINCIPLES OF SECURITIES-BASED VALUATION

How does valuation work when it is based on securities prices?

Any security that is publicly traded offers at least some insight into the potential market value of a particular company. That is, the public financial markets, when operating at or near efficiency, themselves generally serve as a discounting mechanism, reflecting countless scenarios, cash flow forecasts, and industry/economic outlooks into the minute-to-minute price of the security.

However, even in the going-concern context, this valuation methodology has limitations. For instance, consider Apple Inc., probably the most dominant technology company of the current decade (so far). Between June 2009 and June 2010, Apple's stock ranged in value from a low of $133 to a high of $272, implying an equity valuation range of $120 billion to $248 billion. Clearly, many factors that affect Apple's business changed over that 12-month period: an improvement in the U.S. economy, credit issues in Europe, the introduction of the iPad, and so on. But were those variables truly enough to drive a nearly $130 billion increase in the value of Apple's equity? When one considers that, even in less volatile times, more often than not the 52-week range for nearly *any* company's stock reflects a 50 percent to 100 percent variation, the efficient market thesis intuitively seems to lose at least some steam.

This is all the more true in the bankruptcy or workout scenario. That is, the securities-based valuation approach is heavily dependent upon the financial, legal, and operational information about the distressed company in the marketplace being fresh, updated, valid, and properly interpreted. Frequently, this is not the case, particularly since the marketplace may not understand the information that is disclosed during a bankruptcy case. In fact, one bankruptcy court pointed out that "[t]he stigma of bankruptcy alone is a factor that will seriously depress the market value of a company's securities."[25] Similarly, one commentator noted that "the market value of the security will depend upon the investing public's perception of the future prospects of the enterprise. That perception may well be unduly distorted by the recently concluded reorganization and the prospect of lean years for the enterprise in the immediate future."[26] While the trading values of a bankrupt entity's securities can be a valid reference point, it is important to recall—once again—that the tail doesn't wag the dog. As George Bernard Shaw noted, the simple answer—the trading price—is often the wrong answer to a complex problem like valuing a distressed company.

One group of academic researchers takes an even more pragmatic view: "Frequently, investors who specialize in buying the senior debt of bankrupt companies conspire to keep values low so that when a company emerges from bankruptcy proceedings, they get most of its value, including its stock. If the company has been undervalued, the market will send its shares soaring—and they make out like bandits."[27]

So, if the securities-based valuation approach is so doubtful at some times and open to manipulation at others, why even bother to consider it?

The critical word in that question is why *consider* it, rather than why *rely exclusively* on it. Valuation is a mosaic; each data point in isolation is meaningless. But when one steps back and takes in the full view, the picture becomes much clearer.

Therefore, the astute valuation of a distressed entity will focus on the prices of all of its securities, including debt securities. In fact, the prices of different classes of securities of a single distressed company might reflect vastly different recovery and valuation expectations.

Consider, for instance, a bankrupt entity with three layers to its capital structure: (1) secured bank debt with $100 million of face value, trading at 80 cents on the dollar; (2) unsecured promissory notes with $500 million of face value, trading at 40 cents on the dollar; and (3) 40 million shares of publicly traded stock, trading at 25 cents per share. This information is summarized in Exhibit 11-2.

Exhibit 11-2 Range of Enterprise Value Implied by Different Classes of Securities

U.S. Dollars in Millions

	Security's Book Value	Trading Price	Security's Market Value	Implied Enterprise Value
Secured bank debt	$100	$0.80	$80	$80
Unsecured promissory notes	500	0.40	200	300
Equity (40 million shares)	N/A	0.25	10	610

Although it might not be intuitively obvious at first glance, each of these three classes of securities is suggesting an enormously different valuation for the company:

- The *secured creditors* are valuing their bonds at less than par, or $0.80 on the dollar. That is, the secured creditors are indirectly suggesting that their $100 million of bank debt is worth only $80 million, and that all other classes of securities will be wiped out. This sets the low-end enterprise value at $80 million.
- The *unsecured creditors* are similarly valuing their debt at less than par, or $0.40 on the dollar. But doesn't this make the unsecured creditors a bit more optimistic than the secured creditors? Theoretically, the only way that the promissory notes are worth *anything* in a bankruptcy scenario is if the secured bank debt is paid in full, making the unsecured creditors the fulcrum security with roughly 40 percent recoveries. (This oversimplifies credit pricing in order to illustrate the point; many variables will influence the notes' value at any given time.) Thus, the unsecured creditors are indirectly suggesting that their notes are worth $200 million after $100 million is repaid to the secured creditors, with the equity wiped out. This suggests an enterprise value of $300 million.
- If the unsecured creditors might be considered optimistic compared to the secured creditors, the *equity holders* can only be described as positively giddy! At first blush, this might not be particularly obvious, considering that 40 million shares at $0.25 per share values the equity at only $10 million. But what the equity is indirectly saying in this case is that *both* the secured and the

unsecured creditors can be repaid in full (for an aggregate of $600 million), and that there will still be $10 million of equity value left over. This implies a high-end enterprise value of $610 million.

Accordingly, a securities-based valuation analysis of the company reflected in Exhibit 11-2 would suggest a rather remarkable company valuation range of $80 million at the low end to $610 million at the high end. One reason why this might be so is that different constituencies may all simultaneously be ascribing vastly different probabilities to the future performance of the distressed business. (Alternatively, a student of behavioral finance might suggest that this range of valuation expectations reflects the nature and risk tolerance of investors in each asset class—i.e., to grossly stereotype, that secured lenders are risk-averse by nature and likely to ascribe the most conservative valuations to a company, whereas equity investors are the most risk-loving and thus are likely to be the most optimistic about a company's turnaround prospects.)

In any case, securities-based valuation is worth considering, provided that at least a portion of a company's securities are publicly traded.

OTHER VALUATION METHODOLOGIES

What is earnings-based valuation?

Earnings-based valuation focuses on the quality of earnings, normally focusing on earnings from operations and not from extraordinary events. In a normal company, it is based on the recent past and interpreted in the light of management's plans. When applying these valuation methods to distressed companies, analysts should heed the wisdom of legendary investor Warren Buffett: "Earnings can be pliable as putty when a charlatan heads the company reporting them."

When used in the context of distressed companies, the approach is different. As described in the DCF section, valuing a company that is in financial or operational distress generally requires that one forecast out several years (three years is a reasonable forecast period), taking into account many turnaround initiatives, to project earnings well out into the future. An investor might consider what a reasonable earnings-based valuation multiple on "Year 3 earnings" might be, then discount that valuation back to the present day using a discount rate that appropriately reflects the macro- and microeconomic risks that the company faces during the forecast period.

What are some ratios based on earnings, and what do they measure?

- The *average rate of return* is the basic rate of return method that measures profitability. Total net earnings are divided by the number of years the investment will be held, then by the investment's initial acquisition cost, to derive the annual income rate.

- The *internal rate of return (IRR)* is the discount rate that makes the net present value of an investment equal zero. This is most commonly used with discounted cash flow calculations, but it can also be used with earning-based formulas. The formula is $PV = A1 \div (1 + r)^{n1} + A2 \div (1 + r)^{n2} + A3 \div (1 + r)^{n3} + \ldots$, where PV is the present value of the investment; A1, A2, A3 . . . are the interest/payments received in each individual period; r is the rate of return that we need to determine; and n1, n2, n3 . . . are the time periods of receipt from the date of investment.

- *Earnings per share (EPS)* reports the amount of net income that a company has earned for each share of stock outstanding. At present, the definition of EPS is undergoing some adjustment at the FASB.[28] The proposed new statement would clarify that the computation of basic EPS should include both outstanding common shares and instruments whose holders have the right to share in current-period earnings with common shareholders, among other changes. This proposed FASB statement, together with the proposed amendments to International Accounting Standard (IAS) 33, should enhance the comparability of EPS by reducing the differences between the EPS denominator reported under U.S. generally accepted accounting principles (GAAP) and International Financial Reporting Standards (IFRS) as well as by simplifying the application of Statement 128.[29]

- The *price/earnings (P/E) ratio* is the price of a share of stock divided by earnings per share. The ratio can use either historical earnings or future earnings. P/E, by definition, looks only at the value of a company's equity, and does not consider its debt load. Some say that this is a fatal flaw in this ratio.

- *Enterprise value (EV) to EBITDA* is similar to P/E, except that it incorporates a company's net debt (or total debt less cash) into its valuation. More specifically, EV to EBITDA is defined as market capitalization plus total debt minus total cash,[30] divided into EBITDA. By using EBITDA instead of net income, this valuation ratio generally is subject to fewer "below the line" income and expense elements. (That is, the calculation excludes nonoperating income items.) However, it is worth mentioning that both EBITDA and net income still reflect management judgments on items such as accruals. As a result, even EBITDA is not "foolproof." EV/EBITDA is considered best for cash-based businesses, and for industry averages to use as a benchmark. (The flipped multiple EBITDA/ EV is used to calculate return on investment.)

- *Replacement value* suggests what it would cost to replicate the business from the ground up. A buyer might calculate replacement cost if a company appears to be profitable, but the investor does not know what components of the company are producing the profit. Once replacement cost has been established, the buyer's cost of capital is used to discover what kinds of earnings are needed to justify the IRR, or what kind of cash flows must be achieved to justify the discounted cash flow.

- The *interest coverage ratio* measures a company's ability to pay interest—clearly, a critical factor in the valuation of a highly leveraged firm. A simple analysis of this ratio, which is calculated as EBIT divided by annual interest expense, could have tipped investors off to the precipitous declines in equity value that occurred in some of the major overleveraged firms in the recession of 2008–2009.

What are some examples of hybrid valuation approaches?

Given the complexity of valuation, the number of possible hybrid approaches is almost infinite. A dozen or so are most dominant, including the following.

- Cash Flow Return on Equity™
- Cash Flow Return on Investment®
- Cash return on gross investment

- Cash value added
- Discounted cash flow
- Economic Value Added™
- Economic value management
- Enterprise value
- Market value added
- Relative Graham value
- Return on capital employed
- Return on net assets
- Shareholder value added
- Total business return (or total shareholder return)[31]

Any of these could be used to value a distressed business, but in the case of a severely distressed entity, it may be best to stick with assets. The only hybrid techniques that will work will be the ones that include some "economic" concept that gives credit to the distressed entity's goodwill value—beyond earnings, cash flow, and securities values, which may be too low for a meaningful valuation in the distressed firm.

What about comparable transactions? How can they be used to value a distressed business?

Yet another way to value a company is to compare the price to be paid with the price paid for comparable transactions. This was one of the three techniques used in valuing Spansion, Inc., in the recent bankruptcy case discussed earlier. (The other two approaches were discounted cash flow and comparable company values.)

In short, the comparable transactions approach essentially takes the valuation methodologies described earlier and backs into the multiples paid in a particular transaction. It then applies those multiples—with possible adjustments for variables such as expected revenue synergies, cost savings, and other transaction-specific factors—to the company being analyzed to arrive at an implied valuation.

As briefly noted, the comparable transactions approach (similar to the comparable companies approach discussed later) frequently can fail because it is applying valuations of going concerns to a company that is in financial or operational distress. It's the proverbial apples and oranges.

What's more, trying to strip out variables such as revenue synergies and cost savings from the comparable transaction multiples can be fruitless because such variables are usually not publicly disclosed.

How are comparable companies used as a basis for valuation?

The *comparable companies* approach involves identifying a peer group of companies and selecting a market-sensitive multiple for the companies, such as price to earnings, price to book, and total enterprise value to EBITDA (earnings before interest, taxes, depreciation, and amortization), and applying the average of this metric to the financials of the company being valued. The foundation of this approach is the concept that businesses with similar characteristics should have similar valuation in the marketplace. The valuation determined through comparable companies analysis does *not* reflect the control premium a buyer typically pays in an M&A transaction, or the discount that either the public or private capital markets might apply to a bankrupt entity to reflect the future operating uncertainty.

Similar to the comparable transactions analysis, in constructing a comparable companies analysis a peer group of firms is typically chosen from the same industry as the company being valued. These firms should also have similar fundamental characteristics, such as revenues, profitability, and credit quality. While ideally this analysis should target direct competitors, it is often necessary to include a broader array of firms as a practical matter. The analysis should also adjust the capital structures of each comparable company in order to more accurately compare them with the corporation being valued.

Generally, only public companies are used in this process because there is insufficient data available for privately held businesses, which do not publish their financial statements and do not trade on stock exchanges. As a result, a comparable companies analysis can only be conducted when there exists comparable publicly traded companies. Approximately four to eight comparable companies will typically form a representative group for performing this analysis. If few or no companies exist that are both comparable and publicly traded, then this valuation methodology fails and other methods should be applied. For example, in *In re Radiology Assoc., Inc. Litigation*,[32] the bankruptcy court held that differences between proposed comparable companies were so large that any comparable companies comparison was meaningless.

Provided there are sufficient public "comps," a key benefit of the comparable companies process is that it uses publicly traded stock prices to drive the process; the current stock price is generally viewed as one of the best valuation metrics because it represents a balance of the subjective views of numerous investors on various factors affecting the company's future performance. In this sense, the comparable companies methodology provides an up-to-date judgment on the company's risk profile, competitive pressures, cyclicality, and business prospects.

After identifying the list of comparable companies, the comparable valuation multiples are applied to the company being valued to establish a relative valuation range. Multiplying the mean or median price-to-earnings ratio of the comparable companies by the earnings of the company being valued to establish a relative valuation can be helpful to pinpoint a specific valuation, but may be misleading. A better approach is to consider the relative strengths and weaknesses of the company being valued.

This raises yet another challenge in trying to use a comparable companies analysis for a distressed entity: trailing earnings and cash flow for a business in bankruptcy might be temporarily low relative to its normalized earnings power. Accordingly, it may be difficult to apply comparable company multiples to the distressed entity's most recent results. Instead, it is frequently necessary to apply the multiples to projected financial results (one to two years is typical) and, if applicable, discounting the implied valuation back to the present. If applying the comparable companies analysis to projected financial results, be sure to calculate forward multiples using projected financial results of comparable publicly traded companies.

Endnotes

1. Stuart C. Gilson, Edith S. Hotchkiss, and Richard S. Ruback, "Valuation of Bankrupt Firms," *Review of Financial Studies* 13, no. 1 (2000), pp. 43, 45–46.
2. A third element in many situations is, how much is a lender willing to lend against the asset or business?
3. *Bank of America National Trust and Savings Association v. 203 North LaSalle Street Partnership*, 526 U.S. 434, 457, 119 S.Ct. 1411, 1423 (1999) (internal citation omitted).
4. But see *In re SM 104 Limited*, 160 B.R. 202, 228 (Bankr. S.D. Fla. 1993). ("[T]he bidding process itself works to drive the price paid for the equity in the reorganized debtor up towards its fair market value.")

5. In its May 27, 2005, report on AT&T, Proxy Governance Advisory Service notes, "The proxy statement indicates that during the week of January 24–28, 2005, the attorneys for the respective sides essentially completed the proposed merger agreement, including presumably all of the 'social considerations,' such as Dorman becoming president of the combined company and being elected to the SBC board (along with two other AT&T directors) as well as his very lucrative compensation contract, while the critical question of the financial exchange ratio was put to one side." Proxy Governance Advisory Service, AT&T, May 27, 2005, p. 12. This internal client report is quoted with permission.

6. This is the approach taken by Robert A. G. Monks and Alexandra R. Lajoux, *Corporate Valuation for Portfolio Investment: Analyzing Assets, Earnings, Cash Flow, Stock Price, Governance, and Special Situations* (New York: Bloomberg/Wiley, 2010). Our discussion here draws on the Monks-Lajoux framework.

7. This definition is from the ongoing work of the *Conceptual Framework: Joint Project of the International Accounting Standards Board and the Financial Accounting Standards Board*. See "Project Update: Conceptual Framework, Elements and Recognition"; available at http://www.fasb.org/project/cf_phase-b.shtml, last accessed June 12, 2010; and "Notes from Joint Meeting of the IASB and FASB," October 20–21, 2008; available at http://www.fasb.org/news/SDR_10_20-21_08.pdf, last accessed June 12, 2010. The IASB Framework, approved by the International Accounting Standards Committee (IASC) board in April 1989 for publication in July 1989, adopted by the IASB in April 2001, and still current with the IASB, states that "an asset is a resource controlled by the entity as a result of past events and from which future economic benefits are expected to flow to the entity." See "Framework for the Preparation and Presentation of Financial Statements," January 1, 2009; available at http://www.iasb.org/NR/rdonlyres/4CF78A7B-B237-402A-A031-709A687508A6/0/Framework.pdf, last accessed June 12, 2010.

The elements directly related to the measurement of financial position are assets, liabilities, and equity. These are defined as follows:

(a) An asset is a resource controlled by the entity as a result of past events and from which future economic benefits are expected to flow to the entity.

(b) A liability is a present obligation of the entity arising from past events, the settlement of which is expected to result in an outflow from the entity of resources embodying economic benefits.

(c) Equity is the residual interest in the assets of the entity after deducting all its liabilities.

8. Cheryl Moss, Vice President, Friend Skoler & Co., Inc., Saddle Brook, New Jersey, interviewed June 10, 2010.

9. "Uniform Standards of Professional Appraisal from the Appraisal Standards Board of the American Appraisal Foundation"; available at http://www.uspap.org/2010USPAP/USPAP/frwrd/uspap_toc.htm, last accessed June 10, 2010.

10. USPAP 2010–2011, Standards Rule 1-4; available at http://www.uspap
    .org/2010USPAP/USPAP/stds/sr1_4.htm, last accessed June 10, 2010.
11. "Uniform Standards of Professional Appraisal," note 9.
12. This list is adapted from Monks and Lajoux, note 6.
13. Example: "Your investment philosophy requires an average AAR of at least 15
    percent on all fixed asset purchases. Currently, you are considering some new
    equipment costing $96,000. This equipment will have a three-year life, over
    which time it will be depreciated on a straight-line basis to a zero book value.
    The annual net income from this project is estimated at $5,500, $12,400, and
    $17,600 for the three years.
    Analysis:
    The average net income is (5,500 + 12,400 + 17,600)/3 = 11,833.33
    The average investment is (96,000 + 0)/2 = 48,000
    AAR = 11,833.33/48,000 = 24.6%
    This is higher than 15%, so the project should be accepted."
    Ibid.
14. As additional cash investments increase the asset side of the balance sheet, this
    procedure ensures that additional dollars invested do not appear to be dollars of
    return from previous investments. Ibid.
15. See *Matter of Genesis Health Ventures, Inc.*, 266 B.R. 591, 614 (Bankr. D. Del.
    2001).
16. See, for example, *Consolidated Rock Prods. Co. v. DuBois*, 312 U.S. 510, 525-
    526 (1941); *Group of Institutional Investors v. Chicago, Mil., St. P. & Pac. R.R.
    Co.*, 318 U.S. 523, 540-41 (1943).
17. Lawrence P. King, ed., *Collier on Bankruptcy* 7, 15th ed. rev. (1997),
    1129.06[2][a][ii][E] [quoting Peter V. Pantaleo and Barry W. Ridings, "Reorga-
    nization Value," 51 *Business Lawyer* 419, 428 (1996)].
18. No. 02-12740 (Bankr. D. Del. June 13, 2003) (accepting the discounted cash
    flow method "as the appropriate method to determine enterprise value in this
    case," where revenues and earnings were anticipated to experience wide swings
    rather than becoming normalized).
19. 241 B.R. 92, 104 (Bankr. D. Del. 1999) (relying on experts who applied the dis-
    counted cash flow method to a company with volatile cash flows).
20. The analyst has alternatives here, according to one classic financial article.
    "A controversial issue is the question of whether the expected values of net cash
    flows should be discounted with a 'risk-adjusted' rate or whether such flows
    should first be adjusted for risk and then be discounted at a 'risk free' rate."
    Lutz Haegert and R. M. Edelson, "An Analysis of the Kuhn-Tucker Conditions
    of Stochastic Programming with Reference to the Estimation of Discount Rates
    and Risk Premia," *Journal of Business Finance*, September 1974, pp. 319–455.
21. Stanley Foster Reed, Alexandra Reed Lajoux, and H. Peter Nesvold, *The Art of
    M&A: A Merger/Acquisition/Buyout Guide*, 4th ed. (New York: McGraw-Hill,
    2007).

22. See, for example, http://cwmulford.com/CoAnalysis.htm, from Georgia Tech professor Charles Mulford. The Financial Statement Analysis Model consists of several Excel worksheets designed to do a complete financial statement and cash flow analysis of a company. Three years of balance sheet and income statement data are necessary to make the model run.

23. *In re Spansion, Inc., et al., Chapter 11, Debtors. U.S. Bank National Association, as trustee, Plaintiff, v. Wilmington Trust Company, Spansion, Inc., Spansion Technology LLC, Spansion LLC, Cerium Laboratories LLC and Spansion International, Inc. Defendants.* Case No. 09-10690 (KJC), Adv. Pro. No. 09-52274. United States Bankruptcy Court, D. Delaware. April 1, 2010.

24. The authors acknowledge the writings of Phil Weiss of the *Motley Fool* as the source for these two descriptions.

25. *In re New York, New Haven and Hartford R.R.*, 4 B.R. 758, 792 (D. Conn. 1980).

26. Bruce A. Markell, "Owners, Auctions, and Absolute Priority in Bankruptcy Reorganizations," *Stanford Law Review* 44 (1991), pp. 69, 73.

27. Gilson et al., note 1, p. 65, n. 33.

28. See Financial Accounting Standards Board, "FASB Issues Revised Exposure Draft on Earnings per Share," news release, August 7, 2008; available at http://www.fasb.org/news/nr080708.shtml, last accessed June 12, 2010.

29. Financial Accounting Standards Board, "Earnings per Share, an Amendment of FASB Statement No. 128," Exposure Draft (revised), Proposed Statement of Financial Accounting Standards, August 7, 2008; available at http://www.fasb.org/draft/rev_ed_eps_amend_st128.pdf, last accessed June 12, 2010.

30. This approach is suggested by one investor commenting on the Web site motleyfool.com with a blog under the pen name Olikea. He explains: "One of the reasons it is useful to consider the 'enterprise value' as opposed to simple 'market capitalization' is that if company A wished to purchase company B outright, it would not only have to buy up all the shares at the current price (market cap) but it would also have to assume the company's debt. If company B had any cash on hand, this would effectively be an 'instant rebate,' so it gets subtracted from the cost of acquisition." See http://boards.fool.co.uk/Profile.asp?uid=208767628, last accessed June 12, 2010.

31. For a full discussion of these methods, see Monks and Lajoux, note 6.

32. 611 A.2d 485, 490 (Del. Ch. 1991).

CHAPTER 12

Distressed M&A Strategy: The Plan of Reorganization

Begin with the end in mind.

—*Stephen R. Covey,* The 7 Habits of Highly Effective People

OVERVIEW OF THE PLAN OF REORGANIZATION

What is a plan of reorganization, and what function does it serve in the bankruptcy process?

Before a debtor can emerge from Chapter 11, the bankruptcy court must confirm the company's *plan of reorganization* (also known as a *reorganization plan*, a *PoR*, or simply *the plan*). Congress designed the confirmation process for a plan of reorganization to provide democratic checks and balances by having the debtor in possession generally propose a plan of reorganization, the creditors vote on it, and the bankruptcy court confirm it. This design creates a healthy tension between the parties by giving each side negotiating leverage to allow them to arrive at a reasonable compromise. When considering a plan of reorganization, all parties should keep in mind the primary objectives of the bankruptcy process: (1) a fresh start for the business, including a discharge from pre-petition debts, and (2) a fair and equitable distribution to creditors. In this chapter, we explain the process and key issues for proposing, voting on, and obtaining confirmation of a plan of reorganization.

The plan of reorganization is the endgame that all of the parties and their advisors are targeting from the beginning as they maneuver through the bankruptcy process. All of the strategizing, posturing, aligning, negotiating, cajoling, and litigating leads to the climax of the bankruptcy process: the confirmation hearing for the plan of reorganization. The confirmation of a plan of reorganization puts all of the legal and financial theories to the ultimate reality test when the creditors cast their votes either for or against the plan and the bankruptcy court rules on its legality. All is revealed: which negotiating tactics are bluffs, which arguments have merit, which alliances hold firm, which parties switch sides, which ideas can be financed, which recoveries will exceed expectations, and which payouts will disappoint. Because the confirmation process usually involves multiple rounds of proposals, objections, negotiations, and revisions, it is critical that a potential buyer review the latest version of the plan of reorganization.

If, after an exhaustive back-and-forth struggle, the plan of reorganiza- . tion cannot pass the test, the parties may reluctantly conclude that liquidation is the more suitable result for the business. Sometimes the threat of liquidation, which could result in a lose-lose scenario for all parties, is necessary to convince stubborn holdouts to consent to the plan of reorganization. Other times, the opposition can use the threat of liquidation to gain concessions. In rare circumstances, if a stalemate arises during negotiations over a plan of reorganization, the bankruptcy court may dismiss the case altogether, with neither reorganization nor liquidation occurring under federal bankruptcy law.

A key benefit of any plan of reorganization is the legal ability to drag along dissenting minorities, called *holdouts*. Indeed, this benefit may be the reason that the debtor sought a resolution to its issues through federal bankruptcy rather than through an out-of-court workout or a state insolvency proceeding. In this chapter, we explain the techniques involved in confirming a plan of reorganization, such as *cram-down*, *cram-up*, *lockup*, and other concepts, to achieve such drag-along benefits. Also, we describe how minority investors can apply certain defenses to gain negotiating leverage, such as the *best interests of creditors test*, the *feasibility test*, and the *absolute priority rule*.

One way for a potential purchaser to acquire a distressed company is through a plan of reorganization. In general, there are two main approaches to this method. The first approach involves buying the company in a 363 sale that is implemented through a plan of reorganization rather than separately. In this case, the buyer should be prepared to address all of the issues involving 363 sales that we will discuss in Chapter 13 as well as the issues discussed in this chapter. There are some jurisdictions in which the U.S. trustee demands that any sale of a company in bankruptcy be done pursuant to a plan of reorganization rather than as a separate 363 sale. The second approach involves financing a plan of reorganization to take control of the company as it emerges from the bankruptcy process.

In this chapter, we examine the following aspects of the process for confirming a plan of reorganization:

- Exclusivity period
- Plan of reorganization types
- Disclosure statements
- Contents of the plan of reorganization
- Confirmation

Although valuation is never an explicit part of the process for crafting, negotiating, or confirming a plan of reorganization, it is implied and influential at nearly every stage. From determining the fulcrum security to obtaining exit financing to calculating recoveries to evaluating certain tests, the valuation of the company is usually the most important factor. Therefore, all parties typically need to form a view of the company's valuation before assessing a proposed plan of reorganization.

EXCLUSIVITY PERIOD

Who can propose a plan of reorganization?

While at later points during the bankruptcy proceeding, any party to the proceeding may be able to propose a plan of reorganization, only the debtor has the right to do so during the *exclusivity period*. The Bankruptcy Code specifically notes that a bankruptcy trustee, an Official Committee of Unsecured Creditors, any individual creditor, any equity holder, and an indenture trustee may file a plan of reorganization.[1] The entity filing the plan is called the *plan proponent*.

A potential purchaser who does not fall into one of these categories may not file a plan of reorganization because he is not a party in interest. However, if a potential purchaser wishes to make such a filing, he can purchase a creditor's claim and use that creditor's status in the bankruptcy proceeding to propose a plan. Usually, it is more pragmatic for a potential purchaser to align with the debtor or the creditors' committee in order to have a constituency that supports the plan.

What are the exclusivity and solicitation periods?

The *exclusivity period* refers to the stage of the bankruptcy process during which only the debtor may propose a plan of reorganization. The exclusivity period begins on the petition date. Bankruptcy Code section 1121(b) explains that a debtor has 120 days to file a plan of reorganization with the bankruptcy court.[2]

While filing a proper plan of reorganization is a complex undertaking, as a practical matter, the debtor needs to file only a *placeholder plan*—which can be amended at a later date—to satisfy the Bankruptcy Code's technical 120-day requirement; this is because Bankruptcy Code section 1121(c)(2) does not require that the filed plan be confirmable.

The filing of a plan of reorganization automatically triggers the start of the *solicitation period*, which provides another 60 days of exclusivity for the debtor. Therefore, parties will sometimes refer to the debtor's exclusivity period as 180 days, not 120 days, because it is straightforward to file a placeholder plan to receive the automatic extension. The computation of time does not include the day of the event, which means the petition date under these circumstances, and does include the last day. If the last day is a Saturday, Sunday, or legal holiday, then the period runs until the end of the next day that is not one of these days.[3] However, Saturdays, Sundays, and legal holidays are included in counting the number of days in the exclusivity period.

If the debtor—meaning the debtor in possession or the bankruptcy trustee, as the case may be—does not file a plan of reorganization by the 120th day, the debtor's exclusivity period ends automatically, and any party in interest may thereafter file a plan of reorganization.[4] There is no provision in the Bankruptcy Code to restore a debtor's exclusivity once it is terminated.

A potential purchaser should gauge the status of the debtor's exclusivity period when approaching a case. Because of this balance of power at the beginning of a bankruptcy proceeding, a potential purchaser may need to approach the debtor first. If the exclusivity period has already terminated, a buyer should assess which party or parties are gathering the most support for their plan of reorganization. If the exclusivity period is approaching its expiration, a buyer may want to wait and see what happens next.

Can the debtor obtain extensions of the exclusivity and solicitation periods?

Yes. The debtor may request that the bankruptcy court extend the exclusivity and solicitation periods.[5] The debtor must show cause to support the extension request, must provide notice of the request to all parties in interest, and must have a hearing before the bankruptcy court. The debtor may demonstrate cause by explaining the burdens of organizing the company's financial affairs, the time-consuming process of assessing its strategic alternatives, and the difficulties of negotiating with various creditor constituencies.

Multiple extensions are routinely requested and granted in complex Chapter 11 cases, which describes most corporate bankruptcies. A potential purchaser should scan the bankruptcy docket for bankruptcy court orders granting extensions to determine when the extended exclusivity period ultimately ends. Sometimes these orders will contain language indicating that the current extension is the final extension of the exclusivity period, and that requests for further extensions will be denied.

If the debtor fails to request an extension, other parties in interest may make the request instead. Sometimes creditors may prefer that the debtor maintain its exclusivity rather than creating a free-for-all battle among feuding creditors proposing competing plans of reorganization.

A potential purchaser should take special interest in the hearings on requests for extensions of exclusivity periods because key information about the inner workings of the bankruptcy case may be revealed. If the extension request receives one or more objections, the nature of the objections may indicate the goals of various creditors and the status of the negotiations between the parties. The hearing may involve disclosure of the debtor's reorganization process, including perhaps its progress in conducting a sale and soliciting potential bidders. The pleadings and the hearing may reveal information about the debtor's operations, finances, and turnaround as the debtor tries to support its request for more time and the creditors critique the debtor's efforts.

Is there a limit on the amount of time by which the exclusivity period and solicitation period can be extended?

Yes. The Bankruptcy Abuse Prevention and Consumer Protection Act of 2005 (2005 BAPCPA) added new requirements limiting the time granted by extensions to these periods. According to Bankruptcy Code section 1121(d) (2), the 120-day exclusivity period cannot be extended beyond 18 months from the petition date, and the 180-day combined exclusivity and solicitation periods cannot be extended beyond 20 months from the petition date.[6]

Congress was reacting to a perception that bankruptcy proceedings were simply taking too long. For example, United Airlines took three years to confirm its plan of reorganization, and Adelphia took more than four years. In addition, lawmakers were responding to a concern that advisors had an adverse incentive to prolong negotiations over plans of reorganization in order to accumulate excessive fees.

Furthermore, the new limits on exclusivity tipped the balance between secured creditors and bankrupt borrowers in favor of the secured creditors. As discussed previously in Chapter 5, the Bankruptcy Code attempts to balance these competing interests by allowing the debtor to continue to use the collateral that provides security for the lenders, but only as long as the parties agree that the lenders' interests are being adequately protected. Placing limits on exclusivity provides secured creditors with further safeguards, in addition to the adequate protection requirements. Secured creditors can now exert pressure on bankrupt borrowers to create a viable strategy to fix the company expeditiously or else surrender the collateral. Previously, bankrupt borrowers could threaten secured creditors by having their exclusivity periods extended endlessly by sympathetic judges.

Finally, a significant beneficiary of the limits on extensions for exclusivity periods is the potential purchaser of a distressed business. Because the debtor in possession must now deal with strict time limits for creating a plan of reorganization and obtaining sufficient approval votes from creditors for confirmation, the debtor in possession may conclude that a sale of the company is preferable. Negotiating with potential buyers regarding a sale of the company may be easier than negotiating with creditors regarding a plan of reorganization. Usually, potential buyers are sophisticated professionals who understand how to negotiate effectively and transact expeditiously. On the other hand, creditors may be a disorganized band of unsophisticated individuals, small business vendors, and government agencies with inconsistent objectives and irrational expectations. A debtor in possession that is exasperated with the process of unproductive negotiations with various creditors may be susceptible to the overtures of a potential purchaser, especially as the time on its exclusivity clock runs short.

Can the exclusivity period and solicitation period be reduced?

Yes. Under extraordinary circumstances, the bankruptcy court may grant a party in interest's request to shorten the debtor's exclusivity period to less than 120 days or the combined exclusivity and solicitation periods to less than 180 days.[7] The party in interest must show cause for its request and will be subject to a high standard by the bankruptcy court because the 120-day and 180-day periods are perceived as statutory rights of the debtor.

Rather than seek to shorten the exclusivity period, a secured creditor who has lost confidence in management may instead seek to lift the automatic stay in order to seize its collateral,[8] appoint a bankruptcy trustee,[9] or convert the case to a Chapter 7 liquidation.[10]

PLAN OF REORGANIZATION TYPES

What are the various forms that a plan of reorganization may take?

A debtor's plan of reorganization can be a stand-alone plan, a prepackaged plan, or a prearranged plan. Each of these is discussed in this section.

In the absence of a prepackaged or prearranged bankruptcy, a company's bankruptcy process may be characterized as a *free-fall bankruptcy*. Not having arrived at any consensus with its creditors regarding a plan of reorganization, the company may experience a lengthy, contentious, and expensive bankruptcy process that jeopardizes its future. The uncertainty can drive customers to competitors, motivate employees to go elsewhere, and encourage vendors to tighten payment terms. In a free-fall bankruptcy, a potential purchaser may find that the company is especially susceptible to a low bid, but the buyer also risks receiving a company that is in far worse shape than she expected.

What is a stand-alone plan of reorganization?

The term *stand-alone plan of reorganization* refers to a plan of reorganization that does not involve the sale of a company. Instead, the plan contemplates reorganizing the company's operations, restructuring its balance sheet, and enabling it to emerge from Chapter 11 as a going concern.

What is a prepackaged bankruptcy?

The term *prepackaged bankruptcy* (also known as a *prepack*) refers to a pre-petition binding agreement between a debtor and its creditors regarding the terms and conditions for a plan of reorganization. The parties in a pre-packaged bankruptcy seek to leave nothing to chance. The debtor has nego-tiated, disclosed, and documented a plan of reorganization with its creditors during the pre-petition period, and the creditors have agreed to vote in favor of the plan. Although the parties agree on how the company should be reor-ganized and its balance sheet restructured, they believe that they cannot implement their agreement without the powers and protections of the Bank-ruptcy Code, such as a discharge. The debtor then proceeds to file a volun-tary bankruptcy petition and promptly proposes the agreed-upon plan of reorganization. While not all creditors may be involved in this agreement, there must be a sufficient number of approving votes to confirm a plan of reorganization, as described later in this chapter. The intent of the parties in a prepackaged bankruptcy is typically to minimize the length, cost, and disruption of the bankruptcy process. The Bankruptcy Code and Bankruptcy Rules each acknowledge the legitimacy of prepackaged bankruptcies.[11]

When evaluating a prepackaged bankruptcy, a potential purchaser should first determine whether the agreement involves a sale of all or part of the company. If it does not, buyers are likely to be wasting their time trying to convince the parties to withdraw their commitment to a stand-alone plan of reorganization. If it does, then the parties may already have a particular buyer in mind, and that buyer may be very far along in its due diligence, financing, and negotiations. A competing bidder may be at a significant dis-advantage even if there is an attempt to create a bidding process.

If a potential purchaser approaches a distressed company about a sale of all or part of the business pre-petition, the buyer may seek to complete the sale using a prepackaged bankruptcy. The benefits to the buyer are a quick and cooperative bankruptcy process that will minimize objections to the sale pro-cess, the buyer's qualifications, the transaction structure, and the valuation.

Exhibit 12-1 highlights recent examples of prepackaged bankruptcies and shows how quickly the plan confirmation process can occur when there is consensus.

In the Southern District of New York, which is the jurisdiction for many corporate bankruptcies, there is a local rule that provides detailed instructions on the procedures for filing prepackaged bankruptcies.[12]

What is a prearranged bankruptcy?

Like a prepackaged bankruptcy, a *prearranged bankruptcy* (also known as a *prenegotiated bankruptcy*) involves a pre-petition agreement between

Exhibit 12-1 Examples of Recent Prepackaged Chapter 11 Bankruptcies

Debtor	Bankruptcy Court	Petition Date	Plan Confirmed	Number of Days
InSight Health Services Holdings Corp.	D.Del	5/29/07	8/1/07	64
Bally Total Fitness Holding Corporation	SDNY	7/31/07	9/17/07	48
Remy International, Inc.	D.Del	10/8/07	12/16/07	69
Sirva, Inc.	SDNY	2/5/08	5/12/08	97
Vertis, Inc.	D.Del	7/15/08	8/26/08	42
CIT Group Inc.	SDNY	11/1/09	12/10/09	39
Lazy Days R.V. Center, Inc.	D.Del	11/5/09	12/8/09	33
Simmons Company	D.Del	11/16/09	1/5/10	50
Xerium Technologies, Inc.	D.Del	3/30/10	5/25/10	56

a debtor and its creditors regarding the terms and conditions for a plan of reorganization. Unlike in a prepackaged bankruptcy, however, in a prearranged bankruptcy, a binding agreement with a critical mass of creditors has not been reached. The debtor may have obtained lockup agreements from key creditors to support the plan, but it still needs to solicit votes from many other creditors. In some cases, there may be no actual agreement, although the main parties have agreed upon a general outline of the terms before the debtor files a voluntary bankruptcy petition.

With this approach, the parties hope to shorten the company's time in the bankruptcy process because the key terms and overall strategy for the reorganization have already been settled in principle. In addition, the company can announce to its nervous customers, restless employees, anxious vendors, and other unhappy constituents that its bankruptcy process will be quicker and less disruptive because the creditors basically approve of the company's strategy. It is generally beneficial for all parties to keep customers, employees, vendors, and other relationships as calm and cooperative as possible to avoid deepening the company's distress.

Whatever the message that a company may be sending, however, a potential purchaser should still investigate a sale of all or part of the business. Even if the prearranged bankruptcy contemplates a stand-alone plan of reorganization, an agreement in principle is not binding, and certain parties may be more interested in a sale process. Furthermore, any pre-petition agreement in principle in a prearranged bankruptcy is usually tentative, and the passage of time may change the views of certain creditors regarding a sale process.

If a potential purchaser approaches a distressed company about a sale of all or part of the business pre-petition, the buyer may seek to complete the sale using a prearranged bankruptcy if a prepackaged bankruptcy is not feasible. The benefits to the buyer are a quick and cooperative bankruptcy process that will minimize objections to the sale process, the buyer's qualifications, the transaction structure, and the valuation—but not as much as in a prepackaged bankruptcy.

It is important to note that the terms *prepackaged bankruptcy* and *prearranged bankruptcy* are often used loosely and interchangeably by the news media and even by bankruptcy professionals. Therefore, a potential purchaser should confirm with the parties whether a pre-petition agreement was binding or nonbinding and whether it involved a sufficient number of creditors to confirm the plan of reorganization. A review of the bankruptcy docket and the hearing transcript for the first-day motions may also help explain the nature of the agreement between the debtor and its creditors.

Recent examples of prearranged bankruptcies include Reader's Digest Association, Inc.; Lear Corporation; Masonite Corporation; Chiquita Brands, Inc.; and Movie Gallery, Inc.

How does a debtor go about soliciting support for a plan of reorganization?

When soliciting votes for a plan of reorganization, a debtor may seek to obtain *lockup agreements* (also known as *plan support agreements*) from creditors to secure their votes for the plan. Pre-petition lockup agreements are the key mechanism for pursuing a prepackaged bankruptcy. Pre-petition lockup agreements also arise in prearranged bankruptcies, where the debtor seeks to secure the commitment of key creditors. A debtor may seek post-petition lockup agreements as well to secure the commitment of one group of creditors as a prelude to negotiating with another group of creditors.

The Bankruptcy Code implicitly recognizes lockup agreements by noting that notwithstanding the requirement for distributing a disclosure statement to creditors before soliciting their votes for a plan of reorganization:

> [A]n acceptance or rejection of the plan may be solicited from a holder of a claim or interest if such solicitation complies with applicable non-bankruptcy law and if such holder was solicited before the commencement of the case in a manner complying with applicable non-bankruptcy law.[13]

DISCLOSURE STATEMENTS

What is a disclosure statement?

The Bankruptcy Code requires that a *disclosure statement* accompany every plan of reorganization.[14] Whereas the plan of reorganization explains the treatment and resolution of creditors' claims and equity interests, the disclosure statement provides information about the debtor and the debtor's estate so that parties can make informed votes on the plan. Often, the debtor in possession files the disclosure statement with the bankruptcy court prior to filing the plan of reorganization.

Bankruptcy Code section 1125 provides that the debtor's disclosure statement must provide adequate information and must be approved by the bankruptcy court after a notice and a hearing.[15] The disclosure statement is often a highly useful tool for a potential purchaser because it typically contains the most current and detailed information about the financial projections for the company's operations and conclusions about the company's valuation, including the disclosure of reports prepared by the company's advisors, appraisers, and consultants. While the potential purchaser may, of course, have different perspectives on forecasts and valuation, the disclosure statement provides a useful point of comparison. If there is a prolonged negotiation of the plan of reorganization, updated disclosure statements may reveal how the company's performance is improving or worsening. However, the Bankruptcy Code explicitly notes that the bankruptcy court may approve a disclosure statement that does not contain a valuation of the debtor or an appraisal of the debtor's assets.[16]

For situations in which a financial advisor is running a sale process, a potential purchaser should compare the financial information in the disclosure statement to the data contained in a selling memorandum. Whereas an investment bank's selling memorandum usually contains disclaimers regarding the accuracy of the information contained therein, a disclosure statement is an official legal document that is filed by the debtor with the bankruptcy court. As a result, the disclosure statement is likely to be a more reliable and sober representation of the company's situation, with a minimum amount of overblown hype and marketing enthusiasm.

The Bankruptcy Code explains that a debtor may use multiple disclosure statements targeted at different classes of creditors.[17] However, all creditors within the same class must receive the same disclosure statement. For example, a debtor may wish to provide more detail to certain classes of creditors than to others. In practice, this is atypical, but it is worth it for a potential purchaser to ensure that he is receiving the most detailed disclosure statement available.

What does adequate information mean in the context of a disclosure statement?

The Bankruptcy Code defines *adequate information* for a disclosure statement as meaning

> [I]nformation of a kind, and in sufficient detail, as far as is reasonably practicable in light of the nature and history of the debtor and the condition of the debtor's books and records, including a discussion of the potential material Federal tax consequences of the plan to the debtor, any successor to the debtor, and a hypothetical investor typical of the holders of claims or interests in the case, that would enable such a hypothetical investor of the relevant class to make an informed judgment about the plan, but adequate information need not include such information about any other possible or proposed plan and in determining whether a disclosure statement provides adequate information, the court shall consider the complexity of the case, the benefit of additional information to creditors and other parties in interest, and the cost of providing additional information.[18]

One bankruptcy court reviewed many cases and created a list of facts to be disclosed in order to provide adequate information, as shown in Exhibit 12-2.[19]

Although the Bankruptcy Code provides that a bankruptcy court may approve a disclosure statement that does not provide a valuation of the debtor or an appraisal of the debtor's assets,[20] a valuation is usually included, as indicated previously. Therefore, potential purchasers can review the debtor's disclosure statement to get a professional view of the company they seek to acquire. If the company is in a so-called Chapter 22 case, potential purchasers can download the disclosure statement from the prior bankruptcy case to check the valuation methodologies used in that case, which may apply to the current proceeding. Furthermore, if the company's competitors have been through the Chapter 11 reorganization process in the past, potential purchasers can review the disclosure statements in those cases as well.

Exhibit 12-2 Examples of Adequate Information for Disclosure Statements

- The events that led to the filing of a bankruptcy petition
- A description of the available assets and their value
- The anticipated future of the company
- The source of information stated in the disclosure statement
- A disclaimer
- The present condition of the debtor while in Chapter 11
- The scheduled claims
- The estimated return to creditors under a Chapter 7 liquidation
- The accounting method utilized to produce financial information and the name of the accountants responsible for such information
- The future management of the debtor
- The Chapter 11 plan of reorganization or a summary thereof
- The estimated administrative expenses, including attorneys' and accountants' fees
- The collectibility of accounts receivable
- Financial information, data, valuations, or projections relevant to the creditors' decision to accept or reject the Chapter 11 plan
- Information relevant to the risks posed to creditors under the plan
- The actual or projected realizable value from recovery of preferential or otherwise voidable transfers
- Litigation that is likely to arise in a nonbankruptcy context
- Tax attributes of the debtor
- The relationship of the debtor with affiliates

For companies with publicly traded securities, the SEC may comment on whether a debtor's disclosure statement contains adequate information. According to www.sec.gov, the SEC will "review the disclosure document to determine if the company is telling investors and creditors the important information they need to know. . . . Although the SEC does not negotiate the economic terms of reorganization plans, [the agency] may take a position on important legal issues that will affect the rights of public investors in other bankruptcy cases as well." However, the Bankruptcy Code prohibits the SEC and other government agencies from appealing an order of the bankruptcy court regarding whether a disclosure statement includes adequate information.[21]

CONTENTS OF THE PLAN OF REORGANIZATION

How does a bankruptcy court determine whether to confirm a plan of reorganization?

To confirm a plan of reorganization, a bankruptcy court must consider several factors. First, the court must determine whether certain mandatory content is present and whether the plan's other contents are permitted under the Bankruptcy Code. Next, the court ascertains whether the plan satisfies the factors summarized in Exhibit 12-3.

Exhibit 12-3 Plan of Reorganization Confirmation Factors

- The plan complies with all applicable provisions of the Bankruptcy Code.
- The plan proponent complies with all applicable provisions of the Bankruptcy Code.
- The plan is proposed in good faith.
- Payments to be made to professionals under the plan are reasonable.
- The plan proponent discloses the identity and affiliations of directors and officers of the reorganized company and its affiliates.
- The plan proponent discloses the identity and compensation of any insiders to be employed by the reorganized company.
- Any regulators with jurisdiction over the rates charged by a debtor have approved of any rate change provided in the plan.
- The plan passes the best interests of creditors test.
- Unless all classes of claims and interests vote to approve the plan (or are not impaired under the plan), at least one impaired noninsider class has voted in favor.
- Administrative expenses are paid in cash, possibly over time.
- The plan passes the feasibility test.
- All bankruptcy fees are paid.
- If the plan contemplates continuing payments for a pension plan, the payments comply with Bankruptcy Code section 1114.
- All property transfers comply with applicable nonbankruptcy law.
- The plan satisfies the absolute priority rule.

Each of these factors is discussed in more detail later in this chapter. In general, designing a plan of reorganization for confirmation by a bankruptcy court requires the skilled advice of talented professionals.

What does the Bankruptcy Code require in a plan of reorganization?

Regarding the mandatory requirements for a plan of reorganization, Bankruptcy Code section 1123(a) provides[22]

Notwithstanding any otherwise applicable non-bankruptcy law, a plan shall—

(1) Designate, subject to section 1122 of this title, classes of claims, other than claims of a kind specified in section 507 (a)(2), 507 (a)(3), or 507 (a)(8) of this title, and classes of interests;

(2) Specify any class of claims or interests that is not impaired under the plan;

(3) Specify the treatment of any class of claims or interests that is impaired under the plan;

(4) Provide the same treatment for each claim or interest of a particular class, unless the holder of a particular claim or interest agrees to a less favorable treatment of such particular claim or interest;

(5) Provide adequate means for the plan's implementation, such as—

(A) retention by the debtor of all or any part of the property of the estate;

(B) transfer of all or any part of the property of the estate to one or more entities, whether organized before or after the confirmation of such plan;

(C) merger or consolidation of the debtor with one or more persons;

(D) sale of all or any part of the property of the estate, either subject to or free of any lien, or the distribution of all or any part of the property of the estate among those having an interest in such property of the estate;

(E) satisfaction or modification of any lien;

(F) cancellation or modification of any indenture or similar instrument;

(G) curing or waiving of any default;

(H) extension of a maturity date or a change in an interest rate or other term of outstanding securities;

(I) amendment of the debtor's charter; or

(J) issuance of securities of the debtor, or of any entity referred to in subparagraph (B) or (C) of this paragraph, for cash, for property, for existing securities, or in exchange for claims or interests, or for any other appropriate purpose;

(6) Provide for the inclusion in the charter of the debtor, if the debtor is a corporation, or of any corporation referred to in paragraph (5)(B) or (5)(C) of this subsection, of a provision prohibiting the issuance of nonvoting equity securities, and providing, as to the several classes of securities possessing voting power, an appropriate distribution of such power among such classes, including, in the case of any class of equity securities having a preference over another class of equity securities with respect to dividends, adequate provisions for the election of directors representing such preferred class in the event of default in the payment of such dividends;

(7) Contain only provisions that are consistent with the interests of creditors and equity security holders and with public policy with respect to the manner of selection of any officer, director, or trustee under the plan and any successor to such officer, director, or trustee; and

(8) In a case in which the debtor is an individual, provide for the payment to creditors under the plan of all or such portion of earnings from personal services performed by the debtor after the commencement of the case or other future income of the debtor as is necessary for the execution of the plan.

What does the Bankruptcy Code permit (but not require) in a plan of reorganization?

Beyond the mandatory requirements for a plan of reorganization, Bankruptcy Code section 1123(b) authorizes a sponsor of a plan of reorganization to propose other provisions:[23]

Subject to subsection (a) of this section, a plan may—

(1) Impair or leave unimpaired any class of claims, secured or unsecured, or of interests;
(2) Subject to section 365 of this title, provide for the assumption, rejection, or assignment of any executory contract or unexpired lease of the debtor not previously rejected under such section;
(3) Provide for—
  (A) the settlement or adjustment of any claim or interest belonging to the debtor or to the estate; or
  (B) the retention and enforcement by the debtor, by the trustee, or by a representative of the estate appointed for such purpose, of any such claim or interest;
(4) Provide for the sale of all or substantially all of the property of the estate, and the distribution of the proceeds of such sale among holders of claims or interests;
(5) Modify the rights of holders of secured claims, other than a claim secured only by a security interest in real property that is the debtor's principal residence, or of holders of unsecured claims, or leave unaffected the rights of holders of any class of claims; and
(6) Include any other appropriate provision not inconsistent with the applicable provisions of this title.

Must the plan of reorganization propose recoveries for each specific creditor?

No. Under a plan of reorganization, a debtor must group claims with similar seniority or priority into *classes of claims* for determining recoveries to creditors.[24] Accordingly, a plan of reorganization will not focus on explanations of what any individual creditor will receive, but instead will describe more generally how creditors' claims are classified and how each class will be treated. Neither the disclosure statement nor the plan of reorganization will typically provide a guide for matching individual claims with their classes. Therefore, to determine a particular creditor's proposed recovery, an observer must first review the creditor's proof of claim, then determine if there are any unresolved objections to that claim, then identify the class of creditors to which the claim belongs, and finally examine the treatment of that class of creditors in the latest plan of reorganization.

What is an administrative convenience class of claims?

Typically, when a company commences a voluntary Chapter 11 petition, there are various small amounts due to relatively minor creditors. As a practical matter, sending notices to, communicating with, soliciting votes from, and making distributions to these creditors would cost more in administrative and professional fees than the entire amount of the claims themselves. Congress recognized that it is more efficient for all parties to have the debtor simply pay these creditors in full.[25] Therefore, nearly all plans of reorganization contain an *administrative convenience class of creditors*, who are deemed to vote to approve the plan. Generally, the aggregate amount due to the creditors in this class is insignificant.

What is the absolute priority rule?

The *absolute priority rule* refers to ensuring a fair and equitable distribution to all creditors—a fundamental tenet of bankruptcy law—by requiring that more senior creditors be paid in full before more junior creditors receive any recoveries. The priority of distributions is often referred to as the "waterfall," invoking the image of a sequence of buckets in which the next bucket begins to fill from the overflow of the prior bucket.

Bankruptcy Code section 1129(b)(2) codifies the absolute priority rule in a somewhat convoluted manner to arrive at this result. Overall, Bankruptcy Code section 1129(b)(2) examines the treatment of each class of creditors to determine whether the recovery is fair and equitable. By focusing on classes of creditors, the absolute priority rule differs from the *best interests of creditors test*, which focuses on individual creditors.

First, Bankruptcy Code section 1129(b)(2)(A) explains that each class of secured claims must receive the full value of the allowed amount of their liens or the *indubitable equivalent*.[26] In section 506(a)(1), secured claims were adjusted to the full value of the allowed amount of their liens, with the balance of the secured creditors' claims becoming unsecured claims.[27] Therefore, Bankruptcy Code section 1129(b)(2)(A) essentially repeats this concept by explaining that a fair and equitable plan of reorganization must provide the senior creditors with this recovery. As a practical matter, most companies have senior loans with blanket liens on all or substantially all of their assets. Under these circumstances, if the value of the company's assets is less than the amount of the senior loans, the Bankruptcy Code requires the plan of reorganization to provide all recoveries to the senior lenders and none to junior lenders.

Next, Bankruptcy Code section 1129(b)(2)(B)(i) first acknowledges that a plan of reorganization is fair and equitable if it provides full recoveries to a class of unsecured creditors for their allowed claims.[28] If a class of unsecured creditors is receiving partial recoveries, Bankruptcy Code section 1129(b)(2)(B)(ii) provides that for a plan of reorganization to be fair and equitable, all classes junior to this class must receive no recoveries.[29]

Are there any exceptions to the absolute priority rule?

Yes. The *new value exception* involves junior claimants—such as equity holders—receiving partial or even full recoveries despite more senior classes getting partial or no recoveries to induce the junior claimants to provide "new value" to the reorganized company.

Generally, for the exception to apply, this new value must be given in cash or cash equivalents, not "sweat equity." Also, the new value must be a "necessity" to confirm the plan of reorganization, but it is unclear what this really means. If a cash contribution from the pre-petition equity holders is necessary to avoid liquidation and no third party is willing to make a similar investment, it seems doubtful that the reorganizing company is a viable going concern.

Both the absolute priority rule and the new value exception existed under pre-1978 case law. However, although Congress explicitly included the absolute priority rule in the Bankruptcy Code in 1978, it did not mention the new value exception. Therefore, some courts have viewed the new value exception as having been implicitly accepted by Congress when it enacted the absolute priority rule, while others have determined its exclusion to mean

that Congress rejected it. In 1999, the U.S. Supreme Court limited the application of the new value exception. The Supreme Court ruled that such new
value must involve competition and exposure to the financial markets, rather
than be offered exclusively to prior equity holders.[30] Accordingly, applying
the new value exception to a particular bankruptcy case requires the input of
a seasoned bankruptcy attorney who is familiar with the case law of the relevant jurisdiction.

May creditors receive more than 100 percent recoveries?

No. It would be neither fair nor equitable for any creditor to receive more
than 100 percent of its claim, including accrued interest under appropriate
circumstances. The second major component of the "fair and equitable"
requirement is that no creditor or interest holder be paid a premium over
the allowed amount of its claim. Once the participant receives or retains
property equal to its claim, it may receive no more.

The reason for this rule is obvious, and goes back to the basic understanding of debt and equity. Holders of debt traditionally contract for the
payment of interest and repayment of principal, but no more; after that, the
residual goes to equity.[31] As explained by a leading bankruptcy attorney,
"[A] requirement contained in an earlier version of the Code['s fair and
equitable standards] would have assured a dissenting class that no senior
class receives more than 100 percent of its claims, i.e., that it is not provided for more than in full."[32]

However, in solvent debtor cases in which equity holders receive
recoveries, a plan may provide for payment of more than 100 percent of the
principal amount of the debt due to unsecured creditors if they are entitled
to post-petition interest, call protection, and make-whole payments above
and beyond the principal amount of the debt. See Chapter 6 for more details
on post-petition interest and Chapter 14 for a definition of call protection
and make-whole payments. In such rare situations, the amount of these
creditors' claims is increased to include these elements, so that they may
ultimately receive 100 percent recoveries on the increased amounts. Note,
however, that although they may receive more than 100 percent of the principal amount, they are not receiving more than 100 percent of the claim
amount.

What is the best interests of creditors test for a plan of reorganization?

To satisfy the *best interests of creditors test*, a plan of reorganization must provide each individual creditor with a recovery that exceeds the amount that such creditor would receive in a hypothetical liquidation scenario.[33] Unlike the *absolute priority rule*, which addresses fairness among classes of creditors, the best interests of creditors test considers the perspective of each individual creditor.

The concept of liquidation value has multiple interpretations, including forced liquidation value, orderly liquidation value, fair market value, and replacement value. For each of these, the costs of liquidation must then be subtracted from the gross realizable proceeds. For purposes of the best interests of creditors test in a Chapter 11 reorganization, case law is clear that a measure of going-concern value, not foreclosure value, is to be used.[34] While precedent is not entirely clear on this point, it appears that a company should be valued as if it were being sold as a viable enterprise, not broken up into individual assets and sold piecemeal. Potential bidders should be aware that their correspondence with the debtor or its advisors may be used as evidence regarding the company's valuation in a hypothetical sale.

A creditor can waive its rights under the best interests of creditors test by voting to approve the plan of reorganization.[35] Therefore, if a plan of reorganization provides a less-than-liquidation-value recovery for a class of creditors, the votes of *all* of the creditors in that class are required in order to satisfy the requirements of the Bankruptcy Code. Because the best interests of creditors test focuses on individual creditors, it is insufficient for a majority of the class to approve such a plan.

There are many possible reasons why creditors might want to vote for the plan even if it provides less-than-liquidation-value recoveries for them. Particular creditors might have an interest in seeing the company survive rather than be liquidated. For example, insiders might value their continuing post-reorganization employment in addition to their recoveries for their pre-petition wages. Other creditors might place higher value on a smaller recovery in the near term than on an eventual payment following a lengthy liquidation process. Moreover, various creditors may view the value of the reorganized company and the proceeds from liquidating the company differently from the debtor's assertions in the disclosure statement. For example, if some creditors value equity in the reorganized company more highly than the debtor assumes, then they may prefer an equity recovery that appears lower than the amounts that they would receive in a hypothetical liquidation. Finally, in situations where a creditor in the class also has a claim in another class, this creditor may vote for a plan that favors that other class to maximize its overall recovery. The best interests of creditors test provides some protection against such conflicts of interest.

What is a cram-down plan of reorganization?

A *cram-down plan of reorganization* refers to a plan that is confirmed over the objections of other parties. A key factor in choosing federal bankruptcy over an out-of-court workout can be the ability to "cram down" parties who are behaving irrationally, clinging to unrealistic expectations, or negotiating in bad faith. In addition, the ability to cram down a plan can be used to deal with creditors who cannot be located. In practice, many plans of reorganization are confirmed using the cram-down rules contained in the Bankruptcy Code because it is unlikely that all classes of claims and interests will be paid in full or approve the plan.

The crux of a cram-down plan of reorganization, which is not a term that is defined in the Bankruptcy Code, involves the absolute priority rule and the best interests of creditors test. By establishing objective rules in Bankruptcy Code section 1129, Congress created a scheme for fair and equitable recoveries for all creditors and thereby established minimum thresholds for the components of a plan of reorganization. If creditors are unwilling to vote to approve a proposed plan, then their dissent can be disregarded as long as the plan follows these rules, particularly the absolute priority rule and the best interests of creditors test. In essence, these two guidelines provide the framework for the amount of recovery available to each class of creditors.

If these requirements, and others that tend to be more minor issues, are satisfied, the next procedural hurdle is to gain the acceptance of the plan by at least one impaired class (i.e., a class of creditors' claims or equity interests that is receiving a partial recovery).[36] The votes of insiders are excluded from this analysis. Achieving this goal is no small task, and the plan proponent may attempt to show favoritism to gain the support of an impaired noninsider class. The holders of the fulcrum security typically make up this impaired class, making the identity of the fulcrum security an essential element of plan negotiations.

A final requirement for a cram-down plan of reorganization is that the plan does not "discriminate unfairly" with respect to each class of claims that does not approve of but is impaired by the plan.[37] While this term is not defined in the Bankruptcy Code, the legislative history implies that this requirement is meant to protect creditors in classes of claims that have equal priority from different treatment that rises to the level of unfair discrimination.[38] This rule might also protect against discriminatory treatment of classes of creditors that disapprove of the plan. Assertions of unfair discrimination in the classification of claims often arise pursuant to Bankruptcy Code section 1122, such as if similarly situated claims are placed in different classes. As one bankruptcy professional explained:[39]

> Chapter 11 provided a method for allocating reorganization value; that is, since every participant was guaranteed an amount equal to at least the amount of its Chapter 7 dividend, the surplus preserved by reorganization was left for negotiation. The rules of that negotiation are minimal, and found in the confirmation requirements: get consent and meet the other twelve confirmation requirements, or cram down. Cramdown, in turn, still meant meeting the twelve other confirmation requirements, but it also meant preserving vertical and horizontal expectations. Vertical expectations were the province of the fair and equitable rule, with its focus on allocating value to classes in a manner consistent with prebankruptcy priorities. Horizontal expectations among creditors and interest holders of similar priority were left to the unfair discrimination requirement.

Although the concept of a cram-down plan of reorganization may sound objective and straightforward, the fact that bankruptcy courts are courts of equity as well as courts of law ensures a degree of subjectivity and nuance. Indeed, the Bankruptcy Code expressly acknowledges the bankruptcy court's status as a court of equity by requiring that a cram-down plan of reorganization be found by the bankruptcy court to be "fair and equitable" with respect to each class of claims and interests.[40] As a result, overconfidence that a proposed cram-down plan will be confirmed is more likely to stem from hubris than from audacity.

What is a cram-up plan of reorganization?

The tongue-in-cheek term *cram-up plan of reorganization* refers to a bankruptcy court's confirming a cram-down plan of reorganization over the secured creditors' objections. Usually, a cram-down plan involves forcing the agreement of unsecured creditors, but sometimes the unsecured creditors try to turn the tables on the secured creditors. The confirmation requirements regarding secured creditors in Bankruptcy Code section 1129(b)(2) make cram-up plans extremely rare. Bankruptcy courts construe the meaning of *indubitable equivalent* narrowly; accordingly, a debtor has very little ability to force a secured lender to accept modification of its loan after the bankruptcy proceeding has concluded. However, as will be discussed in Chapter 13, some bankruptcy courts may disallow credit bidding by secured creditors in any proposed 363 sales—namely, any of those that in effect guarantees full cash repayment of all secured claims.

Allowing the unilateral modification of the fundamental pre-petition bargain between borrower and secured lender would introduce significant uncertainty into future transactions throughout the financial markets. Such legal uncertainty could increase borrowing costs for all borrowers if lenders perceived increased risks regarding the timing or amount of each borrower's eventual repayment. Moreover, fewer lenders would consider financing a troubled company's out-of-court turnaround because lenders would be concerned about the outcome if the borrower eventually entered bankruptcy. Furthermore, secured lenders might become even more conservative and uncooperative during cash collateral, DIP loan, adequate protection, and carveout negotiations at the beginning of a bankruptcy case because they would have heightened concern about the eventual outcome of the case.

As discussed in Chapter 5, with regard to *adequate protection* and other aspects of the treatment of secured creditors in bankruptcy, bankruptcy law attempts to balance the need of the debtor to reorganize and the need of the secured lender to be repaid. When a bankruptcy case reaches the plan of reorganization stage, these competing interests have been balanced through adequate protection for the senior lenders, who have been forced to patiently await the resolution of the case for months or even years while the debtor has used their collateral to reorganize. As the debtor in possession reaches the end of its bankruptcy journey, there are four main scenarios to examine.

First, if third-party exit financing is available to refinance the senior lenders, there should be no issue because there will be sufficient cash to repay the senior lenders in full, which satisfies the requirements of Bankruptcy Code section 1129(b)(2)(A)(i). The secured creditors received the benefit of their original bargain in that they made a loan, were paid interest, and were repaid their principal.

Second, if the senior lenders' collateral is being sold for at least the amount of the senior loans, there should also be no issue because there will be sufficient cash to repay the senior lenders in full, which satisfies the requirements of Bankruptcy Code section 1129(b)(2)(A)(ii). Once again, the secured creditors received the benefit of their original bargain.

Third, if the debtor in possession seeks a stand-alone reorganization and cannot obtain third-party exit financing, the company must necessarily seek to keep its pre-petition senior lenders in place after exiting from the bankruptcy process. In this scenario, the company's reason for entering bankruptcy did not involve its inability to satisfy the terms and conditions of the original senior credit agreement. Perhaps the company had defaulted on its bonds and its total leverage, but not its senior leverage, was overly burdensome. Or perhaps the company had experienced an unfortunate loss in a litigation battle and needed to resolve its unsecured claims. Or perhaps the company had made a poor acquisition and sought bankruptcy protection in order to shed unwanted assets so that it could pay down its debt to a manageable level. Or perhaps it was clear that the company's equity holders were hopelessly out-of-the-money, and the bankruptcy served the purpose of wiping out the equity and turning over control to the unsecured creditors. The point is that the pre-petition relationship between the secured creditors and the debtor is sound and can remain viable following the consummation of the plan of reorganization.

In the final scenario, the debtor in possession again finds it necessary to keep the pre-petition senior lenders in place after exit, but the original credit agreement no longer makes sense as a result of the passage of time, events of default, changing capital markets, and restructuring of the company's operations. The maturity, interest rate, amortization schedule, and covenants need to be reconsidered. The debtor in possession and the senior lenders will need to negotiate mutually agreeable terms and conditions for the post-exit loan. However, if the debtor in possession cannot obtain third-party exit financing, then the pre-petition senior lenders, who would not be facing any competition, may use their leverage to extract burdensome terms and conditions as the price for the debtor's exiting from bankruptcy without repaying the senior loans. This is where the difficult negotiations begin and the expertise of talented advisors is beneficial. While the debtor in possession cannot force the secured creditors to take less than they are due, the secured creditors, as passive fixed-income investors, are not entitled to recoveries that are more than the amount of their principal balance and accrued interest and fees.

What is the feasibility test for a plan of reorganization?

Another requirement for confirmation is that a plan of reorganization must be *feasible*. Under the Bankruptcy Code, consummation of the plan must not be followed promptly by liquidation or further reorganization, unless that is what the plan already contemplates.[41] While this explicit requirement may seem to state the obvious—after all, Chapter 11 involves reorganization, not liquidation—it is another element that can guide the negotiations between debtors and creditors.

As the debtor—or some other plan proponent—seeks to establish the feasibility of the company's reorganization, it will necessarily produce financial projections and other analyses for the bankruptcy court to review. Demonstrating the existence of going-concern valuation provides supporting evidence for the feasibility test. If a plan of reorganization is feasible, then the reorganized debtor has going-concern value that exceeds the liquidation value. See Chapter 11 of this book for a full discussion of methods of calculating going-concern valuation. The going-concern valuation and supporting reports typically become publicly available on the bankruptcy docket and provide key insights into the company's potential financial performance.

However, these reports should be viewed with a critical—and perhaps cynical—view regarding the motivations of the preparers. Management may be "sandbagging" its projections in order to keep expectations—and recoveries—low. Alternatively, management may be speculating too much if it is under pressure to gain the acceptance of junior creditors. If a battle erupts among multiple parties regarding the validity of the financial projections, the back-and-forth pleadings and in-court testimony may reveal that the most likely outcome is that the parties will compromise by selling the company, thereby providing an opportunity for buyers who are ready and able to close quickly.

What does good faith mean in the context of a plan of reorganization?

A further safeguard designed to state the obvious and balance the negotiations between debtors and creditors is the explicit requirement that a plan of reorganization be proposed in good faith.[42] The bankruptcy court will typically consider the totality of the circumstances to ensure that the plan achieves a fair result that is consistent with the goals and intentions of the bankruptcy laws.[43] For example, the bankruptcy court may evaluate

- Whether the plan was proposed with honesty and good intentions
- Whether there is a basis for expecting that reorganization can be achieved
- Whether there was fundamental fairness in dealing with creditors

On the other hand, bankruptcy courts may view the following factors as indicating that a plan was proposed in bad faith:

- The bankruptcy petition is filed after the debtor has lost litigation in a nonbankruptcy court.
- Classes of creditors are manipulated to meet the requirement that at least one impaired noninsider class accepts the plan.
- The plan proponent is a competitor that is trying to eliminate its competition.
- The plan is being used as a delaying tactic.
- The plan's sole purpose is to evade taxes.

A related requirement is that the plan must not involve any means that is forbidden by any nonbankruptcy law, such as securities laws, antitrust laws, and criminal laws.[44] For example, a debtor is clearly forbidden to pay bribes to creditors to vote in favor of the plan. Another example would involve a plan that creates a monopoly in violation of antitrust law. In general, this requirement is stating the obvious: bankruptcy law exists in the context of other state and federal laws.

What is exit financing?

Typically, as a condition for confirmation of the plan of reorganization, a company needs to raise new capital—called *exit financing*—to pay off the

DIP loan, provide cash for recoveries to pre-petition creditors, and fund the working capital needs for the reorganized business. DIP loans are discussed in detail in Chapter 14 of this book. Unlike DIP loans, exit financing does not have any protection provided by the bankruptcy court because the borrower (i.e., the reorganized company) is outside of Chapter 11 of the Bankruptcy Code. For this reason, exit financing can be more difficult to obtain at times than DIP financing.

In many cases a company's DIP loan is rolled into this new financing package. If the DIP lender is unwilling to convert the DIP loan into exit financing, the company will need to seek new sources of capital. Therefore, as a practical matter, the feasibility of a plan of reorganization may ultimately depend upon whether an exit lender is willing to fund it, regardless of whether creditors are willing to vote to approve it and the bankruptcy court is willing to confirm it.

Most companies exiting bankruptcy emerge with substantially lower leverage ratios than they had when they entered. As a result, the most consistent form of exit financing (in terms of both availability and pricing) is a bank facility of some type. In other cases, the issuer may want to raise awareness of the company among institutional investors. In such cases, the company might consider tapping the public capital markets through a high-yield bond offering.

See Chapter 14 for further information on financing terms and techniques that may be applicable to exit financing.

PLAN CONFIRMATION

Who gets to vote on a plan of reorganization?

All holders of allowed claims and interests get to vote on a plan of reorganization.[45] As discussed in Chapter 4 of this book, claims may be disputed or unliquidated, and therefore invalid; however, the bankruptcy court may temporarily allow these unresolved claims for the purposes of voting. In addition, the bankruptcy court may designate—or disallow—the vote of any holder whose acceptance or rejection of the plan was not in good faith or whose vote was not procured or solicited in good faith or in accordance with the provisions of the Bankruptcy Code.[46]

Is any particular class of creditors more important than others during the plan confirmation process?

The impaired class is especially important to the overall process of confirming the plan of reorganization, and therefore negotiations with that class and its advisors will usually be the most contentious. The *impaired class of creditors*, or the class that receives partial recoveries, is another way to refer to the fulcrum security in the case because the Bankruptcy Code requires that at least one impaired class of creditors must vote to approve the plan of reorganization.[47] Acceptance by an impaired class of insider claims is not acceptable for this purpose because of the unusual influence that insiders typically have over the reorganization process.

Classes that receive full recoveries under the plan are deemed to have accepted the plan.[48] Similarly, classes that receive no recoveries under the plan are deemed to have rejected the plan.[49] The holders of claims or interests in either situation do not need to go through the mechanics of actually voting.

Sometimes a debtor in possession will creatively design classes of creditors in order to create an impaired class that is sympathetic to the debtor in possession and will vote in favor of the plan of reorganization. In general, these attempts to game the system result in vigorous objections by various parties, particularly the U.S. trustee, and are ultimately denied by the bankruptcy court. However, creative attorneys will inevitably continue to try to test the limits in this area.

How many accepting votes are required for a plan of reorganization to be confirmable?

The Bankruptcy Code considers the votes of classes of claims and interests to determine whether a plan has been accepted or rejected.[50] In order for a plan to be confirmable, the Bankruptcy Code requires that each class must either accept the plan or be unimpaired.[51] If a cram-down plan is to be confirmed, then one impaired noninsider class must accept.[52]

To determine whether a class has accepted or rejected the plan, the votes of holders of allowed, undesignated claims or interests within that class are counted both in amount and in number. If at least two-thirds in amount and more than one-half in number vote in favor, the entire class is considered to have accepted the plan. When making these calculations, only votes cast are included; unreturned ballots are of no consequence.

Lockup agreements, prepackaged plans, and prearranged plans all affect the way in which voting will unfold. Also, the contractual provisions affecting certain creditors, such as indentures for bondholders and inter-creditor agreements for secured creditors, may contain additional provisions for voting on a plan of reorganization. For example, if the debt involves bondholders that are governed by a bond indenture agreement, 90 percent of the bondholders may need to approve the plan.

Typically, the claims agent will be responsible for maintaining the official record of allowed claims and interests, soliciting votes among holders of claims and interests, and tabulating the results.

Can a debtor condition a creditor's recovery on how it votes on the plan of reorganization?

Yes, but, as described previously, a plan must provide the same recoveries for all creditors within the same class and cannot discriminate unfairly between classes with equal priority. However, if a plan contains a rights offering (as described in Chapter 14), then a claimant's decision whether or not to participate will probably impact its recovery. In such circumstances, a plan is still fair and equitable because all claimants have a right to participate in the rights offering.

Can a creditor bargain away its right to vote in an intercreditor agreement?

Section 510(a) of the Bankruptcy Code permits the enforcement of subordination agreements among creditors. However, this does not necessarily guarantee senior lenders the right to restrict or control the voting rights of subordinated creditors on a plan of reorganization.[53] Since the *In re 203 North LaSalle Street Partnerships* decision, courts have been ambiguous on the enforceability of voting provisions outlined in intercreditor agreements.[54] Most notably, the court held that Section 1126(a) of the Bankruptcy Code, which provides that the "holder of a claim or interest allowed under section 502 of this title may accept or reject a plan,"[55] means that only the actual holder of the claim may vote and that an agreement giving the right to the senior lender is not enforceable.

What is substantive consolidation and how does it affect voting?

As discussed in Chapter 4 of this book, the bankruptcies of large companies often involve multiple related debtors for each of their subsidiaries and affiliates. As these bankruptcy cases approach the plan confirmation stage, decisions need to be made regarding how to address these multiple debtors. Even though these debtors' bankruptcy cases may have been managed under one lead case number, each debtor technically needs to confirm a plan of reorganization to conclude its case. As a practical matter, bankruptcy courts typically allow related debtors to file one consolidated disclosure statement and plan of reorganization, but such documents must still detail recoveries for various classes of creditors for each individual debtor. Determining such meticulous detail can be extremely time-consuming and expensive. Under certain circumstances, the cost of such efforts to satisfy the requirements of the Bankruptcy Code may outweigh the benefits.

Substantive consolidation is an equitable remedy available to bankruptcy courts to address such circumstances. It is an extreme tool to be employed as a last resort. Under substantive consolidation, the assets and liabilities of related debtors may be consolidated into a single case for the purposes of filing a consolidated plan of reorganization. In other words, all creditors would have claims against one pool of assets. Their claims would still be separated into secured, unsecured, and so on.

When substantive consolidation is applied, there will necessarily be winners and losers among creditors. For example, many large companies are structured with a holding company and multiple operating subsidiaries that own the assets involved in the business. Pre-petition, some creditors may require their debts to be at the operating subsidiaries so that their claims are closer to the assets while other creditors may accept the risk of only having claims against the holding company. These creditors will price their debt with these risks in mind. When the holding company and its operating subsidiaries enter bankruptcy, these creditors will expect to have claims against one of the debtors and not the others. However, under substantive consolidation, all of the creditors will have claims against a collective group of all of the assets. Therefore, the creditors with claims against the operating subsidiaries will have to share their recoveries with the creditors of the holding company. As a result, it is likely that the creditors of the operating companies will receive lower recoveries while the creditors of the holding company will have higher recoveries. Furthermore, creditors of operating companies with higher asset values and lower debt will receive lower recoveries while creditors of operating companies with lower asset values and higher debt will receive higher recoveries. These outcomes are at odds with fundamental bankruptcy principles like fair and equitable recoveries for creditors, which is why substantive consolidation is used sparingly.

The Third Circuit Court of Appeals articulated the key principles for applying substantive consolidation as follows:[56]

- Absent compelling circumstances, courts are required to respect the separateness of corporate entities.
- The harm substantive consolidation addresses is nearly always caused by debtors who disregarded separateness.
- Mere benefit to the administration of the case does not justify substantive consolidation.
- Substantive consolidation is an extreme and imprecise remedy that should be used rarely and only as a last resort after considering and rejecting other approaches.
- Substantive consolidation is a defensive shield, not an offensive sword.

Situations where substantive consolidation may be appropriate include cases where companies disregarded corporate formalities, failed to keep separate books and records for each entity, and comingled assets. These companies' assets may be too tangled to determine the appropriate recoveries for various groups of creditors, making substantive consolidation the only viable solution. It is also important to consider how third parties dealt with the company in transactions. If they typically dealt with the company as a whole without regard to separate corporate entities, then this may point to substantive consolidation.

In addition to affecting recoveries, substantive consolidation also changes voting. Without substantive consolidation, creditors' votes would count toward the plans involving their respective debtors. With substantive consolidation, votes are consolidated along with assets. Depending on the dynamics in the case, this change in voting may affect the negotiations among creditor groups.

Who may object to a plan of reorganization?

Parties in interest may object to a plan of reorganization and attempt to either halt the confirmation process or persuade the bankruptcy court to deny confirmation.[57] Individual creditors, government authorities, and committees may all file objections to a plan. Successful objections to plans will most likely need to be based upon the requirements of the Bankruptcy Code that are explained in this chapter. Legal objections may be enhanced by reasonable arguments that the bankruptcy court should use its equitable powers to promote justice. Whiny complaints about unfair outcomes are commonly filed, but they are rarely successful because the bankruptcy court's equitable powers are supposed to be used sparingly. Typically, a debtor in possession will strive to resolve objections by modifying the plan to attract the votes of the objecting parties. Unresolved disputes will proceed to a hearing before the bankruptcy court for a formal ruling. The bankruptcy court may consider the practical reality that a denial of confirmation of a plan of reorganization would mean that the debtor in possession must return to the drawing board, at significant expense, inconvenience, and delay for all parties.

Notably, a bidder or potential bidder in a proposed sale process does not have standing to object to a plan of reorganization. Also, competitors do not have standing to object to a plan. However, such parties can purchase a creditor's claim in order to gain standing. Alternatively, such parties can use the court of public opinion to pressure the parties, and perhaps the bankruptcy court, via the media to avoid an unfair or unpopular outcome.

What happens if there are competing plans of reorganization?

As explained earlier in this chapter, while only the debtor may propose a plan of reorganization during the exclusivity period, any party may propose a plan if the exclusivity period expires before the debtor's plan is confirmed. Therefore, it is possible for multiple plans to exist and for multiple parties to solicit votes from holders of claims and interests. Each of the plans must comply with all the requirements of the Bankruptcy Code discussed previously. Clearly, this scenario drives up administrative expenses for the debtor's estate, creates confusion among creditors, and makes consensus building more challenging.

Under such circumstances, the Bankruptcy Code explicitly states that the bankruptcy court may confirm only one plan of reorganization.[58] While the bankruptcy court is authorized to make the ultimate decision, the Bankruptcy Code requires that the court consider the preferences of creditors and equity security holders.

What occurs at the confirmation hearing for a plan of reorganization?

The Bankruptcy Code requires that the bankruptcy court hold a hearing regarding the confirmation of the plan of reorganization.[59] Depending on the circumstances, this hearing can be very tense and dramatic, or it can be anticlimactic. Once the date of the hearing is set on the court's calendar, the period leading up to it is usually filled with last-minute dealing, cajoling, objecting, and, hopefully, compromise. If the parties can reach agreement ahead of time—including, often, right on the courthouse steps—the confirmation hearing is mostly a perfunctory process. On the other hand, if controversy persists, then the bankruptcy court will use the confirmation hearing to consider the arguments of all sides. The court may rule orally right at the hearing or may issue its judgment in writing soon thereafter, depending on the circumstances. If the decision is in writing, then it may be a simple order on the bankruptcy docket or a lengthy opinion that becomes case law and is published in databases, such as LEXIS-NEXIS and Westlaw.

However, it is not the purpose of a Chapter 11 plan to be used as a litigating tactic.[60] The Bankruptcy Rules establish procedures for addressing litigation through adversary proceedings before the bankruptcy court. Therefore, it is improper to manipulate a confirmation hearing for such a purpose.

Does the bankruptcy judge have to confirm a plan of reorganization if creditors vote in favor of it?

No, not necessarily. The bankruptcy judge must first make an independent determination that the plan adheres to the various provisions of the Bankruptcy Code. The approving votes of creditors cannot overcome legal deficiencies in the plan.

What is the effect of the confirmation of a plan of reorganization?

The main effect of the confirmation of a plan is the discharge granted to the debtor.[61] The discharge becomes effective as soon as the order confirming the plan becomes final. Like all orders of a bankruptcy court, a confirmation order becomes final 10 days after the date of its entry unless it is appealed or unless the bankruptcy court orders otherwise.[62] Among other things, the discharge means that the property of the debtor's estate is free and clear of all pre-petition claims and interests, unless otherwise provided in the plan.

In general, all provisions of a confirmed plan of reorganization are binding upon the debtor, its creditors, its equity holders, any entity issuing securities under the plan, and any party acquiring property under the plan, regardless of whether such creditor or equity holder is impaired or has accepted or rejected the plan. The debtor (or any new entity organized or to be organized for the purposes of carrying out the plan) is required to implement the plan and comply with any orders of the bankruptcy court, notwithstanding any otherwise applicable nonbankruptcy law, rule, or regulation relating to financial condition (i.e., bankruptcy or insolvency).[63]

What is the difference between confirmation and consummation of a plan of reorganization?

Usually, confirmation of a plan of reorganization is the end of one lengthy process of a bankruptcy case and the beginning of another, called *consummation*, which involves the implementation of the plan. In summary, plan confirmation is a legal result, whereas plan consummation is a practical resolution. Confirmation sets in motion the plan's internal procedures, such as litigation of voidable preference claims and distribution of recoveries to creditors,[64] which lead to consummation. The Bankruptcy Code puts a maximum time limit of five years on distributions made pursuant to a plan,[65] but the actual time frame is usually much shorter. The time period between confirmation and consummation is largely administrative, and the company's operations may exit from the bankruptcy process—either through a 363 sale or as a reorganized company—long before the consummation of the plan is final.

Can the confirmation of a plan of reorganization be revoked?

Yes. Under extraordinary circumstances, the bankruptcy court can revoke its order confirming a plan of reorganization upon request of a party made within 180 days after the entry of the confirmation order.[66] After a hearing on such a request, the bankruptcy court may revoke the confirmation order if and only if the order was procured by fraud. In such a peculiar situation, the revocation order must protect good faith purchasers of assets under the plan and revoke the debtor's discharge.

How does the bankruptcy case end?

At the very end of the bankruptcy process, when everything is complete, the bankruptcy court enters a final decree and closes the case and the docket.[67] In the extraordinary "Chapter 22" case involving High Voltage Engineering, the debtor filed its second case in the same court while its first case was still open. Obviously, the bankruptcy judge who had approved the feasibility of the plan of reorganization in the first case was not amused! In most cases, though, closing the case is the end of the story—and it is a happy one.

But, as mentioned often in this book, buying a company after it has formally exited from Chapter 11 bankruptcy is not the only alternative for acquiring a company that is in financial distress. The next chapter will cover two common alternatives for acquisitions during the bankruptcy process: 363 sales and loan-to-own transactions.

Endnotes

1. See 11 U.S.C. §1121(c).
2. See 11 U.S.C. §1121(b).
3. See Fed. R. Bankr. P. 9006(a).
4. See 11 U.S.C. §1121(c)(2).
5. See 11 U.S.C. §1121(d)(1).
6. See 11 U.S.C. §1121(d)(2).
7. See 11 U.S.C. §1121(d)(1).
8. See 11 U.S.C. §362.
9. See 11 U.S.C. §1104.
10. See 11 U.S.C. §1112.
11. See 11 U.S.C. §1126(b); Fed. R. Bankr. P. 3018(b).

12. See http://www.nysb.uscourts.gov/orders/m387.pdf, last accessed May 28, 2010.
13. See 11 U.S.C. §1125(f).
14. See 11 U.S.C. §1125; Fed. R. Bankr. P. 3016.
15. See Fed. R. Bankr. P. 3017.
16. See 11 U.S.C. §1125(b).
17. See 11 U.S.C. §1125(c).
18. See 11 U.S.C. §1125(a)(1).
19. See *In re Scioto Valley Mortgage Co.*, 88 B.R. 168, 170–171 (Bankr. S.D. Oh. 1988); see also *In re A.C. Williams Co.*, 25 B.R. 173 (Bankr. N.D. Ohio 1982); *In re William F. Gable Co.*, 10 B.R. 248 (Bankr. N.D. W.Va. 1981); *In re Adana Mortgage Bankers, Inc.*, 14 B.R. 29 (Bankr. N.D. Ga. 1981); *In re Metrocraft Publishing Servs.*, 39 B.R. 567 (Bankr. N.D. Ga. 1984).
20. See 11 U.S.C. §1125(b).
21. See 11 U.S.C. §1125(d).
22. See 11 U.S.C. §1123(a).
23. See 11 U.S.C. §1123(b).
24. See 11 U.S.C. §1122(a).
25. See 11 U.S.C. §1122(b).
26. See 11 U.S.C. §1129(b)(2)(A).
27. See 11 U.S.C. §506(a)(1).
28. See 11 U.S.C. §1129(b)(2)(B)(i).
29. See 11 U.S.C. §1129(b)(2)(B)(ii).
30. See *Bank of America National Trust and Savings Ass'n. v. 203 North LaSalle*, 526 U.S. 434, 119 S. Ct. 1411 (1999).
31. Lawrence P. King, ed., *Collier on Bankruptcy* 7, 15th ed. rev. (1999), 1129.04[4][a][ii] (internal citations omitted).
32. Kenneth N. Klee, "All You Ever Wanted to Know about Cram Down under the New Bankruptcy Code," *American Bankruptcy Law Journal* 53 (1979), pp. 133, 142. As he further described in a later article, "The legislative history of the Bankruptcy Code gives but one example of an uncodified aspect of the fair and equitable rule: [A] dissenting class should be assured that no senior class receives more than 100 percent of the amount of its claims. At first glance, this 100 percent limitation appears obvious–it is unfair and inequitable for a claim to be paid more than in full. Court opinions mention this standard without supporting authority precisely because they interpret the terms 'fair' and 'equitable' to have literal meanings as well as to constitute terms of art." See "Cram Down II," *American Bankruptcy Law Journal* 64 (1990), pp. 229, 231 (internal citations omitted).
33. See 11 U.S.C. §1129(a)(7)(A)(ii).
34. See *In re Rash*, 520 U.S. 953, 117 S.Ct. 1879 (1997) (concluding that, for purposes of confirming a cram-down plan proposing to continue operating as a business, collateral should be valued using replacement, not foreclosure, values); *Matters of Treasure Bay Corp.*, 212 B.R. 520, 545 (Bankr. S.D. Miss. 1997)

("To argue that the [unsecured creditors] are not entitled to receive their fair portion of the increase in value between liquidation and going concern value is contrary to *Rash* and applicable principles of the Bankruptcy Code"); *Cellular Information*, 171 B.R. at 930 (using going-concern value); *In re Chateaugay Corp.*, 154 B.R. 29, 33–34 (Bankr. S.D. N.Y. 1993) (holding that Bankruptcy Code section 506(a) requires application of going-concern valuation methodology when property will be used in a postconfirmation going concern); and *Matter of Modern Warehouse, Inc.*, 74 B.R. 173, 177 n.7 (Bankr. W.D. Miss. 1987) (explaining "liquidation of property as a 'going concern,' in chapter 7 or otherwise, is different from liquidation of a non-going-concern").

35. See 11 U.S.C. §1129(a)(7)(A)(i).

36. See 11 U.S.C. §1129(a)(10).

37. See 11 U.S.C. §1129(b)(1).

38. "The requirement of the House bill that a plan not 'discriminate unfairly' with respect to a class is included for clarity," 124 Cong. Rec. 32,407 (1978) (statement of Rep. Edwards); ibid. at 34,006 (statement of Sen. DeConcini) (emphasis added).

39. Bruce A. Markell, "A New Perspective on Unfair Discrimination in Chapter 11," *American Bankruptcy Law Journal* 72 (1998), pp. 227, 247.

40. See 11 U.S.C. §1129(b)(2).

41. See 11 U.S.C. §1129(a)(11).

42. See 11 U.S.C. §1129(a)(3).

43. "In evaluating the totality of the circumstance surrounding a plan, a court has 'considerable judicial discretion' in finding good faith, with the most important feature being an inquiry into the 'fundamental fairness' of the plan." *In re Coram Healthcare Corp.*, 271 B.R. 228, 234 (D. Del. 2001) (concluding that the plan failed to satisfy the requirement that it be proposed in good faith) (internal citations omitted). "It is clear that a court may consider all *post-petition* conduct of the debtor relating to the development and proposal of the plan in evaluating good faith." *SM 104*, 160 B.R. at 244 (denying confirmation) (emphasis in original).

44. See 11 U.S.C. §1129(a)(3).

45. See 11 U.S.C. §§ 502, 1126(a); Fed. R. Bankr. P. 3018.

46. See 11 U.S.C. §1126(e).

47. See 11 U.S.C. §1129(a)(10).

48. See 11 U.S.C. §1126(f).

49. See 11 U.S.C. §1126(g).

50. See 11 U.S.C. §§1126(c), (d).

51. See 11 U.S.C. §1129(a)(8).

52. See 11 U.S.C. §§1129(a)(10), 1129(b)(1).

53. See 11 U.S.C. §510(a).

54. See *In re 203 North La Salle Street Partnership*, 246 B.R. 325 (Bankr. N.D. Ill. 2000). This answer is based on an article by Bob Eisenbach of Cooley LLP: Robert L. Eisenbach, "Second Lien and Intercreditor Agreements: Are Those

Bankruptcy Voting Provisions Really Enforceable?" Cooley LLP; available at http://bankruptcy.cooley.com/2007/01/articles/business-bankruptcy-issues/ secondliens-and-intercreditor-agreements-are-those-bankruptcy-voting-provisions-really-enforceable/, last accessed June 2, 2010.

55. See *In re North LaSalle Street Partnership*, 246 B.R. 325, 331-32 (voting assignment provision not enforced). *Cf. In re Curtis Center Ltd.* 192 B.R. 648, 659-60 (Bankr. ED. Pa. 1996) (voting assignment enforceable).

56. See *In re Owens Corning*, Docket No. 04-4080, 2005 U.S. App. LEXIS 17150 (3d Cir. 2005).

57. See Fed. R. Bankr. P. 3020(b)(1).

58. See 11 U.S.C. §1129(c).

59. See 11 U.S.C. §1128(a); Fed. R. Bankr. P. 3020(b)(2).

60. See *In re Reilly*, 71 B.R. 132, 135 (Bankr. D. Mo. 1987) (denying approval of the disclosure statement). See also *In re HBA East, Inc.*, 87 B.R. 248, 260 (Bankr. E.D. N.Y. 1988) ("Chapter 11 was never intended to be used as a fist in a two party bout. The Chapter is entitled reorganization and not litigation"); and *In re Martin*, 78 B.R. 598, 603 (Bankr. D. Mo. 1987) ("a confirmation hearing in reorganization is not to be used as a litigating tactic").

61. See 11 U.S.C. §1141(d)(1).

62. See Fed. R. Bankr. P. 3020(e).

63. See 11 U.S.C. §1142(a).

64. See Fed. R. Bankr. P. 3021.

65. See 11 U.S.C. §1143.

66. See 11 U.S.C. §1144.

67. See Fed. R. Bankr. P. 3022.

CHAPTER 13

Distressed M&A Strategy: 363 Sales and Loan-to-Own Transactions

The difference between try and triumph is a little umph.

—Unknown

INTRODUCTION TO 363 SALES AND LOAN-TO-OWN TRANSACTIONS

What are some of the ways in which a buyer can structure the acquisition of a troubled company?

While a prospective acquirer can buy a distressed company in part (by buying shares in an insolvent entity, by purchasing a business unit or product line, or by investing in a fund that invests in such entities) or in whole (by acquiring all of the assets or shares of the troubled entity) outside of bankruptcy, there are advantages to structuring a sale within bankruptcy. Key advantages include

- Minimizing the risk of the acquisition's being deemed a fraudulent transfer
- Buying assets free and clear of all claims
- Avoiding successor liability
- Approval of the sale by a neutral and objective bankruptcy judge rather than a potentially conflicted or indecisive board of directors
- Using the provisions of the Bankruptcy Code to overcome the irrational views of holdouts who refuse to consent to the sale

Two primary ways to structure a sale in bankruptcy are known as *363 sales* and *loan-to-own* transactions.

Exhibit 13-1 Completed U.S. 363 Sales, All Sizes, All Industries, All Types (Excluding GM) by Date Announced

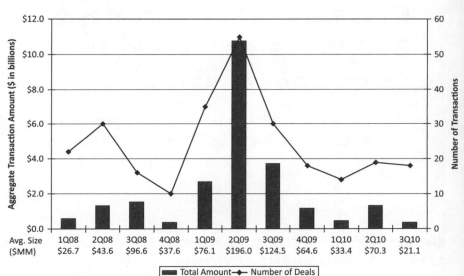

Avg. Size ($MM)	1Q08	2Q08	3Q08	4Q08	1Q09	2Q09	3Q09	4Q09	1Q10	2Q10	3Q10
	$26.7	$43.6	$96.6	$37.6	$76.1	$196.0	$124.5	$64.6	$33.4	$70.3	$21.1

Total Amount—◆— Number of Deals

Source: pipeline.thedeal.com

What are leading examples of recent acquisitions that have been completed in bankruptcy?

As Exhibit 13-1 illustrates, there has been no shortage of distressed sales in the past few years, both out-of-court and via 363 sales. The most notable 363 sales in recent history involved Lehman Brothers, General Motors, and Chrysler. These cases are each profiled in Chapter 3 of this book and highlighted in this chapter.

The Global M&A Network (www.globalmanetwork.com) recently began issuing annual awards to leading examples of deals involving special situations. The 2009 recipients for transactions $100 million and above and above $10 million are profiled in Exhibits 13-2a and 13-2b.

Exhibit 13-2a Example of Exemplary 363 Sale, $100 Million and above

---

ACQUISITION $100 MILLION AND ABOVE

Target: Boscov's Inc.

Buyer: BLF Acquisitions Inc.

Buyer's Advisor: SSG Capital Advisors

Profile: Boscov's, Inc., headquartered in Reading, Pennsylvania, operated nearly 50 family-oriented department stores in the mid-Atlantic region before entering bankruptcy. Since its inception in 1911, the company had remained family owned by the Boscov and Lakin families.

Situation: The company filed a voluntary bankruptcy petition with the Bankruptcy Court for the District of Delaware in August 2008 due primarily to 10 underperforming stores, which were subsequently closed during the beginning of the bankruptcy case. Bank of America provided a $250 million DIP loan, and the company decided to sell the remaining stores via a 363 transaction. In September 2008, the company named Versa Capital Management as the stalking horse bidder. To purchase all of the remaining stores, Versa committed to pay $11 million plus an undetermined amount to pay all secured, priority, and administrative claims submitted in the Chapter 11 case. The company agreed to pay a $4 million breakup fee to Versa if it did not complete the purchase.

Transaction: The Boscov and Lakin families retained SSG Capital Advisors to raise capital to buy the business in a 363 sale. In one of the worst retail and credit environments in recent history and amid turbulent credit markets following the Lehman Brothers bankruptcy, SSG Capital Advisors worked with the families to deliver a $210 million senior credit facility, $50 million in equity from the families and other equity participants, and a $47 million loan to bridge to funding under the Federal HUD 108 program. The deal closed in December 2008. In a period when many retailers were unable to survive bankruptcy, the sale of Boscov's as a going concern was a true holiday success story that was made possible by the collective efforts of the lenders, investors, professionals, and state and local governments that worked hard to get the deal closed.

Exhibit 13-2b Example of Exemplary 363 Sale above $10 Million

---

ACQUISITION ABOVE $10 MILLION

Target: Vivitar
Seller: Syntax-Brillian Corporation
Buyer: Sakar International
Buyer's Advisor: KPMG Corporate Finance
Profile: In November 2006, for $26 million in stock, Syntax-Brillian Corporation acquired privately held Vivitar Corporation, one of the world's largest independent distributors of digital cameras, 35-mm single lens reflex cameras, autofocus cameras, digital videocameras, multimedia players, flash units, binoculars, projectors, and camera accessories.
Situation: Syntax-Brillian Corporation filed a voluntary bankruptcy petition with the Bankruptcy Court for the District of Delaware in July 2008. Though a nondebtor, Vivitar and its assets were part of the security package for Syntax-Brillian's first-lien senior secured lender. Working together with the lender, which was the main significant impaired creditor in the filing, Vivitar engaged KPMG Corporate Finance to find a suitable buyer for Vivitar and create liquidity for the lender. This objective was challenging due to two facts. First, Vivitar was operating with limited capital availability and would likely be forced to cease operations in the very near term if a buyer were not found. Second, until Syntax-Brillian's bankruptcy, Vivitar had operated as a division of Syntax-Brillian, with a limited amount of financial control or reporting capabilities. Consequently, Vivitar engaged KPMG Corporate Finance with the mandate to go to market, find a buyer, negotiate the best deal possible, and close a sale within eight weeks to avoid liquidation.
Transaction: KPMG Corporate Finance conducted a competitive, expedited auction process that generated interest from several diverse counterparties, including liquidators, private equity firms, and strategic investors. KPMG Corporate Finance met the objectives of the company and its lender by closing a sale at the end of August 2008, just seven weeks after Syntax-Brillian's petition date. KPMG Corporate Finance coordinated management meetings and due diligence, and assisted Vivitar and the lender in successfully negotiating a sale at a favorable valuation to Sakar International, Inc., a 30-year-old, family-owned consumer electronics manufacturer based in Edison, New Jersey.

363 SALES

What, exactly, is a 363 sale?

As mentioned in Chapter 2, a *363 sale* (or *363 transaction*) is named after Section 363 of the Bankruptcy Code.[1] The statutory origin of 363 sales is Section 363(b) of the Bankruptcy Code, which requires court approval for asset sales that are outside the debtor's ordinary course of business.[2] Although the original focus of Section 363(b) appears to have been on facilitating the sale of individual wasting assets—such as excess inventory, extraneous equipment, surplus land, and discontinued lines of business—it quickly evolved to encompass sales of entire companies. Section 363 authorizes the leasing of assets to third parties as well as asset sales. While Section 363(b) permits a bankruptcy trustee or a debtor in possession to conduct such asset sales or leases, it provides no such authorization for creditors and creditors' committees. Instead, the role of creditors and creditors' committees is to influence the outcome of 363 sales by negotiating behind the scenes with the debtor or bankruptcy trustee and, when necessary, filing objections and seeking intervention by the bankruptcy court.

Bankruptcy Code section 363 is structured to attract potential buyers who might otherwise shun asset sales involving bankrupt entities. Without an adequate number of bidders, the assets' valuation will be depressed, leading to a suboptimal result for the estate. To maximize the number of potential bidders, Section 363(f) authorizes a bankruptcy trustee or debtor in possession to sell (or lease) the bankruptcy estate's assets *free and clear* of any creditors' claims or equity interests under certain conditions described later in this chapter.[3] Therefore, 363 sales are a means of removing liens on any encumbered assets so that buyers can bid their best price without factoring in discounts for any liabilities, which may be subjective and difficult to calculate. The theory seems to have worked, since most people consider shopping at 363 sales to be bargain hunting, leading to frothy bidding in many previously dire situations.

To maintain the guiding bankruptcy principle of providing a fair and equitable distribution to all creditors, the objective of a 363 transaction is to obtain the *highest and best offer* for the assets that are being sold. Ordinarily, this goal requires the debtor in possession or bankruptcy trustee to conduct an auction or competitive bidding process to demonstrate that the value to the estate is being maximized. The terms, techniques, and issues for conducting bankruptcy auctions are discussed in greater detail later in this chapter.

The procedure for 363 sales begins with the debtor's filing a motion to approve the bidding procedures with the bankruptcy court, allowing parties in interest to object (with valuation being the most common protest). Ultimately, the bankruptcy court has the discretion to determine whether a 363 sale is appropriate, and the decision will focus mostly on the validity and integrity of the sale process, not the resulting valuation. Once the bankruptcy court's order approving an asset sale under Section 363 of the Bankruptcy Code becomes final and nonappealable, the parties can consummate the sale. Once the sale is consummated, the buyer can use the bankruptcy court's order as a valid and practically impenetrable defense against any attempts by the debtor's creditors—whether known or unknown at the time of the sale—to assert claims against the assets that were sold to the buyer. In other words, the court's order is the ultimate evidence proving that the assets were sold free and clear of all claims and interests in a final sale to a bona fide purchaser. These are outcomes that cannot be achieved outside of bankruptcy.

From a public policy perspective, 363 sales may raise concerns related to lack of transparency, the hasty pace of the process, and inconsistent procedures across jurisdictions. Some commentators believe that these issues render the bankruptcy courts and parties in interest vulnerable to unfair dealing, abuse, and sweetheart deals.[4] On the flip side, an opportunistic buyer may exploit these vulnerabilities to bag a bargain.

What kind of bidders participate in a 363 sale?

There are two main categories of bidders: *financial buyers* and *strategic buyers*. Financial buyers include private equity firms and hedge funds (see Chapter 3 for specific names of firms and recent trends). Strategic buyers involve other companies, such as competitors, who have existing operations that could be combined with the assets or businesses being sold. Another type of bidder is a *credit bidder*, which is discussed in detail later in this chapter.

Theoretically, strategic buyers can afford to pay more than financial buyers because they will enjoy strong synergies from the acquisition. Moreover, strategic buyers may have internal sources of capital to finance their bids, whereas financial buyers usually need to raise financing from third parties. Furthermore, since strategic buyers are already knowledgeable about the customers, suppliers, equipment, employees, asset values, and issues in their industry, they should require less time for conducting due diligence. In practice, however, financial buyers are more adroit, swift, and proficient in conducting due diligence, navigating bankruptcy law, and structuring deals than strategic buyers. Many potential strategic buyers are unable to react effectively to the urgency and complexity in a 363 sale.

A debtor in possession may be uncomfortable involving strategic buyers in a 363 sale process and may attempt to exclude such potential bidders altogether. The company may not want to reveal confidential information to its competitors during due diligence that could be used to harm the company in the future. Executives may be concerned that the strategic buyer is gathering valuable information without any real intent to submit a bid. In addition, executives may be concerned that their jobs will be in jeopardy if a strategic buyer prevails at auction and then eliminates duplicative overhead. Furthermore, management may argue that antitrust concerns are too onerous to involve strategic buyers and potentially delay the sale process. Under these circumstances, financial buyers may enjoy significant advantages over strategic buyers.

Sometimes a bidder can be both a financial and strategic buyer. For example, a private equity firm may have an existing portfolio company that is in the same industry as the debtor's business.

Are there any restrictions on which assets can be sold (or leased) in a 363 sale?

Yes. There are restrictions on selling certain assets free and clear, including encumbered assets (i.e., assets with one or more liens), executory contracts, and unexpired leases. In addition, the debtor cannot sell assets upon which the bankruptcy court has already lifted the automatic stay.[5] Furthermore, applicable nonbankruptcy law may prohibit the sale or transfer of certain assets.[6]

In order to sell (or lease) encumbered assets free and clear of all claims and interests, the bankruptcy trustee or debtor in possession, as the case may be, must prove at least one of the following elements to the bankruptcy court:[7]

1. Applicable nonbankruptcy law permits the sale of such assets free and clear of such claims and interests.
2. The entities holding such claims and interests consent.
3. Such interest is a lien, and the price at which such property is to be sold is greater than the aggregate value of all liens on such property.
4. Such interest is in bona fide dispute.
5. Such entity could be compelled, in a legal or equitable proceeding, to accept a money satisfaction of such interest.

Regarding a debtor's executory contracts and unexpired leases, recall that these are assets of the estate. In some cases, these agreements have value that can be sold to a third party, even if the terms of the agreement expressly prohibit such assignment.[8] As discussed in Chapter 2 of this book, the debtor must assume, assume and assign, or reject each executory contract and unexpired lease.[9] In such instances, the Bankruptcy Code authorizes the debtor to assume and assign executory contracts and unexpired leases to third parties, but only if the debtor cures any applicable defaults—such as past due payments—and provides adequate assurance of future performance.[10] This effectively allows the buyer to "cherry pick" below-market executory contracts and unexpired leases, leaving uncompetitive agreements behind with the estate, which can reject them. Frequently, the threat of this tactic alone can be enough to allow some buyers to receive preclosing concessions from counterparties.

Certain exceptions may apply. For example, executory contracts involving intellectual property cannot be assumed and assigned without the counterparty's consent.[11] If the debtor's business is highly dependent upon such contracts, the 363 sale runs the risk of being "held up" by the counterparty.

What are the mechanics of a typical 363 sale?

Exhibit 13-3 summarizes the steps in a typical 363 transaction. Each step is explored in greater detail later in this chapter.

What information does the bankruptcy court include in the notification of the sale process?

Exhibit 13-4 outlines the key information that the bankruptcy court includes in the notification of the sale process.

How can parties object to a 363 sale?

Since the debtor in possession (or bankruptcy trustee, as the case may be) is entitled to propose a 363 sale under the Bankruptcy Code using its business judgment, it is usually difficult to object to the sale itself. Bankruptcy courts typically defer to the debtor in possession's business judgment, and the standard for approval is usually easy to satisfy. Therefore, parties that are

Exhibit 13-3 Mechanics of a Typical 363 Transaction

- The debtor chooses a *stalking horse* (or initial bidder).
- The stalking horse and the debtor negotiate an asset purchase agreement (APA) containing the terms and conditions of an initial bid.
- The debtor files a 363 motion requesting approval of the debtor's proposed stalking horse, bidding procedures, breakup fee, overbid protection, and other such terms.
- After notice and a hearing, the bankruptcy court considers and resolves any objections, then approves the motion.
- The debtor's advisors solicit interest from other potential acquirers in making bids that would exceed the stalking horse's initial bid, using the APA as a template against which qualified bidders may submit qualified bids at an auction.
- Potential bidders indicate their level of interest and their qualifications and, if required, put down a deposit and are allowed to perform due diligence on the assets being sold.
- The debtor holds an auction—usually in the offices of the debtor's attorneys—for all qualified bidders, including the stalking horse.
- Afterward, the court approves the highest and best bidder as the ultimate buyer.
- Only after the winning bid is chosen does the purchaser have an exclusive right to consummate the transaction.
- If a competing bidder prevails (i.e., the stalking horse bidder is not the ultimate buyer), the stalking horse bidder collects its breakup fee and expense reimbursement.

---

seeking to object to a 363 sale often focus on the bidding procedures, declaring that they are inadequate or unfair. For example, objections may challenge the necessity for a stalking horse, the amount of the breakup fee or overbid protection, the length of time that competing bidders have to conduct due diligence, the availability of information for due diligence, the involvement of insiders, or the qualifications for bidders and bids. Sometimes being a nuisance can be sufficient to derail an undesired sale process.

Exhibit 13-4 Information Contained in Judicial Notification of a 363 Sale Process

- The bidding rules
- The date and time for submission of competing bids
- The minimum topping amount (discussed later in the chapter)
- The time and place of the auction
- Minimum bidding increments at the auction
- The amount and terms of the deposit that must accompany the bid
- Requirements that bidders demonstrate the financial where-withal to close
- Markup of the asset purchase agreement that the debtor and the stalking horse agreed to
- Instructions to keep bids confidential until the bidding deadline has passed

How quickly can a 363 sale be completed?

Typically, the time it takes to complete a 363 sale is about 60 days, which is usually sufficient to allow potential bidders to perform due diligence, raise financing, and formulate their bidding strategies. However, the trend in certain jurisdictions, such as the Southern District of New York, has been toward approving 363 sales extremely quickly, especially when there is a perceived emergency or exigent circumstances. This recent trend began in 2008 with the 363 sale of Lehman Brothers to Barclays Capital only four days after the company had filed a voluntary Chapter 11 petition. Lehman's creditors had only two days to examine the deal and file objections, rather than the 20-day period contemplated by the Bankruptcy Rules.[12] The judge in this case explained:

> I know that I need to approve this transaction, and I am absolutely confident in my judgment. But I also know that this is so exceptional relative to the experience that I have had both as a bankruptcy lawyer and judge to know that it could never be deemed as precedent for future cases unless someone could argue that there is a similar emergency. It's hard for me to imagine a similar emergency.[13]

Within the next year, both Chrysler and GM filed voluntary Chapter 11 petitions in the Southern District of New York under similar dire circumstances. In both cases, the bankruptcy court cited the ruling in the Lehman

Brothers case as support for taking similar drastic action using 363 sales (see Chapter 3 of this book for a discussion of each case). Therefore, it is currently unclear whether these cases have changed the expectations of all parties to a bankruptcy proceeding so that lightning-fast 363 sales will become the norm. After all, in most bankruptcy cases, there is usually some sort of emergency or perception of exigent circumstances.

Are a 363 sale and a plan of reorganization mutually exclusive?

No. In practice, professionals typically refer to 363 sales as a distinct process that occurs prior to the confirmation of a plan of reorganization, usually months or even years before the confirmation hearing. As a result, a 363 sale often occurs before the debtor has even proposed a plan of reorganization. However, some bankruptcy cases involve a plan of reorganization that includes a 363 sale of some or all of the business as a key component of the company's strategy.

When a 363 sale occurs prior to the confirmation of a plan of reorganization, the cash proceeds from the sale are usually held in escrow with the bankruptcy court for eventual distribution to creditors following the confirmation of a plan of reorganization (or, in a Chapter 7 liquidation, distributed according to Section 726 of the Bankruptcy Code[14]). Indeed, in some jurisdictions the U.S. trustee requires that a plan of reorganization be filed before a 363 sale is completed so that the debtor's intentions for distributing the cash proceeds from the sale are clearly documented. The point is that the debtor should disclose the whole story to creditors at the time that the creditors are reviewing the debtor's motion to pursue a 363 sale, giving them ample time and opportunity to object to the overall scheme.

Requiring the preparation, solicitation, and confirmation of a plan of reorganization, however, significantly reduces the expediency, expense, and effectiveness of 363 sales, especially when a troubled company is teetering on the brink of liquidation. With these concerns in mind, trends in other jurisdictions are moving in the opposite direction. As described earlier in this chapter, some bankruptcy courts are using their equitable discretion to approve lightning-fast 363 sales that are quicker than Congress even contemplated when enacting the Bankruptcy Code and Bankruptcy Rules.

Are there any limitations on a debtor's decision to sell the entire company in a 363 sale? Why are such sales sometimes criticized as sub rosa plans of reorganization?

When a debtor requests a 363 sale, in effect it is asking the court to waive the usual disclosure, consent solicitation, voting, and confirmation process involved in a traditional plan of reorganization. In addition, a 363 sale is subject to the *business judgment* standard of review (discussed in greater detail in Chapter 10 of this book). This standard is less exacting than the standard of review to which a plan of reorganization is subject—i.e., a judicial determination of whether the plan meets statutory confirmation standards provided by the Bankruptcy Code and Bankruptcy Rules (as discussed in detail in Chapter 12 of this book).

In particular, many courts will be on heightened alert to determine whether the 363 sale process is really a sub rosa or de facto plan because the process runs the risk of making creditors' rights meaningless. The Second Circuit Court of Appeals voiced this concern in the *Motorola* case in 2007: "The reason 'sub rosa' plans are prohibited is based on a fear that a debtor-in-possession will enter into transactions that will, in effect, 'short circuit the requirements of [C]hapter 11 for confirmation of a reorganization plan.'"[15] As a result, a motion for a 363 sale is a significant request, and the debtor must clearly articulate a business justification for the sale. Thought of in a slightly different light, a court will not approve a 363 sale—absent a valid business reason from the debtor—that will fix creditors' recoveries without the procedural protections of a disclosure statement or a plan of reorganization.

Recently, the U.S. government has been an active participant in certain bankruptcies by influencing bankruptcy courts to approve 363 sales that critics called sub rosa plans of reorganization. In the GM bankruptcy, the bankruptcy judge, in making findings regarding the U.S. government's assistance to GM, wrote: "The failure of any of the Big Three (or worse, more than one of them) might well bring grievous ruin on the thousands of suppliers to the Big Three . . . ; other businesses in the communities where [they] operate; dealers . . . and states and municipalities. . . . The U.S. government's fear—a fear this Court shares, if GM cannot be saved as a going concern—was of a systemic failure throughout the domestic automotive industry and the significant harm to the overall U.S. economy."[16] Using similar logic in the earlier Chrysler bankruptcy, a different bankruptcy judge in the same court expanded on and clarified prior case law by ruling that it is not a sub rosa plan for "a debtor [to] sell substantially all of its assets as a going concern and later submit a plan of liquidation providing for the distribution of the proceeds of the sale," if such proceeds both (1) exceed the value that could be received in a liquidation and (2) go directly to the first-priority lenders.[17]

The Bankruptcy Code does not provide any explicit guidance to determine when a 363 transaction is the appropriate sale process. However, one of the earliest major decisions, *In re Lionel Corp.* in 1983,[18] is still used today in framing the analysis. In *Lionel*, the debtor filed a motion to sell its most valuable asset, an 82 percent ownership interest in a separate company that was not part of the debtor's bankruptcy filing, before proceeding with a full plan of reorganization. The asset was not declining in value, and there were no exigent circumstances forcing a quick sale. However, the creditors' committee pressured the debtor to complete the sale so that there would be cash, not stock, to pay creditors later. The bankruptcy court approved the 363 sale, and a group of equity holders appealed. Ultimately, the Court of Appeals for the Second Circuit held that there was no valid business justification for the sale. In so holding, the court noted that, "In fashioning its findings, a bankruptcy judge must not blindly follow the hue and cry of the most vocal special interest groups; rather, he should consider all salient factors pertaining to the proceeding and, accordingly, act to further the diverse interests of the debtor, creditors and equity holders, alike."[19]

The *Lionel* court went on to identify some of the factors to be considered when determining whether there is a business justification for the asset's sale. These are summarized in Exhibit 13-5.

Exhibit 13-5 Considerations for Business Justification for an Asset Sale

- The proportionate value of the asset to the estate as a whole
- The amount of elapsed time since the filing and the likelihood that a plan of reorganization could be confirmed in the near future
- The effect of the proposed disposition on future plans of reorganization
- The proceeds to be obtained from the disposition vis-à-vis any appraisals of the property
- Whether the asset is increasing or decreasing in value[20]

Over the years, subsequent courts have generally molded the factors from *Lionel* into a four-part test: whether the proposed 363 sale reflects (1) a sound business reason, (2) accurate and reasonable notice, (3) an adequate price, and (4) good faith. However, in the Lehman Brothers, GM, and Chrysler cases, the perception of an emergency seemed to overrule the application of these factors.

These transactions all involve sales of companies as going concerns. How are assets sold in a liquidation?

If a bankruptcy case is a Chapter 7 liquidation (or a liquidating Chapter 11 case), section 363 of the Bankruptcy Code, which applies to both Chapter 7 and Chapter 11, authorizes the bankruptcy trustee to liquidate the assets of the estate using the same procedures as for a sale of the company as a going concern. Indeed, 363 sales involving a bankruptcy trustee liquidating assets are much more common, but receive less media attention. The case law precedent generated by 363 sales conducted in the liquidation context is nevertheless relevant to the sales of companies as going concerns.

What about antitrust concerns? Does a 363 sale need to obtain clearance from the DOJ or the FTC?

Yes. As discussed in detail in Chapter 10 of this book, distressed sales remain subject to antitrust law when applicable. The Bankruptcy Code explicitly notes that the Clayton Act applies to 363 sales.[21]

In a 363 sale, how does the debtor make representations and warranties in the purchase agreement?

While the debtor may make the customary representations and warranties in the asset purchase agreement involved in a 363 sale, these representations and warranties typically do not survive closing. In effect, 363 sales are on an "as is, where is" basis, and buyers should heed the warning *caveat emptor*. This has the effect of limiting the liability of directors and officers for breaches of such representations and warranties.

Partly as a result of this nonsurvivability of representations and warranties, the size of the escrow at closing is generally limited in a 363 sale.

Unlike in traditional M&A, escrows in 363 sales are typically reserved for minor price adjustments, such as a working capital true-up.

If a 363 sale is free and clear, what happens to the liabilities?

This hits on a key advantage of the 363 sale process for the buyer: except in limited circumstances, all liabilities remain with the estate. This ordinary rule is subject to some exceptions (known as *successor liability*); one example might be an environmental claim that was not discovered until after the bankruptcy. Another example that ventures into "gray areas" might be product liability in which the cause of action arose after the date of sale.

How does selling assets free and clear shield a buyer from legal risks?

A properly structured 363 transaction facilitates a "free and clear" transfer of assets to the buyer—i.e., free and clear of prior liens and most claims, including claims by creditors that have not been paid at the time of the sale and the risk of subsequent *fraudulent conveyance* claims (discussed in greater detail in Chapter 10). Selling assets "free and clear" in a 363 sale can also provide valuable protection to a buyer from successor liability. Limited exceptions potentially include employment discrimination or product liability, in certain circumstances.[22] It is difficult for a buyer to receive these formidable protections in sales conducted outside of bankruptcy.

What happens to the cash proceeds from a 363 sale?

Once a bankruptcy court has approved a 363 sale and the deal closes, the court decides how the sale proceeds are to be allocated among the secured creditors that have liens on the assets sold. Typically, the liens of the secured creditors automatically transfer from the assets sold and attach to the cash received. In the event that there are additional proceeds above and beyond the allowed secured claims, the bankruptcy court will also allocate cash to unsecured creditors and other claimants in accordance with a plan of reorganization or a plan of liquidation, as the case may be.

Is the Bankruptcy Court's approval of a 363 sale transaction final or appealable?

Parties in interest may appeal a bankruptcy court order approving a 363 transaction to the district court (or the bankruptcy appellate panel, if one exists) and then to the circuit court of appeals (see Chapter 2 for an explanation of the appellate process for bankruptcy court rulings). However, as a practical matter, if the sale order is not stayed, it may be difficult to "unscramble the omelet" and unwind the transaction. This, historically, has been the result of the statutory protections afforded by Section 363(m): "The reversal or modification on appeal of an authorization under subsection (b) or (c) of this section of a sale . . . of property does not affect the validity of a sale . . . under such authorization to an entity that purchased . . . such property in good faith . . . unless such authorization and such sale . . . were stayed pending appeal."[23] This has come to be known as *statutory mootness*.

As of this writing, one recent (2008) appellate decision in the Bankruptcy Appellate Panel for the Ninth Circuit may have chipped away at this historical bedrock. In the *Clear Channel* ruling,[24] the court held that some aspects of a sale order may be appealed and undone, even absent a stay. While the decision has relatively limited application, even within the Ninth Circuit, it will probably influence future APAs—for example, purchasers may negotiate a right to return assets that become encumbered upon appeal, or an escrow might be established to offset a portion or all of this risk.

BIDDING AND AUCTIONS

What are the benefits of being a stalking horse?

In a 363 sale, the debtor typically negotiates with a *stalking horse bidder*, which enters into an APA with the debtor. This APA is then used as the floor bid for negotiations with additional prospective bidders through the auction process. The stalking horse bid prevents the value of the estate from going into free fall by establishing a minimum valuation that is used by the auctioneer in marketing the company. In addition, the stalking horse bid usually triggers media coverage that helps the marketing process as well. Potential buyers who were unaware of the target's bankruptcy case may be intrigued that the stalking horse is getting a bargain price and decide to compete.

The role of stalking horse is frequently coveted, given that it offers several advantages. While there clearly is downside risk in investing considerable time and resources with no assurance of having an "inside track" to getting the deal, the APA that the debtor and the stalking horse sign includes multiple attractive protections. Exhibit 13-6 summarizes some of the most common protections.

In addition to the protections listed in Exhibit 13-6, the stalking horse may have more time to conduct due diligence on the distressed entity than subsequent bidders. Other times, the stalking horse may need to shortcut its due diligence process if the debtor's predicament is particularly urgent. If the stalking horse is dissatisfied with its due diligence, however, it may decide to submit a lower bid to take the additional risks into account.

What guidelines exist for breakup fee percentages?

The Bankruptcy Code and Bankruptcy Rules provide no guidelines for breakup fee percentages. Generally speaking, breakup fees broadly range from 1 to 5 percent of the transaction price. Debtors and their advisors will negotiate a percentage on a case-by-case basis, taking into consideration, among other things, how many parties are seeking to become stalking horse bidders, whether they consider the proposed stalking horse bid to be high or low, the urgency of the 363 sale, and breakup fee trends in other bankruptcy cases.

Courts in some jurisdictions are stricter than those in others in terms of approving the breakup fee and expense reimbursement. For instance,

Exhibit 13-6 Examples of Contract Protections for a Potential Stalking Horse

- The proportionate value of the asset to the estate as a whole
- A breakup fee (also known as a *topping fee*)
- Expense reimbursement, subject to some prenegotiated cap
- Minimum increments for overbids
- Qualification requirements for competing bidders
- Strict deadlines for competing bids and dates for the auction, final court approval, and closing

the Second Circuit Court of Appeals is fairly receptive to such fees (and will generally approve them as long as they represent a reasonable exercise of the debtor's business judgment), whereas the Third Circuit may require proof that the fees are actually necessary to preserve the value of the estate. Here again, experienced legal counsel will know the metes and bounds of what is considered reasonable in different jurisdictions.

Not all breakup fees need to be defined as a percentage of the purchase price. In the unusual bankruptcy case involving General Growth Properties (GGP), the bankruptcy court approved a breakup fee to be paid in warrants for equity in the company if it was sold to another bidder.[25] Although they were contingent upon the future success of the company following bankruptcy, these warrants were valued at hundreds of millions of dollars. The GGP case was the biggest real estate bankruptcy case in U.S. history and involved hundreds of shopping malls. The company attracted strong interest from Simon Property Group, the largest competitor to GGP, and Brookfield Asset Management, a Canadian property manager. Management rebuffed Simon's efforts to pursue a purchase of the company via a 363 sale. Instead, the debtor sided with Brookfield, which had provided a DIP loan earlier in the case, and proposed a plan of reorganization funded by an investor group led by Brookfield to enable GGP to emerge as an independent company. The plan proposed the following:[26]

- An affiliate of Brookfield Asset Management would invest $2.625 billion in exchange for 26 percent of GGP's reorganized stock.
- Fairholme Capital Management would invest roughly $2.79 billion in exchange for 28 percent of GGP's reorganized stock.
- Pershing Square Capital Management would invest about $1.14 billion in exchange for 11 percent of GGP's reorganized stock.
- The plan sponsors would also backstop $1.5 billion in exit financing and a $500 million rights offering for GGP's reorganized stock.

The plan also included a breakup fee to Brookfield in the form of warrants for 120 million shares in GGP's reorganized equity.[27] An investor group led by Simon ultimately raised its bid to $6.5 billion in cash and Simon stock. Both the Simon and the Brookfield-led offers involved the assumption of approximately $15 billion in restructured mortgage debt.[28] After the bankruptcy court approved the debtor's plan involving Brookfield, Simon abandoned its bid.[29]

What is a minimum topping amount?

A *minimum topping amount* (also sometimes referred to as *overbid protection* from the perspective of the stalking horse bidder) is the amount by which competing bids must exceed the stalking horse's bid. Typically, this amount runs in the 3 to 10 percent range, depending on the amount of the sale. For example, if the initial bid by the stalking horse bidder is $2,000,000 with 5 percent overbid protection, no competing bid will be considered unless it exceeds the initial bid by more than $100,000.[30] If a competing bidder submits a bid of at least $2,100,001, then bidding will continue thereafter using the minimum bid increments established by the bidding procedures.

There is usually a relationship between the overbid protection and the breakup fee provided to a stalking horse bidder. In essence, the breakup fee is the portion of the overbid protection that the debtor's estate shares with the stalking horse for assisting with the auction. Therefore, it is rare for the breakup fee to exceed the overbid protection and more common for the breakup fee to be roughly half of the overbid protection.

What sort of contingencies can a bidder include in its bid?

Typically, none. The bidding procedures approved by the bankruptcy court usually require "no outs" bids from qualified bidders. This means that a bid must exclude typical contingencies for due diligence and financing in order to be qualified. Once a bidder is disqualified, there may be no time for that bidder to revise its bid and reenter the auction. Therefore, it is critical that all bidders complete their due diligence and raise sufficient capital prior to submitting their bids.

Can anyone submit a qualified bid?

No. The bidding procedures approved by the bankruptcy court usually contain criteria for qualifying bidders so that the debtor and other bidders can avoid wasting time with bidders who have no credibility. In order to be qualified, a bidder may need to demonstrate its financial capabilities to close a sale if it is the winning bidder. Sometimes a qualified bidder will need to put a refundable deposit in escrow at the time it submits its bid. These deposits are usually refunded promptly after the auction, except for the runner-up bidder's deposit, which is often withheld until the sale to the winning bidder is consummated. If the winning bidder fails to consummate the sale, the runner-up bidder may prevail ultimately.

May a secured creditor be a bidder during an auction for a sale of the company?

Yes. Just because a party is a secured creditor in a bankruptcy proceeding does not prevent it from bidding for the company in a sale process. Unlike other bidders, who typically must present all-cash offers, a secured creditor may bid some or all of its secured claim as well as cash, which is known as *credit bidding*. This makes sense because if the secured creditor presented an all-cash bid, some or all of the cash would simply be used to pay off the secured creditor itself.

More specifically, a creditor may bid up to the full amount of its secured claim to acquire the asset to which its lien is attached. In exchange, the indebtedness on the asset is canceled in the amount of the bid. If the amount of the potential debt forgiveness exceeds a cash bid from a third party, the court may rule that the credit bid is the "highest and best" bid.

What limitations are there on credit bidding?

Only a secured creditor with a valid, perfected lien on a particular asset may credit-bid for that asset. This can get tricky when the lender seeks to credit-bid for a basket of assets that includes other collateral. In such scenarios, the court may have to allocate value among the collateral and the noncollateralized assets. If the secured creditor has a blanket lien on all or nearly all assets of the company, the secured creditor can credit-bid for the entire enterprise.

In terms of dollar amount, the maximum credit bid is the face amount of the lender's secured claim. The economic or market value of the underlying collateral is not considered. For companies in distress, the difference between face and market value can be significant, meaning that many credit bidders can compete effectively at auction without needing to contribute any additional cash (i.e., beyond the cash used to invest in the secured claim). While this favorable attribute will be little consolation to a lender who funded the loan at par, a distressed investor that bought the secured claim in the secondary markets at a low price can gain much greater buying power at auction.

From a mechanical standpoint, if there is a syndicate of lenders, the secured creditor may credit-bid only with the consent of lenders holding at least 50 percent of the dollar amount of a bank loan group's secured debt. Additional mechanics are often hammered out in the intercreditor agreement.

In a recent development, the Third Circuit Court of Appeals ruled that a secured creditor can be prohibited from credit bidding if the 363 sale is part of a plan of reorganization. In the *Philadelphia Newspapers* case, the debtors proposed a plan of reorganization that specifically limited the right of the secured lenders to credit-bid. The secured creditors' claims amounted to more than $300 million and involved blanket liens on substantially all of the debtors' property. The debtors' plan proposed selling at auction nearly all of their assets, except for an office building valued at $29.5 million, free and clear of all liens. The plan would distribute the cash received at the auction, which the debtors estimated at $37 million, plus the office building, subject to a two-year rent-free lease, to the secured creditors. The debtors argued that their plan provided indubitable equivalent recoveries to the secured creditors, so credit bidding was not appropriate. The debtors' motion to approve bidding procedures for their plan's 363 sale named a stalking horse bidder composed of former and current management and equity holders. The bankruptcy court sided with the secured creditors and denied the debtors' motion with respect to credit bidding.[31] On appeal, the district court reversed,[32] and the Third Circuit Court of Appeals affirmed.[33] The district court noted that the Bankruptcy Code does not provide secured creditors with any statutory right to credit-bid when a debtor chooses to sell its collateral under the indubitable equivalent principle in a plan of reorganization. This decision left open a secured creditor's right to object to a 363 sale because the proceeds would not provide the indubitable equivalent of its claims. Also, secured creditors can still argue over whether a debtor is reasonably exercising its business judgment.

Although this Third Circuit case and another Fifth Circuit case[34] create new uncertainty for secured creditors, they can mitigate these risks by bidding at auctions using cash just like other bidders. In theory, if a secured creditor's cash bid prevails, the secured creditor will simply receive its cash back (less the administrative expenses in the case) as its recovery under the plan of reorganization.

How can credit bidding chill the overall bidding activity in an auction?

Both financial and strategic buyers may be discouraged by a secured creditor who is credit-bidding in an auction for several reasons. First, the secured creditor has the benefit of experience with the company as a lender, and therefore has probably been able to perform deeper due diligence. Second, the secured creditor has probably gained a more intricate understanding of the nature and value of the assets involved, including the accuracy and validity of asset appraisals. Third, by credit-bidding, the secured creditor is not investing new capital and thus does not need to raise fresh financing to fund its bid, giving it an advantage over other bidders. Fourth, the secured creditor may have an adverse incentive, wanting the valuation to be bid up as high as possible because the proceeds will be used to pay the claims of—don't forget—the secured creditor. As a result, a distressed investor who bought the secured claims will fortuitously profit if a third party tops the credit bid. Finally, if the holder of the secured claim, such as a hedge fund, bought the claim at a discount, it can bid up to the face value of its entire claim, giving it a significant advantage over other bidders who are bidding real cash for 100 percent of their bids.

As one bankruptcy court explained:[35]

> [I]f an undersecured creditor was allowed to credit-bid, this "bidding in" could give rise to "roundhousing" whereby an undersecured creditor can bid in excess of its secured claim, up to and including the total amount of both its secured and unsecured claims, confident in the knowledge that substantially all, if not all, of the funds paid for the reorganized debtor would be returned in partial or total satisfaction of its claims. By doing so, such a creditor could appropriate all going-concern value in the debtor to itself and share no infusion of value through the bid price with other creditors.

Is it possible for multiple potential bidders to team up by submitting one bid?

It depends upon whether forming teams will enhance the auction and increase the amount of the winning bid. Understandably, collusion among bidders is expressly prohibited by the Bankruptcy Code.[36] Collusion among bidders reduces the level of bidding activity by potentially decreasing the number of qualified bidders and diminishing the amount of the bids submitted. Therefore, collusion undermines the fair and equitable result sought to be provided by an auction and causes the winning bid to fall short of the highest and best value for the assets being sold. Accordingly, the Bankruptcy Code authorizes the debtor in possession (or trustee, as the case may be) to unwind a sale involving collusion and to seek punitive damages.

On the other hand, it may be advantageous for multiple bidders to form a team to buy a package of assets that they can divide afterward. If the debtor in possession is selling multiple business units as a package, then an auction may attract more bidders if they are allowed to form teams. The bankruptcy court may consider whether such teams are advantageous to maximizing the value of the debtor's estate but, alternatively, may require that the business units be sold separately in multiple 363 sales.

Usually, the debtor in possession and the bankruptcy court may permit lenders and buyers to form teams to bid on assets at 363 sales. A financial buyer will often need to obtain financing from a third party, so this sort of team is typically not considered collusion if the third party (e.g., a bank) would not otherwise be involved in a bid for the debtor's assets. Sometimes, the debtor's financial advisor may seek one particular lender to provide terms for a loan for any bidder to consider using to finance its bid. Such prequalified loans are known as *staple financings* because they are hypothetically stapled to the front cover of the offering memorandum circulated by the financial advisor to prospective bidders. In difficult capital markets, identifying staple financing may help increase interest among prospective bidders to participate in an auction.

Can a bidder be disqualified from the sale process for not following the rules?

Not necessarily (although that's an imperfection of the 363 sale process). Ultimately, the debtor may waive any number of would-be rule "infractions."

Such infractions often involve bids that are late or are otherwise noncon-forming (e.g., no marked-up asset purchase agreement, missing a description of financing ability, contemplating a modified package of assets, and so on). While this will undoubtedly seem unfair to conform-ing bidders, ultimately the process is focused on a single objective: maximizing the recovery on the assets of the estate for the benefit of all parties in interest in the case.[37] To borrow a legal phrase, then, one might argue that, in practice, the bidding procedures are only "honored in the breach."

If maximizing recoveries is the single objective of a 363 transaction, does that mean that price is the dominant differentiating factor among various bids?

Not necessarily. Remember, the key is trying to flesh out a "higher and better" bid. A factor such as certainty of closing (which could be influenced by financing ability, antitrust considerations, or third-party contract con-sents) can be a meaningful differentiator during the bidding process. It is critical to evaluate how a bankruptcy court will use its equitable powers and apply relevant case law precedents to determine what sort of bid could be deemed best even if it is not highest.

Can a losing bidder get its expenses reimbursed?

Perhaps. If a losing bidder can demonstrate that its bids made a meaning-ful and necessary contribution to the value received by the debtor's estate, then the losing bidder may be able to recover some or all of its expenses as an administrative expense. Bankruptcy Code Section 503(b) provides for the allowance of administrative expenses where the requesting party shows that the fees are "actually necessary to preserve the value of the estate."[38] For example, following its approval of a 363 sale in the *Foamex Int'l* case,[39] the Bankruptcy Court for the District of Delaware ordered up to $1 million in reimbursement of certain expenses to Wayzata Investment Partners, the losing bidder, whose participation in the auction enabled bidding to soar by approximately $50 million beyond the initial stalking horse bid.

LOAN-TO-OWN TRANSACTIONS

What is a loan-to-own transaction?

A *loan-to-own* transaction can take multiple forms, but it generally refers to the purchase of debt (typically at a discount) with the ultimate goal of converting the debt to equity in order to take control of the underlying asset or the broader business.

Loan-to-own transactions usually involve the origination or purchase of pre-petition secured debt or the funding of a DIP loan, which is discussed in detail in Chapter 14 of this book.

From time to time, a loan-to-own transaction might be combined with a rights offering (in which larger creditors acquire warrants in the debtor's new equity, with the cash being used to take out smaller creditors) or the purchase of the expected fulcrum security. (As Chapter 4 describes in more detail, a *fulcrum security* is the position on the debtor's capital structure that is most likely to be paid at least partly in equity.) In some circumstances, the purchaser may also acquire a portion of the debtor's equity or management control (e.g., voting power or board seats) as a means of further entrenching itself as a vocal participant in the restructuring process.

What's a typical scenario in which a loan-to-own transaction makes sense strategically?

The loan-to-own technique can be a useful precursor to credit bidding in a 363 sale. A typical scenario is one in which a distressed investor buys pre-petition secured debt at a discount in the secondary markets, rolls over the pre-petition secured debt into a DIP loan, requires that it become the stalking horse (i.e., negotiates stalking horse designation as part of the DIP loan agreement), insists upon an expedited marketing process, and credit-bids at the auction. Throughout the process, the distressed investor will probably attempt to take action and make statements that will chill bidding by other interested parties and co-opt those parties that it cannot drive away.

Consider, for instance, a secured bond with a $100 face value, where the market value of the underlying collateral has declined to $50. A purchaser that steps in to buy the bond at $45 ahead of a 363 transaction can credit-bid up to $100 for the asset with no additional cash outlay. A scenario such as this, where the credit bid sets an artificially high bidding threshold,

understandably would dissuade many would-be competitors from even bidding on the asset. Even if they did manage to outbid the initial purchaser,
the return on the purchaser's invested capital could still be enormous,
depending on how the court distributes the estate's cash proceeds.

This example, however, also illustrates a key issue that some creditors
will raise about a loan-to-own transaction—namely, that recoveries for
unsecured creditors would be zero. Because the distressed investor would
probably have acquired the pre-petition secured debt in the secondary markets, the estate would not have received any cash from that transaction. Nor
would the estate have received any cash from the credit bid, which, by the
strategy's very definition, is cashless. Therefore, critics argue that this loan-
to-own scenario is a thinly disguised liquidation with the predetermined
result that value accrues only to the most senior lenders.

In situations such as the preceding example, what recourse do junior creditors have?

Junior creditors—such as second-lien lenders and unsecured claimants—
might consider challenging the loan-to-own tactic under at least one of
three different arguments: equitable subordination, recharacterization, and
fundamental unfairness. (The following discussion briefly summarizes
equitable subordination and recharacterization. Chapter 5 discusses these
concepts in greater detail.)

First, junior claimants might pursue the remedy of *equitable subordination*, depending on the precise circumstances of the preceding example.
As noted earlier in this book, the bankruptcy court is a court of equity as
well as a court of law. This means that a bankruptcy court can exercise its
discretion to produce fair and just results—which includes potentially subordinating prior claims on a debtor's assets.

Second, the junior claimants might pursue the similar, albeit distinct,
remedy of *recharacterization*. Under this remedy, the court has the power
to ignore the form of a transaction and instead give effect to its substance.
This may include treating the purchaser's claim on the debtor's asset(s) as
equity, rather than debt. Like a finding of equitable subordination, not only
would this preclude a credit bid, but it would also be likely to wipe out
most, if not all, of the distressed investor's potential return (i.e., the rechar-
acterized claim would face a fate similar to that of the interests of other
equity holders) and could even cause a loss on the investment.

Third, the junior claimants might argue that it would be fundamentally unfair to the competitive bidding process for the bankruptcy court to allow the purchaser to credit-bid up to the face value of its lien. As a court of equity as well as a court of law, the bankruptcy court has the authority under Section 363(k) of the Bankruptcy Code to deny or limit the purchaser's rights in certain circumstances.[40]

What are some of the downside risks of a loan-to-own strategy?

There are at least four key downside risks with such a strategy:

- *Limited financing.* Generally, loan-to-own purchases are all-cash transactions, with little or no third-party financing available. Sellers may sometimes provide financing, but it will most likely be a very low loan-to-value and will have a recourse component.
- *Lender liability.* Lender liability can potentially be alleged based on numerous legal theories, although the most common claims involve the implied covenant of good faith and fair dealing that is imposed on every party to a contract. This covenant requires that neither party to a contract take any action that deprives the other party of the benefits of the agreement. This means that a lender must take care not to gain an opportunistic advantage over the borrower in a way that suggests that the lender is not acting in good faith. To mitigate the risks of lender liability, an acquirer should fully evaluate the selling lender and its reputation, including any history of lender liability claims that it may have faced. The would-be buyer should also analyze how the debt was serviced by the selling lender and any other relevant facts concerning the course of conduct between the borrower and the selling lender.
- *Potential original issue discount (OID) issues.* A portion of any gain on the subsequent sale of acquired debt purchased at a discount might be taxable at ordinary income—rather than capital gains—tax rates. Alternatively, in certain circumstances, the discount from the original face amount of the acquired debt

might be includible in current-year ordinary income as the carrying value of the debt accretes toward maturity. This is an area in which experienced tax counsel is particularly helpful.

- *Potential fiduciary duties.* "Buy your own" may trigger fiduciary duty issues between affiliated funds, or equitable subordination claims. Some investment funds, particularly in the private equity arena, used the credit market dislocation in 2009 to buy back the debt of selected portfolio companies. This strategy, sometimes referred to as "buy your own," can trigger at least three key issues:

  1. An investment fund's organizational documents may preclude the fund's purchasing debt in a debtor that is controlled by an affiliated investment fund.

  2. Even where the organizational documents allow it, a "buy-your-own" strategy poses the risk of equitable subordination claims by third parties.

     An affiliated party's purchase may trigger cancellation of debt, or COD, income to the portfolio company in an amount equal to the difference between the adjusted issue price of the debt purchased and the purchase price paid for the debt. Chapters 8 and 9 discuss the accounting and tax implications of COD income in greater detail; however, as a general rule, parties are related if they are at least 50 percent owned by the same persons. (As an aside, during the residential mortgage meltdown in 2008–2009, the mortgage company ResCap used this strategy to its advantage. The company bought back some of its own debt at a discount and booked an accounting gain; this increased the company's book value and staved off tripping covenants for an additional quarter.)

- *Reputation.* Last but not least, using the loan-to-own tactic has the potential to harm an investor's reputation in the marketplace. While the investor may get one particular deal done at a bargain price, doing so may impair its ability to win deals in the future. As the noted English satirist Joseph Hall wrote: "A reputation once broken may possibly be repaired, but the world will always keep their eyes on the spot where the crack was."

With these risks in mind, we next turn to considerations for refinancing a business (a possible alternative to either a 363 sale or a loan-to-own transaction) and, if a sale process is inevitable, how a buyer can finance the purchase of a company in distress.

Endnotes

1. See 11 U.S.C. §363.
2. See 11 U.S.C. §363(b).
3. See 11 U.S.C. §363(f).
4. See, for example, Elizabeth B. Rose, "Chocolate, Flowers and Section 363(b): The Opportunity for Sweetheart Deals without Chapter 11 Protections," *Emory Bankruptcy Developments Journal* 23 (2006), p. 249.
5. See 11 U.S.C. §§362, 363(d)(2).
6. See 11 U.S.C. §363(d)(1).
7. See 11 U.S.C. §363(f).
8. See 11 U.S.C. §363(l).
9. See 11 U.S.C. §365.
10. See 11 U.S.C. §365(b).
11. See 11 U.S.C. §365(n).
12. Bankruptcy Rule 4001(d)(2) sets the default notice provision for filing objections to motions related to asset sales at 15 days, and then Bankruptcy Rule 4001(d)(3) provides that a hearing before the bankruptcy court on the motion and any objections should be held no less than 5 days after an objection is filed, for a total of 20 days. See Fed. R. Bankr. P. 4001(d)(2) and 4001(d)(3).
13. *In re Lehman Brothers Holdings Inc.*, Case No. 08-13555 (Bankr. S.D.N.Y. 2008).
14. See 11 U.S.C. §726.
15. *Motorola, Inc. v. Official Comm. of Unsecured Creditors*, 478 F.3d 452, 466 (2d Cir. 2007) (quoting *Pension Benefit Guar. Corp. v. Braniff Airways, Inc. (In re Braniff Airways, Inc.)*, 700 F.2d 935, 940 (5th Cir. 1983).
16. See *In re General Motors Corp.*, 407 B.R. 463, 477 (Bankr. S.D.N.Y. 2009). (Gerber, J.).
17. See Opinion Granting Debtors' Motion Seeking Authority to Sell, Pursuant to 11 U.S.C. §363, Substantially All of the Debtors' Assets [Dkt. No. 3073], Chrysler LLC, *et. al.*, Case No. 09-50002 (AJG), (Bankr. S.D. N.Y. April 30, 2009).
18. *Comm. of Equity Sec. Holders v. Lionel Corp. (In re Lionel Corp.)*, 722 F.2d 1063, 1071 (2d Cir. 1983).
19. Ibid.
20. Ibid.
21. See 11 U.S.C. §363(b)(2).
22. There may be other limitations on "free and clear" transfers. For instance, in one recent decision, the Court of Appeals for the Ninth Circuit held that a credit

bid by a secured creditor does not convey title free and clear of junior consensual liens, even though that might be possible in confirmation of a Chapter 11 plan. *In re PW, LLC (Clear Channel Outdoor, Inc.)*, 391 B.R. 25 (9th Cir. 2008).

23. See 11 U.S.C. §363(m).

24. *Clear Channel Outdoor, Inc. v. Knupfer (In re PW, LLC)*, 391 B.R. 25 (B.A.P. 9th Cir. 2008).

25. *In re General Growth Properties, Inc.*, Case No. 09-11977-alg (Bankr. S.D.N.Y. 2009).

26. Jamie Mason, "Simon Bows out of GGP Pursuit," May 7, 2010; http://pipeline .thedeal.com/tdd/ViewArticle.dl?id=10005425993, last accessed June 15, 2010.

27. Ibid.

28. Ibid.

29. Ibid.

30. Eric S. Prezant, "Acquisitions and Dispositions of Assets of Troubled Companies," Vedder, Price, Kaufman & Kammholz; available at http://www.vedderprice.com/ docs/pub/273d54ad-1f15-41b7-95a6-b2e137c855a9_document.pdf, last accessed June 2, 2010.

31. See *In re Phila. Newspapers, LLC*, Case No. 09-11204 (SR, CJ) [Dkt. No. 1234] (Bankr. E.D. Pa. Oct. 8, 2009).

32. See *In re Phila. Newspapers, LLC*, 418 B.R. 548 (E.D. Pa. 2009).

33. See *In re Phila. Newspapers, LLC*, 2010 U.S. App. LEXIS 5803 (3d Cir. 2010).

34. See *In re Pacific Lumber*, 584 F.3d 229 (5th Cir. 2009) (finding that a plan proposing the transfer of property to a named buyer for cash provided the indubitable equivalent to secured creditors, who had objected after the auction was over, and therefore preserving their right to credit-bid was not imperative).

35. See *In re Moonraker Assocs., Ltd.*, 200 B.R. 950, 955 (Bankr. N.D. Ga. 1996).

36. See 11 U.S.C. §363(n).

37. As the Southern District of New York noted in *In re Ames Dept. Stores, Inc.*, "One of the policies fundamental to the bankruptcy process is that of the Trustee to marshal and maximize estate assets. Section 363(b) fosters that policy by allowing the sale of all, or substantially all, of the debtor's assets outside the context of a plan of reorganization." 136 B.R. 357, 359 (Bankr. S.D.N.Y. 1992).

38. See 11 U.S.C. §503(b).

39. See *In re Foamex Int'l Inc.*, No. 09-10560 (KJC) (Bankr. D. Del.).

40. See 11 U.S.C. §363(k).

CHAPTER 14

Distressed M&A Strategy: Financing and Refinancing Considerations

Don't throw good money after bad.

—Proverb

INTRODUCTION TO DISTRESSED M&A
FINANCING AND REFINANCING

When working with companies in distress, buyers and others will encounter many important financing issues. While the basic principles of financing remain the same, there are some terms and techniques that are unique to distressed situations—or at least have special meaning there. There are new lessons to be learned, special exceptions to customary rules that become important, and conventional wisdom that needs to be reconsidered. As leading restructuring professionals will remind their clients: "If the answers were obvious, we wouldn't be here." Bear in mind, however, that financing—perhaps more than any other topic discussed in this book—is in a constant state of flux. This overview will probably need refreshing as capital markets evolve and financial engineering innovates.

From the perspective of a company in distress, a financing transaction typically entails refinancing the company's existing capital structure to provide the company with additional "runway" to conduct an operational turnaround, wait for industry cycles to turn, or endure a recession. Of course, if the company suffers from operational issues, burdensome litigation, unfavorable agreements, regulatory change, or other fundamental problems, "Band-Aid" refinancing may simply mask the symptoms, and bankruptcy may inevitably be the only way to cure the company's ailments. Unfortunately, many distressed companies complete refinancing transactions that simply postpone an inevitable bankruptcy and facilitate futility rather than serve as effective solutions.

Overall, the company's goals during a refinancing include increasing liquidity, extending debt maturities, relieving financial covenants, and avoiding bankruptcy. Sometimes the refinancing involves the company's negotiating with its existing creditors to change the terms of its existing debt. Other times, the refinancing involves the company's transacting with new funding sources to pay off some or all of its existing debt. Indeed, the availability of the capital markets to facilitate the refinancing with fresh capital gives the company leverage to negotiate with its existing creditors, who may be fatigued and want to become disentangled from the company. If the company is unable to close a refinancing transaction before its liquidity dries up, however, then bankruptcy may be its only remaining option. The exorbitant cost, risky uncertainty, and time-consuming distraction faced by all parties in bankruptcy usually pressure them to reach an out-of-court compromise. However, as discussed throughout this book, the problem of uncooperative holdouts may force the other parties to resort to a cram-down plan of reorganization and other tactics that can be accomplished only in bankruptcy.

If the company and its creditors cannot reach agreement, the capital markets do not offer helpful alternatives, or the parties become fatigued with the negotiating process, the company may decide to pursue a distressed sale as another alternative to bankruptcy. A financial buyer of a distressed company may have access to capital that is superior to that of the company and its creditors. A strategic buyer of a distressed company may have readily available cash to partially finance the transaction. In either situation, buyers will want to become familiar with the refinancing concepts in this chapter because they are also useful financing techniques for distressed M&A. Many of these refinancing concepts can also be used as techniques for obtaining fresh capital for new financing as well. In addition, this chapter addresses how buyers of distressed companies may employ special financing methods, such as seller takebacks and earn-outs.

After explaining several financing and refinancing concepts, the remainder of this chapter describes general terms, practices, and legal considerations involved in negotiating and completing a financing transaction.

When you are seeking to apply the different financing and refinancing concepts discussed in this chapter to an actual distressed situation, we recommend that you create a chart analyzing the sources and uses of the proposed financing transaction. One way or another, the sources of capital must equal the uses of capital in order to complete a financing or refinancing. Therefore, it is helpful to make sure that you understand the flow of funds well. Creating a useful sources and uses chart can help minimize costly miscommunications between the company and its counterparties, between clients and their advisors, and among various professionals within a particular firm.

OVERVIEW OF REFINANCING METHODS

What are some refinancing methods that a distressed business can employ to avoid selling the company or entering bankruptcy?

Depending upon the state of the capital markets, alternatives for refinancing a troubled company may include

- Amend and extend agreements with existing lenders
- Refinancing a cash flow loan with an asset-based loan
- Factoring receivables
- Terming out payables
- Debt exchange offers
- Debt-for-equity swaps
- Rights offerings and warrants
- Private investment in public equity (PIPE)
- Government-supported transactions

The sections that follow provide an overview of each of these alternatives. For a specific situation, an investment banker can explore current market conditions and summarize the pros and cons of various decisions. The investment banker will probably need to work with legal counsel to review the company's existing credit agreements for provisions that may hinder refinancing efforts.

What are some examples of provisions in existing credit agreements that may hinder refinancing efforts?

Creditors are passive investors who are not involved in day-to-day operations, as management is, or strategic decision making, as boards of directors are. Therefore, it is understandable that credit agreements typically create triggers to sound alarms when financial performance falls outside of the initially anticipated parameters and impose boundaries on the company's activities outside of the ordinary course of business. In Chapter 2 of this book, we discussed the former provisions, which can result in an out-of-court workout or Chapter 11 reorganization. In this chapter, we will focus on the latter provisions, which can hinder a company's refinancing efforts and thus may precipitate a distressed sale or bankruptcy.

- A *negative pledge* is an undertaking by the borrower not to pledge to someone else assets that may be subject to the lender's lien or to no lien. It generally is used to bar junior liens on collateral that is subject to the lender's senior lien. Although in theory the rights of the holder of a junior lien should not impinge on the senior lender's rights in the collateral, in practice lenders strongly prefer not to be accountable to a second-lien holder with regard to their stewardship over the collateral on which they have a first lien. In the eyes of a senior lender, the holder of a junior lien is someone who can second-guess your actions in realizing upon the collateral and sue you if you slip up, or even if you don't.
- *Prepayment penalties* are incentives for borrowers to avoid refinancing for a specified period of time. Lenders often impose prepayment penalties in loan agreements in order to make sure that they recoup their up-front investment of time and effort in underwriting and documenting the loan. Also, lenders may have included the loan in their internal plans and are relying upon the income stream generated by the interest payments and recurring fees. Typically, borrowers and lenders include in the loan agreement a schedule of prepayment penalties as a declining percentage of the loan balance over the life of the loan. For example, there may be a 3 percent prepayment penalty if the loan is paid off prematurely in the first year,

a 2 percent penalty in the second year, a 1 percent penalty in the third year, and no penalty thereafter. Prepayment penalties are similar to *call protection* in bonds.

- *Call protection* for bonds, similar to prepayment penalties for loans, is an incentive for borrowers to avoid early retirement of the debt. Bondholders seek to maintain the duration of their investment by discouraging early payoff, especially if interest rates are expected to decline and bondholders fear that they will no longer be able to find similar yields in the marketplace. The terms of call protection vary from bond to bond and are typically three to five years. For example, "NC-5" means that the bond is noncallable for five years. Some bonds are "NCL," meaning that they are noncallable for the life of the debt. While the company may prepay, the cash premium required is usually overly burdensome, motivating the company to find another alternative.

- *Make-whole provisions* are a form of prepayment penalty whereby, upon a unilateral decision by the borrower to prepay the loan, the lender is due—in addition to the customary principal and accrued interest—the present value of all future payments according to a prearranged formula. This provision "makes the lender whole" for all of its future profits and accounts for its theoretical opportunity cost when the loan is called prematurely.

- Limitations on payment of *dividends* and other distributions to equity holders may be included. Often there is an outright prohibition at least for a specified time period, or until certain financial tests are satisfied. However, the lender may permit distributions of dividends to stockholders of an S corporation for the purpose of paying federal, state, and local income taxes on the company's income.

- *Transactions with affiliates* may be prohibited. Key exceptions may be those that are expressly agreed upon and those that are conducted on an "arm's-length" basis for services that are definitely required by the borrower in the ordinary course of business.

- Restrictions on *lending money to or guaranteeing the obligations of third parties* may be included.

- *Minimum amortization payments* are required principal payments that the borrower must make at certain intervals. When
  operations begin to struggle, these payments can become especially onerous.
- *Excess cash flow sweeps* are sometimes included in credit
  agreements. These provisions calculate the amount of cash
  remaining after operating expenses, debt service, and capital
  expenditures. The borrower may be forced to use a percentage
  of any excess cash above and beyond these amounts to amortize the debt. For distressed companies, this "use it or lose it"
  requirement can force companies to make suboptimal decisions
  regarding how to manage cash.

Therefore, the primary goal of a refinancing transaction may be to
loosen these restrictions with a new lender, thereby increasing the company's
liquidity and flexibility.

REFINANCING METHODS: AMEND AND EXTEND AGREEMENTS

What does "amend and extend" mean?

When a borrower violates its financial covenants, lenders may agree to
amend the loan agreement by waiving prior defaults and extend the maturity
of the loan to give the borrower time to improve its performance or refinance the loan. In exchange, these lenders will typically extract an amendment or waiver fee (which has generally ranged from 5 to 25 basis points in
recent years) plus an average spread increase of roughly 200 basis points for
the interest rate. Chapter 3 of this book discusses trends regarding amend
and extend agreements during the 2008–2009 global economic crisis.

Whether a lender agrees to amend and extend depends on many factors
ranging from the credibility of the management team's turnaround plan to
internal politics within the lender's organization. Typically, lenders will weigh
the cost and risk of bankruptcy, on the one hand, against the economic advantage of an amend and extend agreement, on the other. If the lender feels that
its collateral position is stable, then an amend and extend agreement is more
likely to be signed. However, if the lender feels that its principal is at risk,
then it is less likely to agree to delay foreclosure or other remedies.

Why are these agreements sometimes called "amend, extend, and pretend" agreements?

Bankruptcy professionals sometimes jokingly say that "amend and extend" really means "amend, extend, and pretend" when a distressed company needs a fundamental fix. Lenders may want to report the loan as "performing" rather than "defaulted," so they may enter into an "amend and extend" agreement to postpone recognizing the problem in the current reporting period and disclosing it to their regulators and stockholders. In other situations, lenders may want to forestall foreclosure until a later period if they believe that asset values are artificially low at present. Critics of these practices will point to Japan's economic malaise in the 1990s, when banking regulators turned the other way while lenders kept "zombie" loans on their balance sheets and refused to recognize defaults and to realize losses of principal.

If there is more than one lender involved in a loan agreement, do all the members of a lending group have to approve every waiver and amendment?

Frequently, leveraged loans are made by groups of banks, or *syndicates*. In some cases, the banks involved in making the loan will be parties to the loan agreement, with one of their number designated as the *agent bank*. In other cases, only one bank will sign the loan agreement, but it will sell off participation interests to other banks. Although the number of participants in a loan makes no difference to the borrower from a legal standpoint, the practical implications of having to deal with multiple lenders can be serious and troublesome.

Generally, a percentage of the syndicate, rather than all the lenders, needs to approve every waiver and amendment. Certain provisions related to interbank matters, such as the percentage of lenders in a syndicate needed to grant waivers, are generally contained in a separate document, which is sometimes called the *participation agreement*. The borrower is not a party to the participation agreement and may not even be allowed to see it. Although arrangements for providing approval for waivers and amendments vary widely, it is not unusual for participation agreements to provide that certain changes in the loan (such as changes in interest rates, due date, and principal amount) are so fundamental that all lenders must consent, whereas other changes can be approved by banks holding at least a 51 percent interest (or in some cases a 66.6 percent interest) in all loans outstanding or in lending commitments. The lenders may appoint a *steering committee* to negotiate such matters on behalf of the group.

REFINANCING METHODS: REFINANCING A CASH FLOW LOAN WITH AN ASSET-BASED LOAN

What is the difference between financing senior debt with a cash flow loan and an asset-based loan?

Asset-based loans (also known as *ABL loans*) are a form of senior debt financing with a first lien that is available from most banks as a last resort alternative to cash flow loans. Whether it is an ABL loan or a cash flow loan, a credit facility may involve a revolver only, a revolver and a term loan, or a revolver and multiple term loans, and may work in conjunction with other tranches of debt, such as second-lien loans, mezzanine loans, or high-yield bonds. As with conventional credit facilities, there may be one lender or an agent plus a syndicate of lenders. Whereas cash flow loans use EBITDA (earnings before interest, taxes, depreciation, and amortization) or another measure of cash flow to determine the total amount available in the credit facility, asset-based loans focus on the value of each category of assets on the company's balance sheet. Therefore, an asset-based loan can be a welcome financing alternative when a distressed company is experiencing a cash flow crunch amid significant uncertainty. However, if a company is failing as a result of issues that are plaguing its entire industry, then asset values throughout the industry may plunge because everyone is seeking to sell assets, but there are no buyers. Under such circumstances, an asset-based loan may not be very helpful for refinancing the company's cash flow loan and providing relief in a liquidity crisis. Exhibit 14-1 compares the features of an asset-based loan with those of a cash flow loan.

While balance sheets follow GAAP and show the lower of cost or market value for assets, asset-based lenders typically focus on *net orderly liquidation value* (NOLV). Depending upon the situation, NOLV may or may not differ from historical cost and fair market value. Orderly liquidation value does not imply a rushed "fire sale" that is poorly marketed. Instead, orderly liquidation value assumes taking a reasonable period of time to conduct a marketing process for the assets that will allow a sufficient

Exhibit 14-1 Comparison of Cash Flow Loans and Asset-Based Loans

	Cash Flow Loans	Asset-Based Loans
Revolving line of credit	Available	Available
Term loans	Available	Available
Permit junior liens	Depends upon lender	Depends upon lender
Interest	Fixed or floating	Usually floating
Covenants		
Minimum EBITDA	Likely	Unlikely
Maximum capex	Likely	Unlikely
Total leverage ratio	Likely	Unlikely
Senior leverage ratio	Likely	Unlikely
Fixed charge coverage ratio	Likely	Possibly
Borrowing base	No	Yes
Lockbox account	Inactive	Active
Annual budgets	Yes	Possibly

number of potential buyers to learn about the sale, evaluate the assets, and submit bids at an auction. Once orderly liquidation value is calculated for each asset on the balance sheet, liquidation costs—such as the expenses for liquidators, advertising, storage, and shipping—are subtracted to determine NOLV. ABL lenders will usually engage a professional appraiser—at the borrower's expense—to determine NOLV. Professional appraisers adhere to a set of standards called the Uniform Standards of Professional Appraisal Practice and may bring specialized industry knowledge from recent relevant auctions.[1] (Chapter 11 of this book discusses the applicable professional standards for appraisers.)

Once the appraiser finalizes her report, ABL lenders then apply *advance rates* to the NOLV of each asset category to calculate the initial maximum amount of the loan, which is known as *total availability* (or sometimes simply *availability*). The difference between the amount that has been drawn on the credit facility and total availability is called *excess availability*. Furthermore, the loan will be subject to a *maximum availability* that acts as an absolute cap on the amount of the loan, regardless of the result of the formula for calculating total availability. As the company operates throughout the life of the loan, the amounts of total availability, loan balance, and excess availability will fluctuate regularly. When total availability exceeds the maximum loan amount, the difference between total availability and the maximum loan amount is called *suppressed availability*, which is liquidity that the company cannot access with the existing lender. If the company needs to access its suppressed availability and the lender refuses to modify the maximum loan amount, the borrower can try to refinance the existing ABL loan with another ABL lender.

In the loan agreement, ABL lenders will require borrowers to provide periodic updates on the balances of each asset category by filing a borrowing base certificate (defined later in this chapter) with the ABL lender. Typical ABL loan agreements also provide for periodic collateral inspections by the ABL lender's representative, rights to periodically charge the borrower for an updated appraisal, identification of any assets that are in the possession of third parties, and submission of an annual budget. Frequently, ABL loan agreements will require the borrower to maintain *minimum excess availability*, which effectively requires the borrower to pay for a loan that is larger than the amount that it can borrow.

Another common feature of asset-based loans involves a *lockbox account*—usually located at the lender's financial institution—into which all cash inflows, such as collection of accounts receivable from customers, must be deposited. This enables the lender to keep a close eye on the company's cash flow and to gain access to the cash in the lockbox as a remedy following a default. Therefore, distressed companies that refinance a cash flow loan with an asset-based loan will need to rearrange their cash management practices, including (1) updating wiring information and account numbers for customers to provide payment, (2) setting up the lockbox account for cash inflows and a separate operating account for cash outflows, (3) expecting a regular cash flow sweep from the lockbox account to pay down the revolver balance, and (4) getting used to formally requesting revolver draws frequently to provide cash in the operating account to pay upcoming invoices to vendors, payroll to employees, and other disbursements. If a company's finance department was accustomed to maintaining large cash balances in bank accounts and remaining unconcerned about the exact timing of cash inflows and outflows, converting to the cash management practices required by an ABL lender may be a startling, time-consuming change.

Like other lenders, ABL lenders will probably charge closing fees, prepayment penalties, unused line fees on revolvers, and reimbursement of legal bills and other out-of-pocket expenses. The borrower will need to balance incurring charges for unused availability with the risk of suffering suppressed availability that the company will eventually need.

The last section of this chapter discusses general considerations for acquisition financing that also apply to asset-based financing.

How are advance rates determined?

With respect to advance rates, every situation is different in terms of the nature of the collateral, the state of the industry, the competitiveness of the credit markets, and the strength of the borrower's internal accounting controls. The ABL lender will typically reevaluate these issues twice a year and may adjust the advance rates (typically only downward) if there has been a material change. After all of these considerations have been taken into account, a lender will then impose ineligibility limitations on the applicability of the stated advance rates, resulting in *net advance rates* that actually govern the amount of availability under the borrowing base.

In a typical situation, eligible receivables will be those that are not more than 90 days old or past due, have been created in the normal course of business, arise from bona fide sales of goods or services to financially sound parties unrelated to the borrower or its affiliates, and are not subject to offset, counterclaim, or other disputes. Many ABL lenders will also impose ineligibility requirements to address customer concentration issues and foreign accounts receivable. The ABL lender will then advance up to a specified percentage (typically 70 to 90 percent) of eligible receivables.

ABL loans also typically advance amounts against a company's inventory. To be eligible, inventory will generally have to be of the kind normally sold by the borrower (if the borrower is in the business of selling goods) and will be limited to finished goods that are boxed and ready for sale, not in the hands of or in transit to a customer. In such circumstances, an advance rate of 50 percent is not uncommon. Odd lots of finished goods are likely to receive lower advance rates. In addition, in many circumstances, ABL lenders will lend against raw materials or work-in-process inventory. However, a lower advance rate—perhaps 15 percent—will be applied to such unfinished goods because of the problems an

ABL lender would experience in attempting to liquidate them. For example, there may be a limited market for raw materials that are not sold by the original manufacturer, and work in progress may be totally unsalable without investing time and capital to create a finished good. Finally, ABL lenders may also impose an *inventory sublimit*—an absolute dollar ceiling on the amount of inventory to which the advance can be applied. The inventory sublimit attempts to strike an artificial balance between the percentage of the lender's collateral arising from receivables and that arising from inventory in the overall ABL loan.

For a quick back-of-the-envelope estimate of a company's total availability to get started, a good rule of thumb for net advance rates is

- *Accounts receivable:* 75 percent of NOLV
- *Inventory:* 50 percent of NOLV
- *Property, plant, and equipment:* 10 percent of NOLV
- *Intangibles:* 0 percent

If NOLV is not readily available, you can substitute book value for a preliminary evaluation. It will then become important to remember to inquire about the differences between book value and NOLV during due diligence.

As noted in this example, an ABL lender may be unwilling to agree to an advance rate for hard-to-value assets like intangibles (e.g., trademarks, patents, customer lists, and blueprints). Even though the borrower receives no availability as a result, ABL lenders will typically still require that their liens include this collateral, which is known as *boot collateral*. This is one of the reasons why borrowers turn to ABL lenders as a last resort.

For businesses that experience noticeable swings in net working capital throughout the year, ABL lenders are likely to impose seasonally adjusted advance rates on inventory, reflecting that some inventory is more valuable at certain times of year than at others. For example, stockpiles of conversation heart candies are less valuable around Memorial Day than right before Valentine's Day. Under these circumstances, ABL lenders may even agree to advance more than 100 percent of cost at certain times of the year, reflecting the marketplace reality that NOLV will exceed costs (i.e., it will reflect the markup between wholesale prices and costs).

Under certain circumstances—not all of them welcome—an ABL lender may agree to allow the loan balance to exceed the total availability calculated by the borrowing base. These situations are known as *overadvances* (or, cynically, as an *airball*). By agreeing to overadvances, ABL lenders are essentially moving beyond asset-based lending and returning to evaluating the loan on a cash flow basis.

What is a borrowing base?

A *borrowing base* is a requirement, agreed to by both the borrower and the ABL lender, concerning the amount and quality of assets that the borrower must have in order to borrow from the lender. The borrower must regularly provide a *borrowing base certificate* to the lender, reporting the balance of each asset category included in the borrowing base (e.g., receivables, inventory, and so on), deducting ineligibles, applying the advance rates to the eligible assets in each category, calculating the total availability, comparing the total availability to the maximum loan amount, and reporting the excess availability, if any. It is common for ABL lenders to require stressed and distressed companies to provide borrowing base certificates weekly. Typically, the company's chief financial officer must sign off on each borrowing base certificate.

Are there any other conditions that apply to subsequent draws on the revolving line of credit in an ABL loan?

Yes. In most loan agreements, the lender's obligation to honor subsequent draws upon the revolver is subject to a variety of conditions beyond the borrowing base. Chief among them is reaffirmation by the borrower that the original representations and warranties made in the loan agreement are still true and valid. Typical representations and warranties that are included in loan agreements are discussed later in this chapter in the section about acquisition financing. For example, the borrower may need to represent each time that there have been no material adverse changes in the business and that no covenant default exists. If the requisite conditions are not met, the lender is not required to lend. These conditions may pose challenges for distressed companies as their situation deteriorates, leaving executives with the ethical dilemma of whether to be dishonest when reaffirming representations and warranties in order to continue accessing the liquidity they need if they are to keep the company afloat. Therefore, both borrower and lender should pay careful attention to whether the required representations and warranties are realistic and appropriate, given the context of the loan, to avoid a prompt default after closing or to create untrustworthy relationships.

REFINANCING METHODS: FACTORING RECEIVABLES

What is factoring?

Factoring is a type of short-term financing obtained through the outright sale of accounts receivable to a third party, known as a *factor*. Factors may be independent companies specializing in this type of financing, or they may be subsidiaries of other companies, such as banks. A sale to a factor is usually *nonrecourse*—that is, the factor pays the company a discounted rate for the accounts receivable and takes its chances on getting repaid, having no recourse if the bills are uncollectible. The discount is usually 10 to 20 percent of the face value of the invoice. Distressed companies may resort to factoring their receivables to increase liquidity, but they will sacrifice profitability if they do so because of the discount involved. For example, if a company sells a product for $100,000 at 25 percent gross margin ($25,000) to a customer on 45-day terms and then factors the receivable at 90 percent to get the cash promptly ($90,000), it will lose 10 points of gross margin ($10,000), for a resulting profitability of only 15 percent ($15,000).

REFINANCING METHODS: TERMING OUT PAYABLES

What does terming out payables entail?

When a company becomes distressed, its vendors are likely to be one of the first groups to notice: they begin to realize that the company is taking longer to pay their bills, they need to call the company's accounts payable department more frequently and receive responses that are less satisfactory, and their orders may stop following previous patterns and returns may become more common. As discussed in Chapter 6 of this book, vendors receive general unsecured claims for unpaid invoices if the company enters bankruptcy.

Therefore, as vendors become nervous about a company's future, they often tighten their payment terms—such as requiring cash-on-delivery (COD) terms—and attempt to minimize any write-downs or write-offs in the event that the company files a voluntary bankruptcy petition.

In this context, if a company wants to pursue an out-of-court workout to avoid a Chapter 11 reorganization, it may need to go to its vendors and renegotiate payment terms for overdue invoices (e.g., invoices that are more than 90 days past due). Clearly, the company will be in no condition to pay all of its overdue invoices in full. Although the vendors will feel that they deserve full payment because they provided goods or services to the company, they will eventually need to concede that they would receive only partial recoveries in a Chapter 11 reorganization. Therefore, the phrase *terming out payables* refers to the occasional practice in which a distressed company agrees with its vendors to make partial or full payments of overdue invoices over a much longer period of time, perhaps 18 months or two years. In effect, the company attempts to transform current liabilities into long-term debt. The exact details will depend upon the company's circumstances, including how much cash it can pay the vendors upon signing the agreement, how much the vendors would be likely to receive in a hypothetical bankruptcy, and how persuasive the management team can be during emotional and stressful conversations with irate vendors. Because terming out payables is often unfamiliar territory for its employees, distressed companies may seek the expertise of turnaround consultants to manage negotiations with vendors.

REFINANCING METHODS: DEBT EXCHANGE OFFERS

What is a debt exchange offer?

A *debt exchange offer* (or simply an *exchange offer*) is a debt-for-debt exchange that enables a company to refinance its existing debt on a noncash basis by offering existing bondholders the opportunity to exchange their existing bonds (typically trading at a significant discount to face value) for newly issued debt. This new debt frequently has a face amount equal to, or slightly higher than, the current market value of the existing debt. It usually also has a later maturity date than the existing bonds. In so doing, the company has both reduced its total outstanding indebtedness and extended its maturity schedule. In favorable capital markets, the company may even be able to reduce its cost of borrowing (i.e., coupon or interest rate) as well.

As an inducement to enter into such an exchange, the company frequently will offer bondholders two important credit enhancements (in addition to the modest increase in face value over current market value): (1) new debt that is more senior in the company's capital structure than the existing bonds, and (2) in some cases, a higher coupon rate than current market rates for similarly rated companies. Thus, not only is there an incentive to tender into the offer, but there is also a strong disincentive to *not* tender, as nontendering holders of the existing debt will find themselves "leapfrogged" in the capital structure. Recent examples of debt exchange offers include those by Realogy Corporation, Harrah's Entertainment, and ResCap.

To illustrate, assume that XYZ Corp. has three tranches of debt: (1) a $100 million senior secured credit facility; (2) $200 million of senior subordinated bonds; and (3) $300 million of junior subordinated bonds. The coupon and maturity dates of each tranche are summarized in Exhibit 14-2. Assume further that the junior subordinated bonds are trading at 35 cents on the dollar as a result of XYZ Corp.'s financial distress, and that XYZ Corp. had previously carved out approval in its existing credit agreements to issue an incremental senior secured bank debt facility with a second lien.

Exhibit 14-2 Example of a Debt Exchange Offer

Existing Debt	Face Value	Coupon	Maturity
Senior secured debt, first lien	$100	8.00%	Jan 2014
Senior secured debt, second lien	$ 0	N/A	N/A
Senior subordinated debt	$200	9.00%	Jan 2015
Junior subordinated debt	$300	10.00%	Jan 2011
Total debt and weighted averages	$600	9.33%	27 months

After Debt Exchange	Face Value	Coupon	Maturity
Senior secured debt, first lien	$100	8.00%	Jan 2014
Senior secured debt, second lien	$120	10.00%	Jan 2014
Senior subordinated debt	$200	9.00%	Jan 2015
Junior subordinated debt	$ 0	N/A	N/A
Total debt and weighted averages	$420	9.05%	47 months

Note: USD in millions

XYZ could tender for the junior subordinated bonds at 40 cents on the dollar (almost a 15 percent premium to the current market value) in exchange for second-lien senior secured bank debt maturing on January 1, 2014. If the tender offer is successful, XYZ Corp. would reduce its overall indebtedness by $180 million (or 30 percent), lower the effective interest rate on its entire debt structure to 9.05 percent from 9.33 percent, and extend its weighted average maturity to 47 months from 27 months. (See Exhibit 14-2.) While this may not fix whatever fundamental business issues XYZ Corp. might be facing, it at least buys the company some breathing room. It would also increase XYZ's book value by $180 million, or the amount of the cancellation of debt (COD) income.

The "catch" in this scenario is that XYZ Corp. would have to pay income tax on the $180 million of COD income, as described in Chapter 8 of this book. However, as also described in that chapter, the American Recovery and Reinvestment Tax Act of 2009 allows companies to defer until 2014 the recognition of such income arising in 2009 or 2010, at which point the income must be reported ratably over a five-year period. In addition, the company may have net operating losses (NOLs) that absorb this tax gain—particularly if the company's financial performance has been fading over time and the company has been unprofitable in recent years.

Are these transactions sometimes considered "coercive"?

Yes. The "leapfrog" dilemma can brand them as "coercive debt exchanges."

REFINANCING METHODS: DEBT-FOR-EQUITY SWAPS

What is a debt-for-equity swap?

In a *debt-for-equity swap*, a company exchanges debt for a predetermined amount of equity. The value of a swap in such cases is usually determined by current market valuations. However, as in a coercive debt exchange, the issuer may offer a higher exchange value to give debt holders an incentive to tender. A company might select a debt-for-equity swap, rather than a debt-for-debt exchange in order to maintain a debt-to-equity ratio below some targeted level or to avoid interest payments or future maturities on such debt.

Exhibit 14-3 Example Debt-for-Equity Swap

Existing Capital Structure	Face Value	Coupon	Interest Expense
Senior secured debt, first lien	$100	8.00%	$ 8
Senior subordinated debt	$200	9.00%	$18
Junior subordinated debt	$300	10.00%	$30
Shareholders' equity (book value)	$100	N/A	N/A
Debt/equity ratio and annual interest	6.0×		$56

Pro Forma Capital Structure	Face Value	Coupon	Interest Expense
Senior secured debt, first lien	$100	8.00%	$ 8
Senior subordinated debt	$200	9.00%	$18
Junior subordinated debt	$150	10.00%	$15
Shareholders' equity (book value)	$160	N/A	N/A
Debt/equity ratio and annual interest	2.8×		$41

Note: USD in millions

Exhibit 14-3 illustrates an example. Assume that rather than offering junior subordinated bondholders a debt-for-debt exchange, XYZ Corp. announces an exchange offer for half of the outstanding bonds (still trading at 35 cents on the dollar) at a 15 percent premium to market value. This offer would reduce the amount of junior subordinated debt to $150 million from $300 million. In so doing, XYZ Corp. would issue $60 million of new equity ($150 million of face value × 35 cents on the dollar × 15 percent market premium). The transaction would also lower XYZ Corp.'s debt-to-equity ratio to 2.8× from 6.0×, and its annual interest expense to $41 million from $56 million.

REFINANCING METHODS: RIGHTS OFFERINGS AND WARRANTS

What is a rights offering?

There are many different varieties of *rights offerings* with many different names. Such an offering is also sometimes referred to as *preemptive rights*, *subscription rights*, and *oversubscription privileges*. At its core, a rights offering involves a company's providing existing investors with *rights certificates* that give them the short-term right, but not the obligation, to purchase new shares in the company, at a specified price (the *subscription price*), before the company sells shares to new investors (typically, the public). In most cases, the subscription price is set lower than the current market price. (While no financial terms have been set in stone in recent years, a 20 percent discount to projected market value is relatively common.) Where the rights certificates are issued to shareholders, such shareholders usually receive one right for each share of stock owned as of the *rights record date.*

From the shareholders' perspective, a rights offering offers preexisting investors an opportunity to avoid dilution and thus maintain their proportionate ownership of the company after the financing. From the company's standpoint, a benefit of selling shares to existing shareholders is that marketing costs will be less than those for selling to the general public.

A rights offering is not only relevant in a workout scenario; in fact, the alternative is also increasingly common in bankruptcy—particularly as a component of the plan of reorganization and the exit financing package.[2] Creditors are offered the right, based on the size of their claims, to purchase securities issued by the reorganized debtor upon emergence from bankruptcy. This structure often includes an *oversubscription feature* (also known as a *backstop*): in exchange for the right to buy additional securities, sponsoring creditors usually agree to purchase some or all of the securities that are not sold during the initial offering. (In contrast, an "uninsured" rights offering would be one in which there is no third-party agreement to pre-purchase the unsubscribed rights.)

This oversubscription feature can be very effective. Claim holders who find the credit appealing can purchase additional securities, often at attractive prices, when the market for a debtor's securities is otherwise illiquid. When secured debt is being converted to equity, an oversubscription provides a method for holders of unsecured claims to recover a greater share of their claims. In addition, unsecured creditors usually can choose between exchanging their claims for cash or exchanging them for newly issued securities of the debtor. The new securities carry an implied value that exceeds the monetary offer, reflecting the greater risk inherent in owning securities of a company that is emerging from bankruptcy. In addition to receiving securities in exchange for claims, creditors can purchase additional debt or equity securities, on a pro rata basis, according to the value of their claims. This is crucial to a rights offering because it may enable a debtor to raise additional cash apart from an exit financing.

Are rights offerings subject to SEC registration requirements?

Generally no, and the securities issued may be freely traded pursuant to section 1145 of the Bankruptcy Code[3]—provided that the securities satisfy section 1145's "principally/partly" test. This test requires that the overall consideration for the rights certificates must consist "principally" of the existing claim and "partly" of cash or other property. This means that the value of the existing claim must exceed the value of the cash or other property paid in.

The Bankruptcy Code does not define the term *exceed*, although greater than 50 percent should be sufficient.[4] If the rights certificates do not pass this test, they are not freely transferable unless they are formally registered or unless they qualify for another registration exception. As a practical matter, if this occurs, participants and backstop guarantors are likely to force the reorganized debtor to register its securities so that they can sell them. However, registration will limit the ability to dispose of securities quickly on the open market.

What are warrants, and what are usually the key terms?

A *warrant* is the right (but not the obligation) to purchase securities (usually equity) from a company at a specific price on or before a specific date. A warrant is essentially an *option*, with one key difference: the holder of a warrant typically purchases a newly issued security directly from the issuer, whereas the holder of an option usually buys a previously issued and outstanding security from another investor. A warrant is also similar to a rights certificate, discussed previously, except with respect to timing: whereas a warrant might have a term of two to five years, a rights certificate usually expires much faster—in many cases, as soon as one month or less.

Equity warrants might be attached to a credit facility that provides the lender with a so-called *equity kicker*, allowing the lender to capture more financial upside if the company is successful. This feature is particularly common in distressed scenarios, where the prospect of merely earning a fixed return on capital at risk may be insufficient incentive to attract debt financing.

Key provisions in a warrant will address how many shares can be acquired upon exercise of the warrant; the amount of the "exercise price" (the amount to be paid to acquire the shares); the period of time during which exercise may occur (which, to prevent interference with any future sale of the company, should not extend beyond the date of any such sale); any restrictions on transfer of the warrant; and any situations in which the warrant holder may have to register shares or participate in registrations by the company for a public stock offering under the securities laws. There are also lengthy and technical provisions providing for adjustment in the number of shares for which the warrant can be exercised to prevent dilution if there are stock splits or dividends or if shares are sold to others at less than full value.

REFINANCING METHODS: PRIVATE INVESTMENT IN PUBLIC EQUITY (PIPE)

What exactly is a PIPE?

A *PIPE*, or private investment in public equity, is a private placement of publicly traded securities, contractually structured to provide future liquidity through an effective resale registration agreement. The term *PIPE* has also been expanded to include (1) a registered direct offering, (2) a venture/sponsor-style private placement with associated governance considerations, (3) a private "equity line" or equity dribble-out program, and (4) to some extent, a "wall crossed" follow-on offering.[5] Recent examples include KKR's $300 million investment in Eastman Kodak, TPG Capital's $255 million investment in Armstrong World Industries, and Leonard Green's $425 million investment in Whole Foods.

In a *traditional PIPE*, an investor buys a security at a fixed price or a fixed conversion ratio. This security typically involves common stock (sold at a fixed price that is at a discount to the market), convertible debt (which may have either a fixed or floating coupon), and/or convertible preferred stock with a fixed conversion ratio. A *structured PIPE*, in contrast, typically involves a convertible security with an adjustable conversion price that is linked to the market price of the underlying common stock during a period prior to conversion. As with a traditional PIPE, the coupon on a structured PIPE can be either fixed or floating. In any of these scenarios, warrants may also be issued as part of the deal.

Transactions such as these are particularly common when a public company's stock is illiquid, or when the investor insists upon control provisions (e.g., board representation, enhanced voting rights, veto rights, or preemptive rights and antidilution protections) that it ordinarily would not be able to obtain through an open market purchase. PIPEs also offer the benefit of speed (ranging from a few days to several weeks), as a full registration statement is typically not necessary. In certain circumstances, an issuer may be able to sell more than 20 percent of its equity via a PIPE without shareholder approval (a threshold test for both the New York Stock Exchange and Nasdaq), although many technical requirements apply.

REFINANCING METHODS: GOVERNMENT-SUPPORTED TRANSACTIONS

What is an example of a government-supported transaction?

Probably the most common example is a transaction supported by the Federal Deposit Insurance Corporation (FDIC), such as loss sharing on loan portfolios in order to facilitate acquisitions. Despite the recent media focus on such transactions, the FDIC first introduced loss sharing in selected purchase and assumption (P&A) transactions as far back as 1991. The original goals of loss sharing were to (1) sell as many assets as possible to the acquiring bank, and (2) have the nonperforming assets managed and collected by the acquiring bank in a manner that aligned the interests and incentives of the acquiring bank and the FDIC. Under loss sharing, the FDIC agrees to absorb a significant portion of the loss—typically 80 percent—on a specified pool of assets and offering even greater loss protection in the event of financial catastrophe. The acquiring bank is then liable for the remaining portion of the loss. Recent examples include (1) BB&T's acquisition of Colonial Bank, (2) the acquisition of BankUnited by private equity investors WL Ross & Co., Blackstone Group, and Carlyle Group, and (3) the acquisition of IndyMac Bank (renamed OneWest Bank) by hedge fund investors J.C. Flowers & Co., Paulson & Co., MSD Capital, and a fund controlled by famed investor George Soros. For a thorough discussion of the FDIC's loss sharing transactions, we recommend *Managing the Crisis: The FDIC and RTC Experience,*[6] which examines the challenges faced by the FDIC and the Resolution Trust Corporation (RTC) in dealing with troubled banks and thrifts during the financial crisis of the late 1980s and early 1990s.

Other examples of government-supported transactions include the bankruptcies of General Motors and Chrysler. These cases are highlighted in Chapter 3.

POST-PETITION FINANCING CONSIDERATIONS

How can a debtor obtain post-petition secured financing to fund its reorganization throughout its bankruptcy case?

A DIP (debtor-in-possession) loan is post-petition secured debt that is used to fund a company's operations during a bankruptcy proceeding. Most DIP loans are asset-based revolving credit facilities for working capital purposes, so the explanation of ABL loans earlier in this chapter applies to DIP loans. As with other credit facilities, there may be one lender or an agent plus a syndicate of lenders.

Historically, DIP lending typically was done by commercial banks and specialized finance companies that funded moderate-sized facilities—up to a few hundred million dollars.[7] Over the last several years, however, many larger DIP facilities have been brought to market, including a $1.0 billion deal for Quebecor World, Inc. in 2008; a $1.75 billion deal for Dana Corp. in 2006; and a $1.7 billion deal for Delta Air Lines in 2005, and the investor base for DIP loans expanded to institutional lenders, hedge funds, and CDOs/CLOs.[8] As explained by The Deal Pipeline:[9]

> Despite the credit crunch, 2009 was a record-setting year for debtor-in-possession financing by almost any measure. . . . [Excluding] DIPs lent by the U.S. Treasury Department and Export Development Canada in the megabankruptcies of General Motors Corp. (which received $33.3 billion in DIP financing) and Chrysler LLC ($4.96 billion) . . ., debtors had secured $21.41 billion in DIP financing through Nov. 15, still more than 2008's total and way ahead of the pace through the same period in 2006 and 2007.

Exhibit 14-4 gives the volume of DIP loans raised in recent years.

Exhibit 14-4 Bankruptcy Financing: Debtor-in-Possession Lending

Year	No. of Deals	Volume ($bill.)
2001	85	$7.7
2002	130	13.6
2003	134	7.6
2004	151	7.7
2005	165	14.0
2006	218	9.5
2007	235	13.6
2008	345	18.6
2009	404	62.4

Source: The Deal Pipeline

In theory, DIP loans should be the safest investments for lenders to make, with risks akin to those of Treasury bills but much higher yield from interest and fees. After all, the lender already knows that the business is in severe financial distress, so the underwriting assumptions can be very conservative. Moreover, the DIP lender is the first party to be repaid at the end of the bankruptcy proceeding, giving it the best position in the capital structure, called a *superpriority claim*. In addition, the assets are under the supervision of the bankruptcy court, giving the DIP lender extra protection from the misdeeds of the borrower or other creditors. Furthermore, the bankruptcy process provides increased transparency for the company's operations and affairs. Finally, while technical defaults are common because the uncertainty of operating in bankruptcy makes it difficult to set financial covenants accurately, it is extremely infrequent for debtors to experience a payment default on DIP loans. As illustrated in Exhibit 14-5, DIP loans have become sufficiently mainstream that they are rated by rating agencies.[10]

Despite an overall default rate of approximately 0.5 percent and attractive asset coverage ratios,[11] however, not all DIP loans are safe bets. Notable examples of bankruptcy cases involving a DIP loan that suffered a payment default include

- *Marvel Entertainment Group.* After Marvel filed a voluntary bankruptcy petition in December 1996, competing plans of reorganization filed by Ronald Perelman and Carl Icahn

Exhibit 14-5 Public, Unmonitored DIP Loan Ratings Assigned by Moody's

Debtor in Possession	Date Rated	Facility Description	Rating
Buffet's Inc.	4/23/2008	$85MM DIP Term Loan (New Money)	Ba3
		$200MM DIP Term Loan (Roll-over)	B3
Dana	3/28/2006	$750MM DIP Revolver	B3
Corporation		$700MM DIP Term Loan	B3
	1/11/2007	$650MM DIP Revolver	B1
		$900MM DIP Term Loan	B2
Delphi	11/7/2005	$1.75 Billion DIP Revolver	B1
Corporation		$250MM DIP Term Loan	B1
Northwest Airlines, Inc.	8/9/2006	$1.225 DIP Facility	Ba2
Quebecor	2/11/2008	$400MM DIP Revolver	Ba2
World, Inc.		$600MM DIP Term Loan	Ba3
R.J. Tower	4/6/2005	$300MM DIP Revolver	Ba2
Corporation		$425MM DIP Term Loan	Ba3

resulted in a stalemate. As a result, the $100 million DIP loan was not repaid to a lender group headed by Chase Manhattan Bank at its June 1997 scheduled maturity date. The DIP lenders consented to a forbearance agreement and received current interest and partial principal amortization until Marvel emerged from bankruptcy in October 1998. At exit, the DIP loan was fully repaid, but not as contemplated by the loan agreement's original payment terms.

■ *Winstar Communications.* Winstar filed a voluntary bankruptcy petition in April 2001 as a result of a liquidity crunch that management blamed on Lucent Technologies' failure to honor its contractual commitments. Lenders CIBC, Citicorp, Credit Suisse First Boston, Bank of New York, and Chase Manhattan Bank provided Winstar with a DIP loan of up to $300 million. Subsequently, industry issues, including the crash of the telecom bubble and excess capacity, resulted in futile restructuring efforts by the debtor and its creditors. Furthermore, the debtor spent millions of dollars of its scarce liquidity on post-petition litigation with Lucent. Ultimately, Winstar's assets were sold in December 2001 for $38 million, implying a recovery in the 20 to 30 percent range for the DIP lenders. However, the DIP lenders also received rights to Winstar's litigation against Lucent, hired separate counsel, and succeeded in characterizing Lucent as an insider for the purpose of voidable preference claims, which significantly strengthened their case.[12]

What is required for the bankruptcy court to approve a DIP loan?

Occasionally, a company has sufficient cash collateral to continue funding its operations without incurring a DIP loan. However, if a company is experiencing enough financial distress to prompt a bankruptcy filing, then its available cash is usually insufficient to fund its operations. The Bankruptcy Code provides certain requirements for obtaining bankruptcy court approval for post-petition financing in either a Chapter 7 liquidation or a Chapter 11 reorganization. First, a debtor is required to seek unsecured, post-petition debt for the estate in the ordinary course of business (e.g., payment terms from vendors) that will receive priority payment as an administrative expense (see Chapter 4 of this book).[13] Next, if that approach proves insufficient, a debtor may request that the bankruptcy court approve unsecured post-petition debt outside of the ordinary course of business (e.g., new unsecured notes) that will receive priority payment as an administrative expense.[14] If offering funding sources administrative expense status that ranks *pari passu* with the debtor's other administrative expenses fails to attract sufficient capital, then the debtor can request that the bankruptcy court approve the estate's incurring debt on one of the following terms:[15]

- Unsecured post-petition debt that will receive administrative expense status, but with priority payment over all other administrative expenses
- Secured post-petition debt with a lien on unencumbered property of the estate (assuming that such property exists)

- Secured post-petition debt with a junior lien on encumbered property of the estate (which can be problematic if one or more junior liens already existed pre-petition)

As a last resort, if the debtor can demonstrate that all of these tactics have proved inadequate to attract sufficient capital to fund the business during the bankruptcy proceeding, then the debtor may request that the bankruptcy court approve the estate's incurring secured post-petition debt with a senior or equal lien on encumbered property.[16] However, the debtor must also demonstrate that the interests of the holders of the existing pre-petition liens on such encumbered property are adequately protected (see Chapter 5 of this book for details on adequate protection).[17] The debtor has the burden of proof with respect to adequate protection in these circumstances.[18]

Given this framework, Congress appears to have intended for debtors to incur secured post-petition debt with first liens on the property of their estates only under extreme conditions. However, DIP loan markets are often inefficient, with few parties that are willing to devote the time and effort of underwriting, negotiation, and documentation. Therefore, DIP lenders typically face no consequences for demanding the best position and protection possible, knowing that the distressed company really has no viable alternatives. As a result, the last resort alternative has become much more common than Congress may have originally intended it to be. When the pre-petition secured lenders agree to become the post-petition secured lenders (in exchange for converting their pre-petition secured claims into post-petition secured claims in addition to advancing fresh capital), this is called a *rollover DIP loan*. When a new funding source becomes the post-petition secured lender (maintaining the status quo with the pre-petition secured lenders), this is called a *new money DIP loan*, which may also be a *priming loan* if the liens provided to the new money DIP loan result in the subordination of the liens of the pre-petition secured lenders (as opposed to the new money DIP loan paying off all of the pre-petition secured claims). Each of these situations is discussed further in this chapter. Also, there may be a hybrid scenario in which the new funding source receives first liens on some property while the pre-petition secured lenders retain their first liens on other property and receive second liens on the property securing the new money DIP loan.

In addition to the Bankruptcy Code's requirements, an increasing number of bankruptcy courts have enacted local rules or general orders that specify procedures and restrictions for DIP loans. Therefore, the parties should review these regulations for the relevant jurisdiction prior to completing negotiations regarding the DIP loan agreement. Otherwise, they may be unpleasantly surprised when they arrive in court seeking approval for their agreed-upon terms.

What considerations should a prospective lender keep in mind before making a post-petition loan?

First and foremost, a new lender should consider competition with existing pre-petition lenders. If there is excess collateral value above and beyond the amount of the pre-petition senior lender's loan, its secured claim is deemed to be oversecured; in such a case, a bankruptcy court might hold that the pre-petition senior lender has *adequate protection*, as long as the *equity cushion* is significant enough (Chapter 5 of this book explores these concepts in greater detail). This may open the door to an incremental post-petition loan secured by the excess collateral. Key considerations that a prospective lender should keep in mind in such circumstances include the following:

- What is the nature, extent, and value of the existing collateral?
- What adequate protection is necessary for use of the cash collateral?
- Is a priming lien available?

In general, it is usually unwise to engage in a legal battle regarding priming liens because it is too costly and difficult to prevail. Therefore, if the pre-petition senior lenders are undersecured (i.e., the value of the company's collateral is insufficient to cover the amount of the senior loans), then a prospective lender might want to avoid the opportunity altogether. Otherwise, the prospective lender may find itself becoming an innocent bystander drawn into litigation between the debtor and its pre-petition senior lenders over priming liens. Ultimately, the debtor may agree to pursue a rollover DIP loan with its pre-petition senior lenders, leaving the prospective lender with nothing to show for its time-consuming efforts. These issues are discussed later in this chapter.

Whether the pre-petition senior lenders are oversecured or undersecured, the prospective lender should consider its bargaining stance with both the company and competing new lenders. Factors to consider might involve

- Does the company really need the new loan? Or is the company looking at it as a public relations tool or as an insurance policy against a future asset sale?
- Does the company have a substantial number of unencumbered assets? This may increase competition for the post-petition loan.
- Are there any imperfections in the liens of the pre-petition senior lenders? If so, there may be additional collateral available for post-petition liens.
- Is there a controlling shareholder that may want to issue the loan instead of allowing a third-party lender to step in? Courts will often scrutinize the terms of such insider loans before approving them. A third party lender may be wasting its time if its term sheet is being used to prove that an insider's proposal is reasonable.

Can a pre-petition secured lender become a DIP lender?

Yes. There is no legal restriction on a pre-petition secured lender's becoming a DIP lender. In fact, becoming the DIP lender may be a smart strategy for the pre-petition lender because bankruptcy courts will often permit a pre-petition lender to roll over its pre-petition loan into the post-petition DIP loan, thereby promptly resolving any issues with its pre-petition claims, such as defects in improperly perfected liens. It is generally easier for the debtor to choose the pre-petition lender to become its DIP lender to avoid contentious litigation over adequate protection or priming. Naturally, unsecured creditors that are seeking to challenge the lender's pre-petition secured claims will object to rollover treatment, but they may need to acquiesce if no alternative capital sources are available. Once the bankruptcy court's approval of the DIP lender's superpriority claim has become final and non-appealable, the post-petition lien is no longer subject to challenge.

A rollover may involve a gradual process in which collections of pre-petition accounts receivable are used to pay down the pre-petition loan. Alternatively, the lender may advance a new post-petition loan to pay off the pre-petition loan in its entirety, thereby converting the lender's pre-petition loan to a post-petition loan.

A rollover will attract intense scrutiny from the bankruptcy court and the U.S. trustee because it circumvents the Bankruptcy Code. The lender may be trying to improve its undersecured position early in the bankruptcy case, when the valuation of its collateral remains vague and other parties are not yet ready to challenge the lender's status. In addition, the lender may require other parties to waive their ability to challenge the enforceability of the lender's pre-petition credit agreement and the validity of its liens, perhaps in violation of the debtor's fiduciary duties to other creditors. Moreover, the DIP lender may be able to use its leverage to extract procedural protections for its post-petition claims that would not have been available for its pre-petition claims. Furthermore, early in the case, when a DIP loan is being negotiated, it is often difficult to estimate the ultimate amount of administrative expenses, which could affect the recoveries to the lender's pre-petition secured claims but are paid after the amounts due on the lender's post-petition claims.

A potential purchaser can glean information about the case by examining the actions of the pre-petition secured lender. The pre-petition lender is often in the best position to become the DIP lender because it is already familiar with the company's business, collateral, management, and capital structure. Therefore, its advance rates on the assets provide informed guidance regarding the floor of value for those assets. On the other hand, the pre-petition lender may be tired of the loan and want to have it refinanced by fresh capital, signaling that there may be underlying issues with the industry, company, and/or management that should concern a potential purchaser as well. For similar reasons, a potential purchaser may also examine the interest rate and fees being charged by a DIP lender compared to those in other bankruptcy cases to assess whether the company may involve extraordinary risks. The cost of the DIP loan may also indicate the pricing of the acquisition financing that the potential purchaser may use to buy the company in a 363 sale.

What are the advantages to an existing, pre-petition lender of making a post-petition loan?

The Bankruptcy Code, as well as certain practicalities of the corporate reorganization process, provides many incentives for a pre-petition senior lender to continue to support a debtor after the company has filed for bankruptcy protection.

First, as noted earlier in this chapter, becoming the DIP lender may be a smart strategy for the pre-petition lender because bankruptcy courts will often permit a pre-petition lender to roll over its pre-petition loan into the DIP loan, thereby promptly resolving any issues with its pre-petition claims. These might include improving the pre-petition lender's priority, validating pre-petition liens, reducing the threat of litigation, and obtaining waivers to any avoidance claims (such as preferences and fraudulent transfers) against the lender.

Similarly, the lender might attempt, as a condition for extending a post-petition loan, to *cross-collateralize* both its pre-petition and post-petition loans and advances against the debtor's post-petition assets. This request would be subject to court approval; it is also worth mentioning that this strategy has met with mixed success historically. Frequently, the likelihood that a court will approve such a request hinges on whether the cross-collateralization is *forward* (i.e., the lender is seeking a lien on pre-petition collateral to secure post-petition debt) or *backward* (i.e., the lender is seeking a lien on post-petition collateral for outstanding pre-petition indebtedness). Courts are more likely to approve forward cross-collateralization on the theory that the lender is not improving the position of an existing claim, but rather is merely exacting a lien on or interest in what may well be the only tangible assets that the debtor can offer as security for future advances. In contrast, some courts have denied a request for backward cross-collateralization under the argument that the action would constitute an *ex parte* (i.e., without notice) derogation of other creditors' rights.

Third, the debtor's continued existence as a going concern might be critical to the value of the pre-petition lender's collateral. Thus, facilitating working capital to the debtor may, in effect, be in the lender's self-interest. Likewise, the pre-petition lender may be able to sign a DIP financing agreement that enhances its control over its pre-petition and post-petition collateral.

Fourth, unlike other pre-petition lenders, the senior lender that rolls into a DIP loan will frequently increase the likelihood that it will be paid interest at the contract rate on its pre-petition debt.

Finally, the action may minimize the risk of alternative financing and a priming fight, as well as litigation over adequate protection issues.

Can a new money DIP loan cause the liens of a pre-petition lender to be subordinated?

While the legal answer is yes, the practical answer is no. A *priming loan* is a theoretical form of a new money DIP loan in which the debtor borrows secured post-petition debt from a new lender in exchange for granting a senior or equal lien on encumbered property.[19] If it is permitted by the bankruptcy court, this action would subordinate—called *priming*—the liens of the pre-petition secured lenders.

In nearly every situation, a priming loan is legally impractical because of the significantly contentious litigation—known as a *priming fight*—that will inevitably result regarding whether the new money DIP loan should gain priority repayment terms over any pre-petition secured debts of the company. A priming fight will also involve bitter arguments regarding the valuation of the company's collateral, whether capital is realistically available on less onerous terms, and whether the pre-petition secured creditors are adequately protected (e.g., by an equity cushion). The pre-petition secured creditors will vigorously contest the implications of impairing their security interests in the debtor's collateral, including infringing on their constitutional property rights in the estate. All of these issues will inevitably drive up administrative expenses, increase uncertainty in the marketplace when the newly bankrupt debtor is highly vulnerable, and harm relationships among parties who eventually will need to agree on a plan of reorganization. Therefore, finding a compromise to avoid a full-blown priming fight is almost always the best option. A compromise could include paying down some or all of the pre-petition secured claims, pursuing a hybrid scenario with a partial new money DIP loan and partial rollover DIP loan, increasing the post-petition interest rate for the pre-petition secured creditors, paying a fee to the pre-petition secured creditors, and/or agreeing to a certain course of action during the bankruptcy case, such as a 363 sale.

What has been the impact of intercreditor agreements and second-lien debt on DIP loans?

The current wave of business bankruptcy cases has been shaped by the dramatic rise of second-lien debt and intercreditor agreements. Because companies are entering Chapter 11 reorganization with notably more secured debt than in previous periods, little collateral is available to secure post-petition financing. Indeed, the second-lien lenders may already be underwater, leaving no room for a DIP lender's secured claims without an undesirable priming fight. As one academic study discovered:[20]

> With the debtors' balance sheets overly-encumbered, the use of cash collateral and DIP financing approval were the most contentious issues creditors faced with second lien lenders. Despite provisions in intercreditor agreements that address the use of cash collateral and approval of DIP financing, approval of both were issues in 10 of the 16 cases examined (Dura Automotive, Aerosol Packaging, Werner, Calpine, Performance Transportation Systems, American Remanufacturers, New World Pasta, Meridian Automotive, Tower Automotive, and Westpoint Stevens). Second lien lenders have not been hesitant to challenge cash collateral and DIP financing waivers on the basis of the enforceability of these waivers, adequate protection of their collateral and the priming of their debt. . . .
>
> The difficulty of securing DIP approval from second lien lenders is compounded by the fact that often an opportunistic hedge fund is the first lien lender providing the DIP, and the hedge fund will subject the debtor to onerous and punitive covenants that reduce the possible recovery of second lien lenders. For example, second lien lenders objected to expensive DIP financing provided by Black Diamond Capital in both the Werner and New World Pasta bankruptcies, and second lien lenders objected to the costs of DIP financing provided by first lien lender Credit Suisse in the Meridian bankruptcy.

How are DIP loans eventually paid off?

The loan agreements for DIP loans will include a maturity date, which is usually the earlier of the consummation of the plan of reorganization and the target time frame for completing the bankruptcy case. However, predicting this time frame is an inexact science, so the debtor may need to negotiate one or more extensions, which are likely to involve another fee for the lender. In unusual cases, the debtor may refinance a DIP loan from one lender with a subsequent DIP loan from another lender. Upon the consummation of a plan of reorganization, the exit financing to fund the plan must, as a practical matter, provide for paying off the DIP loan. However, it is common for the DIP lender to agree to fund the exit financing as well. In such circumstances, the DIP loan effectively rolls over into the exit financing, much like pre-petition loans can roll over into DIP loans. Plans of reorganization and exit financing are discussed further in Chapter 12 of this book.

FINANCING USING CONTINGENCY PAYMENTS

Why do acquisitions of distressed businesses include contingency payments as part of the deal structure?

Outside of bankruptcy, many leveraged acquisitions involve contingency payments structured with a takeback by the seller of debt, stock, or a portion of the future earnings stream. This is particularly likely to occur if there are material outstanding issues at the end of due diligence, there is significant uncertainty about the company's future prospects, there is pressure to get a deal closed quickly, and/or the parties have trouble agreeing on the purchase price. Contingency payments are often an effective means of compromising in negotiations to get a deal closed rather than having both sides walk away. In such deals, the seller takes only part of the purchase price in cash, with the understanding that the buyer will pay more if certain conditions (i.e., contingencies) are met.

While contingency payments are possible in out-of-court workouts and inherent in many plans of reorganization, they are less compatible with 363 sales, which normally require that qualified bids involve cash only.

What are seller notes, and why do acquisitions of distressed businesses use them?

In one form of contingency payment, the seller takes back a note from the buyer in lieu of cash. Sometimes the note has a junior lien on the company's assets. If the note is subordinated to other debt, it is called a *seller's subordinated note* or simply a *seller note*.

If debt is taken back, it may be structured as a simple installment sale, or it may involve accompanying warrants. In either case, the claims of the seller are generally junior to those of other creditors, such as the senior lenders to the buyer.

In essence, a seller note is akin to a very large escrow. Typically, most acquisitions require that a portion of the cash paid be held back in an escrow account for a period of time. If the seller breaches representations or warranties in the purchase agreement, then the buyer may look to the cash in the escrow account before needing to collect directly from the seller. Similarly, if there is a seller note, the buyer may cease payments on it as a remedy for breaches of representations and warranties by the seller.

Therefore, because the seller knows that the seller note will give the buyer leverage in post-closing litigation or arbitration, the seller is more likely to be accurate and thorough in its disclosures during due diligence and legal documentation.

A seller note is probably an impractical solution for paying stockholders of publicly held companies because of the delays and disclosures involved in getting a prospectus registered under federal securities laws to accompany the offer of debt or other securities.

Why do sellers consider takeback financing, including junior class financing?

Sellers are generally reluctant to take back stock or debt that is junior to all other debt. Still, a seller benefits from such subordinated financing by receiving an increased purchase price, at least nominally, and obtaining an equity kicker or its equivalent. The seller may well be aware, and should be prepared to face the fact, that the note or stock will realize its full value only if the acquired company prospers, and that there is a real risk that this part of the purchase price will never be paid. Obviously, this is especially true when selling a distressed company. However, as discussed in Chapter 1 of this book, it is common for sellers to remain in a state of denial regarding what ails their businesses, so they may nevertheless believe that takeback financing has considerable value.

By the same token, however, the upside potential that the seller can realize if the transaction is successful can be much greater than what it could receive if no part of its purchase price were contingent or exposed. There may also be cosmetic advantages to both buyer and seller in achieving a higher nominal price for the target company, even though a portion of that price is paid in a note or preferred stock with a market value below its face value. Thus, for example, if a seller has announced that it will not let its company go for less than $100 million, but has overestimated its value, the seller may eventually be pleased to settle for $60 million cash and a $40 million 10-year subordinated note at 4 percent interest. The note will go onto the seller's books at a substantial discount. (The amount of the discount will be useful for the buyer to discover if he later wishes to negotiate prepayment of the note in connection with a restructuring or a workout.)

What are the relative advantages of using subordinated debt and preferred stock for takeback financing?

Preferred stock has the advantage of increasing the equity listed on the balance sheet and thus helps protect the highly leveraged company from insolvency and makes it more attractive to senior and high-yield bond lenders. Remember that to avoid fraudulent transfer claims (see Chapter 10 of this book), an insolvent corporation cannot transfer its property to anyone else without receiving reasonably equivalent value. Thus, if solvency is an issue, the seller and lenders may feel more comfortable with including some preferred stock on the balance sheet. Also, increasing the amount of equity on the balance sheet can make the company look better during credit checks by vendors when they are reevaluating payment terms.

Subordinated debt offers considerable advantages to the seller, however. Payments are due whether or not there are corporate earnings, unless otherwise restricted by subordination provisions. Taking back a note, rather than preferred stock, bespeaks a greater degree of separation and greater appearance that the amounts due will be paid. The seller may intend to sell the paper it takes back, and it can get more for a note than it could get for preferred stock. The seller may be able to obtain security interests in the acquired company's assets (junior to the liens of the acquisition lenders, of course), but no such security interest accompanies preferred stock.

From the buyer's point of view, a note has the major advantage of generating deductible interest payments rather than nondeductible dividends. Preferred stock has the important disadvantage of preventing a buyer from electing pass-through tax status as an S corporation. For both reasons, be sure that if a note does emerge, it is not subject to reclassification as equity by the IRS. Accepting the seller's preferred stock can also have other adverse tax consequences.

Absent unusual circumstances, if the buyer can persuade the senior and high-yield bond lenders to accept a seller's subordinated note rather than preferred stock in the post-closing capital structure, the seller should have no objections. Alternatively, the lenders and the seller may accept preferred stock that is convertible into a note at the buyer's option once the company achieves a certain net worth or cash flow level. As a last resort, the buyer may persuade the seller, six months or a year after closing, when its debt has been somewhat reduced, to convert the preferred stock into a note.

How can a seller obtain an equity kicker in the company it is selling?

Sometimes, as mentioned before, a seller note has the same effect as an equity kicker because it serves to inflate the sales price beyond the company's real present worth, and it can be paid only if the company has good future earnings. It is also quite possible for the seller simply to retain a post-closing minority stake in the common stock of the acquired company. Alternatively, the seller can obtain participating preferred stock, in which dividend payments are determined as a percentage of earnings or as a percentage of dividend payments made to common stockholders, and in which the redemption price of the preferred rises with the value of the company. Some of these choices have tax significance.

What is an earn-out?

An *earn-out* is another form of contingent payment to finance a distressed M&A transaction. An earn-out involves paying a portion of the purchase price to the seller based on the future earnings of a company. A common type of earn-out provides for additional payments to a seller if the earnings exceed agreed-upon levels. Another type of earn-out may provide that certain debt that is given to the seller as part of the acquisition price is "anticipated" and paid off early if earnings exceed agreed-upon levels.

Earn-outs require consideration of various factors: the type of contingent payment (cash or stock), the measurement of performance (operating income, cash flow, net income, or something else), the measurement period, maximum limits (if any), and the timing of payments.

Why would the parties use an earn-out?

The parties may disagree on the value of the business because they have different opinions about the projected profit stream. Often, the buyer is relying on the seller's projections of future cash flow in setting the price. For companies in distress, the seller's financial forecast may appear particularly rosy in light of its recent poor performance. In such situations, the buyer and seller may disagree on the seller's ability to realize the projected results. The buyer should be willing to pay a higher price for greater cash flow if the projected cash flow is realized by continuing the seller's prior business practices and, for example, waiting for a cycle to turn and pricing and volume to recover. However, if the buyer expects to implement significant changes to turn around a failing business, then the buyer may feel that the seller does not deserve to share in the rewards of the buyer's efforts. Indeed, the buyer may feel that she is fixing the bone-headed mistakes that the seller has been making for years, so the seller should not reap any benefit. On the other hand, the seller may feel that the buyer would never have the opportunity to buy the company at such a low value in order to fix the company. An earn-out permits the buyer to pay a reasonable price that takes into account the risks of the turnaround plus a premium if and when improved cash flow is eventually realized post-closing. It also allows the seller to realize the full value of the business if the return to historical profitability is as straightforward as was represented to the buyer.

Earn-outs can be particularly useful for buying a strategic business unit or product line from a large company. These divestitures are often called *corporate orphans* or *carveouts*. For these transactions, because there are probably no separate audits, direct and indirect transfer costs can distort financial results, and estimates of post-closing overhead requirements may be unclear, it is extremely challenging to verify in due diligence the level of profitability that the business would generate under the buyer's ownership. Therefore, the best solution may be to sell the business with an earn-out to discover whether or not it is profitable, and if it is, how profitable. Indeed, sometimes the buyer may prefer that some insiders remain because they will know where all the bodies are buried, will be aware of untapped upside, and may have themselves artificially depressed the earnings.

Why are earn-outs difficult to administer?

To illustrate the challenges in administering an earn-out, suppose the seller receives an additional payment in each of the first three years after the sale, provided that in each of those years, the acquired company realizes operating income of $1 million or more. Although simple in concept, earn-outs raise a number of definitional problems. First and foremost, the buyer and seller must agree on the critical definition of operating income. The buyer will want to be sure that this income comes from continuing operations and not from extraordinary or nonrecurring events. Furthermore, the earn-out may require that the acquired company be operated separately and consistently with past practices. If the buyer wants to combine certain of its operations or modify them, such changes will be difficult to factor into the levels of earnings to be achieved, particularly if they are not decided upon until after the sale.

What concerns will the seller have in an earn-out?

The seller is interested in ensuring that changes in the operation of the company after the sale do not affect the company's ability to attain the targeted earnings. The seller may thus seek agreements that goodwill will be ignored in making the calculations and that the company will continue to be operated in a manner that is consistent with past practice and will not be charged with new administrative overhead expenses. The seller may also focus on depreciation, interest charges, and intercompany transactions with the buyer's company if the sale involves a strategic buyer rather than a financial buyer.

The seller may want to receive credit for the target's postacquisition results. In the previous example, suppose the $1 million level is not achieved. If in the first three years the company earns, respectively, $800,000, $1 million, and $1.2 million, the seller may feel entitled to receive the total contingent payment. Even though operating income did not exceed $1 million in the first year, the average for the three years was $1 million. To deal with this issue, the parties may agree on a sliding scale or averaging approach and a maximum overall payment.

The parties will also focus on when the buyer makes a contingent payment to the seller. Typically, the debate is whether payments are made after each year's earnings are reported or in a lump sum at the end of the period, and whether prior years' payments are recoverable based upon performance in future years. If the period is three years, for example, the buyer may try to recoup the payment in Year 1 from the seller if the financial results in Years 2 and 3 fall below expectations. The seller, naturally, will feel that the suboptimal performance of the business in Years 2 and 3 was the fault of the buyer's mismanagement, not the condition of the well-run company that the seller delivered at closing.

Are there any tax and accounting considerations with earn-outs?

For sellers, earn-outs can spread out income in taxable transactions, with resulting tax benefits. To have a tax-free reorganization, contingent shares must be issued within five years of the closing.

The buyer may also obtain a tax deduction if the earn-out is paid as compensation under an employment agreement. Postclosing employment (or consulting) agreements may be provided to sellers in lieu of an earn-out. For example, if certain sellers are actively involved in managing the business while other sellers are passive investors, it may be appropriate to provide the active sellers with additional consideration in the form of a postclosing employment agreement, which may include noncompete and nonsolicitation clauses. However, compensation provided by such agreements may be ordinary income to the recipient.

Why are earn-outs not more common?

Ultimately, no legal agreement can provide complete protection for both parties in earn-out agreements; there are far too many variables. The buyer and the seller must rely on either the provisions expressed in terms of the intent or good faith of the parties or their reasonable business judgments. Therefore, each side may want to investigate the reputation and trustworthiness of the other. By the time the buyer and the seller have gone through a turbulent acquisition closing with each other, they may find little comfort in earn-out arrangements. For these reasons and others discussed later, many painfully negotiated (meaning that expensive fees were paid to lawyers) earn-out agreements are bought out, renegotiated away, or simply stricken from the purchase agreement at or near the closing of the transaction.

From the buyer's perspective, buyers of distressed businesses will often come to realize in due diligence that the turnaround required is much greater than they originally expected when they negotiated the terms of the deal with the seller. If so, they may resent sharing the fruits of their post-closing efforts and ingenuity with the seller (i.e., the party who marketed the company as being in good condition). Moreover, in determining the financial projections upon which the earn-out is to be based, the buyer may not want to reveal his turnaround strategies to the seller for fear that the seller will back out of the deal and proceed to implement the buyer's good ideas. In other cases, where an earn-out might initially look feasible, the buyer may determine that it needs all of the upside potential to attract investors or lenders, leaving no upside to share with the seller via an earn-out. Furthermore, during the sale process, the lead buyer may determine that other potential buyers have dropped out, yet the distressed company urgently needs to complete a sale. In such circumstances, the buyer may feel that she has the seller between the proverbial rock (bankruptcy) and hard place (reduced purchase price) and can use the buyer's negotiating leverage to remove contingent payments like earn-outs from the purchase agreement at or near closing.

From the seller's perspective, if the seller deduces the buyer's good ideas from the buyer's focus in due diligence and in negotiating the earn-out, then the seller may decide to drop the earn-out and demand more upfront cash to capture more of the value at closing. The seller may feel that although the buyer was initially hesitant to pay a full price—making the earn-out an acceptable compromise—due diligence has calmed the buyer's fears and made the buyer excited about the opportunity's upside, meaning that an earn-out is no longer necessary. Also, the seller may determine that the buyer is "half pregnant" after spending considerable resources on due diligence and legal fees, and will not back away from the deal if the terms are sweetened to favor the seller. Separately, during due diligence, the seller may have developed legitimate concerns about the buyer's ability to operate the company successfully and may not want the hassle of policing the earn-out once the buyer is in command. For example, the buyer could overspend on R&D, advertising, and so on, reaping the benefits many years in the future, but reducing the amount paid to the seller via the earn-out by reducing reported earnings in the initial post-closing years. If the seller really wants a clean break so that he can move on to other endeavors, the last thing he will want is to ride herd on the proper application of the definition of direct expenses, which is often the essence of properly administering an earn-out.

How can the seller in a contingency payment deal protect its collateral?

If the contingent consideration is secured by a lien on certain pledged property, the buyer may need to promise to

- Keep the business and pledged property adequately insured
- Limit sales of pledged property (e.g., inventory) to merchandise sold in the ordinary course of business

- Require that the pledged property be kept free of any other liens (a negative pledge)
- Bar leases of the pledged property by the borrower
- Provide key staff life insurance for principal executives of the borrower

How can the seller in a contingency payment deal make sure that the buyer will comply with the business plan?

If an acquisition involves contingent consideration, the buyer may be asked to promise to

- Use the proceeds of the loan only for the stipulated purposes
- Engage only in the kinds of business contemplated by the lenders
- Refrain from merging or selling all or substantially all of the company's assets, or any portion thereof in excess of a specified value, without the seller's consent
- Limit capital expenditures, lease payments, borrowings, and investments in affiliates and third parties to agreed-upon amounts
- Prevent a change in the ownership or control of the company without the seller's consent
- Bar acquisitions of other businesses
- Make changes in the acquisition agreement, subordinated debt instruments, or other material documents

CONSIDERATIONS FOR ACQUISITION FINANCING

After agreeing to terms with the seller, what should a purchaser consider when raising senior debt to finance the remainder of the post-closing capital structure?

After the need to borrow is minimized by maximizing the amount of contingent payments and minimizing the overall purchase price, the next step is to organize and orchestrate the borrowing program. The art of structuring a financing is to allocate the revenues and assets of the acquired company to lenders in a manner that does the following:

- Maximizes the amount loaned by the most senior and highly secured and thus lowest-interest-rate lenders
- Leaves sufficient cash flow to support, if needed, a layer of subordinated, higher-interest-rate "mezzanine" debt, as well as any seller notes
- Provides for adequate working capital and is consistent with seasonal variations and foreseeable one-time bulges or dips in cash flow
- Permits the separate leveraging of distinct assets that can be more advantageously set aside for specialized lenders, such as sale-leasebacks of office buildings or manufacturing facilities
- Accommodates both good news and bad—that is, permits debt prepayment without penalty if revenues are sufficient and permits nonpayment and nonenforcement of subordinated debt if revenues are insufficient
- Avoids and, where necessary, resolves conflicts between lenders

Customarily, these results are achieved through layering of debt. (For more on debt subordination in the context of a bankruptcy, see Chapter 2 of this book.)

What does a senior lender consider when underwriting an acquisition loan?

A number of considerations are key to a lender's underwriting:

- Liquidation value of the collateral
- Credibility of the borrower's financial projections
- Whether the borrower's projections show enough cash flow to service the debt (including junior debt) with a healthy cushion
- Whether proposed asset liquidations are likely to take place in time and in sufficient amount to amortize the term debt (or reduce the revolver commitment)
- Potential company profitability and industry prospects

- The amount of junior debt (and the capacity of the junior creditor to assist the borrower with additional funds in a workout scenario)
- The backgrounds, talent, tenure, and integrity of the management team
- The strength of accounting controls and practices
- The amount of equity being invested by the buyer

How is proposed acquisition financing presented to prospective lenders?

The normal medium of acquisition financing is the so-called bank book, a brief narrative description of the proposed transaction and the target company. The bank book (also known as an *offering memorandum* or *confidential investment memorandum*) indicates what financing structure is contemplated and includes projections of earnings sufficient to cover working capital needs and to amortize the debt, along with a balance sheet setting forth the pledgeable assets. (Because the balance sheet will typically value assets based on GAAP, an appraisal of actual market and/or liquidation value, if available, may be attached or referenced.)

What happens after the bank book is presented to a lender?

If the loan officer believes that the bank may be willing to make a loan that meets the dollar amount and general terms requested by the buyer, she will seek to obtain as much information as possible about the company from the buyer. This information will include proxy statements, 10-Ks and 10-Qs if the target is a public company, and audited financial statements or tax returns if it is not. The loan officer will also send out a team of reviewers to visit the company's facilities and interview its management and will obtain an internal or outside appraisal of the assets. This review can take from half a week to a month or more. Banks are aware that they are in a competitive business and generally move quickly, particularly if the loan is being considered by several of them simultaneously.

The loan officer will then prepare a write-up recommending the proposed loan and will present it to the bank's credit committee. The committee may endorse the recommendation as made, approve it with changes (presumably acceptable to the buyer), or turn it down. If the proposal is approved, the loan officer will prepare a *commitment letter* setting forth the bank's binding commitment to make the loan. This letter thereafter becomes the loan officer's governing document in future negotiations.

What does the commitment letter contain?

Apart from the bare essentials (the amount of the loan, how much will be term and how much revolver, the maturity of the term loan and amortization provisions, and interest rates), the commitment letter will also set forth the bank's proposals on the following:

- Fees to be paid to the bank
- Voluntary prepayment rights and penalties under the term loan
- What collateral is required; whether any other lender may take a junior lien on any collateral on which the bank has a senior lien; and whether the bank is to receive a junior lien on any other collateral subject to another lender's senior lien
- How the funds are to be used
- The amount of subordinated debt and equity that may be required as a condition to the making of the senior loan
- Payment of the bank's expenses

The commitment may also set forth in some detail lists of covenants, default triggers, reporting requirements, and conditions to closing, including legal opinions to be furnished by the borrower's counsel; it also usually contemplates additional closing conditions and covenants that may be imposed by the bank as the closing process evolves. The commitment letter will also contain an expiration date, typically a very early one. For example, it may provide that the offer to make the loan will expire in 24 hours if it is not accepted in writing by the borrower, or it may allow as much as two weeks.

Are the terms of the commitment letter negotiable?

Yes, but the best, and often the only, time to negotiate is when early drafts of the commitment letter are being circulated or when the loan officer sends the buyer an initial proposal letter before credit committee approval.

Buyers should be careful to involve their lawyers and other advisors at that stage, and not wait until later to get into details. Be sure you understand the lender's procedures. The proposal letter may be the only opportunity to negotiate a document in advance; sometimes commitment letters appear only after the credit committee has met. Afterward, the lender's expectations are likely to become inflexible, and the loan officer will probably find it awkward to resubmit the proposed loan to the credit committee. The borrower typically does not know how much latitude the loan officer has to modify the commitment letter without returning to the credit committee. Because time is of the essence in the typical acquisition, and a new credit action can result in delay, it is also frequently not in the borrower's interest to return to the credit committee.

Once the commitment letter is signed, how long will the commitment remain open?

The lender's commitment to make a loan will typically provide that definitive documentation must be negotiated, prepared, and signed by a certain date. Sometimes the time allowed is quite short: 30 or 45 days. Sometimes closing on the acquisition will be protracted because of the need to obtain regulatory consents, such as FCC consents to change of ownership of television stations. If the buyer wants to extend the length of a commitment, he can sometimes pay an additional fee to the bank.

What fees are typically charged by banks for lending services?

Bank fees tend to be as varied as the ingenuity of lenders can devise and as high as borrowers can accept. In some cases, the lender may charge a fee upon the delivery of the commitment letter signed by the bank (the *commitment letter fee*) and a second commitment letter fee upon its execution by the borrower. Both such fees will probably be nonrefundable, but they may be credited against a third fee due from the borrower at closing on the loan (the *closing fee*).[21]

If the loan has been syndicated, the bank may charge an *agency fee* or *management fee* for its services in putting together the syndicate. This will typically be an ongoing fee (as opposed to the one-time commitment letter and closing fees), payable quarterly or monthly as a percentage of the total facility (0.25 percent per annum is not uncommon).

The total amount of fees charged by a bank at the closing typically ranges between 1.0 and 2.5 percent. The percentage depends on the speed demanded of the bank, the complexity of the transaction, the size of the banking group (the more lenders there are, the more expensive it is), and the degree of risk. A short-term bridge loan will probably involve a higher front-end fee than a long-term facility because the bank has less opportunity to earn profit by way of interest over the life of the loan.

For revolvers, in addition to the front-end fees, there will usually be an *unused line fee* (also known as a *commitment fee* or *facility fee*), which is typically around 0.5 percent, from time to time on the amount that is undrawn and available.

If the borrower will need letters of credit, the bank will typically assess a *letter of credit fee* (typically 1 to 1.5 percent per annum) on the amount committed under a standby or commercial letter of credit.

Finally, the bank will often seek *early termination fees* on the unpaid balance of the term loans. Like call protection and makewhole provisions for bonds, these fees are intended to compensate the bank for economic losses that it may suffer if the borrower terminates the term loan prior to its maturity because of a cheaper financing source, thus depriving the bank of the anticipated profit on the loan for the balance of the term. These fees may step down in amount the longer the term loan is outstanding. This is usually worth spending some chips to negotiate. After the distressed company turns around, the buyer will probably want to refinance the senior loan as quickly as possible to escape a whole panoply of burdensome covenants. As discussed earlier in this chapter, these fees are likely to pose a problem during refinancing efforts.

Typically, whether the loan is made or not, the commitment letter will require that the borrower be liable for all of the lender's out-of-pocket expenses and obligations for fees and disbursements of the bank's outside counsel. This provision is not negotiable; banks never expect to pay their own counsel for work done in connection with a loan. Such fees are always assessed against the borrower or, if the loan does not close, the intended borrower.

Can a letter of credit facility be combined with an acquisition loan?

Yes. If the business uses letters of credit in its ongoing operations (for purposes such as assuring payment for raw materials or foreign-sourced goods), it can generally obtain a commitment from the lenders to provide such letters of credit up to a stipulated aggregate amount. The letter of credit facility will typically be carved out of the revolving line of credit, will be collateralized by the same collateral that secures the revolver, and will have the effect of limiting availability under the revolver to the extent of the aggregate letter of credit commitment. In such circumstances, draws on letters of credit will be treated as draws on the revolver.

Acquisition loan agreements typically contain a lengthy list of conditions to closing. Are there any that are likely to be particularly troublesome?

Although the points of sharpest contention vary from transaction to transaction, there are some that crop up regularly. They include the following:

- *Requirements regarding perfection and priority of security interests in collateral.* If, for example, first liens on inventory in various jurisdictions are to be given to the lenders, certain events must occur. *First,* lien searches have to be completed and reports received and reviewed (there are professional companies that can be hired to conduct computerized searches of liens on record in any state or county office); *second,* documents terminating old liens have to be prepared, signed, and sent for filing; and *third,* documents perfecting new liens have to be prepared, signed, and sent for filing.
- *Related filing schedules.* Once all that has been done, filing must be coordinated in each of the jurisdictions so that it occurs contemporaneously with the funding of the new loan and the payoff of the old loan. In a complex, multijurisdictional transaction, such coordination, if it is to be done successfully, requires a combination of monumental effort and plain old good luck (and, of course, excellent lawyers). Not infrequently, lenders have some flexibility concerning the filing of termination statements in connection with the old loan being discharged and will allow a reasonable period after closing for this to be accomplished.
- *Counsel opinions.* Few deals crater over the failure of counsel for the borrower to deliver required opinions, but it is not

unheard of for a closing to be delayed while final points in the opinions are negotiated between counsel for the bank and counsel for the borrower. Problems typically occur in local counsel opinions and relate to the validity of the bank's lien in a particular jurisdiction. There is no magic solution, but early involvement of local counsel for the borrower is always a good idea.

■ *Auditors' opinions.* Auditors may not provide opinions as to the solvency of borrowers, and are highly unlikely to provide comment formally on the reliability of financial projections provided by the borrower to the bank. However, they now routinely make assessments of internal controls, because of the requirement under Section 404 of the Sarbanes-Oxley Act.

■ *Governmental consents and approvals.* In certain transactions, the approval of a governmental entity is a central element in the transaction. For example, a sale of a television station cannot be effected without requisite approvals from the FCC. The timing of such approvals, even if they are reasonably assured, is outside the control of the parties, and the failure of a government agency to act when expected can wreak havoc on the schedule for closing an acquisition.

■ *Material litigation and adverse changes affecting the company.* Some loan agreements give the buyer and/or lender the right to back out if the target gets hit by a major lawsuit that, if successful, could seriously harm the company's business. If this contingency does occur, the burden is on the seller's counsel to persuade both the buyer and the bank that the suit is unlikely to succeed or that, if it is successful, it would not be material to the company or its operations. Similarly, bad economic news can cause either the buyer or the bank to halt the process, resulting in either a negotiated price reduction or a termination.

What purposes do the representations and warranties in the loan agreement serve?

The representations and warranties are intended to corroborate and complete the information on the acquired company upon which the lender based its credit decision. They constitute, in effect, a checklist of potential problem areas for which the borrower is required to state that no problem exists, or to spell out (by way of exceptions or exhibits) what the problem is. Thus, typical warranties will state that

- The financial statements of the borrower that have been submitted to the bank are correct. (Although it is comforting to have this conclusion backed by an auditor's certification, the auditor's report is usually laced with qualifications.)
- There are no liens on the borrower's assets, except as disclosed to the bank or permitted pursuant to the loan agreement.
- The transactions contemplated will not conflict with laws or any contracts to which the borrower is a party or by which it is bound (the so-called noncontravention representation).
- There are no lawsuits pending or threatened against the borrower that are likely to have a material adverse effect on it if they are decided against the borrower, except as disclosed to the bank.
- The loan will not violate any margin rules, if applicable.
- The borrower has no exposure under ERISA.
- The borrower is not a regulated public utility holding company or investment company (because, if it were, various governmental orders would be required).
- The borrower is "solvent" (so as to mitigate concerns about fraudulent transfer risks).
- The borrower's assets (and principal office) are located in the places specified. (This information is needed to ensure that perfection of security interests in the collateral is effected by filing notices in the correct jurisdictions.)

What happens if a representation is wrong?

A breached representation can have two practical consequences for a borrower: (1) if such a breach occurs, the bank may refuse to make a requested loan advance, either at or after the closing, and (2) breach of a representation or warranty can trigger a default under the loan agreement.

The first consequence—bank refusal to fund—should not be surprising. The truth and accuracy of the representations is typically a condition for the initial loan made at the time the loan agreement is signed and also for any subsequent draws on the revolving line of credit. If, for example, the borrower has warranted in the loan agreement that it has no significant environmental problems, and subsequently it is discovered that it has been guilty of illegal dumping of hazardous wastes, the bank will probably have the right under the loan agreement to shut off further draws on the revolving line of credit. Such a decision could be catastrophic for a company that is precluded from financing itself from cash flow because its loan agreement requires that collected receivables be deposited in a lockbox account that is under the lender's control (such accounts are discussed earlier in this chapter with respect to asset-based loans).

The second consequence—a default under the loan agreement—triggers the remedies that a lender generally has under a loan agreement, one of which is the right to *accelerate* the loan, that is, to declare all loaned amounts to be immediately due and payable, even though the revolver may not expire until the end of the current year and the amounts due under the term loan may not be otherwise due for several years. See Chapter 1 of this book for further discussion on defaults.

The right to accelerate is, in a practical sense, the right to trigger the bankruptcy of the borrower, and for that reason it is unlikely to be exercised except in those cases where a lender determines that its interests will be better protected by putting the borrower in bankruptcy than through other means. See Chapter 2 of this book for considerations regarding restructuring alternatives, such as out-of-court workouts, federal bankruptcy, and state insolvency proceedings.

What techniques can be used to take some of the bite out of default provisions?

There are basically two default softeners: the use of *grace* or *cure* provisions and the concept of *materiality*.

A grace period is a period of time following the due date for the making of a payment during which that payment may be made and default avoided. Five days' grace beyond the due date is not uncommon; sometimes 10 or even 15 days may be granted.

Cure periods apply to events of default triggered by covenant breaches. Generally, the lender will attempt to limit the application of cure periods to those covenants that are capable of being fixed (e.g., a duty to submit financial reports) but deny them for covenants that are designed to provide early warning of trouble (e.g., breach of financial ratios). The latter category of covenants typically cannot be cured and will require a waiver or amendment to avoid default. Sometimes the cure period will not begin to run until the lender has given the borrower notice of a failure to perform; in other cases, the cure period will begin to run when the borrower should have performed, whether the lender knew of the borrower's failure or not. Cure periods vary greatly from transaction to transaction and from provision to provision. However, 5-day, 10-day, and 30-day cure periods are seen from time to time, and sometimes the concept of counting only "business days" is used to extend the period by excluding Saturdays, Sundays, and nationally recognized holidays.

The concept of materiality arises when a representation turns out to be untrue, but the effect of this inaccuracy is not materially adverse to the borrower or the collateral, or to the lender's position. Therefore, the parties may agree in the loan agreement that a breach of a particular representation or warranty must be material in order to constitute a default. Materiality may not be applicable to every representation and warranty in the loan agreement.

Endnotes

1. See http://www.uspap.org/2010USPAP/toc.htm, last accessed June 2, 2010.
2. The discussion that follows is drawn from Wendell H. Adair Jr. and Brett Lawrence, "Rights Offerings: Raising Cash without Registering Securities," Stroock & Stroock & Lavan LLP; available at http://www.stroock.com/SiteFiles/Pub306.pdf, last accessed June 2, 2010.
3. See 11 U.S.C. §1145.
4. Shai Y. Waisman, "Rights Offerings: A Practitioner's Guide," *Weil, Gotshal Bankruptcy Bulletin*, October 2007; available at http://www.weil.com/news/pubdetail.aspx?pub=8453, last accessed June 2, 2010.
5. Julie Spellman Sweet, "PIPEs: A Review of Key Legal Issues," in R. Scott Falk and Sarkis Jebejian (eds.), *Mergers & Acquisitions: What You Need to Know Now, 2009* (New York: Practicing Law Institute, 2009).
6. Available at http://www.fdic.gov/bank/historical/managing/history1-07.pdf, last accessed June 2, 2010.
7. See "Moody's Comments on Debtor-in-Possession Lending," Moody's Investors Service, October 2008; http://www.moodys.com/cust/content/content.ashx?source=StaticContent/Free%20Pages/Credit%20Policy%20Research/documents/current/2007300000539803.pdf, last accessed June 13, 2010.

8. Ibid.
9. See John Blakeley, "The New DIPs," January 22, 2010; http://www.pipeline.thedeal.com/tdd/ViewBlog.dl?id=33060, last accessed on June 14, 2010.
10. "Moody's Comments," note 6.
11. Ibid.
12. See *Schubert v. Lucent Technologies (In re Winstar Communications, Inc.)*, 554 F.3d 382 (3d Cir. 2009).
13. See 11 U.S.C. §364(a).
14. See 11 U.S.C. §364(b).
15. See 11 U.S.C. §364(c).
16. See 11 U.S.C. §364(d)(1)(A).
17. See 11 U.S.C. §364(d)(1)(B).
18. See 11 U.S.C. §364(d)(2).
19. See 11 U.S.C. §364(d)(1)(A).
20. Gordon Lu, "Bankruptcy Implications of Second Lien Loans"; http://www.turnaround.org/cmaextras/Paper—BankruptcyImplications.pdf (internal citations omitted), last accessed September 13, 2010.
21. Borrowers should pay fees only to reputable institutions. Advance-fee loan rackets have proliferated in recent years. Check with your local Better Business Bureau offices.

CONCLUSION

It is only under the shelter of the civil magistrate that the owner of ... valuable property, which is acquired by the labour of many years, or perhaps of many successive generations, can sleep a single night in security.

—Adam Smith, Wealth of Nations, Book V,
"Of the Expences of the Sovereign, or Commonwealth," Part II, Chapter V, 1776

In such condition there is no place for industry, because the fruit thereof is uncertain, and consequently no culture of the earth, no navigation nor use of the commodities that may be imported by sea, no commodious building, no instruments of moving and removing such things as require much force, no knowledge of the face of the earth, no account of time, no arts, no letters, no society, and, which is worst of all, continual fear and danger of violent death, and the life of man solitary, poor, nasty, brutish, and short.

—Thomas Hobbes, Leviathan, *Chapter XIII,*
"Of the Natural Condition of Mankind as Concerning Their Felicity and Misery,"
1651

The world assumed by the formal bankruptcy process is the world envisioned by Adam Smith, in which each person sleeps securely, knowing that there are laws to protect private property from undue seizure. Unfortunately, however, that same world can all too often revert to a Hobbesian state of nature. Both have been characterized as "capitalism." Which kind of capitalism do we want for ourselves and future generations?

While it is bad enough that a troubled company faces numerous complex problems in carrying out its operations, the situation can be exacerbated by bad behavior on the part of the parties involved. As we have described throughout this book, the Bankruptcy Code and Bankruptcy

Conclusion

Rules do a great deal to encourage a collaborative process among the various parties involved in a distressed situation. Unfortunately, however, no law can mandate good manners, force ethical conduct, or require a conscience. While good faith and fair dealing are laudable goals, they are extremely difficult to enforce. Cunning minds will always find loopholes in the law and distort legislators' good intentions to produce unintended consequences. Although bankruptcy judges have equitable powers at their disposal to preserve the integrity of the system, their actions are typically more reactive than proactive, muting their effectiveness through delayed decision making followed by lengthy appeals.

As you participate in distressed M&A, we urge you to keep the following adage in mind: "Sheep get sheared; pigs get fat; hogs get slaughtered." While one person's crisis is another person's opportunity, it can also become another person's slaughterhouse when buyers exhibit overzealous, nefarious, or underhanded behavior. Being overly agreeable, eager to please, or downright gullible is usually an invitation for exploitation. The distressed M&A process can sometimes bring out the worst in people who are seeking to make a living off the misfortune of others.

Regrettably, there are many examples of bad behavior to examine:

- Dishonest managers who commit fraud, embezzlement, misrepresentation, and self-dealing
- "Vulture" investors who thwart the bankruptcy process to divert value to themselves
- "Chainsaw" turnaround managers who cut bone, not just fat, when reducing expenses
- Overzealous attorneys who bill for outrageous amounts, far beyond the value that they create
- Greedy investment bankers with "heads I win, tails you lose" engagements
- Selfish executives who put their own interests ahead of the needs and rights of their creditors and investors (and the corporate directors who let them do it)
- "Terrorist" creditors' committees that demand greenmail

While the underlying cause of this bad behavior is straightforward—it is greed, plain and simple—it is unclear why so many more people are unable to resist their urges. Why can't the power of civilization and the voice of conscience prevail?

Stress may be a mitigating factor. The panic surrounding troubled companies is palpable, and for good reason: financial forecasting is uncertain, unresolved problems spawn new ones, time is of the essence, and viable alternatives disappear from view as soon as they appear. When fear supplants hope, people tend to go into crisis mode and make suboptimal decisions, adversely affecting employees, vendors, customers, and other constituents who lack strong voices and oversight. Under such harsh circumstances, many parties feel that they are trapped in a zero-sum game, and executives, creditors, and advisors alike will form opinions as to which parties will come out being winners and which will be losers. For the parties who are predicted to be the losers, the stakes are incredibly high, including potentially crippling financial disaster, career-ending job loss, and unbearable emotional depression.

As we discussed in Chapter 1 of this book, denial can be very strong as a company descends into the death spiral, and, as psychologists have concluded when examining the stages of grief, denial is frequently followed by anger. This anger often manifests itself as a fierce battle among the parties involved with a distressed company, in which only the professionals come out ahead (because of hourly billing). All parties involved in steering a company through troubled financial waters need to consider carefully the long-term impact on their reputations and profits of the incentives they create when they establish or agree to compensation systems.

In reality, many distressed situations present an opportunity for creative solutions to complex problems. Some people shun this challenge, while others embrace it. Special situations often demand fresh perspectives, "out-of-the-box" thinking, and renewed hope, but it is typically easier to make snap decisions and pursue the path of least resistance. In nearly every predicament, however, there exists an opportunity to play the hero of the story rather than the villain. If cooler heads prevail, a narrow path out of the quagmire can very often be discovered. While it is easy to toss around platitudes like "win-win," it is much more difficult to design mutually beneficial solutions and even harder to implement them under urgent conditions with limited liquidity and intense pressure. As Nobel Prize for Peace recipient Nelson Mandela said, "It always seems impossible until it's done." Indeed, Exhibit C-1 illustrates how perseverance and cooperation can reveal hidden value.

Exhibit C-1 How Did Rearranging the Puzzle Create an Extra Piece?

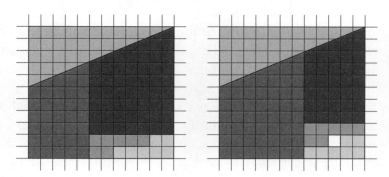

We hope that the detailed discussion throughout this book will increase people's awareness and enhance their comprehension of the many issues involved in dealing with troubled companies so that markets will become more efficient and valuations will rise to realistic levels. We also anticipate that dispelling common myths about troubled companies, the bankruptcy process, and distressed M&A will lead to more favorable outcomes for all parties involved. At the very least, we hope that victims in these situations will use the tools provided here to defend themselves against the vultures that are preying upon them.

Perhaps, in time, legislators will move to improve the process so that it can achieve a fairer, more equitable recovery for creditors and equity holders while giving debtors an even fresher start. In the meantime, if writing this book and having you read it saves just one more person from losing a job, allows just one more plant to avoid consolidation, keeps just one more company from liquidating, or encourages just one more bidder to participate in an auction, it will have been well worth the effort.

INDEX

Page numbers followed by n indicate notes.

A

Absolute priority rule, 123, 350–353
Acceleration of debt, 32, 115
Accounting:
  accrued interest on pre-petition debt, 237–238
  cancellation of debt income, 248–251
  carryovers and carrybacks, 238–240
  Chapter 11, 235–239, 251–252
  earn-outs, 442
  firms for solvency opinions, 294
  fresh start accounting/reporting, 251–266
  insolvency, definitions of, 250–251
  net operating loss (NOL), 238–251
  pre-petition vs. post-petition liabilities, 236–237
  reorganization under FASB Accounting Standards Codification (ASC 852), 235–236, 251–252
  restructuring (*See* Workouts)
  timing and inflection points, 213–214
  (*See also* Fresh start accounting/ reporting; Net operating loss)
Accounting rate of return (ARR), 312
Accrued interest on pre-petition debt, 237–238
Acid test ratio, 313
Acquisition financing (loan), 444–454
  bank book, 446–447
  commitment letter, 447–448
  default provisions, 453–454
  fees charged, 448–449
  lender underwriting, 445–446
  loan agreement conditions, 450–451
  purchaser post-closing capital structure, 444–445
  representations and warranties, 451–453
Adelphia, 146, 201, 338
Adequate information, disclosure statement, 344–345
Adequate protection, 132, 356, 429
Ad hoc committee of creditors, 199–201

Adjusted basis, 214
Administrative convenience class of creditors, 350
Administrative expense carveout, 178
Administrative expenses, 115, 117
Advance rates, asset-based loans, 411, 413–415
Advisors, 173–210
  appraisers, 205–206
  auditors, 11, 30n8, 451
  bankruptcy court oversight, 175–176
  bankruptcy lawyers, 180–185
  claims agents, 204–205
  compensation, 178–179, 183–185, 189–190, 196, 205
  corporate lawyers vs. bankruptcy lawyers, 180
  counsel opinions, acquisition loan agreement, 450–451
  financial, 186–189
  leading firms:
    bankruptcy lawyers, 173, 183–184
    claims agents, 204–205
    financial advisors, 174
    liquidators, 205–206
    restructuring advisors, 186–188
    turnaround consultants, 174, 191–193
  solvency opinions, 294
Aetna, 300n40
Affiliate transactions, 407
Agency fee, 448
Agent bank, 409
Airball, asset-based loans, 415
Alix, Jay, 174, 191
Allocation of repayment, fraudulent transfers, 289–290
Allowed claims, 122
Altman, Edward, 7, 42, 205
Amending and extending existing agreements, refinancing, 72–73, 408–410
American Bankruptcy Institute (ABI), xiv, 69, 71, 179

American Recovery and Reinvestment Act of 2009 (ARRA), 230, 239
American Society of Appraisers, 310–311
Antilayering covenants, 135
Antistuffing rule, 247
Antitrust, 208, 282–287, 386
Apollo Management, 92
Appeals, 49, 388
Apple Inc., 5–6, 320
Applicable Federal Rate (AFR), 226
Applicable high-yield discount obligation (AHYDO), 227, 233n6
Appraisers, 205–206
Asset-based loans (ABLs), 410–416
Asset swap, 218
Assets:
    defined, 329n7
    intangible, 255–257
    transfer to creditors, workout, 230–232
    valuation, 310–314
Assignment for the benefit of creditors (ABC), 62
Association for Corporate Growth (ACG), xiv
Auctions (*See* 363 sales, bidding and auctions)
Auditors, 11, 30n8, 451
Auletta, Ken, 78
Automatic stay, 58, 63
Average collection period, 312
Average rate of return, 324

B

Backstop, 421
Backward collateralization, 433
Bank book, 446–447
Bankruptcy Abuse Prevention and Consumer Protection Act of 2005 (BAPCPA), 53, 55, 57, 117, 120, 175–176, 187, 293, 337
Bankruptcy Appellate Panel (BAP), 49
Bankruptcy Code:
    absolute priority rule—section 1129(b), 350–352, 356–357
    advisors—section 327/1103, 176
    automatic stay—section 362, 58
    bankruptcy, types of, 38–43, 50–51

best interests of creditors test, 350, 353–354
Chapter 1, 38
Chapter 3, 38
Chapter 5, 38
Chapter 7 liquidation, 38, 53, 68–69, 71, 106, 162, 232n1
Chapter 7 trustee, 108–109
    (*See* Bankruptcy trustees)
Chapter 9, 38
Chapter 11 (*See* Chapter 11 reorganization, Bankruptcy Code)
Chapter 11 trustee, 107–108 (*See also* Bankruptcy trustees)
Chapter 12, 39, 55
Chapter 13, 39
Chapter 15, 39
"Chapter 22," 40–43, 71, 344
"Chapter 33," 41, 77
"Chapter 44," 77
collateral protections—section 361, 140–141
cram-down plan, 354–356
cram-up plan, 356–358
creditors, treatment of, 114–115
creditors' committee (*See* Creditors' committee)
debtor vs. creditors' committee, 152
debtor in possession (DIP), 104, 106–109
debtor's estate—section 541, 99–100
defined, 36
discharge—sections 523/524, 116
disclosure statement—section 1125, 343–344
disinterested person—section 101(14), 177
examiner—section 1106(a)(3), 197
exclusivity period—section 1121(b), 335–339
executory contracts—section 365, 58–59
fraudulent transfers—section 547, 287–288
insolvent, defined, 8
intercreditor agreement—section 501(a), 362
involuntary bankruptcy—section 303(b), 37
lockup agreements, 342

Bankruptcy Code (*Cont'd.*)
plan of reorganization confirmation—
section 1129, 361, 366
plan of reorganization requirements—
section 1123(a), 347–349, 352
prearranged bankruptcy, 340–342
prepackaged bankruptcy, 340
pre-petition creditors becoming DIP
lender, 431–434
rights offerings and warrants—section
1145, 422
sale of company as going concern—
section 363 (*See under* 363 sales)
unexpired leases—section 365, 58–59
Bankruptcy courts:
appeals of decisions by, 49, 388
Delaware, District of, 47, 70, 142–145,
180–181, 273–276
jurisdiction of, 45–47
New York, Southern District of (SDNY),
47, 70, 78–80, 82, 84, 180, 340,
382–383
valuation determination by, 306–307
Web sites, 47–48
Bankruptcy Judges, United States Trustees,
and Family Farmer Bankruptcy Act
(1986), 55
Bankruptcy lawyers, 180–185
corporate lawyers vs. bankruptcy
lawyers, 180
pro hac vice, 182
retention, 280
solvency opinions, 294
(*See also* Advisors)
Bankruptcy Reform Act (1994), 55
Bankruptcy remote entity, 44–45, 100
Bankruptcy Rules, 43, 54–55, 176, 366
Bankruptcy trustees, 58, 105–109, 196,
282, 335, 380
Bankruptcy Week, xiv
BankUnited, 424
BAPCPA (*See* Bankruptcy Abuse
Prevention and Consumer Protection
Act of 2005)
Basis, 214
BB&T, 424
Bear Stearns & Co., 36

Berry-Hill Galleries, 158–159
Best interests of creditors test, 350,
353–354
Bid submission, in 363 sales, 391–392
Bidders, in 363 sales, 377–379
Board of directors:
bankruptcy trustee appointments, 282
business judgment rule, 271–273
D&O insurance, 273, 280
duty of care, 270
duty of good faith, 270–271, 274–275
duty of loyalty, 270, 274
fiduciary director duties, deepening
insolvency, 277, 279–280
fiduciary duties, 270–282
legal risks, 270–282
managing debtors, 111–113
personal liability, 272–273
resignation from, 280–281
retention of legal counsel, 280
shareholder sale of large block of stock,
273–274
Bond indenture, 14
Bonds (*See* High-yield bonds)
Borrowing base and certificate, asset-based
loans, 415
Borrowing capacity, 225 (*See also*
Asset-based loans)
Boscov's Inc., 375
BP, 12
Brandt v. Hicks, Muse, 277
Breakup fee, 389–391
Breeden, Richard C., 80
Buckhead America Corp., In re, 276–277
Buffett, Warren, 10, 323
Business failure, 3–30
company reasons for, 3–12
default, 16–22
high-yield bonds, 13–22
industry, reasons for, 3–4
M&A opportunities presented by, 22–29
management reasons for, 3–6
terms to describe troubled companies,
27–28
Business judgment rule, 17, 105, 271–273
Buyer promises, contingency payment
financing, 444

C

Call protection, bonds, 13, 160, 407
Cancellation of debt (COD), 226–228,
    230–231, 248–251, 400
Carryover basis, 215
Carryovers and carrybacks, 238–240
Carveouts, 178, 440
Case management/electronic case files
    (CM/ECF), 121
Cash collateral, 105, 124n19, 137–138
Cash current debt (CCD) coverage, 320
Cash flow-based valuation, 314–320
Cash flow deterioration, as warning sign,
    9–10
Cash flow loan refinanced with asset-based
    loans, refinancing, 410–416
Cash flow statements, 314–316
Cash flow sweeps, refinancing, 408
Chapter 11 reorganization, Bankruptcy
    Code:
  advisors, 197, 201
  bankruptcy accounting, 235–239, 251–252
  Chapter 11 trustee, 107–108 (See also
      Bankruptcy trustees)
  cost of bankruptcy, 51–53
  cram-down plan, 354–356
  debtors and creditors, 101, 106
  distressed M&A opportunities, x
  exclusivity and solicitation period
      extensions, 337
  free-fall bankruptcy, 339
  restructuring alternatives for distressed
      companies, 38–43, 50–51, 54
  trends in distressed M&A and investing,
      68–71, 74, 81–82
  (See also specific chapter procedures
      under Bankruptcy Code)
Chief restructuring officer (CRO), 36,
    109–111
Chrysler, 75–75, 77, 84–85, 374, 382, 386
CIT Group, 77, 82
Claims, 116–123
  administrative expenses vs., 117
  allowed vs. disallowed, 122
  call protection, 160
  classes, 349–350, 361
  contingent, 118

counterparties to contracts, 113, 154
critical vendors, 154–157
described, 116
disputed vs. undisputed, 119–120
employees, 7–8, 80, 113, 115, 132,
    153–154, 162
environmental clean-up and toxic torts,
    161, 164–165
fraudulent, 122
governments, 113, 132, 154
insider, 120–121
landlords, 113, 153–154
legal vs. equitable, 119
liquidated, 118
make-whole provisions, 160
mass torts, 161
matured vs. unmatured, 118
pari passu, 117, 143, 154
pension plan termination, 160–163
plaintiffs, 8, 113, 132, 154
post-petition interest payments, 157–158
pre-petition interest payments, 157–159
pre-petition principal payments, 159
priority (See Priority of claims)
proof of, 121–122
suppliers, 7, 113, 115, 132, 153–157
trading, 91
typical holders, 154
union contract rejection, 161, 163–164
utilities, 113, 154
vendors, 7, 113, 115, 132, 153–157
Classes of claims, plan of reorganization,
    349–350, 361
Claims agents, 204–205
Claims trading, 88, 90–91
Clayton Act, 282, 386
Clear Channel Outdoor, Inc., 388
Closing fee, 448
Collateral:
  acquisition loan agreement conditions, 450
  adequate protection (Bankruptcy
      Code section 361), 140–141
  equity cushion, 140, 429
  insufficient, 138–139
  pre-petition creditors, 141
  protections, contingency payment
      financing, 443–444

Collateral (*Cont'd.*)
secured creditors, 127–128, 137–142
security interest in (*See* Liens)
undersecured vs. oversecured, 138–139
value of, 140
Commitment fee, 449
Commitment letter, 447–448
Comparable companies valuation
methodology, 326–328
Comparable transaction valuation
methodology, 326–328
Competing plans of reorganization
confirmation, 365–366
Competitors in financial distress, as
warning sign, 12
Comprehensive Environmental Response,
Compensation, and Liability Act
of 1980 (CERCLA, Superfund),
164–165
Confidential investment memorandum, 446
Confirmation, plan of reorganization,
360–368
Confirmation hearings, plan of
reorganization, 366
Conseco, 77, 83–84
Consummation vs. confirmation, plan of
reorganization, 367
Contingency payment financing, 436–444
buyer promises, 444
collateral protections, 443–444
earn-outs, 439–443
effectiveness of, 436
equity kicker, 439
seller notes, 436–437
takeback financing, 437–438
363 sales, 391
Contingent claims, 118
Continuity of business enterprise,
Section 382, 240–241
Corporate orphans, 440
Cost approach to value, 256
Cost of bankruptcy, 51–53
Cost basis, 215
Covenant-lite bonds, 10, 20–22
Covenants, high-yield bonds, 14–16
Cram-down plan of reorganization,
354–355

Cram-up plan of reorganization,
356–358
Credit agreements, refinancing, 406–408
Credit bidding, in 363 sale, 378, 392–394
Credit Card Accountability, Responsibility,
and Disclosure Act (2009), 55
Credit line, as warning sign, 12
Credit Lyonnais, 275–276
Credit ratings and credit rating agencies,
12, 19–21, 30n8
Credit-related developments, as warning
sign, 12
Creditors, 113–123
administrative expenses, 115, 117
Bankruptcy Code treatment of, 114–115
claims, 116–123
claims trading, 91
discharge, 116
generally accepted accounting principles
(GAAP) treatment of, 114–115
mezzanine financing, 132
pre- and post-petition, 115
second-lien, 130–135
secured (*See* Secured creditors)
solvency, 7–8
unsecured (*See* Unsecured creditors)
workouts, 33
(*See also* Bankruptcy Code; Claims)
Creditors' committee, 152–153,
165–171
Bankruptcy Code, 165
chairperson, 167–168
counsel, 185
forcing a sale of the company, 171
roles and responsibilities, 165
341 formation meeting, 169–170
Crisis management consultants, 174,
189–194 (*See also* Advisors)
Critical vendors, 154–157
Cross-collateralized loans, 433
Cross default, 17
Cross-streaming, fraudulent transfers,
291–292
"Crown jewels," sale of, as warning
sign, 11
Cure period, default, 453–454
Current ratio, 313

D
Dana Corp., 425, 427
Days' sales outstanding, 312
The Deal, xiv, 67, 183, 185, 187, 192, 425
Debt (*See* Asset-based loans; Claims;
    Creditors; High-yield bonds; Liens;
    Obligor; Second-lien loans)
Debt/EBITDA ratio, 7
Debt/equity ratio, 7, 313–314
Debt exchanges, refinancing, 218, 417–420
Debt-for-debt swap, 218
Debt-for-equity swap, 218, 419–420
Debt vs. lien subordination, 135
Debt maturity schedule, 12
Debt restructuring (*See* Workouts)
Debt/total assets ratio, 314
Debtor in possession (DIP), 101–109
    authority of, 102–103
    in bankruptcy, 57
    claims trading, 91
    described, 101–102
    duties of, 104
    fraudulent transfers, right to sue, 290
    management by, and Bankruptcy Code,
        106–109
    plan of reorganization, 360
    363 sale, 379–380
Debtor-in-possession (DIP) loans, 425–435
    acquiring and examples of, 425–428
    in bankruptcy, 57
    bankruptcy court approval of, 428–430
    claims trading, 91
    described, 102–103
    exclusivity and solicitation period, 335–339
    intercreditor agreements and second-lien
        debt effects, 434–435
    lender considerations, 430–431
    losing possession (*See* Bankruptcy trustees)
    new money, 433
    paying off, 435
    plan of reorganization, 360
    from pre-petition secured lender, 431–433
    for reorganization financing, 425–435
Debtors, 99–113
    administrative expenses, 115, 117
    bankruptcy filing, 43
    bankruptcy trustees to manage, 107–109

board of directors to manage, 111–113
claims, 116–123
chief restructuring officer (CRO) to
    manage, 109–111
debtor in possession (DIP), 101–109
debtor's estate, 99–100
defined, 99
managing, 104–113
multiple subsidiaries and bankruptcy, 101
nondebtors/nondebtor entities, 100–101
related, 100
Debtor's estate, 99–100
Deepening insolvency, fiduciary director
    duties, 277, 279–280
Default, 16–22, 119, 453–454
    cure periods, 453-454
    events of, 16
    interest, 16
    (*See also* Restructuring alternatives for
        distressed companies)
Delaware, District of, 47, 70, 142–145,
    180–181, 273–276
Delphi, 74
Delta Air Lines, 425
DIP (*See* Debtor in possession)
Direct method of reporting, cash flow
    statements, 315
Disallowed claims, 122
Discharge, 116
Disclosure statements, 104, 257, 343–345
Discounted cash flow (DCF), valuation
    methodology, 316–319
Disinterested person, 177
Disputed claims, 119–120
Disqualification, in 363 sale, 395–396
Disqualified debt instrument, 227–228
Distress pension plan termination, 162–163
Distressed investors, 87–94
Distressed M&As, trends in (*See* Trends in
    M&A and investing)
Dividends payable, 112–113, 407
D&O insurance, 273, 280
Doctrine of necessity, 155–156
Dodd-Frank Act (2010), 56, 209
Doherty, Joseph W., 179
Dow Corning Corp., In re, 237
Drucker, Peter, 314

Dubai World, 110
Due diligence, traditional vs. distressed
    M&A, 23
DuPont formula for return on equity, 312
Duty of care, board of directors, 270
Duty of good faith, board of directors,
    270–271, 274–275
Duty of loyalty, board of directors, 270, 274

E
Early termination fee, 449
Earnings-based valuation, 323–325
Earnings per share (EPS), 324
Earn-outs, 439–443
EBIT/interest expense ratio, 7, 325
EBITDA, 324–325, 410–411
Efficiency indicators, asset valuation, 312
Elrod Holdings, 147
Emerging Communications, 274
Employee Retirement Income Security
    Act of 1974 (ERISA), 104, 109,
    160–162, 208
Enron, 76–77, 82–83, 95n22
Enterprise value (EV) to EBITDA, 324–325
Environmental clean-up, 161, 164–165
Equitable interests, 119
Equitable subordination, 142–147, 398
Equity:
    defined, 329n7
    for tax purposes, 227
Equity cushion, 140, 429
Equity definition of insolvency, 8
Equity holders, securities-based valuation,
    322–323
Equity kicker, 422–423, 439
Equity value, net operating losses, 246–248
Events of default, 16
Examiners, 197–199
Excess availability, asset-based loans,
    411–412
Excess cash flow sweeps, 408
Exchange offer, 218, 227, 230, 417–419
Exclusivity period, plan of reorganization,
    335–339
Executory contracts, Bankruptcy Code,
    58–59
Exit financing, plan of reorganization,
    359–360

Expense reimbursement to losing bidder, in
    363 sale, 396
Extinguishment of debt, workout, 222–223

F
Facility fee, 449
Factoring, 416
Failing firm defense, antitrust, 282–287
Failure (*See* Business failure)
Fair market value (FMV), 246–247
Fair valuation, 8, 289
Fair value allocation, fresh start,
    253–255
FASB ASC 805/852, 235–236, 251–253
Feasibility test, plan of reorganization, 358
Federal bankruptcy (*See* Chapter 11
    reorganization, Bankruptcy Code)
Federal bankruptcy courts
    (*See* Bankruptcy courts)
Federal Deposit Insurance Corporation
    (FDIC), 56, 207–208, 424–425
Federal Rules of Bankruptcy Procedure
    (Bankruptcy Rules), 43, 54–55,
    176, 366
Federal Trade Commission (FTC), 208,
    282–284, 286, 386
Fees charged, acquisition financing,
    448–449
Feingold, Kenneth, 53
Fiduciary duties, board of directors,
    275–282, 400
Filing schedules, acquisition loan
    agreement, 450
Financial advisors, 174, 186–189
Financial buyers, in 363 sale, 378
Financial crisis (2007–2009), 36, 51,
    67–73, 152–153
Financial distress warning signs, 9–12
Financial ratios:
    asset valuation, 311–314
    cash flow-based valuation, 319–320
    common, 7, 10–11, 15
    Debt/EBITDA ratio, 7
    Debt/equity ratio, 7, 313–314
    Debt/total assets ratio, 314
    earnings-based valuation, 324–325
    EBIT/interest expense ratio, 7, 325

Financial ratios (*Cont'd.*)
  Enterprise value (EV) to EBITDA,
    324–325
  Price/earnings (P/E) ratio, 324
  Quick ratio, 313
  Working capital ratio, 313
Financial weakness, antitrust, 287
Financing, 425–455
  acquisition, 444–454
  cash flow, 316
  contingency payments, 436–444
  debtor-in-possession (DIP) loans,
    425–435
  loan-to-own transactions, 399
  (*See also* Refinancing)
Fitch rating agency, 12, 19
Foamex Int'l Inc., In re, 396
Forbes, xi
Forbes, B. C., xi
Foreclosure, 62–63
Forum shopping, 45
Forward collateralization, 433
Fraudulent claims, 122
Fraudulent transfers, legal risks, 287–298
  allocation of repayment, 289–290
  bankruptcy after acquisition, 290–291
  BAPCPA impact, 293
  cross-streaming, 291–292
  described, 287–288
  insolvency, meanings of, 288–289
  liens and obligations, 291
  right to sue, 290
  solvency opinions, 294
  step-transactions, 293–294
  363 sales, 387
  upstreaming, 291–292
"Free and clear" of claims, in 363 sales,
    377, 387
Free cash flow from operations,
    calculating, 315
Free-fall bankruptcy, 339
Fresh start accounting/reporting,
    251–266
  balance sheet, 257–266
  defined, 251
  disclosures, 257

  fair value allocation, 253–255
    implementing, 253
    intangible asset recognition, 255–257
    reorganization value, 252–253
    time to adopt, 251–252
Fulcrum security, 90–91, 114, 152–153, 397
Funds (cash) flow statements, 314–316
Funds specializing in insolvent entities, 87,
    92–93

G
General growth properties (GGP),
    112–113, 189–190, 390–391
General Motors, 76–77, 80–82, 110, 374,
    382, 384, 386
Generally accepted accounting principles
    (GAAP), 8–9, 114–115
Gheewalla, 276
Global M&A Network, 374–376
Going concern, 51, 68, 90, 102, 215–216,
    309–310
  (*See also* 363 sales)
Going-out-of-business (GOB) sales,
    205–206
Good faith, plan of reorganization, 359
Government agencies, 207–209
Government consents/approvals, loan
    agreement, 451
Government-supported transaction,
    refinancing, 424–425
Grace period, 16, 453
Great Recession (2007–2009), 36, 51,
    67–73, 152–153

H
Harrah's Entertainment, 418
Hart-Scott-Rodino Antitrust Improvements
    Act (1976), 282
Hedge funds, 87, 93–94
High Voltage Engineering, 368
High-yield bonds, viii–ix, 12–22
Highest and best offer, in 363 sale, 377
Holdouts, plan of reorganization, 334
Horizontal Merger Guidelines, 285–286
Houlihan Lokey, 187
Hybrid valuation approaches, 325–326

I

Impaired class of creditors, 361
Improvement in position test, 129
Income:
  cancellation of debt (COD), 226–228,
    230–231, 248–251, 400
  from restructuring, 217–221, 225–226
Income approach to value, 256
Indenture, bond, 14
Indirect costs of bankruptcy, 52
Indirect method of reporting, cash flow
  statements, 315
Indubitable equivalent, 350–351
Industry:
  bankruptcy cases by, 87
  high-yield bond default by, 17, 119
  reasons for business failure, 3–4
IndyMac Bank, 424
Infirmities, 91
Informal committee of creditors,
  199–201
Information in judicial notification of 363
  sale, 380, 382
Insider claims, 120–121
Insolvency:
  bankruptcy petitions, 49–50
  company reasons for business failure, 8–9
  defined, 8, 30n7
  vs. failing condition, antitrust, 285
  fraudulent transfers, 288–289
  as reason for business failure, 6–8
Insufficient collateral, 138–139
Intangible assets, 255–257
Intercreditor agreements, 133–135, 362,
  434–435
Interest coverage ratio, 7, 325
Internal rate of return (IRR), 324
Internal Revenue Code (IRC):
  asset transfer to creditor—section 1001,
    230–232
  cancellation of debt (COD) income—
    section 61/108, 216, 230, 248–249
  insolvency, definitions of, 250–251
  net operating loss (NOL)—section
    172/382, 216, 238–242
International Shoe, 283–284, 286

Inventory sublimit, asset-based loans, 414
Inventory turnover, 312
Investing cash flow, calculating, 316
Investment bankers (*See* Advisors;
  Financial advisors)
Investment Company Act (1940), 112–113
Involuntary bankruptcy, 37
Involuntary pension plan, termination
  of, 163

J

Jobs, Steve, 5–6
Judicial foreclosure, 63
Junior credit recourse, 398–399
Junior creditors (*See specific topics*)
Junk bonds (*See* High-yield bonds)
Jurisdiction of bankruptcy courts, 45–47

K

Kaiser Aluminum, 287
Key employee retention programs
  (KERPs), 120
Kmart, 110, 156–157
Kreisler, 147

L

Large public company bankruptcies,
  67–68, 71, 77–87
Late payment pattern, 9
Law firms (*See* Advisors; Financial
  advisors)
"Leapfrogging," debt exchange offer,
  418–419
Lear Corporation, 257–266
Leasing assets, in 363 sale, 377, 379–380
Legal precedents, bankruptcy court, 47
Legal risks, 269–302
  antitrust considerations, 282–287
  equitable subordination, 142–147, 398
  fiduciary duties, board of directors,
    270–282
  fraudulent transfers, 287–298
  intercreditor agreements, 133–135, 362,
    434–435
  lender liability, 142, 192–194, 399
  recharacterization, 142, 144–145, 398

Legal risks (*Cont'd.*)
    representations and warranties, 386–387,
        451–453
    substantive consolidation, plan of
        reorganization, 363–364
    successor liability, in 363 sale, 387
    voidable preferences, bankruptcy, 59–60
    zone of insolvency, 275–279
Lehman Brothers, 52–53, 70, 74, 76,
    78–79, 110, 198–199, 374, 382, 386
Lender liability, 142, 192–194, 399
Less-than-liquidation value, plan of
    reorganization, 353–354
Letter of credit fee, 449
Leverage indicators, asset valuation,
    313–314
Leverage ratio, 7, 313–314
Liabilities, 23, 329n7
Liens, 130–137
    adequate protection, 132
    debt vs. lien subordination, 135
    defined, 130
    fraudulent transfers, 291
    intercreditor agreements, 133–135
    perfecting, 135–137, 142
    second-lien loans, 130–135
    tranches of secured loans, 130–131
Line of credit, asset-based loans, 415–416
Lionel Corp., In re, 385–386
Liquidated claims, 118
Liquidation, 309–310, 386
Liquidators, 205–206
Liquidity:
    indicators of, asset valuation, 313
    as reason for business failure, 5–6
Loan-to-own transactions, 397–401
Local counsel, 180–182
Lockbox account, asset-based loans, 412
LoPucki, Lynn, 45, 54, 179

M
M&A, traditional vs. distressed, 23
Make-whole provisions, 160, 407
Management:
    as business failure reason, 3–6
    debtor in possession (DIP), 106–109
    of debtors, 104–113

incentives to distort valuation, 306
    replacing, 106–107 (*See also* Bankruptcy
        trustee; Chief restructuring officer)
    workouts, 36
Management fee, 448
*Managing the Crisis: The FDIC and RTC
    Experience,* 425
Market approach to value, 256–257
Marvel Entertainment Group, 426–427
Mass tort claims resolution, 161
Material deferral of payments, 229
Material litigation, loan agreement, 451
Matured claims, 118
Maximum availability, asset-based
    loans, 411
McDonald, Lawrence G., 78
Mezzanine financing, 132
    (*See also* High-yield bonds)
Milken, Michael, 13
Miller, Henry, 31, 174
Minimum amortization payments, loan
    agreement, 408
Minimum excess availability, asset-based
    loans, 412
Minimum topping amount, in 363
    sale, 391
Mistakes in management, 6–7
Modification of debt terms, workout,
    217–223, 226, 228–230
Moody's rating agency, 12
Motorola, 384
Multiple subsidiaries and bankruptcy, 101

N
National Association of Bankruptcy
    Trustees, 109
Nature of debt instrument, 229
Negative pledge, refinancing, 406
Net advance rates, asset-based loans, 413
Net operating loss (NOL), 238–251
    bankruptcy accounting, 238–251
    cancellation of debt (COD) income,
        248–251
    debt exchange offer, 419
    defined, 238
    fair market value (FMV) calculation,
        246–247

Net operating loss (NOL) (*Cont'd.*)
   limitations [Internal Revenue Code (IRC)
     section 382], 240–242
   maintaining in Chapter 11, 239
   ownership changes (IRC section 382),
     242–244
   role of, 240
   Section 382 limitations, 240–248
Net orderly liquidation value (NOLV),
   410–411, 414
New instrument with "substantially
   different terms," workout, 221–225
New money DIP loan, 429, 434
New value exception, 351–352
New York, Southern District of (SDNY)
   courts, 47, 70, 78–80, 82, 84, 180,
   340, 382–383
New York Times, 52
Nonassenting creditor, assignment for the
   benefit of creditors (ABC), 62
Nondebtors/nondebtor entities, 100–101
Nontroubled debt restructuring, 223–225
Nortel Networks, 110

O
Obama, Barack, 52
Obligor, changes in, 229
Offering memorandum, acquisition
   loan, 446
Official committee of equity holders,
   201–204
Official committee of unsecured creditors
   (*See* Creditors' committee)
Offset (*See* Setoff)
Oliver v. Boston University, 274
Operating cash flow (OCF) ratio, 315,
   319–320
Orderly liquidation value (*See* Net orderly
   liquidation value)
Original issue discount (OID) bonds, 118,
   227, 237, 399–400
Overadvances, asset-based loans, 415
Overbid protection, in 363 sale, 391
Overleverage, 6–8, 24
Oversecured collateral, 138–139
Oversubscription, refinancing, 420–423
Ownership changes, 242–246, 251

P
PACER (*See* Public Access to Court
   Electronic Records)
Pacific Gas & Electric (PG & E), 77, 86
Pari passu claims, 117, 143, 154, 428
Participation agreement, refinancing,
   409–410
Pass-through entities, 239, 250, 267n8
Payment default, 16
Payment expectations, changes in, 229
Payment penalties, 406–407
Penn Central, 75
Pension Benefit Guaranty Corporation
   (PBGC), 162–163, 208
Pension plan, termination of, 160–163
Perfected liens, 135–137, 142
Person, definition in bankruptcy, 99
Petition date, Bankruptcy Code, 36, 115
Phila. Newspapers, In re, 393
Plan of reorganization, 333–371
   absolute priority rule, 350–353
   Bankruptcy Code requirements—section
     1123(a), 347–349, 352
   bankruptcy court confirmation, 346–347
   best interests of creditors test, 353–354
   claim priorities, 349–352
   classes of claims, 349–350
   confirmation, 360–368
   consummation vs. confirmation, 367
   contents of, 346–360
   cram-down, 354–355
   cram-up, 356–358
   definition and function, 333–335
   discharge, 116
   disclosure statements, 343–345
   exclusivity period, 335–339
   exit financing, 359–360
   feasibility test, 358
   good faith, 359
   reorganization value, 252–253
   revocation of confirmation, 368
   solicitation period, 335–339
   soliciting votes for, 342
   stand-alone, 339
   sub rosa, 384–385
   substantive consolidation, 363–364
   363 sales, 383

Plan of reorganization (*Cont'd.*)
    types of, 339–342
    voting on, 360–364, 366
    (*See also* Bankruptcy Code; Chapter 11)
Plan support agreements, 342
Post-petition creditors and liabilities, 115,
    129, 236–237
Post-petition financing, 425–435 (*See also*
    Debtor-in-possession loans)
Post-petition interest payments, 157–158
Power of sale clause, 63
Powers, William C., Jr., 82
Pre-petition creditors and liabilities, 115,
    117, 129, 141, 236–237, 431–434
Pre-petition interest payments, 157–159
Pre-petition principal payments, 159
Prearranged bankruptcy, 340–342
Preemptive rights, refinancing, 420–423
Preferred stock, takeback financing, 438
Prenegotiated bankruptcy, 340–342
Prepackaged bankruptcy, 170, 339–340
Present fair salable value, 289
Price of distressed companies, 22–24,
    88–90, 308–309, 396
Price/earnings (P/E) ratio, 324
Priming loan, 429, 434
Priority of claims, 122–123, 154, 349–353
Private equity funds, 87, 93
Private investment in public equity (PIPE),
    refinancing, 423–424
*Production Resources Group, L.L.C. v.
    NCT Group, Inc.,* 276
Professional advice, bankruptcy, 52
    (*See also* Advisors; Bankruptcy lawyers)
Pro hac vice, bankruptcy lawyers, 182
Proof of claim, 119, 121–122
Proof of interest, 122
Protecting Employees and Retirees
    in Business Bankruptcies Act
    (pending), 56
Public Access to Court Electronic Records
    (PACER), 104, 120–121, 180
Publicly traded for tax purposes,
    workout, 229
Purchase agreement, in 363 sales, 386–387
Purchaser post-closing capital structure,
    444–445

Q
Quebecor World, Inc., 425
Quick ratio, 313

R
Radiology Assoc., Inc. Litigation, In re, 327
Radnor Holdings, 142–143
Rates of default, 17–19
Rating agencies, 12, 19–21, 30n8
Ratings downgrade, as warning sign, 12
Ratios (*See* Financial ratios)
Real estate investment trust (REIT), 112–113
Realogy Corporation, 418
Reasonable period of time, 8
Reasonably equivalent value, 302n62
Rebuttable presumption, 107, 124n21
Recharacterization, 142, 144–145, 398
Reclamation claim, 117
Recovery from bankruptcy, 71
Refinancing, 403–425
    amend and extend existing agreements,
        408–410
    with asset-based loans (ABLs), 410–416
    debt exchanges, 417–420
    debt-for-equity swap, 419–420
    existing credit agreement provisions
        which may hinder, 406–408
    factoring receivables, 416
    government-supported transaction,
        424–425
    overview of methods, 405–408
    private investment in public equity
        (PIPE), 423–424
    rights offerings and warrants, 420–423
    special considerations, 403–405
    terming out payables, 416–417
    (*See also* Financing)
Related debtors, 100
Reorganization plan (*See* Plan
    of reorganization)
Reorganization value, fresh start,
    252–253
Replacement value, 325
Representations and warranties, 386–387,
    451–453
Reputation, loan-to-own transactions, 400
ResCap, 418

Resignation from board of directors, 280–281
Restricted asset sales/leases, 379–380
Restructuring, described, 28
Restructuring alternatives for distressed companies, 31–65
bankruptcy, 36–60
factors determining, 32
out-of-court restructuring, 31–33
state insolvency proceeding, 60–63
workouts (debt restructuring), 33–36
Restructuring charges, constant, as warning sign, 11
Retention of advisors (*See* Advisors; Bankruptcy lawyers)
Return on assets (ROA), 312
Return on equity (ROE), 312
Revocation, plan of reorganization confirmation, 368
Revolving line of credit, asset-based loans, 415–416
Right to sue, fraudulent transfers, 290
Rights certificates, 421
Rights offerings, 397, 420–423
Rights record date, 421
Risks, legal (*See* Legal risks)
Rollover DIP loan, 429, 431–432
Rowan, Marc, 92

S
Sale of "crown jewels," as warning sign, 11
Sale of high-yield bonds, 13–14
Sale proceeds allocation, in 363 sales, 387
Sarbanes-Oxley Act (2002), 451
Schlotzsky's, 147
Second-lien loans, 130–135, 434–435
(*See also* Collateral; Intercreditor agreement; Liens)
Section 382 limitations, 240–248
Secured creditors, 127–149
bankruptcy concern, 127–128
collateral, 127–128, 137–142
constitutional property rights, 128
defined, 114, 128
equitable subordination, 142–147
lender liability, 142, 192–194, 399

liens, 130–137
loss of secured status, 142–147
recharacterization, 142, 144–145, 398
recovery, 35, 64n2
securities-based valuation, 322
setoff, 128–129
(*See also* Collateral; Intercreditor agreement; Liens)
Securities, rights offerings and warrants, 420–423
Securities-based valuation, 320–323
Securities and Exchange Commission (SEC), 30n8, 207, 345, 422
Security changes, significant modification of debt terms, 229
Seller notes, 436–437
Senior debt instruments, high-yield bonds vs., 14–15
Separable intangible assets, 255–256
Setoff, 128–129
Shareholder sale of large block of stock, 273–274
Significant modification of debt terms, workout, 228–229
Single purpose entity, 44–45, 100
Smith, Adam, 457
Smith v. Van Gorkom, 272
Solicitation period, 335–339
Soliciting votes for plan of reorganization, 342
Solvency, as reason for business failure, 6–8 (*See* Insolvency)
Solvency opinions, fraudulent transfers, 294
Sources and uses statements, 314–316
Southern District of New York (SDNY) courts, 47, 70, 78–80, 82, 84, 180, 340, 382–383
Spansion, Inc., In re, 23, 319, 326
Special counsel, 182–183, 185
Special-purpose entity (SPE), 44–45, 100
Special situations, 27, 160–165
Speed of transaction, in 363 sales, 382–383
Split rated bonds, 20–21
Stalking horse bidder, 103, 170, 381, 388–389
Stand-alone plan of reorganization, 339
Standard pension plan, termination of, 162

Standard & Poor's rating agency, 12, 19–20
Staple financings, 395
State insolvency proceeding, 60–63
Statement of cash flow, 314–316
Statute of Elizabeth laws, 287
Statutory mootness, in 363 sale, 388
Step-transactions, fraudulent transfers, 293–294
Stepped-up basis, 215
Strategic buyers, in 363 sale, 378–379
Stressed companies, 28
Structural factors, investing in distressed companies, 88–89
Structured PIPE, 423–424
Sub rosa plans of reorganization, 384–385
Subject to compromise, pre-petition vs. post-petition liabilities, 236
Subordinated debt, takeback financing, 438
Subscription rights, refinancing, 420–423
Subsidiaries, multiple, and bankruptcy, 101
Substantive consolidation, plan of reorganization, 363–364
Successor liability, in 363 sale, 387
Superpriority claim, 426
Suppliers, as critical vendors, 155–157
Suppressed availability, asset-based loans, 412
Syndicates, refinancing, 409

T
Takeback financing, 437–438
Tax issues:
    earn-outs, 442
    equity for tax purposes, 227
    (*See also* Workouts, tax issues)
Technical default, 16–17
Terming out payables, refinancing, 416–417
Testing period, ownership changes, 242
Thermadyne Holdings, 187
Third-party restrictions, refinancing, 407
Thornburg Mortgage, 77, 85–86
341 formation meeting, 169–170
361 protections, 140–141
    (*See also* Adequate protection; Secured creditors)

363 sales, 373–396
    antitrust concerns, 386
    appeal bankruptcy court's approval of, 388
    assets sold in liquidation, 386
    bidding and auctions, 388–396
        bid submission, 391–392
        bidder participation in, 377–379
        breakup fee percentages, 389–391
        contingencies, 391
        credit bidding, 392–394
        disqualification, 395–396
        expense reimbursement to losing bidder, 396
        minimum topping amount, 391
        overbid protection, 391
        price, as dominating factor, 396
        stalking horse bidder, 381, 388–389
    collusion, 395
    completed U.S. sales (2008–2010), 374
    defined, 377–378
    financial advisors, 186–189
    "free and clear" of claims, 377, 387
    information contained in judicial notification of, 380, 382
    leading examples, 374–376
    liquidations, 386
    objections to, 380–381
    plan of reorganization and, 383
        sub rosa, 384–385
    procedure begins, 378
    representations and warranties in purchase agreement, 386–387
    restricted asset sales/leases, 379–380
    sale of company as a going concern, 51, 68, 90, 102
    sale proceeds allocation, 387
    speed of transaction, 382–383
    structured within bankruptcy, 373
    subject to business judgment standard of review, 384–386
    successor liability, 387
    typical process, 380–381
Total availability, asset-based loans, 411
Toxic torts, 161, 164–165
Traditional investment bankers, 186–187
Traditional management consultants vs. turnaround consultants, 189–191

Traditional vs. distressed M&A, 23
Traditional private investment in public
  equity (PIPE), 423
Tranches, 17, 130–131
  (*See also* Classes of claims; *Pari passu*
  claims)
Treasury regulation, modification of debt
  terms, 228
Trends in distressed M&A and investing,
  67–96
bankruptcy, in light of Great Recession,
  67–71
bankruptcy cases, notable, 75–87
distressed investing, in light of market
  rally (2009–2010), 74–75
distressed investors, 87–94
distressed M&A deals, 72–74
Troubled companies, terms to describe,
  27–28
Troubled debt restructuring (TDR),
  218–221, 223
Trust fund doctrine, 275–276
Trust fund tax, 237
Trust Indenture Act (1939), 14
Trustees:
  appointments of, 58, 108–109, 282
  bankruptcy, 105–109, 196, 282,
    335, 380
  Chapter 7 and Chapter 11, 107–109
  U.S. Trustees, 170, 195–197, 201–202
Turnaround consultants, 36, 110–111, 174,
  189–194
Turnaround Management Association
  (TMA), xiv, 173, 179
*203 North LaSalle Street Partnerships,
  In re,* 362
Twyne's Case, 301n61

U
Underperformers, 27
Undersecured collateral, 138–139
Underwriting, acquisition financing,
  445–446
Undisputed claims, 119–120
Unexpired leases, 58–59
Uniform Commercial Code (UCC),
  135–137, 142

Uniform Fraudulent Conveyance Act
  (UFCA), 287–289
Uniform Fraudulent Transfer Act (UFTA),
  8, 287
Union contract, rejection, 161, 163–164
United Airlines, 338
United States v. Kirby Lumber, 226, 248
Unmatured claims, 118
Unsecured creditors, 151–172
  claims, 154–165
  creditors' committee, 152–153, 165–171
  functions, during bankruptcy, 151–153
  securities-based valuation, 322
  (*See also* Claims; Creditors; Creditors'
    committee)
Upstreaming, fraudulent transfers, 291–292
U.S. Circuit Courts, 45–49, 137–138, 166
U.S. Constitution:
  on bankruptcy, 36, 44, 61
  on property rights of secured creditors, 128
U.S. Department of Justice (DOJ), 208,
  282–286, 386
U.S. Trustees, 170, 195–197, 201–202

V
Valuation, 305–331
  appraisers, 205–206
  asset, 310–314
  bankruptcy vs. traditional, 307–308
  cash flow-based, 314–320
  collateral, 140
  comparable companies, valuation
    methodology, 326–328
  comparable transactions, valuation
    methodology, 326–328
  determination, and bankruptcy courts,
    306–307
  determined by Bankruptcy Court,
    306–307
  discounted cash flow (DCF) analysis,
    valuation methodology, 316–319
  fair, 289
  fair value, 253–255
  importance, 305–306
  management incentives to distort, 306
  methods of, 307–328
  to minimize purchase price, 308–309

Valuation (*Cont'd.*)
  net orderly liquidation value (NOLV),
    410–411, 414
  present fair salable value, 289
  traditional vs. distressed M&A, 23
Valukas, Anton R., 78, 198
Vivitar Corporation, 376
Voidable preferences, bankruptcy, 59–60
Voluntary bankruptcy, 37
Voluntary bankruptcy petition, filing,
    43–47, 49–50
Voting on plan of reorganization,
    360–364, 366
Vulture funds, 92, 458

W
Warning signs of financial distress, 9–12
Warrants, 420–423
Washington Mutual (WaMu), 70, 79, 88
Wasting assets, in 363 sale, 377
Winstar Communications, 147, 427–428
Worker, Homeownership and Business
    Assistance Act (2009), 239
Working capital ratio, 313
Workouts:
  accounting for, 213–233
  asset swap, 218
  asset transfers to creditors, 230–232
  borrowing capacity, 225
  common issues, 217
  as debt extinguishment, 222–223
  defined, 27, 33
  exchange of debt, 218, 227, 230
  "financial difficulty," 232n2

income creation, 217–221
modification of debt terms, 217–223, 226,
    228–230
new instrument with "substantially
    different terms," 221–225
nontroubled debt restructuring, 223–225
process of, 34–36
publicly traded for tax purposes, 229
tax issues, 214–231
  basis, 214–217
  cancellation of debt (COD), 226–228,
    230–231
  common, 217
  deductibility of interest on new
    instrument, 227–228
  going concern, 215–216
  income from restructuring, 225–226
  tax basis, 214–217
  tax deductibility of interest on new
    instrument, 227–228
  tax-free structure, 216–217
timing and inflection points, 213–214
troubled debt restructuring (TDR),
    218–221, 223
WorldCom, 76, 79–80
W.T. Grant, 75

Y
Yield, modification of debt terms,
    228–229

Z
Zone of insolvency, 275–279
Z-Score, 7

H. Peter Nesvold, Esq., C.F.A., C.P.A., is a managing director in equity research at Jefferies & Co. in New York. Given his diverse background in finance, law, and accounting, Peter offers unique insight into the interrelated issues impacting securities analysis and transaction structures. Previously, he was a portfolio manager/analyst at Lazard Asset Management, a senior managing director in equity research at Bear Stearns, and an M&A attorney at Shearman & Sterling. He coauthored *The Art of M&A* and *The Art of M&A Structuring*. After receiving his B.A. in economics from the College of Arts & Sciences at the University of Pennsylvania, he graduated cum laude from Fordham Law School, where he achieved Order of the Coif and was elected editor in chief of his law journal.

Jeffrey M. Anapolsky, Esq., M.B.A., is a high-yield credit analyst at T. Rowe Price in Baltimore. He has over 10 years of experience advising, operating, and investing in special situations involving bankruptcies, liquidations, and workouts. Previously, he was a bankruptcy attorney at Akin Gump Strauss Hauer & Feld, a restructuring advisor at Wasserstein Perella, and a distressed investor at Sun Capital Partners and American Capital. After receiving a B.S. in finance from the Wharton School of Business and a B.A. in mathematics from the College of Arts & Sciences at the University of Pennsylvania, magna cum laude, he graduated from the J.D./M.B.A. program at Harvard Law School and Harvard Business School.

Alexandra Reed Lajoux, M.B.A., Ph.D., is chief knowledge officer of the National Association of Corporate Directors. She is the author of *The Art of M&A Integration* and coauthor of *The Art of M&A, The Art of M&A Due Diligence, The Art of M&A Structuring*, and *The Art of M&A Financing and Refinancing*. A graduate of Bennington College, she holds an M.B.A. from Loyola University in Maryland and a Ph.D. from Princeton University.